I0820779

CALATRAVA

Philip Jodidio

CALATRAVA

Santiago Calatrava
Complete Works 1979–Today

TASCHEN

CONTENTS

APPENDIX

EINLEITUNG

INTRODUCTION

THE SECRET OF PHILANTHROPY

"I started out wanting to go to art school," recalls Santiago Calatrava. "Then, one day, I went to buy some things in a stationery store in Valencia, and I saw a little book with beautiful colors. It had yellow and orange ellipses on a blue background, and I bought it immediately. It turned out to be about Le Corbusier, whose work was a discovery for me. I saw images of the concrete stairways in the Unité d'Habitation, and I said to myself, what an extraordinary sense of form. The point of the book was to show the artistic aspects of the architect's work. As a result of buying it, I transferred to architecture school."[1]

Born near Valencia in 1951, Calatrava went to primary and secondary school there. Beginning in 1959, he also attended the Arts and Crafts School, where he started formal learning in drawing and painting. When he was 13, his family took advantage of the recent opening of the borders of Franco's Spain, and sent him to France as an exchange student. After graduating from high school in Valencia, he went to Paris to attend the École des Beaux-Arts, but he arrived in 1968, in the midst of the student uprising. He returned to Valencia and, seduced by a small colorful book, enrolled in the Escuela Técnica Superior de Arquitectura, where he got a degree in Architecture and did postgraduate work in urbanism.

Where others might have ended their studies, Calatrava decided to continue. Attracted by the mathematical rigor that he perceived in certain works of historic architecture, and feeling that his training in Valencia had given him no clear direction, he decided to begin postgraduate studies in Civil Engineering and enrolled in 1975 at the ETH (Federal Institute of Technology) in Zurich. He received his Ph.D. in 1981. This decision certainly changed his life in many ways. It was during this period that he met and married his wife, Robertina Marangoni, who was a law student in Zurich. Professionally speaking, the keys to Santiago Calatrava's current activity are also to be found in Zurich. As he says: "The desire to start over from zero was extremely strong for me. I was determined to set aside all of what I worked with in architecture school and to learn to draw like an engineer and to think like one too. I was fascinated by the concept of gravity and resolute in feeling that it was necessary to work with simple forms. I could say that my taste for simplicity in engineering comes in part from my observation of the work of the Swiss engineer Robert Maillart. With simple forms he showed that it is possible to create a strong content and to elicit an emotional response. With the proper combination of force and mass, you can create emotion."

ENGINEER, ARCHITECT, ARTIST

Calatrava's early interest in art, and the aesthetic sense that drew him to the small book on Le Corbusier would remain another constant factor in his work, and one of the things that sets him apart in the world of contemporary architecture. Referring to a 2005 exhibition of his art and architecture held at New York's Metropolitan Museum of Art, Calatrava says: "I think that the curator in charge, Gary Tinterow, understood my way of working, because he titled the show 'Sculpture into Architecture' rather than the reverse. Architecture critics haven't gotten over being perplexed by my work." Indeed, while noting that the last time the Metropolitan showed the work of a living architect was in 1973, Nicolai Ouroussoff, when reviewing this show, wrote in *The New York Times*: "No one would argue that Mr. Calatrava's sculptures would make it into the Met on their own merits; as art, they are mostly derivative of the works of dead masters like Brancusi," going on to a rather brutal conclusion: "One wishes he had left the sculpture back in his studio."[2] This comment above all seems to show a lack of understanding of Calatrava's sculpture. "In sculpture," he says, "I have used spheres and cubes, simple forms often related to my knowledge of engineering. It is a sculpture that gave rise to the Turning Torso (Malmö, Sweden, 1999–2004, see page 276). I must admit that I greatly admire the liberty of a Frank Gehry, or Frank Stella as a sculptor. There is a joy and a liberty in Stella's work that is not present in my sculpture, which is always based in the rough business of mathematics."[3] Calatrava is quite clear about saying that he has always disliked the art gallery circuit, almost never showing his sculpture. He also underlines the fact that "the reaction I receive from artists is very positive. Art is much freer than architecture, because, as Picasso said, some artists work with marble and others with shit." This is not to say that Santiago Calatrava is at all naive about the difficulty of his task. In 1997, he wrote: "Architecture and sculpture are two rivers in which the same water flows. Imagine that sculpture is unfettered plasticity, while architecture is plasticity that must submit to function, and to the obvious notion of human scale (through function). Where sculpture ignores function, unbowed by mundane questions of use, it is superior to architecture as pure expression. But through its rapport with human scale and the environment, through its penetrability and interiority, architecture dominates sculpture in these specific areas."[4]

Calatrava goes so far as to suggest that art must be considered to be a source of ideas for architecture. "Why do I make drawings of the human figure? The artist or the architect can send his message across time by the very force of form and shadow. Rodin wrote: 'Harmony in living bodies is the result of the counterbalancing of masses that move; the Cathedral is built on the example of the living body.'[5] Let me give you an example of the importance of art for 20th-century architecture. When Le Corbusier wrote 'Architecture is the masterly, correct, and magnificent play of masses brought together in light' in 1923,[6] how many people knew that he was borrowing from the thought of the sculptor Auguste Rodin? In 1914, in his book *Les Cathédrales de France*, Rodin wrote: 'The sculptor only attains great expression when he gives all his attention to the harmonic play of light and shadow, just as the architect does.'[7] The fact that one of the most famous phrases of modern architecture was inspired not by an architect but by a sculptor underlines the significance of art."

Aside from his consistent interest in art, Santiago Calatrava has also brought a related passion to his own very personal definition of architecture—that of movement: implied but also real, that is to say, physical motion. From the early folding doors of his Ernsting's Warehouse (Coesfeld-Lette, Germany, 1983–85, see page 36) to the more recent 115-ton Burke Brise Soleil of the Milwaukee Art Museum (Milwaukee, Wisconsin, 1994–2001, see page 232), he has come back again and again, in his sculpture and his architecture, to the unusual concept of repetitive, physical movement. Why?

---

1 Santiago Calatrava in conversation with the author, Zurich, February 22, 2006.
2 Nicolai Ouroussoff, "Buildings Shown as Art and Art as Buildings," *The New York Times*, October 25, 2005.
3 Santiago Calatrava in conversation with the author, Zurich, February 22, 2006.
4 Julio González, Dessiner dans l'espace, Skira, Kunstmuseum Bern, 1997. "L'architecture et la sculpture sont deux fleuves dans lesquels coule une même eau. Imaginons que la sculpture est plastique pure et que l'architecture est plastique soumise à la fonction et avec une évidente notion de l'échelle humaine (à travers la fonctionnalité). Tandis que la sculpture ignore le cadre de la fonctionnalité –, – elle est étrangère à la servitude dérivée des questions d'utilisation et donc elle est, pour ainsi dire, supérieure à l'architecture en tant qu'expression purement plastique. L'architecture au contraire soumet son expression plastique et à ces exigences. Par contre, celle-ci, de par son rapport à l'échelle humaine, à l'échelle de l'environnement de par don intériorité et sa pénétrabilité, elle l'emporte dans ces domaines spécifiques sur la sculpture."
5 Auguste Rodin, *Les Cathédrales de France*, Armand Colin, Paris, 1914. "L'harmonie, dans les corps vivants, resulte du contre-balancement des masses qui se déplacent: la Cathédrale est construite à l'exemple des corps vivants."
6 Le Corbusier, *Vers une architecture*, 1923. "L'architecture est le jeu savant, correct et magnifique des volumes assemblés sous la lumière."
7 Auguste Rodin, *Les Cathédrales* op cit. "Il n'atteint à la grande expression qu'en donnant toute son étude aux jeux harmoniques de la lumière et de l'ombre, exactement comme fait l'architecte."

"There is a cinematic element in 20th-century art," replies Calatrava. "Artists like Alexander Calder, Naum Gabo or Moholy-Nagy created sculptures that move. I love their work and it gives me a great emotion. My doctoral thesis 'On the Foldability of Frames' had to do with the fact that a geometric figure can be reduced from three dimensions to two and ultimately to just one. Take a polyhedron and collapse it, making it into a planar surface. Another transformation reduces it to a single line, a single dimension. You can view this as a problem of mathematics or topology. All the mystery of the omnipresent Platonic solids is summed up in the polyhedron. After thinking about these questions, I looked at ancient sculpture in a different light. Works such as the *Discobolus* by Myron create a tension based on an instant of movement, and that is how I became interested in the problem of time, time as a variable. Einstein said 'God does not play dice with the Universe,' and so it became apparent to me that everything is related to mathematics and the unique dimension of time. Then I thought about statics (the branch of physics concerned with physical systems in static equilibrium) and realized that there is nothing static about them. Everything is potential movement. Newton's second law of motion states that the acceleration of an object is dependent upon two variables: the net force acting upon the object and the mass of the object. Mass and acceleration are related, and thus there is time in force. I realized that architecture is full of things that move, from doors to furniture. Architecture itself moves and with a little luck becomes a beautiful ruin. Everything changes, everything dies, and there is an existential meaning in cyclical movements. I wanted to make a door of my own, one that would have a poetic meaning and transform itself into a figure in space, and that is how the Ernsting's project came about."

THE ESSENCE OF ARCHITECTURE

The fact that some are uncomfortable with the multiple forms of expression chosen by Santiago Calatrava is probably the best indication that he is on to something important. In 2016, he completed one of the most complex and politically sensitive projects imaginable in the United States, the World Trade Center Transportation Hub (see page 320) in the midst of the area that New Yorkers have come to call Ground Zero. "We think he is the da Vinci of our time," said Joseph Seymour, the former executive director of the Port Authority of New York and New Jersey, the client for the station. "He combines light and air and structural elegance with strength." Standing amid new towers and next to the 9/11 Memorial, the Hub clearly places the original vision of Santiago Calatrava at the heart of the American consciousness of one of the most traumatic events of recent times. Nor is praise for Calatrava rare, even in the closed world of architecture. In 2005, Santiago Calatrava became the second Spaniard (after Josep Lluís Sert in 1981) to win the prestigious American Institute of Architects' Gold Medal. The AIA Committee on Design declared: "Santiago Calatrava's work seeks out the essence of architecture. His architecture expands the vision and expresses the energy of the human spirit, captivating the imagination and delighting us in the wonders of what sculptural form and dynamic structure can accomplish. Santiago Calatrava defines the reason for the Gold Medal. His vision elevates the human spirit through the creation of environments in which we live, play, and work."

Santiago Calatrava does not seem to be perturbed by the coexistence of art, architecture, and engineering in his own thought. And yet, with his combined interests, Calatrava is indeed close to the heart of one of the most intense debates in the recent history of construction and design. As Sigfried Giedion wrote in his seminal book *Space, Time and Architecture*: "The advent of the structural engineer with speedier, industrialized form giving components broke up the artistic bombast and shattered the privileged position of the architect and provided the basis for present-day developments. The 19th-century engineer unconsciously assumed the role of guardian of the new elements he was continually delivering to the architects. He was developing forms that were both anonymous and universal." Giedion retraces the debate about the role of engineering by citing a number of essential dates and events. Among them: "1877: In this year the question entered the Académie, when a prize was offered for the best paper discussing 'the union or the separation of engineer and architect.' Davioud, one of the architects of the Trocadéro, won the prize with this answer: 'The accord will never become real, complete, and fruitful until the day that the engineer, the artist, and the scientist are fused together in the same person. We have for a long time lived under the foolish persuasion that art is a kind of activity distinct from all other forms of human intelligence, having its sole source and origin in the personality of the artist himself and in his capricious fancy.'"[8] Though neither Giedion's insistence on the "anonymity" of the work of the engineer, nor Davioud's reference to the "capricious fancy" of the artist seem to fit well with Calatrava's powerful originality, he does appear to meet the Frenchman's requirements for an accord between art, engineering, and architecture. Then, too, Joseph Seymour's reference to the "da Vinci of our time" also comes to mind.

The catalog of Santiago Calatrava's 1993 exhibition at the Museum of Modern Art in New York underlines the close relationship of his work to that of other groundbreaking engineers: "Calatrava is part of the distinguished heritage of 20th-century engineering. Like those of the preceding generations—Robert Maillart, Pier Luigi Nervi, Eduardo Torroja, and Félix Candela—Calatrava goes beyond an approach that merely solves technical problems. Structure, for these engineers, is a balance between the scientific criterion of efficiency and the innovation of new forms. Calatrava considers engineering 'the art of the possible,' and seeks a new vocabulary of form that is based on technical know-how, yet is not an anthem to techniques."[9] The first figure cited, Robert Maillart (1872–1940), graduated from the ETH in Zurich in 1894 and went on to create some of the most spectacular modern bridges, and to make innovative use of concrete. His Giesshübel Warehouse in Zurich (1910) employed a concrete slab "mushroom ceiling" for the first time, permitting Maillart to do away with the use of beams. As Matilda McQuaid writes: "Maillart was one of the first engineers of this century to break completely from masonry construction and apply a technically appropriate and elegant solution to reinforced-concrete construction. Although the technical idea in Calatrava's work is neither the primary motivation, as with Maillart, nor understated, it informs the overall expression of the structure. His work becomes an intertwinement of plastic expression and structural revelation, producing results that possibly can be best described as a synthesis of aesthetics and structural physics."[10]

Although he naturally admires the work of Maillart, Santiago Calatrava is quick to point out that his bridges are very different from those of his predecessor, if only because of their sites. "Maillart's bridges," says Calatrava, "are often set in beautiful mountain scenery. His achievement was to successfully introduce an artificial element into such magnificent locations. Today," he continues, "I believe that one of the most important tasks is to reconsider the periphery of cities. Most often public works in such areas are purely functional, and yet even near railroad tracks, or spanning polluted rivers, bridges can have a remarkably positive effect. By creating an appropriate environment, they can have a symbolic impact whose ramifications go far beyond their immediate location."[11]

Calatrava's work has undoubtedly been influenced by that of Félix Candela, who was born in Madrid in 1910, and emigrated to Mexico in 1939, where he created a number of remarkable thin-shelled concrete structures, such as the Iglesia de la Virgen Milagrosa (Narvarte, Mexico, 1955), a design entirely based on hyperbolic paraboloids. Another Spaniard, the Madrid engineer Eduardo Torroja (1899–1961), was fascinated by the use of organic or vegetal forms whose undeniable sculptural presence may well spring from the influence of Gaudí. Many of Santiago Calatrava's references are to Spanish, and more specifically Catalan, architects or artists. "What fascinates me in the

---

8 Sigfried Giedion, *Space, Time and Architecture*, Harvard University Press, Cambridge, Massachusetts, 5th edition, 1976.

9 Matilda McQuaid, *Santiago Calatrava, Structure and Expression*, The Museum of Modern Art, New York, 1993.

10 *Ibid.*

11 Santiago Calatrava in conversation with the author, Zurich, June 1997.

personality of Goya, for example," says Calatrava, "is that he is one of the first artists to renounce the idea, as Rembrandt had before him, of serving any one master. What I admire in Miró's work," he continues, "is its remarkable silence, as well as his radical rejection of everything conventional." Although Gaudí provides him with an example like that of Maillart, Calatrava seems more at ease speaking about the sculptor Julio González. "The father and grandfather of González were metalworkers for Gaudí on projects like the Park Güell. Then they went to Paris, and that is where the work of Julio González with metal comes from. With all due modesty," concludes Calatrava, "one might say that what we do is a natural continuation of the work of Gaudí and of González, a work of artisans moving toward abstract art."[12]

The kind of art that Santiago Calatrava is referring to is apparent in his most successful bridges and buildings, and yet it remains difficult to describe in words. Another of the essential figures of 20th-century engineering, the Italian Pier Luigi Nervi, attempted such a definition in a series of lectures he delivered at Harvard in 1961: "It is very difficult to explain the reason for our immediate approval of forms which come to us from a physical world with which we, seemingly, have no direct tie whatsoever. Why do these forms satisfy and move us in the same manner as natural things such as flowers, plants, and landscapes to which we have become accustomed through numberless generations? It can also be noted that these achievements have in common a structural essence, a necessary absence of all decoration, a purity of line and shape more than sufficient to define an authentic style, a style I have termed the *truthful style*. I realize how difficult it is to find the right words to express this concept. When I make these remarks to friends, I am often told that this view of the near future is terribly sad, that perhaps it would be better to renounce voluntarily the further tightening of the bonds between our creations and the physical laws, if indeed these ties must lead us to a fatal monotony. I do not find this pessimism justified. Binding as technical demands may be, there always remains a margin of freedom sufficient to show the personality of the creator of a work and, if he be an artist, to allow that his creation, even in its strict technical obedience, becomes a real and true work of art."[13]

ALONG THE STEEL RAILS

The reason for Calatrava's long presence in Zurich is one of circumstances. Having completed his own studies, he stayed on there because his wife, Robertina, had not yet completed hers. Then, as luck would have it, he won a 1982 open competition to design the new Stadelhofen Station (1983–90, see page 52). To say that this unusual building is centrally located would almost be an understatement. Set into a green hill near Bellevueplatz and off Theaterstrasse close to the lake, it is tightly integrated into a largely traditional urban environment. "In order to understand the Stadelhofen Railway Station," says Santiago Calatrava, "you have to view it as an extremely urban project, one which entailed the repair of the urban fabric. There is a clear contrast between the radical nature of the technical and architectural solutions chosen, and the attitude toward the city that is extremely gentle. Any number of links have been created—not only bridges and access points, but also connections with the streets which didn't exist before. Small park areas, such as the veil of greenery hanging over the upper level, were created." Indeed, when approaching the station from the city, the visitor first encounters a very traditional pavilion that originally housed the station, before entering or descending into the areas designed specifically by Calatrava. "It was obvious from the outset," continues the architect, "that the respect given to buildings over 100 years old in Switzerland precluded any attempt to demolish or substantially modify the old station house. I did not find that aspect illogical, however, because it fits into a reading of the city which remains intact."[14] Nevertheless, once the traveler has gone past the old pavilion, he enters a very different world that seems closer to the imagination of Gaudí than to that of the stolid burghers of Zurich. Although Calatrava points out that Zurich does have something of a tradition of radical architecture, with houses by figures such as Marcel Breuer, it is clear that with the

Stadelhofen Station he indulged for the first time in his career on a large scale in the kind of innovative design for which he has become famous.

The curved 40 x 240-meter site required construction during the continued operation of the commuter train line, and was modified to include a large shopping area below ground. The whole has an organic unity that the circumstances could not have simplified. Like an extravagant flying dinosaur that has come to nest against this hillside, the structure is articulated by a pattern of repeating elements, with enormous anthropomorphic gates leading to the underground shopping mall where one quickly gets the impression of being in the concrete belly of the beast. There is a continuity in the dark metal above ground and the riblike concrete below that establishes a clear hierarchy of spaces and forms; all of this while placing an obvious emphasis on the legibility and functional clarity of the station.

Though it may be that the whole of Stadelhofen Railway Station gives the impression of being conceived around a kind of dinosaur metaphor, the substance of Calatrava's design is more complex, or perhaps different. "In reality, what I have attempted is what I would call a dialectic of transgression, which is based on the vocabulary of structural forces. In Stadelhofen, for example, there are a series of inclined columns. Though this appears to be an aesthetic decision, it is in fact related to the necessity of holding up the structure. Naturally there were various solutions for this type of support. They could have been simple cylinders for example, but I chose to articulate them in the shape of a hand. This is where the question of metaphors becomes interesting. How better to express the function of the columns than to invest them with the sense of the physical gesture of carrying?"[15]

Though Santiago Calatrava's name is often cited with reference to bridges, he is also a recognized specialist of railroad stations, including the Oriente Station in Lisbon or the slightly later Liège-Guillemins facility in France. One of the buildings that contributed most to his burgeoning reputation, however, was the Lyon-Saint-Exupéry Airport Railway Station (1989–94, see page 104). This 5600-square-meter station located at the formerly called Lyon Satolas airport was one of the then new generation of rail facilities designed to serve France's growing network of high-speed trains (TGV). The juxtaposition of rail, air, and local transport facilities at a single location makes for a particularly efficient system. The 120-meter-long, 100-meter-wide, and 40-meter-high passenger terminal, which opened on July 7, 1994, is based on a central steel element weighing 1300 tons. Calatrava's station seems to echo Eero Saarinen's TWA Terminal at Kennedy Airport (1957–62) in its suggestion of a bird in flight, but it is more exuberant than its American ancestor. The plan of the complex, with its link to the airport, also resembles a manta ray. A total of six train lines run below the main building and stop at a 500-meter-long covered platform, also designed by Calatrava. The middle tracks, intended for through trains moving at over 300 kilometers per hour, are enclosed in a concrete shell, a system that required careful calculation of the "shock waves" surrounding the TGV. Shared by the French national rail company (SNCF), the Rhône-Alpes region, and the Rhône Department, the total cost of this facility exceeded 600 million francs.

When asked about the image of a prehistoric bird, Calatrava responds in a typically oblique, yet informative manner: "I am merely an architect," he says, "not an artist or someone who is seeking to foment a revolution. It might be interesting to note that Victor Hugo in his novel *Notre-Dame de Paris* compares the cathedral to a prehistoric monster. Despite the fact that he may have had an excellent knowledge of architecture, and that he was a very conscientious writer, he did not hesitate to use such an unexpected metaphor in describing Notre-Dame Cathedral. I honestly am not looking for metaphors. I never thought of a bird, but more of the research which I am sometimes pretentious enough to call sculpture."[16] Indeed, both the drawings and the sculpture by Calatrava that are most

---

12 *Ibid.*
13 Pier Luigi Nervi, *Aesthetics and Technology in Building, The Charles Eliot Norton Lectures*, 1961–1962, Harvard University Press, Cambridge, Massachusetts, 1965, p. 186.
14 Santiago Calatrava in conversation with the author, Zurich, June 1997.
15 *Ibid.*

closely related to the Lyon station seem to find their origin not in the metaphor of a bird, but in a study of the eye and the eyelid, a recurring theme in his work. "The eye," says Calatrava, "is the real tool of the architect, and that is an idea that goes back to the Babylonians."

The swooping front of the Lyon-Saint-Exupéry Station that runs right into the earth has been compared to the beak of a bird, but Calatrava once again seems to have had an entirely different idea in mind. "The 'beak' was formed as the result of complex calculations of the forces playing on the structure. It also happens to be the assembly point for the water run-off pipes. Naturally, I did my best to minimize the mass of that point, without any thought of an anthropomorphic design," he says. Admitting that the use of his own sculptures as a starting point for the design represents as much of an aesthetic choice as would a consciously anthropomorphic concept, Calatrava says: "Call it irrational if you will, but I would say that there is no path to follow. I want to be like a boat in the sea. Behind it there is a trail, but in front there is no path."[17]

TREES ON THE HILL

Calatrava's work on the spectacular Oriente Station in Lisbon (see page 212) is a vital example of his method and explains a good deal of his early success. Following the catastrophic earthquake of 1755, Lisbon oriented itself toward the interior, turning its back almost literally on the broad vistas of the Tagus estuary. This tendency was amplified in more recent times, as poor landfill on the river's edge became the site for industrial facilities. The 340 hectares that comprised the so-called Redevelopment Area, with Expo '98 and the Oriente Station at its heart, were occupied until the 1990s by fuel depots, container warehouses, the city's slaughterhouse, and sewer or waste treatment facilities. Although much of Lisbon's glorious past remains inscribed in its streets and squares, its intimate relation to the Tagus, formerly the source of unimaginable wealth, was almost lost in the mists of time.

It is in this context that the Association of Portuguese Architects launched an "Ideas Contest for the Riverside Zone" in 1988. The construction of the Belém Cultural Center (1988–92) near the river's edge represents a first significant step toward the rehabilitation of Lisbon's historic ties to the Tagus. An even more important political and cultural decision began to take form in November 1993 when Parque Expo '98 SA confided a first "Urbanization Plan for the Redevelopment Area" to the architect Luís Vassalo Rosa. From the outset, the intention of the developers of this tract was to create something more than the typically ephemeral architecture of a World Fair. Situated at the eastern extremity of the city, with five kilometers of waterfront on the Tagus, the Redevelopment Area is close to the Vasco da Gama Bridge. Inaugurated on March 29, 1998, this impressive structure spans the 12-kilometer width of the Tagus, rising as high as 45 meters. Symbolically, the completion of a bridge named after the great explorer and the placement of Expo '98 could not have sent a clearer signal. Lisbon, and indeed Portugal, were intent on reclaiming their historic heritage, and once again to open out onto the Tagus and the world beyond.

Santiago Calatrava was chosen to build the Oriente Station following a limited competition in which Terry Farrell, Nicholas Grimshaw, Rem Koolhaas, and the late Ricardo Bofill also participated. The Oriente Station is, together with Álvaro Siza's Portuguese Pavilion, undeniably the most architecturally significant structure to emerge from Expo '98. The station, with its 200 000 visitors per day, was clearly the centerpiece of the plan to revive the waterfront in the east of the city. The most spectacular aspect of the project is undoubtedly the 78 x 238-meter covering over the eight raised railway tracks, whose typology recalls that of a stand of trees. Rather than emphasizing the break between the city and the river implied by the station, Calatrava has sought, here as elsewhere, to open passageways and reestablish links. This will is made manifest by the fact that the architect has cut into the elevated mound on which the railway tracks run, in order to effectively build the station below them. The complex includes two large glass-and-steel awnings over the entrances, one measuring no less than

112 meters in length and 11 meters in width. There is a bus station and car park, a metro station below (not designed by Calatrava), and a longitudinal gallery including commercial spaces that were included in the architect's brief. Ticketing and service facilities are located five meters below the tracks, with an atrium marking the longitudinal gallery five meters lower, and the opening on the river side intended as a main access point.

Seen from a distance, or for that matter from within, the most visible aspect of the Oriente Station is indeed its treelike design. At least two other projects by Santiago Calatrava have also called on the structural typology of the tree or forest: his unbuilt design for the Cathedral of St. John the Divine in New York (1991) and the BCE Place: Galleria and Heritage Square in Toronto (1987–92). St. John the Divine, one of New York's best-known churches, was originally built in a neo-Romanesque style by Heins & La Farge in 1892 and "gothicized" by Cram & Ferguson in 1911. Calatrava's project would have added a new south transept and a "bio-shelter" perched 55 meters above ground level. Obviously related in its symbolism to the Garden of Eden, the bio-shelter would have been completed with structural elements below derived from the form of trees. Placed in the existing attic of the nave, this garden would not have changed the profile of the building, but would have brought natural light into the church. Philip Johnson, a jury member, pointed out the relationship of Calatrava's design to the decor of the church, and, indeed, the tree typology does bring to mind the origins of Gothic architecture. The image of the tree is also at the heart of the Bell Canada Enterprises Place: Galleria and Heritage Square (see page 74). Here, Calatrava worked with the New York office of Skidmore, Owings & Merrill to create a six-story, 115-meter-long white-painted steel and glass passageway connecting two towers. As *The New York Times* wrote: "This gallery is nothing if not Gaudí-esque." It also recalls a forest path in a metaphorical sense. The use of white steel and glass is also premonitory of the tree-related designs for the platforms of the Oriente Station.

Whether it be in Toronto or in New York, Santiago Calatrava called on the tree metaphor for different reasons—related in the first instance to a large urban space set between high towers, and in the second to the neo-Gothic design of St. John the Divine. The fact that the tree is one of the most obvious models for the column or early church nave forms only reinforces its undeniable biological presence. In each instance, the words of Nervi—"our immediate approval of forms which come to us from a physical world"—come to mind. In the case of the Oriente Station, Calatrava explains that very specific circumstances related to his own understanding of Lisbon led him to the unusual canopy design. He says: "I went to Lisbon at least five times during the competition for the Oriente Station, if only to take in the mood of the city. It may be obvious to say so, but Lisbon is a very beautiful city. Like Rome, it is built on hills, which means that there are often remarkable views. You are in the city and yet able to look at it at the same time. There is also the monumentality of the Tagus, which is at this point the widest river in Europe. The Sea of Straw is incredibly vast. The urban history of Lisbon is very ancient, and yet it retains a clarity in its composition."[18]

When Calatrava speaks of the platform design of the Oriente Station, he refers to "trees on a hill." The "hill" in this instance is the high mound on which the railway tracks run. To explain the tree metaphor, he again refers to his visits to Lisbon during the competition. "There are numerous parks in the city with trees," he says. "I immediately felt that the elevated tracks called for a wooded hillside. This was a very explicit idea in my mind. For the competition, I cited a melancholic poem by Fernando Pessoa, which evokes the idea of going to the 'arvoredo,' the woods. I wanted to accentuate the transparency of the station. In an urban environment, which will undoubtedly become even more dense, the Oriente Station will resemble an oasis. It will be a place where people will come to rest!"

---

16 *Ibid.*
17 *Ibid.*
18 Santiago Calatrava in conversation with the author, Paris, September 1998.

When asked why in this instance he has preferred a vegetal metaphor to the anthropomorphic designs he seems more at ease with, Calatrava replies: "Imagine that you create an elevated square. This is obviously not an introverted type of architecture. I am on a hillside in Lisbon and I look around me. What is lacking? Some protection from the sun and the rain."[19]

A slightly later design by Calatrava, for the Liège-Guillemins Railway Station (see page 254), shows some changes in his thinking and illustrates reasons for the differences between the pared-down simplicity of his bridges and the more complex feeling of his larger buildings. "Bridges, by their very nature, necessitate a strict economy of means. You have the bridge surface, the arc that supports it, and the foundations, with each representing about one third of the cost. Given the simplicity of the function of a bridge, there is only limited margin for intervention. On the other hand, in a railway station, there are at least 16 types of decisions which can have an aesthetic impact, from the choice of metal window frames to the lighting design and so on. It is up to the skills of the designer to obtain the result he has imagined within the economic constraints of such a project." Despite this fundamentally different situation, it can readily be seen that Calatrava's taste for "transgression" or innovation pushes him equally to design unusual bridges and unexpected stations. "Take the case of the TGV Station in Liège," he continues. "We reinvented the façade completely. Or rather there is no façade. That, in my opinion, is a fundamental transgression. In the place of a traditional façade, there will only be large openings signaled by metal awnings overhanging the square in front of the station." As Calatrava points out, this design decision has important consequences on the functional layout of the station. In a more symbolic vein it might be asked how a station with no façade can be identified as such. "The setting is an urban one, and it seemed to me that the first vision that travelers or visitors would have of the station would be important," explains Calatrava. "My solution was two-fold. As it is located on a hill, and is approached from above, there is a view of the city and of the layout of the station. The plan thus becomes the real façade. In order to improve the rapport between the city and the station, we proposed to create a square in front of it."[20] It would seem that this strategy of absence or of a kind of minimalism brings the Liège Station closer to the bridges in its concept than some of Santiago Calatrava's earlier buildings. As for his taste for "transgression," it becomes apparent that Calatrava's careful methods imply a respect for the economic and functional conditions of a project, and seek out a specific reasoning within the gamut of available technical possibilities. His ideas work and engage public interest because they spring from the fertile imagination of the architect-engineer, but also because they respect, from the outset, the fundamental forces at play.

WINGS AND A PRAYER

Calatrava's sensitivity to urban design is undoubtedly what won him the competition in Lisbon, but also in Liège, or more recently in Manhattan for the symbolically charged World Trade Center Transportation Hub. He seems to genuinely feel that the architect can elevate a place such as a railway station and give it a sense of the sacred. When asked if his idea is to make spaces that are comfortable and humane or rather to reach for something more, his answer reveals much about his creative process. "Everything is based on man," he says, "but in man's complexity, the sacred exists, or there wouldn't be so many people crowding into the Pantheon in Rome to see the round hole in the dome. What about railway stations? If you take the example of the modern stations in Switzerland—in Zurich or Basel for example—you get the feeling that you are in a shopping mall. Grand Central Terminal in New York seems to come from a different planet. By exalting abstract values, architecture is capable of being a catalyst for enormous events. But if you go at it with a purely functionalist attitude, you don't catalyze anything. You wind up with a mediocre shopping mall. The feeling that I get in the Central Hall of Grand Central Terminal is the product of great intelligence. It gives a particular sense, even a sacred aspect to commerce. While sacrificing nothing of its utility, the station becomes an act of celebration.

Look at all that has sprung up around the void at the heart of Grand Central—the Seagram Building and Park Avenue itself. In America, no building resembles the Pantheon so closely in these terms. Look at what the architects have placed in the center of the great hall—a clock and a small stand intended to give away timetables—two elements intended to give, rather than to take, from travelers. We need beauty and beauty can generate great things."[21]

When describing his plans for the World Trade Center Transportation Hub (see page 320), Calatrava lists his materials as "glass, steel, concrete, stone, and light." Calatrava has understood that light must shine into the very heart of one of the darkest events in recent American history, and in that he touched the sensitivity of New Yorkers even before the wings of his station rose up out of the ground. Although suggestive of motifs from many traditions (the Byzantine mandorla, the wings of cherubim above the Ark of the Covenant, the sheltering wings on Egyptian canopic urns), the form of his glass roof is summed up, according to Santiago Calatrava, by the image of a bird released from a child's hands. Whatever its symbolism, the complex will also address the overly intricate layering of lower Manhattan's transport system, born of a century of progressive extensions, enlargements, and changes of direction. Working with skilled specialists, as he has in other rail facilities, Calatrava has found elegant solutions to extremely complex technical problems. The generosity that the architect evokes in the design of Grand Central Terminal is at the heart of his WTC project, and it is expressed largely through space and light. As the formal description goes: "The part of the building visible at street level is an arched oval of glass and steel, approximately 107 meters long, 35 meters across at its widest point, and 49 meters high from the lower concourse to the apex of the skylight. The steel ribs that support this structure extend upward into a pair of canopies, which resemble outspread wings and rise to a maximum height of 51 meters. On the main concourse—approximately 10 meters at street level, and 40 meters below the apex of the glass roof—visitors will be able to look up at a column-free, clear span." Echoing Santiago Calatrava's own feelings about the importance of an uplifting design, Michael Bloomberg, the former Mayor of New York, declared: "Today we unveil the design of downtown's new PATH station and we imagine that future generations will look at this building as a true record of our lives today as we rebuild our city. What will they see in Santiago Calatrava's thrilling work? They'll see creativity in design, and strength in construction. They'll see confidence in our investment in a stunning gateway to what will always be the 'Financial Capital of the World.' They'll see a seamless connection to the PATH train, city subways, and, ultimately, to our regional airports. And they'll see optimism—a building appearing to take flight—just like the neighborhood it serves."

ACROSS THE RIVER AND THROUGH THE TREES

As Santiago Calatrava says himself, designing a bridge involves a very specific set of issues, not the least of them symbolic. "If you look back over the history of 19th- and 20th-century bridges," says Calatrava, "many are very special and significant structures. They were given stone cladding, sculpted lions or railings, even angels holding lamps, as is the case on the Alexander III Bridge in Paris. This attitude disappeared as a result of World War II," he continues. "Hundreds of bridges all over Europe had to be rebuilt quickly. It was out of necessity that a school of purely functionalist bridge design sprang up. A good bridge was a simple one, and above all a cheap one." Calatrava obviously feels that this functionalist school of bridge design has far outlived its postwar usefulness. "Today, we have to rediscover the potential of bridges," he declares. He cites the examples of European cities like

---

19 *Ibid.*

20 Santiago Calatrava in conversation with the author, Zurich, June 1997.

21 Santiago Calatrava in conversation with the author, Zurich, February 22, 2006.

Florence, Venice, or Paris to highlight the fact that through their usefulness, but also their permanence, bridges of the past have had a key role in forming impressions of the cities themselves. To make his point Santiago Calatrava goes so far as to say that building a bridge can be a more potent cultural gesture than creating a new museum. "The bridge is more efficient," he says, "because it is available to everyone. Even an illiterate person can enjoy a bridge. A single gesture transforms nature and gives it order. You can't get any more efficient than that," he concludes.[22]

The success of Calatrava's own efforts to give a new meaning to bridges might best be summed up by the example of the Alamillo Bridge and the La Cartuja Viaduct (Seville, 1987–92, see page 80). Standing out at one of the entries to Expo '92, the spectacular 142-meter-high pylon is inclined at a 58-degree angle (the same as that of the Great Pyramid of Cheops), making it visible from much of the old city of Seville. The Alamillo Bridge has a 200-meter span, and runs over the Meandro de San Jerónimo, an all but stagnant branch of the Guadalquivir River. It is supported by 13 pairs of stay cables, but, above all, the "weight of the concrete-filled pylon is sufficient to counterbalance the deck, therefore backstays are not required."[23] Although Calatrava had originally imagined a second bridge, inclined in the opposite direction, like a mirror image of the first one, to cross the nearby Gaudalquivir, budgetary considerations made the client, the regional government of Andalusia, opt for only one span together with the 500-meter-long La Cartuja Viaduct.

Aside from his own copiously illustrated notebooks which make clear the thinking that went into creating the innovative form of the Alamillo pylon, Calatrava here called quite directly on the inspiration provided by *Running Torso*, a sculpture he created in 1986, in which inclined stacked marble cubes are balanced by a tensioned wire. Indeed, many of the drawings that Calatrava hangs on the walls of his Zurich home depict figures in motion. *Running Torso* is clearly inspired, as its title implies, by the tension and forces of a body moving forward. Although the specific use that Calatrava makes of this analysis is very personal, the result does retain something of the "truthful style" evoked by Pier Luigi Nervi.

Despite the ease with which the uninformed person can indeed appreciate the beauty of a bridge, the method that leads to these forms is quite complex. "It is an intuitive process, which is to say a system that relies on the synthesis of a number of factors," he says. His description of bridge design deserves to be quoted at length: "I believe that first and foremost, the location of a bridge must be considered. On certain sites, for example, you could not employ an arc because it is not feasible to transfer the loads to the shore in an appropriate manner. Then, too, waterborne traffic must be considered. The height of a bridge can be determined by the type of boats which must past beneath it. The choice of materials is also essential—wood, steel or concrete might be used according to the local circumstances—and cost factors. These elements and others lead, by a process of elimination, toward certain possible structural solutions. It is then that not only the type of bridge itself, but also its impact on its environment begin to give it form. And then, too, the engineer must make the calculations necessary to be certain that the design he imagines is indeed viable. I create a model which links mathematical science to nature, permitting an understanding of the behavior of nature. We are always confronted with the forces of nature," he concludes.[24]

Another of Santiago Calatrava's bridges, the Campo Volantín Footbridge (Bilbao, Spain, 1990–97, see page 118) is exemplary in terms of his thoughts on peripheral or industrial urban spaces, as well as a proficient exercise in engineering resulting in an unexpected form. Crossing the Bilbao River in a location intended to link the city center with the rundown commercial area called Uribitarte, it calls on the principle of the inclined arch which Calatrava first used in an unbuilt 1988 project for a new bridge on the Seine, between the 12th and 13th arrondissements, linking the Gare de Lyon and the Gare d'Austerlitz. Here, an inclined parabolic arch spanning 71 meters supports a curved walkway that makes for a visually arresting design. Yet, that curve is more than artistic license. As Sergio Polano explains: "The torsion created at the points of suspension of the uprights by the eccentricity of the weight is balanced by the counter-curve of the walkway, thus transferring the load to the concrete foundations," the whole suggesting "a pendulum in suspended motion."[25] Where actual physical motion is not part of the design, Santiago Calatrava's work often brings to mind the sort of tension he evokes in a sculpture like the *Discobolus*.

A number of bridges by Calatrava confront radically different locations with the language of simplicity and efficiency that has come to characterize his river or canal crossings. Calatrava's bridge in Venice, the aptly named Fourth Bridge on the Canal Grande (1999–2008, see page 248), is only the fourth crossing to be built over the famous canal since the 16th century. Connecting the railway station and Piazzale Roma, the 94-meter bridge has a central arch with a very large radius and a transparent glass deck which has been the object of some critiques. Again, elegance and a deft capacity to deal with local pride and political complexities have allowed Santiago Calatrava to build where others have tried and failed in the past.

THE VERTICAL CHALLENGE

From the largely horizontal world of bridges, Calatrava has ventured boldly into the verticality of towers on numerous occasions in his career, though he now seems to be concentrating even more on such design. The best known of his earlier towers is the Montjuïc Communications Tower (Barcelona, Spain, 1989–92, see page 86), which was built at the time of the Olympic Games. Some 130 meters high, with an inclined stem, the tower has been compared to a javelin being thrown, yet Calatrava's own approach, as usual, seems to be quite unexpected. His drawings make clear that the inclined design is inspired by the shape of a kneeling human figure making an offering. Similarly, the plan of the tower would seem at first sight to be inspired by Masonic symbols such as the compass. Santiago Calatrava insists that this particular impression is incorrect, and that it is once again the human eye that inspired him. Naturally the eye is also one of the Masonic symbols, but the reasoning and content of the Montjuïc Tower are clearly multifaceted, just as its engineering creates a surprisingly dynamic shape. As the catalog of the 1993 exhibition at MoMA explains: "Symbolically, the tower refers to the ritual events of the Olympic Games. Its singular form does not contradict the laws of statics, because the center of gravity at the base coincides with the resulting vertical of its dead load. The inclination of the stem coincides with the angle of the summer solstice in Barcelona and acts as a sundial as the sun travels across the circular platform at the base of the stairs. These characteristics heighten the existence of the two major avenues in Barcelona, La Meridiana and El Paralelo, denoting the avant-garde vocation of this city and referring to the technical advances of the period."[26]

Fifteen or so years later, Calatrava designed three very different towers, the Turning Torso, based on his drawings of a male torso; the 80 South Street Tower in New York, made of 12 cantilevered, glazed cubes inspired by a series of sculptures he made up to 20 years earlier; and, most surprisingly, the Chicago Spire, a 160-story, 610-meter-high tower that would have become the tallest building in the United States. In each instance, the architect shows that he in no way feels that towers are outdated as symbols, or as functional, efficient forms of design. Both the Turning Torso and the 80 South Street Tower embody his idea of using the science of statics to give the impression of the movement inherent in the concept of mass. Based on mathematical calculations, these works escape the realm

---

22 Santiago Calatrava in conversation with the author, Zurich, June 1997.
23 Dennis Sharp (ed.), *Santiago Calatrava*, Architectural Monographs, no. 46, Academy Editions, London, 1996.
24 Santiago Calatrava in conversation with the author, Zurich, June 1997.
25 Sergio Polano, *Santiago Calatrava, Complete Works*, Gingko, Electa, Milan, 1996.
26 *Santiago Calatrava, Structure and Expression*, MoMA, New York, March–May 1993.

of dry science to evoke the body or the uplifting sentiment that only a great building can inspire. The Turning Torso (Malmö, Sweden, see page 276) was inaugurated in 2005, while the Chicago Spire (see page 344) and 80 South Street Tower projects were abandoned because of the 2008 financial crisis.

The New York Times evoked Brancusi in describing Calatrava's sculptures, in itself not a disparaging comparison, and yet it may be true that the architect-engineer seems to call on examples from the early 20th century more readily than on recent thought and art. Calatrava quotes Einstein, who famously said: "God does not play dice with the Universe." But at the time, the master of modern physics was reacting to the advances of Quantum Theory, and in particular Werner Heisenberg's *Uncertainty Principle*, which stated, with reference to subatomic particles, that: "The more precisely the position is determined, the less precisely the momentum is known in this instant, and vice versa." Where many artists and architects since then (1927) have embodied the reasoning of uncertain times in their work, why is it that Calatrava seems so firmly anchored in another era—one where Platonic solids might have ruled rather than the complexity described by the theories of Benoît Mandelbrot, for example. "In the 1980s," says Calatrava, "there was indeed experimentation in architecture that had to do with the Chaos Theory and the sort of mathematics used to predict the movement of a stock exchange or the weather. But there is a programmatic element in Einstein's famous sentence that I would like to underline. Order exists, and I am tempted to say that we have already gone beyond the Chaos Theory and begun to think of the order of design. Personally, I have never wanted to render anything explicit in architecture other than order. I have indeed always referred to pure geometry and to controlled movement. The only place chance may enter into my work is when I make a sketch. Where current architecture is concerned, I note that those who choose models based on uncertainty, in the form of disorder or deconstruction if you will, must refer strongly to engineering when they seek to give some maturity to their work. People like Daniel Libeskind proudly refer to their past experience with mathematics, and it is obvious that the science of engineers is essential to their architecture. I might be so bold as to say that I have always played the game from the center. Even the roof of the Bodegas Ysios (Laguardia, Álava, Spain, 1998–2001, see page 264) is based on a sinusoid curve. In my sculpture I have obviously used simple forms, and 20 years later, a sculpture, allied with the idea of the human body was the basis for the Turning Torso."[27]

A PAVILION LIKE A FALCON, A CHAPEL LIKE A PRAYER

As Santiago Calatrava carried forward the mature phase of his career, his works testified that he had no intention of becoming duller as time goes by. Work in his native city of Valencia saw the inauguration of a final phase of the cultural complex he started in 1991, the Opera House (1996–2006, see page 198). The Tenerife Auditorium (Santa Cruz de Tenerife, Canary Islands, Spain, 1991–2003, see page 146) similarly confirmed the boldness of his designs and brings forth the recurring theme of the eye, the instrument of his passion. Working against the clock and on an enormous scale, Santiago Calatrava also completed the Athens Olympic Sports Complex (OAKA, Athens, Greece, 2001–04, see page 292) including no less than 199 000 square meters of plazas; 94 000 square meters of pathways; 61 000 square meters of green areas; 29 000 square meters of water elements; 130 000 square meters of service facilities; and 178 000 square meters of parking lots and roads. It is easy to see where Calatrava has been, but not as obvious to tell where he will go in the future. This very point may well be a key to understanding his thought. "Imagine that you don't know where you are going," he says. "The baggage you bring with you is what you carry inside. For me this is almost a situation of paranoia, or of schizophrenia. I have a sense of forms born of 14 years of university studies—I have encountered mathematics and I love them. When I look at the work of Picasso, Cézanne or Matisse, all of which moves me, I must notice that they never engaged in the abstraction, except in limited details of their works. They worked to create an emotion and I am also born of their universe. I have long been inspired by a simple phrase of Michelangelo, '*l'architettura dipende dalle membra dell'uomo.*' To use the human body as a means of expression is and will remain important." In a recent discussion, Santiago Calatrava seemed to be most enthusiastic about plans for a future large exhibition of his artwork. At his home and studio in Zurich, he paints and draws, including figure studies from live models. Aside from the highly visible World Trade Center project, before 2020, Calatrava also completed the Museum of Tomorrow in Rio (2010–15, see page 394). The forms of each of these projects confirm the architect's desire and ability to challenge the conventional limits of contemporary buildings. His work stands out from its surroundings, giving a sense that modernity can still be exhilarating.

For this edition of the TASCHEN monograph, Santiago Calatrava sat down with the author to discuss some of his most recent work, which includes a monumental sculpture in Chicago and a surprising small chapel in Naples, entirely renovated and redecorated with pieces conceived by him and executed with the collaboration of local artisans. The plunge into the past represented by the Church of San Gennaro intervention (Naples, Italy) is contrasted with the architect's ongoing plans to build a remarkable tunnel and bridge crossing of West Bay (Doha, Qatar) and an even more surprising tower in Dubai, two projects that have been on hold for some time.

PJ *What brought you to create a large sculpture in Chicago?*

SC I have always been interested in creating artworks at the same time as my work on architecture. A person from Chicago contacted me subsequent to my 2015 show of sculptures in New York. At the invitation of The Fund for Park Avenue, I installed seven large-scale pieces on the central island of Park Avenue between 52nd and 65th Streets. I was delighted at the idea of creating a large 8.8-meter-high sculpture in Chicago (see page 352), which has a justified reputation for being one of the birthplaces of modern architecture. In the past 50 years or so, a number of significant public artworks have been installed in the city, including a 15-meter-high untitled sculpture by Picasso (1967), Anish Kapoor's *Cloud Gate* (2004), Jaume Plensa's *Crown Fountain* (2004), Joan Miro's *Chicago* (1981), Jean Dubuffet's *Monument with a Standing Beast* (1984), and Alexander Calder's bright red *Flamingo* (1973).

The placement of my work *Constellation* at the fork in the Chicago River is excellent: despite being in front of a large tower, it has a certain autonomy. It was challenging to create a work in the context of so many large buildings. I could have used naturally colored stainless steel, aluminum or bronze. But the scale of the piece made bronze a very difficult option. I decided to use aluminum with a bright red color if only because I admire the work of Alexander Calder. I particularly admire his use of movement in the mobiles. My son Gabriel and I created the design for an exhibition of the small-scale work of Calder in 2015 (*Multum in Parvo*, Dominique Lévy Gallery, New York). I also chose bright red for Chicago so that my work would contrast with the greenish glass tower behind it.

PJ *What is the status of other work that you have in the Gulf Region?*

SC We have two projects that have been on hold in the region: the Sharq Crossing destined to link the two sides of West Bay in Doha (see page 408) and the Dubai Creek Tower (see page 416). These have been delayed as the countries concerned put an emphasis on more urgent work: the upcoming FIFA World Cup for Qatar and the 2020 Expo Dubai for the UAE, but they will both advance. The foundations for the tower have been completed.

PJ *As we speak, you have almost completed a surprising project in Naples, Italy: the renovation of an 18th-century chapel. Here it seems that you have worked more as an artist than as an architect.*

---

27 Santiago Calatrava in conversation with the author, Zurich, February 22, 2006.

SC The Director of the Capodimonte Museum in Naples is the Frenchman Sylvain Bellenger, who previously worked in the Cleveland and Chicago museums as well as having directed the Chateau de Blois in France (1992–99). He organized an exhibition of my work called "In the Light of Naples" at the end of 2019. Part of his work was also the rehabilitation of the 134-hectare Real Bosco (or Royal Park) of Capodimonte. Within the park there are about ten buildings, including the Real Fabbrica di Capodimonte-Istituto Superiore ad Indirizzo Raro Caselli, which was a porcelain factory. Another of the buildings in the park is the Church of San Gennaro (see page 442), built in 1745 by the important architect and stage designer Ferdinando Sanfelice at the behest of Charles of Bourbon. Sylvain Bellenger imagined that my exhibition could be the occasion to renovate the chapel, which had been closed for several decades. I felt that an installation in that chapel, or perhaps more clearly a restoration, could be carried forward by calling on the artisans of the region. The first of these was the neighboring porcelain factory. We then turned to the royal textile factory of Caserta, San Leucio, which is still in activity, and to the master glassmaker Antonio Perotti, from Vietri sul Mare, to participate in the project. We are still working on a new altar with local bronze-working artisans, and the liturgical vestments. I have given all the drawings for my designs to the museum. These were inspired in good part by the surrounding park and forest environment and the project was essentially financed by the Region of Campania.[28]

A HYMN TO THE LIVING WORLD

No matter how significant mathematics and the science of engineering are in the work of Santiago Calatrava, it is art and emotion that drive him to create works that surpass the mundane calculation of forces. "Life is like a collection of pearls," says Calatrava. "You find one here and another there on your road. What is the sense of function in architecture? It is love, the love that one gives others, the generosity of the architect. There is a great secret in architecture and that is its philanthropic nature, and that philanthropy can be understood in the terms of function. A building functions well out of love for men. The secret of philanthropy in architecture is in its function. Beauty is given through intelligence or intuition. In architecture it is necessary to draw every detail. Each act, except the emotion that sets you on your way, is an act of intelligence. Architecture is what makes beautiful ruins; it is the most abstract of all the arts."[29] And so, even as he refers to "beautiful ruins," Santiago Calatrava has focussed more and more on art forms that are less abstract, including porcelain and textiles, for the chapel in Naples. His large sculptures are, indeed, closer to abstraction than his drawings or watercolors. All these works speak of an indefatigable love of life itself in its many forms. His architecture, which often literally moves, is also a hymn to the living world.

---

28 Santiago Calatrava in conversation with the author, Zurich, January 17, 2022.

29 Santiago Calatrava in conversation with the author, Zurich, February 22, 2006.

ALPINE BRIDGES

Switzerland. 1973–1979.

Project

ALPINE BRIDGES

Location

SWITZERLAND

Calatrava was well aware of the engineering tradition of the ETH in Zurich and it is significant that one of his first published works is this series of bridges that in many ways take up where the famous Swiss engineer Robert Maillart left off.

Calatrava war sich der Ingenieurtradition der ETH in Zürich bewusst, und es ist bezeichnend, dass eines seiner ersten publizierten Werke diese Serie von Brücken ist, die dort anknüpft, wo der der berühmte Schweizer Ingenieur Robert Maillart aufgehört hat.

Calatrava était très au fait des traditions d'ingénierie de l'ETH de Zurich et il est significatif que l'un de ses premiers travaux publiés ait été cette série de ponts qui, à de nombreux égards, reprend le problème là où l'ingénieur suisse Robert Maillart l'avait laissé.

Between 1973 and 1979, Santiago Calatrava designed a series of bridges that mark the beginnings of his career. Inspired by the Swiss mountains and the work of Robert Maillart (1872–1940), one of the most famous graduates of Zurich's ETH, he evolved toward progressively more daring and spectacular concepts. He describes this work in his own terms as follows: "After passing my architectural exams in Valencia, Spain, I enrolled at the Federal Institute of Technology (ETH) in Zurich, Switzerland, in 1973 to study civil engineering. I had spent many holidays visiting various regions of Switzerland and was fascinated by its beautiful mountain landscape. I had also developed an interest in the concrete bridges of Robert Maillart, whose work I had studied as an architecture student and which was primarily located in Switzerland."

WALENSEE BRIDGE

"During my third year of study, the 'Brückenbau' course (bridge construction) provided my first opportunity to design a bridge. The site, near Walensee, faced the beautiful Churfirsten mountains. The exercise was to design a bridge spanning from a mountain tunnel across a ravine. My design proposed continuing the shape of the concrete tunnel shell, while permitting the sun to illuminate the roadway. I achieved this by cutting and modifying the shape of the tubular section to the structural requirements of the span. The tensile forces were carried over the pylon supports by the upper portion of the elliptical shell, while the compressive forces were taken along the road deck."

ACLETA BRIDGE

"In the spring of 1979 I commenced my thesis work at the ETH with a bridge design in Disentis, Switzerland. The location is a splendid Alpine area of the Vorderrhein valley on the way from Reichenau toward the Oberalp Pass. The road to Disentis crosses two impressive bridges. One designed by Robert Maillart in 1905 over the Rhine in Tavanasa; the other, the Lavina Tobel Bridge in Tamins, was designed by Max Bill in 1966. I initially produced two series of bridge designs. The first series was based on the classical concrete arch bridge designs of Maillart and variations on those principles. The second series followed my earlier explorations in 'free cantilever' bridges. This series of four variations to the 'free cantilever' model was primarily concerned with controlling the interacting forces contained at the pylon and deck connection, and allowing these forces to become the formal expression of the bridge. The third design variation looked to increase the structural efficiency of the method explored in the second variation. In order to produce longer free spans, I increased

As Calatrava explains, his mastery of the requirements of engineering allows him to explore the gamut of shapes that can resist the forces applicable to such bridges. With his knowledge of fundamentals, he is left free to invent sculptural solutions to given problems.

Wie Calatrava erklärt, kann er dank seiner umfassenden technischen Kenntnisse die Skala der Formen ausschöpfen, die den auf solche Brücken einwirkenden Kräften standhalten können. Dies ermöglicht es ihm, plastische Lösungen zu erdenken.

Comme l'explique Calatrava, sa maîtrise des contraintes techniques lui permet d'explorer toute la gamme des formes susceptibles de résister aux forces engendrées par ce type de ponts. Sa connaissance le rend libre d'inventer des solutions sculpturales.

the static height of the pylon to deck connection by extending the lateral arms of the support pylon above the road deck. The tensile forces would therefore be transferred through cables embedded in the concrete pylon walls in a similar manner as that previously described for the Walensee Bridge. The fourth design variation, in contrast to the shell structure of the Walensee Bridge, proposed a reduction in the thickness of the pylon's lateral walls containing the embedded tension cables in an effort to create a prestressed concrete shell structure. This development proved to be a short step from removing the concrete shell in which the cables were embedded and leaving them exposed. I would explore this variation shortly."

BIASCINA VIADUCT

"After completing my thesis, and becoming a licensed Civil Engineer at the end of spring 1979, I worked as an assistant in the Architecture Department at the ETH. In order to study for her law exams, my wife and our son moved to her parents' house near Locarno, in southern Switzerland. I spent every weekend traveling by train from Zurich to Locarno and back. After passing through the Gotthard, the trains' spiral descent through the mountain tunnels to the valley below provided several stunning views of the Biascina Bridge, which was being built at the time for the transalpine Gotthard Highway. During these trips I began to sketch my own ideas for the design of this bridge. I applied the principles developed during my thesis explorations in 'free cantilever' design and realized a clear span of 300 meters by liberating the embedded tension cables from the prestressed concrete shells of the pylon supports."

SKETCHES FOR THE IABSE SYMPOSIUM IN ZURICH

"During the fall semester of 1979, while I was working as an assistant in the Architecture Department at the ETH and writing my Ph.D. thesis, the International Association for Bridge and Structural Engineering (IABSE) decided to hold its 50th anniversary symposium in Zurich the following year. A professor in the Civil Engineering Department at the ETH, Mr. Christian Menn, was invited to speak on 'Modern Bridge Design and Construction.' He asked me to design a bridge that might be presented during his lecture. I presented him with several design variations for very tall pylon bridges that would make it possible to cross deep Alpine valleys, one of which was presented at the symposium. In these variations I explored the effects of different pylon cross sections, such as 'cross,' 'double T,' rhomboid, hexagonal, and whole box, as well as diverse methods of connecting the cables to the top of the pylon."

ALPINE BRÜCKEN

Die Anfänge von Santiago Calatravas Laufbahn als Architekt standen im Zeichen einer Reihe von Brückenentwürfen zwischen 1973 und 1979. Beflügelt von der schweizerischen Bergwelt und dem Werk Robert Maillarts (1872–1940), eines der berühmtesten Absolventen der ETH Zürich, gerieten seine Konzepte zunehmend spektakulär. Er selbst beschreibt diese Arbeiten wie folgt: „Nachdem ich meine Architekturexamina in Valencia bestanden hatte, schrieb ich mich 1973 an der Eidgenössischen Technischen Hochschule in Zürich für Bauingenieurwesen ein. In vielen Ferien hatte ich die Schweiz bereist und war von der wunderbaren Bergwelt fasziniert. Außerdem interessierten mich die Betonbrücken Robert Maillarts, dessen überwiegend in der Schweiz befindliches Werk ich als Architekturstudent kennengelernt hatte."

WALENSEE-BRÜCKE

„Während meines dritten Studienjahres gab mir der Kurs ‚Brückenbau' die erste Gelegenheit, eine Brücke zu entwerfen. Dem Baugelände in der Nähe des Walensees liegen die markanten Gipfel der Churfirsten gegenüber. Ich musste eine Brücke konzipieren, die sich von einem Bergtunnel über eine Schlucht spannte. Mein Entwurf sah vor, die Form des Tunnelgehäuses aus Beton fortzusetzen; außerdem sollte das Sonnenlicht auf die Straße fallen. Ich erreichte dies, indem ich die Form des Röhrenquerschnitts modifizierte, um sie den konstruktiven Erfordernissen der Öffnung anzupassen. Die Zugkräfte wurden durch den oberen Teil des elliptischen Gehäuses über die Stützpfeiler aufgenommen, während die Druckkräfte entlang der Straßendecke geführt wurden."

ACLETA-BRÜCKE

„Im Frühjahr 1979 begann ich meine Abschlussarbeit an der ETH mit einem Brückenentwurf in Disentis/Schweiz. Die Stelle liegt in einer großartigen, alpinen Region des Vorderrheintales auf dem Weg von Reichenau zum Oberalppass. Die Straße nach Disentis überquert zwei imposante Brücken. Die eine, 1905 von Robert Maillart entworfen, überspannt den Rhein bei Tavanasa, während die Lavina-Tobel-Brücke in Tamins 1966 von Max Bill erbaut wurde. Zu Anfang konzipierte ich zwei Serien von Brückenentwürfen: Die erste Serie fußte auf der klassischen Betonbogenbrücke Maillarts und Abwandlungen dieser Grundregeln. Für die zweite Serie mit vier Variationen zog ich meine früheren Versuche mit freitragenden Auslegerbrücken heran. Dabei ging es in erster Linie darum,

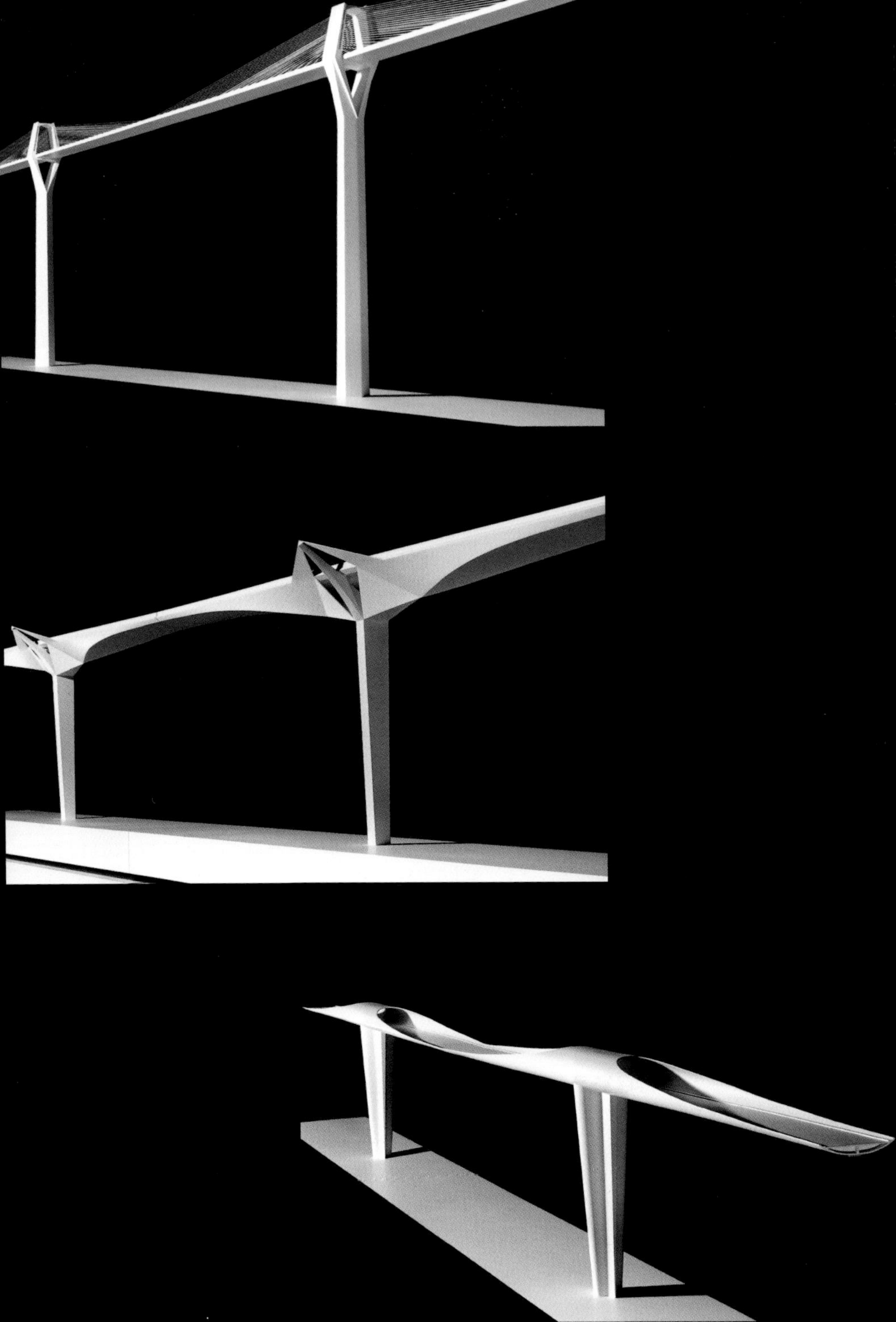

Although it would appear that Calatrava's earlier sketches had a more summary character than his more recent work, the idea of the lightness and broad span of the bridge seen to the right is clearly in his mind— an indication of his future design goals.
Collection Tom F. Peters

Obwohl Calatravas frühere Skizzen zusammenhängender erscheinen als seine neueren Arbeiten, spielt die Idee der Leichtigkeit und großen Spannweite der Brücke (rechts) offensichtlich eine Rolle – ein Hinweis auf seine späteren Designziele.
Collection Tom F. Peters

Bien qu'il semble que les croquis anciens de Calatrava possèdent un caractère plus sommaire que ceux réalisés pour ses œuvres plus récentes, il avait déjà en tête l'idée de légèreté et de grande portée comme le montre le pont illustré à droite – indication sur ses futurs objectifs conceptuels.
Collection Tom F. Peters

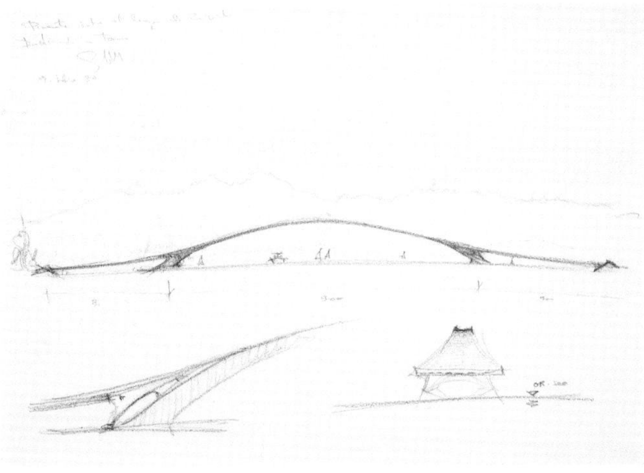

die in der Pfeiler- und Tafelverbindung enthaltenen interagierenden Kräfte, die der Brücke ihre Form geben, zu beherrschen. Die dritte Entwurfsvariante sollte die konstruktive Effizienz der zuvor ausgeloteten Methode steigern. Um größere Spannweiten zu erreichen, steigerte ich die statische Höhe der Pfeiler-Tafel-Verbindung, indem ich die Seitenarme des Stützpfeilers über der Straßentafel verlängerte. Ähnlich wie zuvor bei der Walensee-Brücke beschrieben, würden die Zugkräfte daher durch in die Betonwände des Pfeilers eingebettete Seile übertragen. Im Gegensatz zur Gehäusekonstruktion der Walensee-Brücke sah die vierte Entwurfsvariante vor, die Stärke der Seitenwände des Stützpfeilers mit den eingebetteten Seilen zu reduzieren, um eine Spannbetonschalenkonstruktion zu schaffen. Von dieser Entwicklung war es nicht mehr weit bis zur Entfernung der Betonumhüllung der Seile, die dann frei sichtbar wären. Ich sollte diese Variante kurze Zeit später erproben."

BIASCINA-VIADUKT

„Nachdem ich im Frühjahr 1979 meine Abschlussarbeit beendet und die Prüfung zum Bauingenieur abgelegt hatte, war ich als Assistent an der Architekturabteilung der ETH tätig. Meine Frau musste sich damals auf ihre juristischen Examina vorbereiten und zog deshalb mit unserem Sohn ins Haus ihrer Eltern bei Locarno im Süden der Schweiz. Ich fuhr in dieser Zeit an jedem Wochenende mit dem Zug von Zürich nach Locarno und zurück. Nach dem Passieren des Gotthard eröffneten sich auf der kurvenreichen Talfahrt durch zahllose Tunnel einige fantastische Ausblicke auf die Biascina-Brücke, die damals für die transalpine Sankt-Gotthard-Straße gebaut wurde. Auf diesen Reisen begann ich,

A concern for great simplicity and elegance is seen in these two sketches, one dealing with the problem of curvature and the other with great height in the support pylons. As always, Calatrava takes into account the fundamental engineering required to attain such a reduced form of expression.
Collection Tom F. Peters

Diese beiden Skizzen veranschaulicen, welche Rolle Einfachheit und Eleganz spielen. Die eine zeigt das Problem der Krümmung, die andere die enorme Höhe der Stützpylone. Wie immer berücksichtigt Calatrava die grundlegende Technik, die erforderlich ist, um solch klaren Ausdruck zu erzielen.
Collection Tom F. Peters

Le souci de grande simplicité et d'élégance se remarque dans ces deux croquis, l'un traitant du problème d'une courbe et l'autre de la hauteur des pylônes. Comme toujours, Calatrava prend en compte les principes fondamentaux de l'ingénierie pour atteindre à une forme d'expression aussi concentrée que possible.
Collection Tom F. Peters

meine eigenen Ideen für die Gestaltung dieser Brücke zu skizzieren. Ich wendete die für meine Abschlussarbeit entwickelten Prinzipien für freitragende Auslegerkonstruktionen an und realisierte eine freie Spannweite von 300 m, indem ich die ummantelten Spannseile von den Spannbetonhülsen der Pylonenstützen befreite."

ENTWÜRFE FÜR DAS IABSE-SYMPOSIUM IN ZÜRICH

„Im Lauf des Herbstsemesters 1979, während ich als Assistent am Fachbereich Architektur der ETH an meiner Doktorarbeit schrieb, entschied die International Association for Bridge and Structural Engineering (IABSE), das Symposium zur Feier ihres 50-jährigen Bestehens im folgenden Jahr in Zürich zu veranstalten. Christian Menn, Professor im Fachbereich Bauingenieurwesen der ETH, war eingeladen, über das Thema ‚Modern Bridge Design and Construction' zu sprechen. Er bat mich, eine Brücke zu entwerfen, die er während seines Vortrags vorstellen könnte. Ich legte ihm mehrere Entwürfe für sehr hohe Pylonenbrücken über tiefe Alpentäler vor. Einer davon wurde bei dem Symposium gezeigt. Mit diesen Varianten erforschte ich die Auswirkungen verschiedener Pylonenquerschnitte, wie Kreuz, Doppel-T, Raute, Hexagon und Viereck, sowie verschiedene Methoden, die Seile mit der Spitze des Pylons zu verbinden."

PONTS ALPINS

De 1973 à 1979, Calatrava conçut une série de ponts qui marquent les débuts de sa carrière. Inspiré par les montagnes suisses et l'œuvre de Robert Maillart (1872–1940) l'un des plus fameux diplômés de l'ETH de Zurich, il évolua peu à peu vers des concepts de plus en plus audacieux et spectaculaires. Il décrit ainsi ces ouvrages : « Après avoir obtenu mon diplôme d'architecte à Valence (Espagne), je me suis inscrit à l'Institut fédéral de technologie de Zurich (ETH), en 1973, pour étudier le génie civil. J'avais déjà passé plusieurs fois des vacances en Suisse et visité diverses régions. J'étais fasciné par la beauté des paysages alpins. Je m'étais également intéressé aux ponts en béton de Robert Maillart (pour la plupart en Suisse), dont j'avais étudié l'œuvre quand j'étais étudiant. »

PONT DU WALENSEE

« Au cours de ma troisième année d'études, le cours de construction de ponts *(Brückenbau)* m'offrit l'opportunité d'en dessiner un pour la première fois. Le site, près du Walensee, faisait face au superbe massif des Churfisten. L'exercice consistait à imaginer un ouvrage franchissant un ravin au sortir d'un tunnel. Mon projet proposait de prolonger la forme de la coque en béton du tunnel, tout en laissant le soleil éclairer la route. J'y suis parvenu en coupant et modifiant la section tubulaire en fonction des contraintes structurelles imposées par la portée. Les forces de traction étaient transférées aux supports du pylône par la partie supérieure de la coque elliptique, et les forces de compression réparties le long du tablier. »

PONT D'ACLETA

« J'ai commencé ma préparation de thèse à l'ETH au printemps 1979 par un projet de pont à Disentis, en Suisse. Il s'agissait d'une magnifique région de la vallée du Haut-Rhin, entre Reichenau et le col de l'Oberalp. La route pour Disentis franchit deux ponts impressionnants, l'un dessiné par

Robert Maillart en 1905 pour franchir le Rhin à Tavanasa, l'autre, le pont de Lavina Tobel à Tamins, conçu par Max Bill en 1966. Au départ, je proposai deux séries de projets. La première s'appuyait sur les principes de ponts à arche classiques en béton de Maillart et quelques variations sur ce concept. La seconde était dans la ligne de mes explorations antérieures de ponts en "porte-à-faux libre". Cette série de quatre variantes consistait d'abord dans le contrôle des forces interactives qui œuvraient à la connexion entre le pylône et le tablier pour leur permettre de se transformer en expression formelle du pont. La troisième proposition visait à accroître l'efficacité structurelle de la méthode explorée dans la seconde. Pour obtenir des portées plus longues, j'augmentai la hauteur statique de la connexion pylône-tablier en étendant les bras latéraux du pylône de soutien par-dessus le tablier. Les forces de traction seraient alors transférées par des câbles noyés dans les parois en béton du pylône de manière similaire à celle décrite pour le pont du Walensee. La quatrième variante, par contraste avec la structure en coque du pont du Walensee, proposait de réduire l'épaisseur des parois latérales du pylône contenant les câbles en tension pour créer une structure en coque de béton précontraint. Ce développement n'était pas loin de supprimer la coque de béton dans laquelle les câbles étaient insérés et de les rendre apparents, ce que j'allais bientôt étudier. »

VIADUC DE BIASCINA

« Après avoir soutenu ma thèse et être devenu ingénieur civil diplômé à la fin du printemps 1979, j'ai travaillé comme assistant au département d'architecture de l'ETH. Pour se préparer à ses examens de droit, ma femme emménagea avec notre fils dans la maison de ses parents près de Locarno, en Suisse méridionale. Chaque week-end, je faisais l'aller-retour en train entre Zurich et Locarno. Après avoir franchi le Gothard, la descente en zigzag vers la vallée à travers une série de tunnels offrait des vues stupéfiantes sur le pont de Biascina que l'on construisait en même temps que l'autoroute transalpine du Gothard. Au cours de ces voyages, j'ai commencé à tracer des croquis à partir de mes idées personnelles sur cet ouvrage. J'ai appliqué les principes mis au point lors des recherches exploratoires pour ma thèse sur les "porte-à-faux libres", et réalisé une portée sans soutien de 300 mètres en dégageant les câbles des coques en béton précontraint des pylônes. »

CROQUIS POUR LE SYMPOSIUM DE L'IABSE À ZURICH

« À l'automne 1979, alors que je travaillais comme assistant à l'ETH et rédigeais ma thèse de doctorat, l'International Association for Bridge and Structural Engineering (IABSE) décida de tenir le symposium de son cinquantième anniversaire à Zurich l'année suivante. Un professeur du département de génie civil de l'ETH, Christian Menn, m'invita à y parler de « La conception et la construction de ponts modernes ». Il me demanda de concevoir un exemple qui pourrait être présenté à l'occasion de cette conférence. Je lui soumis plusieurs variantes d'un projet d'ouvrage à très hauts pylônes qui permettrait de franchir les vallées alpines. L'une fut présentée au symposium. J'y explorais les effets de différentes sections de pylônes comme la croix, le "double-T", l'ovale, l'hexagone et la boîte, ainsi que diverses méthodes pour connecter les câbles au sommet du pylône. »

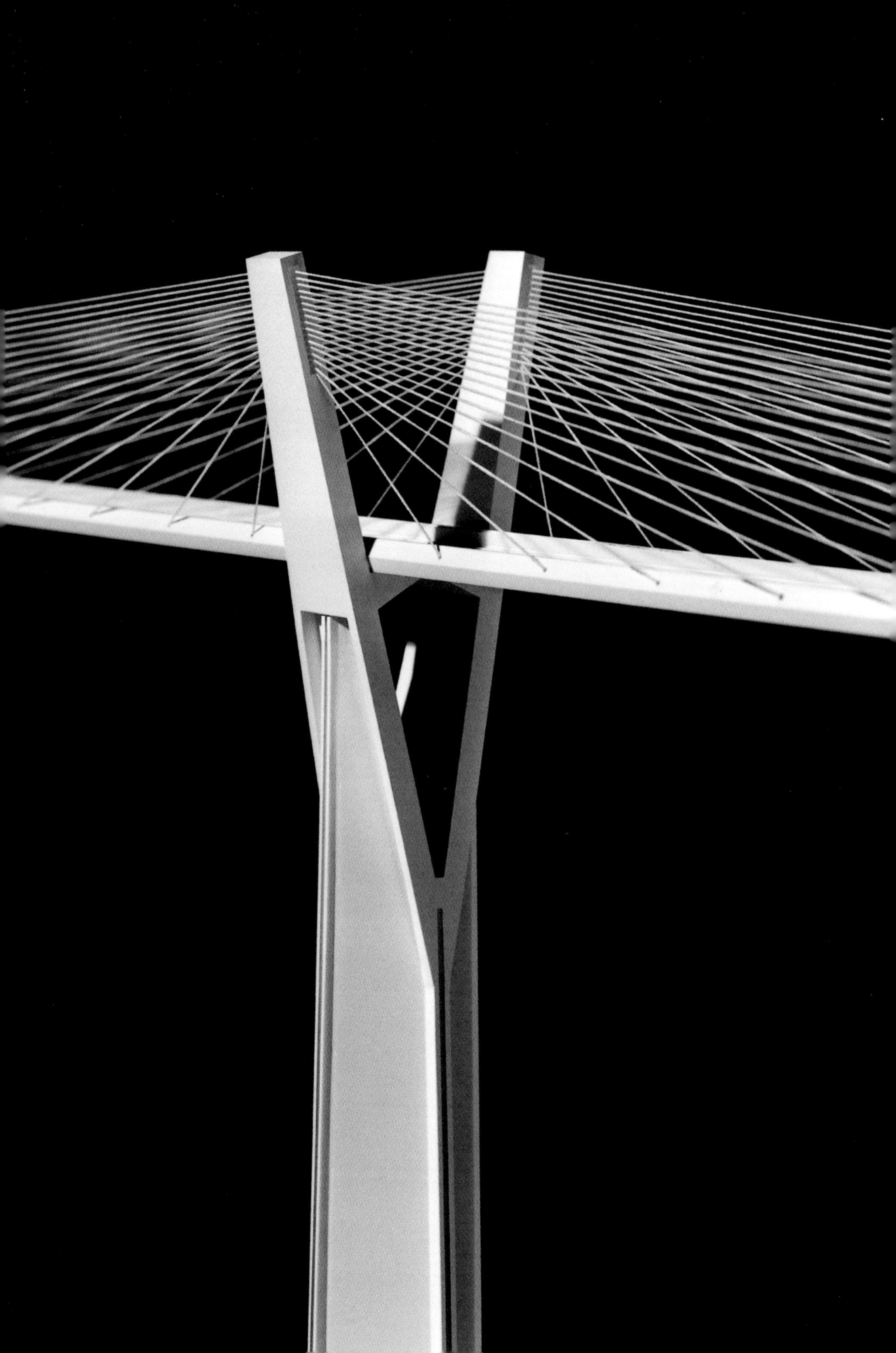

ERNSTING'S WAREHOUSE

Coesfeld-Lette, Germany. 1983–1985.

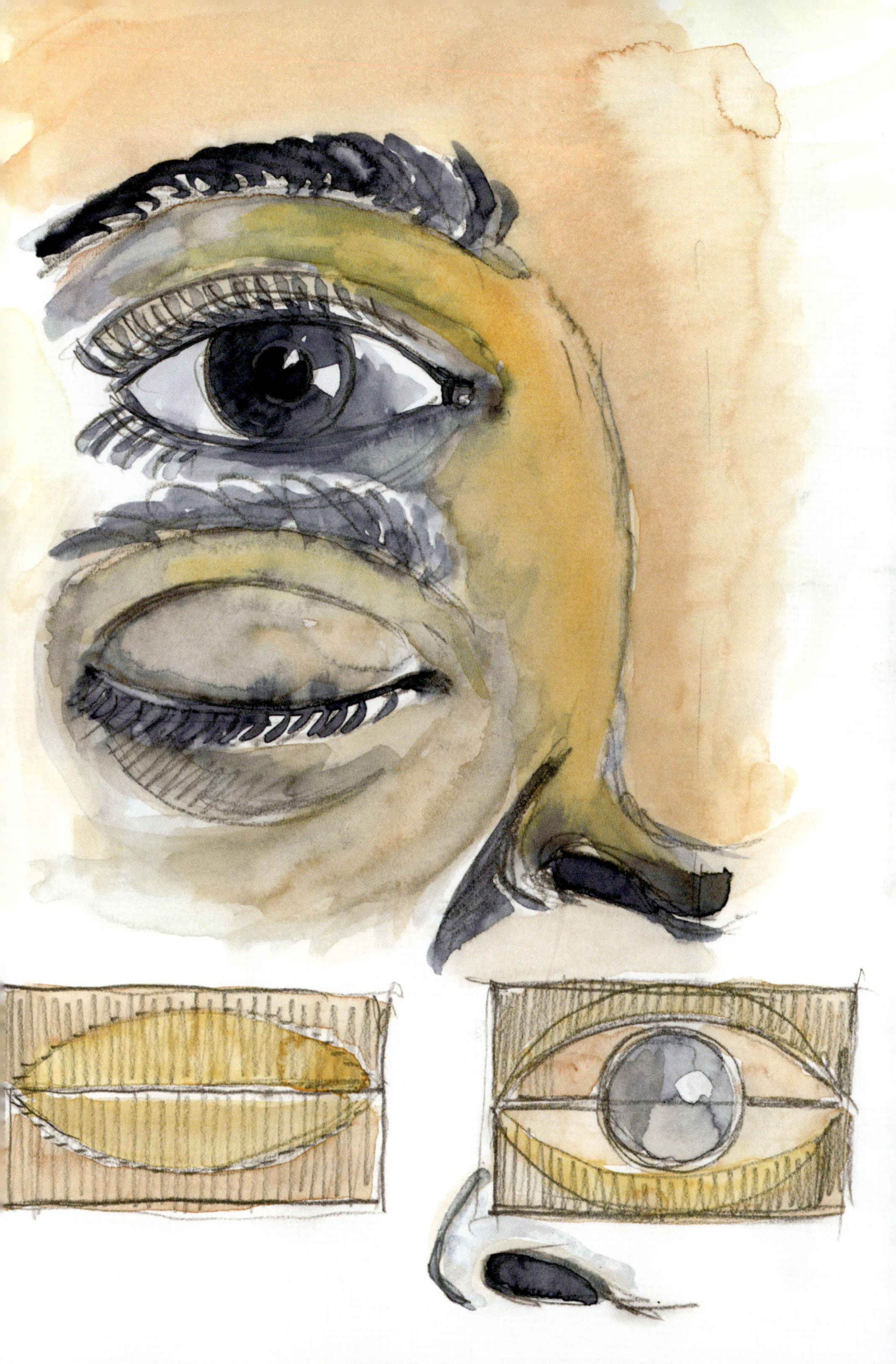

Detalle de las
puertas abiertas

Project

ERNSTING'S WAREHOUSE

Location

COESFELD-LETTE, GERMANY

Client

ERNSTING'S COMPANY

One fact that sets Santiago Calatrava apart from other architects and engineers is that even relatively technical drawings, such as this sketch for Ernsting's cargo door, become works of art, giving an attractive appearance to a detail that would usually be expressed in a much drier form.

Ein Umstand, der Calatrava von anderen Architekten und Ingenieuren unterscheidet, ist, dass selbst eher technische Zeichnungen wie diese Skizze für Ernsting's Ladetor zu Kunstwerken werden und einem normalerweise schnörkelloser dargestellten Detail ein reizvolles Aussehen verleihen.

L'un des points qui distinguent Calatrava des autres architectes et ingénieurs est que, même des dessins relativement techniques comme ce croquis des portes de l'entrepôt Ernsting's, deviennent des œuvres d'art et confèrent un aspect séduisant à des détails généralement exprimés de façon beaucoup plus sèche.

Santiago Calatrava's fascination with human or natural form and function is clearly part of his design process. This interest has led him to create bridges that have been described in terms of "frozen movement," but has also inspired him to actually introduce movement into some of his buildings. Then, too, his drawings and sculptures participate actively in the search for innovative solutions. All of these elements are present in the Ernsting's Warehouse, which he was commissioned to complete after an invited competition involving Fabio Reinhart and Bruno Reichlin. Ernsting's is a well-known German clothing manufacturer with a reputation for seeking quality in its working environments. In the case of the Coesfeld-Lette campus, the warehouse that Calatrava worked on in the 1980s is now located opposite a more recent structure by David Chipperfield, the Service Center (1998–2001), an elegant minimalist design surrounded by a garden conceived by the noted Belgian landscape architects Jacques and Peter Wirtz. Calatrava worked with an initial warehouse form proposed by Gerzi, a specialist in facilities for the textile industry. He decided to cover the Gerzi structure with untreated aluminum, a typical industrial material, seeking to make each façade different while maintaining the overall unity imposed by the cladding. The aluminum is treated according to light patterns, corrugated on the south where it "responds to sunlight as if it were a giant sculpture," or with a specially formed S-profile on the north where the façade receives only midday sun. The most surprising feature suggested by Calatrava is to be found in the form of the three large loading bay doors, measuring 13 x 5 meters. The hinged aluminum ribs rise to form a concave arch as they open, creating canopies. A sculpture by Calatrava with a "form based on the human eye" was part of the design process. "Here," says the architect, "the form became an experiment in kinetics, used to investigate the mechanical transformation of planes in a building."

Die Faszination, die menschliche oder naturgegebene Formen und Funktionen auf Santiago Calatrava ausüben, ist eindeutig Teil seiner Entwurfsarbeit. Dieses Interesse führte dazu, dass er Brücken konzipierte, die als „gefrorene Bewegung“ beschrieben wurden, inspirierte ihn aber auch, tatsächlich Bewegung in einige seiner Bauten zu integrieren. Darüber hinaus sind seine Zeichnungen und Skulpturen Teil seiner Suche nach innovativen Lösungen. Alle diese Elemente sind in Ernsting's präsent, mit dessen Fertigstellung er im Anschluss an einen geschlossenen Wettbewerb mit Beteiligung von Fabio Reinhart und Bruno Reichlin beauftragt wurde. Ernsting's ist ein bekannter deutscher Bekleidungshersteller, der Wert auf sehr gute Arbeitsumgebungen legt. Dem Lagerhaus in Coesfeld-Lette, an dem Calatrava in den 1980er-Jahren arbeitete, steht jetzt ein neuerer Bau von David Chipperfield gegenüber. Dieses Servicezentrum (1998–2001) ist ein elegantes, minimalistisches Gebäude, umgeben von einer Gartenanlage von den bekannten belgischen Landschaftsarchitekten Jacques und Peter Wirtz. Calatrava musste mit einer vorgegebenen Lagerhausform von Gerzi arbeiten, einem Spezialisten für Bauten der Textilindustrie. Er entschied, den Gerzi-Bau mit unbehandeltem Aluminium, einem typischen Industriematerial, zu ummanteln. Dabei war er bemüht, jede Fassade anders zu gestalten und dabei doch die von der Verkleidung vorgegebene Einheitlichkeit zu wahren. Das Aluminium ist dem Lichteinfall entsprechend behandelt, gewellt auf der Südseite, wo es „auf Sonnenlicht wie eine riesige Skulptur reagiert“, und mit einem speziell geformten S-Profil auf der Nordseite, wo die Fassade nur zur Mittagszeit Licht erhält. Das überraschendste von Calatrava entworfene Detail betrifft die Form der drei breiten, 13 x 5 m großen Tore der Laderampen. Die schwenkbaren Aluminiumrippen erheben sich beim Öffnen zu einem konkaven Bogen und bilden Vordächer. Eine Skulptur Calatravas mit einer „auf dem menschlichen Auge basierenden Form“ beeinflusste seinen Entwurfsprozess. „Hier“, sagt der Architekt, „wurde die Form zu einem kinetischen Experiment, um die mechanische Transformation von Flächen in einem Gebäude zu erkunden.“

La fascination de Calatrava pour les formes et les fonctions humaines ou naturelles appartient de toute évidence à son processus de conception. Cet intérêt l'a conduit à créer des ponts au sujet desquels on a pu parler de « mouvement figé », mais aussi à introduire vraiment le mouvement dans certains de ses projets de bâtiments. Ses dessins et ses sculptures participent activement à sa recherche de solutions innovantes. Tous ces éléments sont présents dans l'entrepôt Ernsting's dont il reçut commande à l'issue d'un concours restreint auquel participèrent Fabio Reinhart et Bruno Reichlin. Ernsting's est un fabricant de vêtements allemand très réputé, connu pour rechercher une certaine qualité dans ses lieux de travail. L'entrepôt de la zone d'activités de Coesfeld-Lette, conçu par Calatrava dans les années 1980, se trouve aujourd'hui en face d'une structure plus récente, le Centre de services (1998–2001) signé David Chipperfield, élégante réalisation minimaliste entourée d'un jardin conçu par les célèbres paysagistes belges Jacques et Peter Wirtz. Calatrava a travaillé sur un bâtiment initial de Gerzi, un spécialiste des installations pour l'industrie textile. Il décida d'habiller cette structure d'aluminium brut, matériau typiquement industriel, et chercha à différencier chaque façade tout en maintenant l'unité d'habillage de l'ensemble. L'aluminium est traité en fonction du type de lumière : ondulé au sud, où il « réagit à la lumière du soleil comme un sculpture géante », ou profilé en « S » et spécialement mis au point pour la façade nord touchée par le soleil uniquement à la mi-journée. L'élément le plus étonnant reste cependant la forme des portes des trois grands sas de chargement de 13 x 5 mètres. Leurs deux parties articulées en aluminium s'élèvent pour former un arc concave qui se transforme en auvent. Une sculpture de Calatrava, « dont la forme est inspirée de celle de l'œil humain », a joué un rôle dans cette conception. « Ici », dit l'architecte, « la forme est devenue une expérimentation cinétique utilisée pour étudier la transformation mécanique des plans d'un bâtiment. »

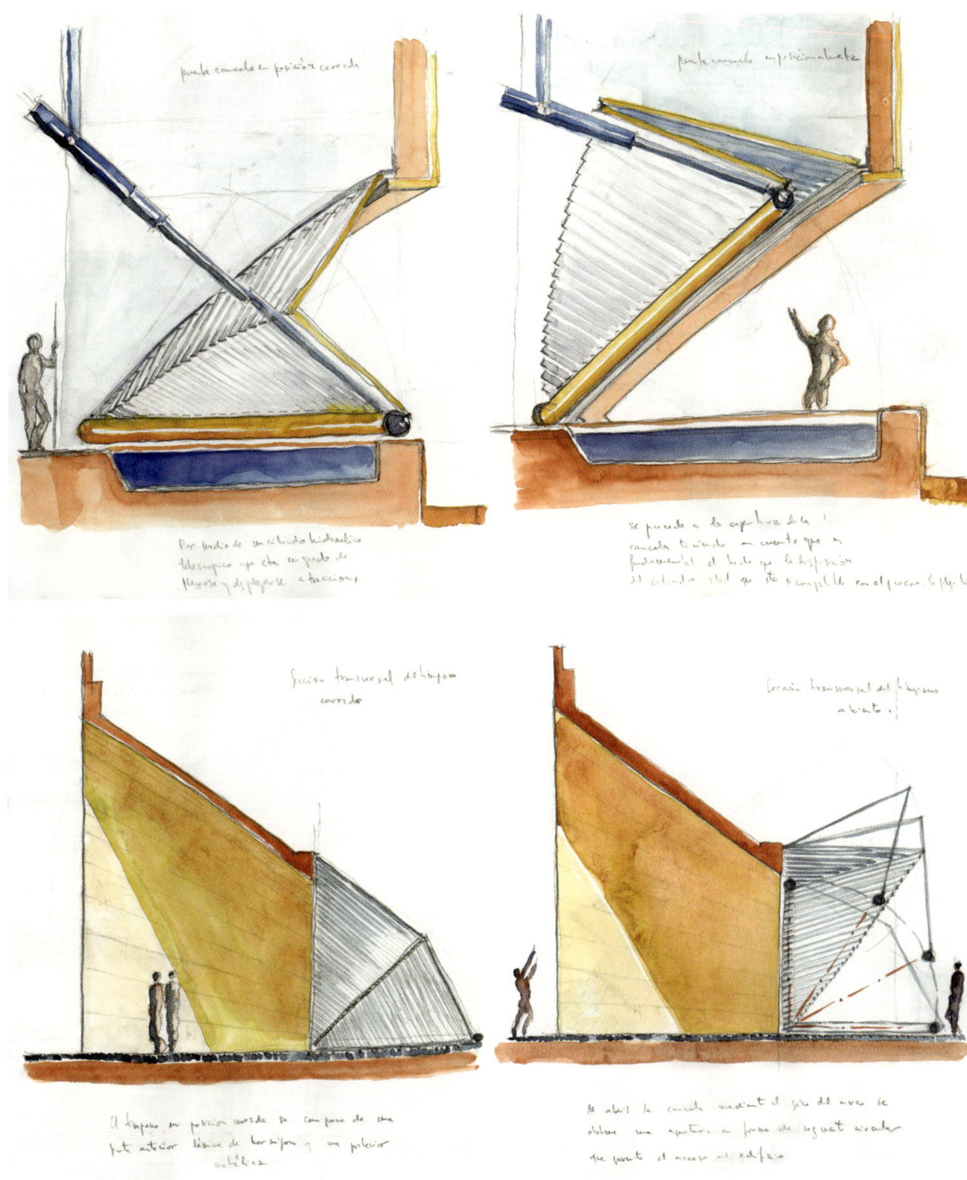

Calatrava's sketches reveal the mechanisms of his folding doors, inspired by such natural forms as the human eye and adapted to the requirements of the materials employed.

Calatravas Skizzen zeigen die Funktionsweise seiner Falttüren, die von naturgegebenen Formen wie dem menschlichen Auge inspiriert und den Bedingungen der verwendeten Materialien angepasst sind.

Les croquis de Calatrava expliquent le mécanisme de ces portes repliables, inspirées de formes naturelles comme celle de l'œil humain et adaptées aux contraintes des matériaux employés.

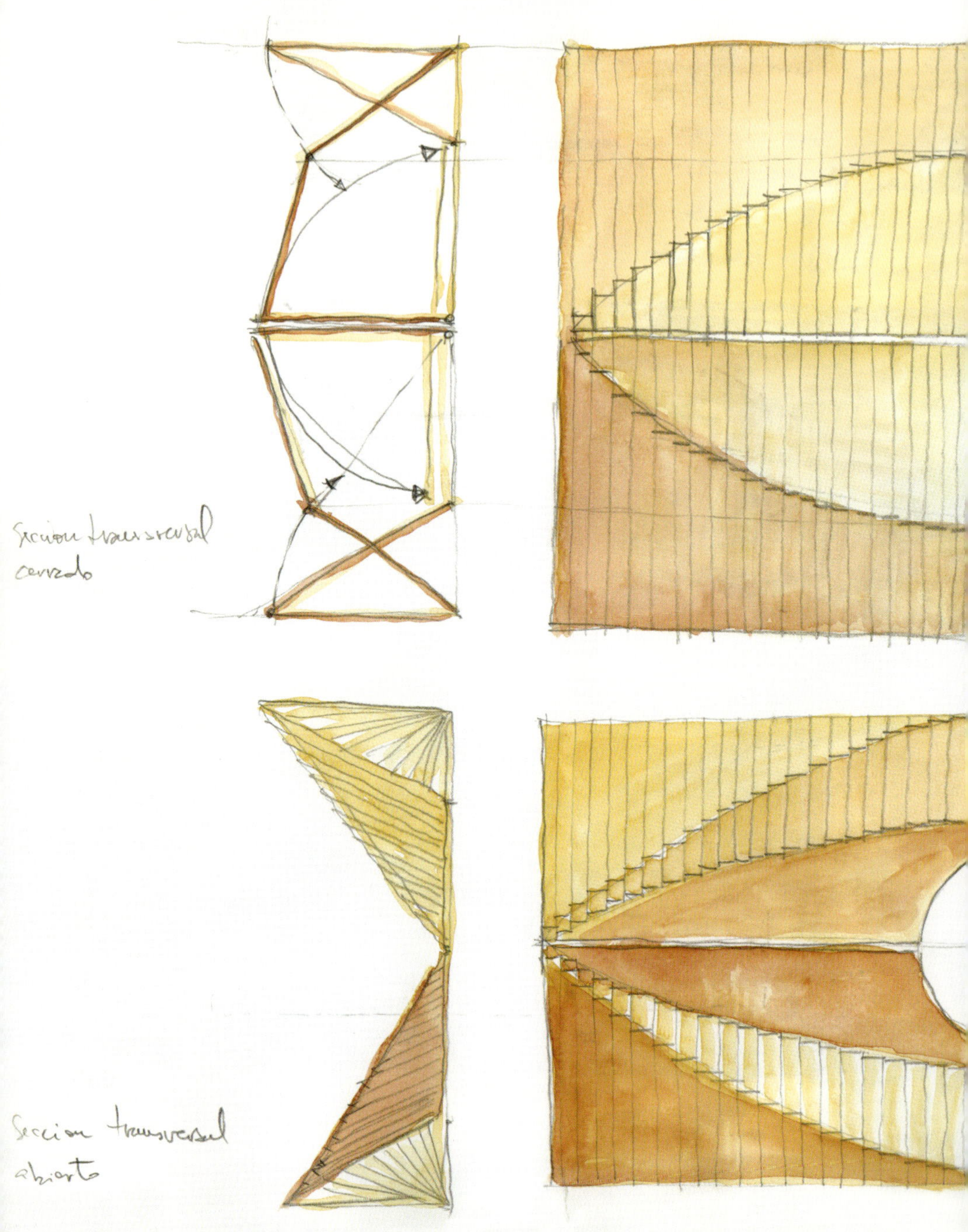
Seccion transversal
cerrado
Seccion transversal
abierto

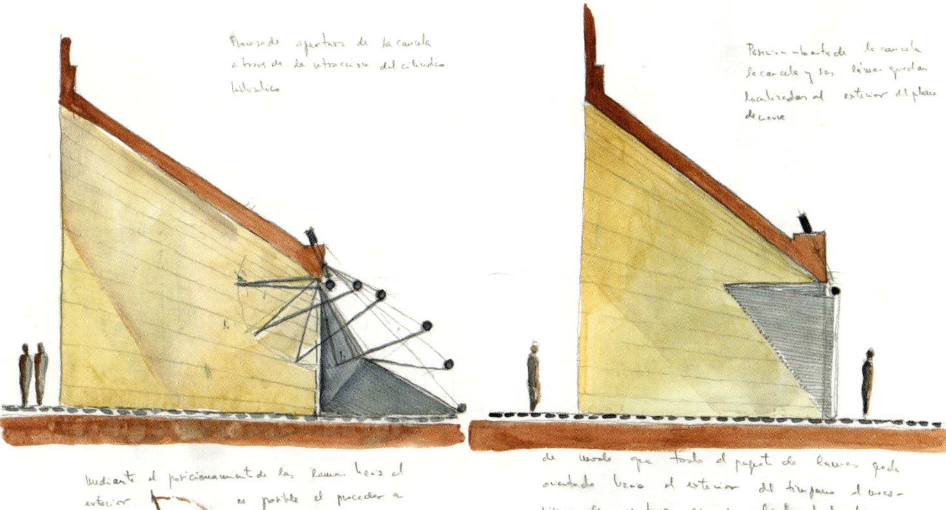

Simplicity and elegance are the hallmarks of Ernsting's doors. Although warehouse architecture has often given rise to innovative and economically viable solutions, Calatrava brings a new level of sophistication to this project.

Schlichtheit und Eleganz kennzeichnen Ernsting's. Wenngleich die Architektur von Lagerhäusern schon häufig zu innovativen und wirtschaftlich vertretbaren Lösungen führte, bringt Calatrava einen neuen Grad von Raffinement in dieses Projekt ein.

La simplicité et l'élégance sont le signe distinctif des portes Ernsting's. Bien que l'architecture d'entrepôts ait souvent suscité des solutions innovantes et économiques, Calatrava lui apporte un degré supplémentaire de sophistication.

Fachada Sur
Fachada oeste

The undulating metal surface of the warehouse brings something of the regularity that one might expect in such circumstances, and yet the curtain-like walls are also harmonious with the more inventive doors of the cargo bays.

Die gewellte Aluminiumverkleidung des Lagerhauses schafft etwas von der unter diesen Umständen zu erwartenden Regelmäßigkeit, und doch harmonieren die vorhangartigen Wände mit den innovativeren Toren der Laderampen.

L'enveloppe en métal ondulé de l'entrepôt offre la régularité attendue pour ce type de construction, tandis que les murs-rideaux sont en harmonie avec les portes, plus originales, des quais de chargement.

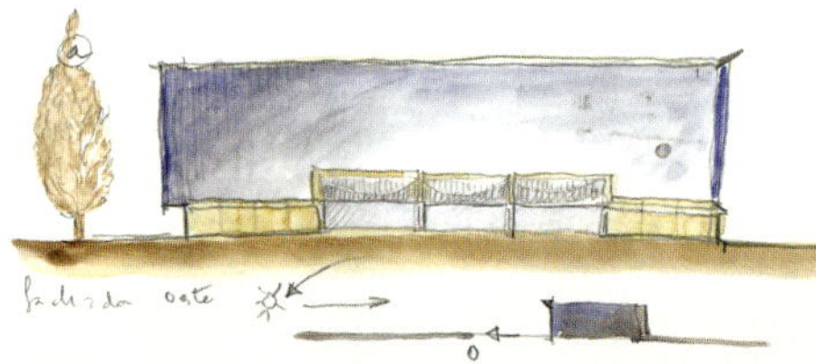

Calatrava's examination of the site led him to complete a series of drawings (above) that place his own design in its future context, next to other structures. The surprising sketch of a whale to the right plays on the sort of zoomorphic inspiration that runs throughout the architect's work.

Calatravas Ortsbegehung veranlasste ihn, eine Reihe von Zeichnungen (oben) anzufertigen, die sein Design in seinen künftigen Kontext neben anderen Gebäuden stellen. Die verblüffende Skizze eines Wals (rechts) spielt mit jener Art zoomorpher Inspiration, die das gesamte Werk des Architekten prägt.

Étudiant le site, Calatrava a réalisé une série de dessins (ci-dessus) qui place le projet dans son futur contexte, à côté d'autres constructions. La surprenante présence d'une baleine, à droite, est un clin d'œil à l'inspiration zoomorphique qui court dans toute l'œuvre de l'architecte.

Con el ojo lateral y las puertas todo
el edificio cobra una dimensión de ballena
y así gana de organismo vivo lo que
hace pensar que
de camiones
con mercancías y el funcionamiento del interior
como máxima de la mercancía
¡¡¡ el edificio como organismo viviente !!!

El ojo mecanico

El elemento primario en la composicion global es el ojo mecanico para ser construido en el nicho lateral.

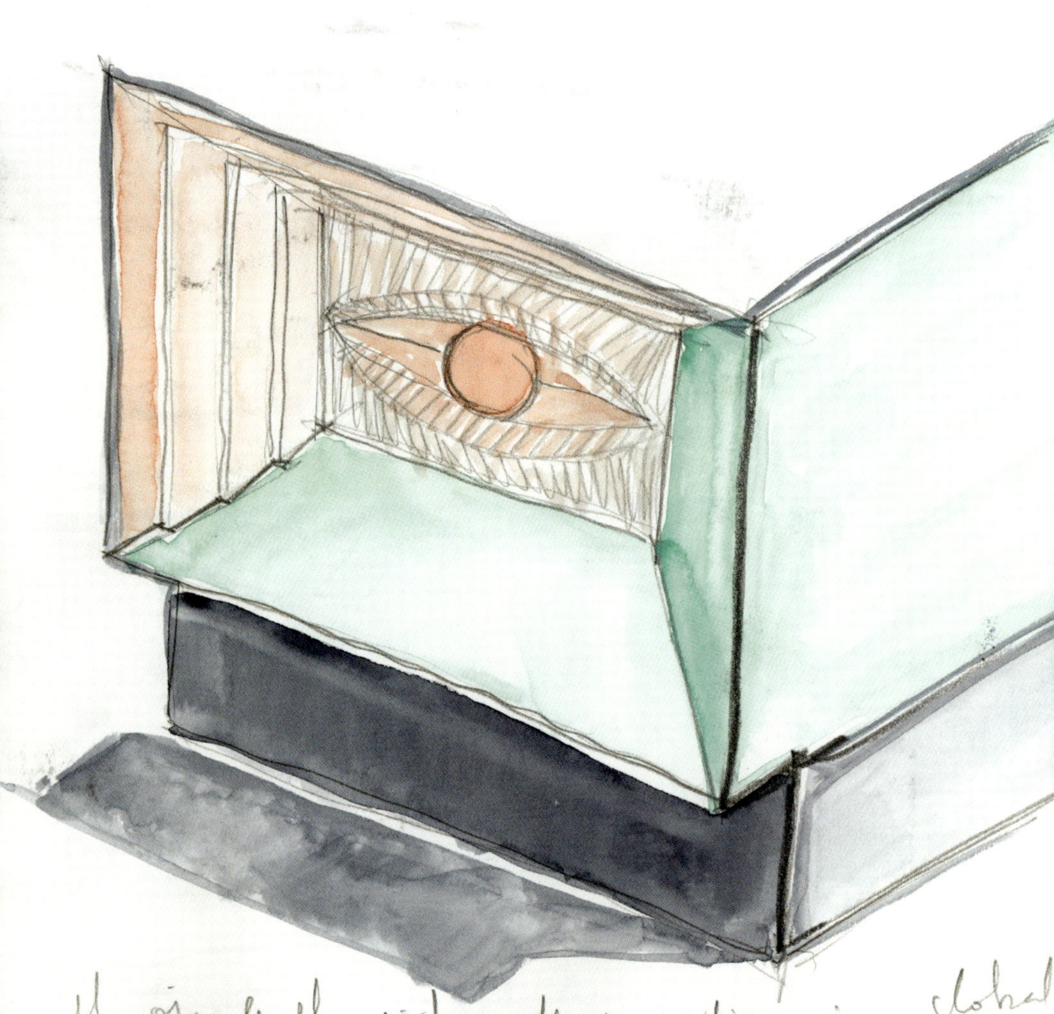

El ojo en el nicho da una dimension global a el edificio

The architect's real tool is neither a computer nor a pencil, but his eye. The eye is at the center of a creativity that extends to a wide and diverse range of forms, inspired by the human body, but also by the animal world.

Das wahre Werkzeug des Architekten ist weder ein Computer noch ein Bleistift, sondern sein Auge. Es steht im Zentrum einer Kreativität, die ein breites, variantenreiches, vom menschlichen Körper und der Tierwelt inspiriertes Formenspektrum umfasst.

L'outil essentiel de l'architecte n'est ni l'ordinateur ni le crayon mais son œil. L'œil est au centre d'une créativité qui couvre une grande variété de formes inspirées par le corps humain, mais aussi par le monde animal.

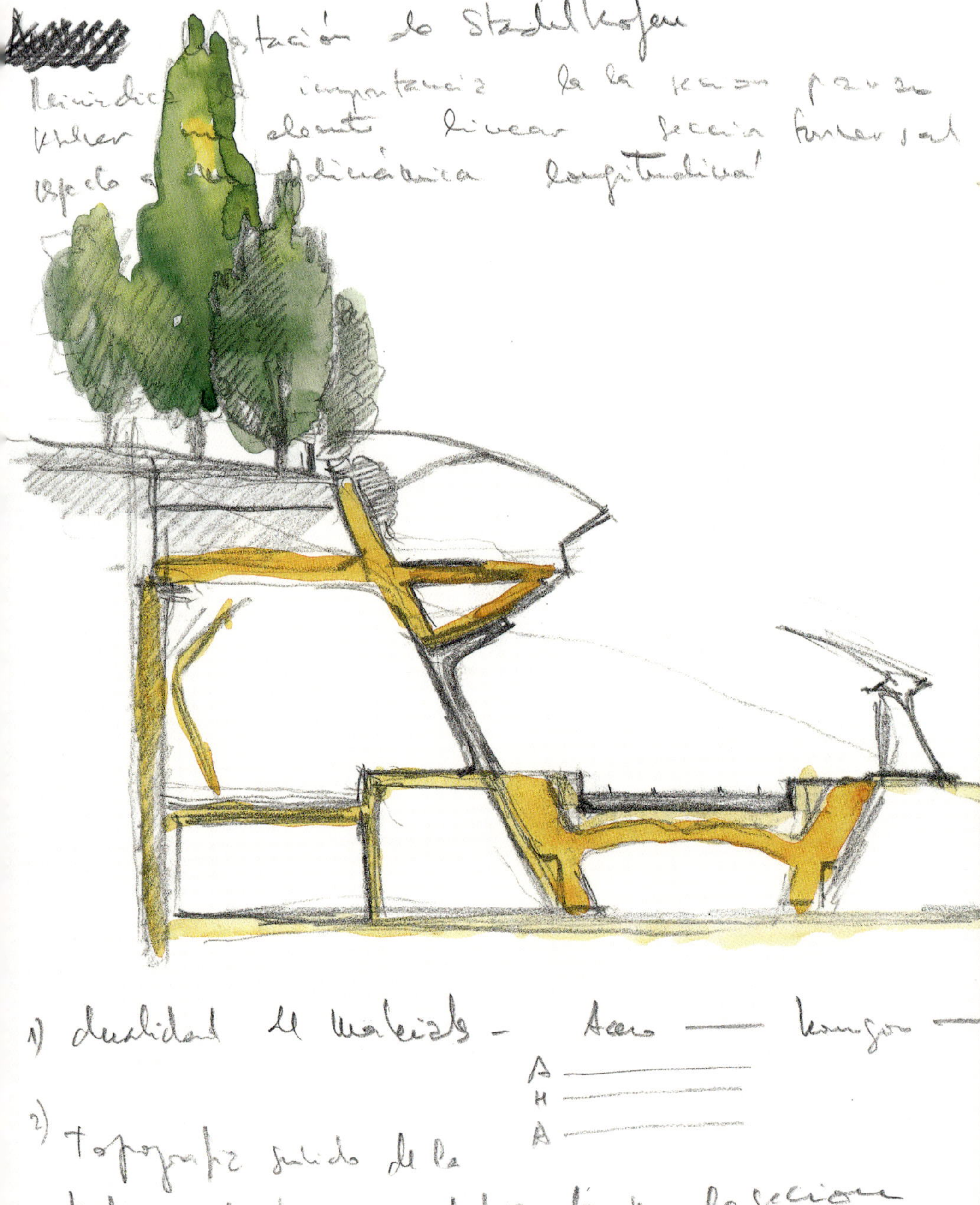
Estación de Stadelhofen
importancia
lineal
dinámica longitudinal
1) dualidad de materiales — Acero — hormigón —
A
H
A
2) Topografía
tectónica del terreno
por la sección
3) MASAS
4) Iconografía

STADELHOFEN STATION

Zurich, Switzerland. 1983–1990.

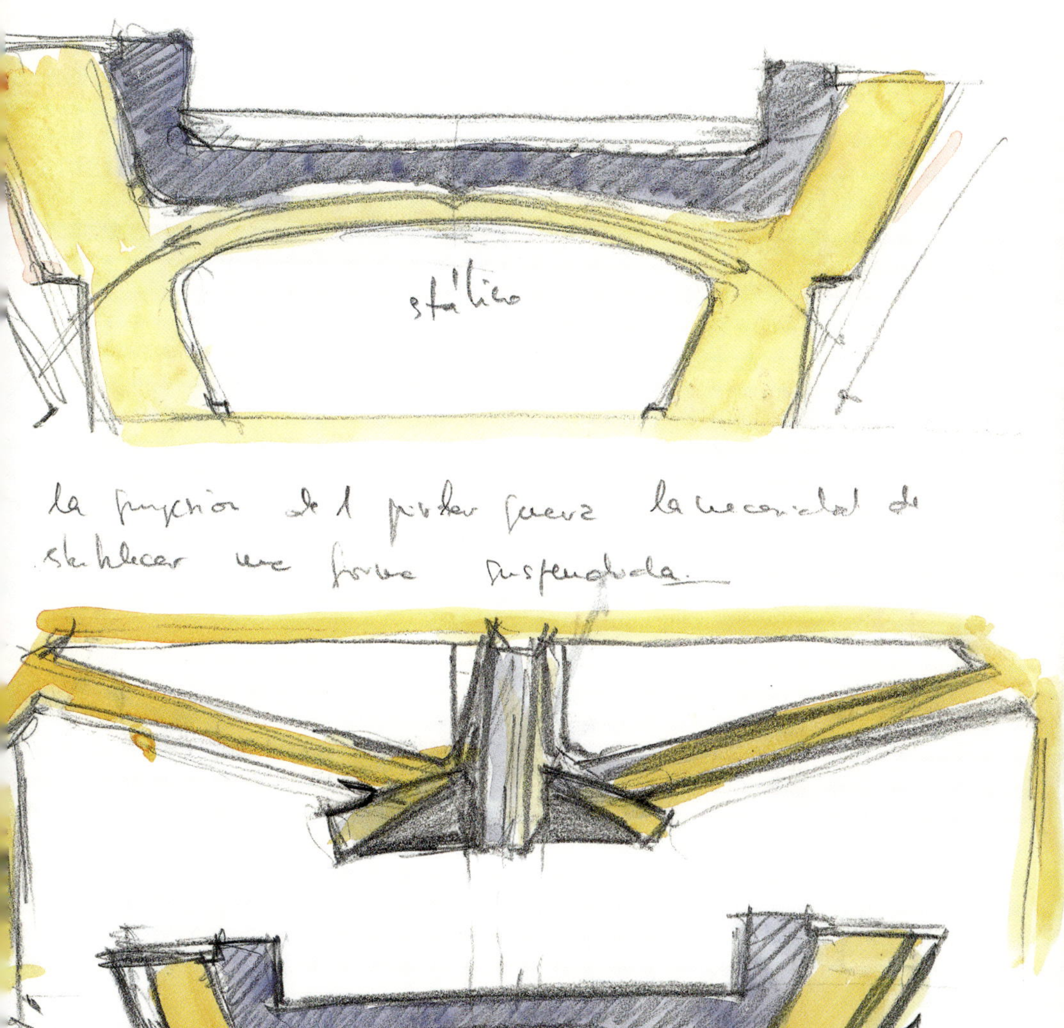

Posible ubicación de la estación de ferrocarril

Project
STADELHOFEN STATION

Location
STADELHOFEN SQUARE, ZURICH, SWITZERLAND

Client
SWISS FEDERAL RAILWAYS, BERN

Length
270 METERS

It might be difficult to identify the sketch to the left were it not part of the architect's material for the Stadelhofen Station. Calatrava imagines people in specific areas of the finished space well before the first concrete is poured.

Es fiele möglicherweise schwer, die Skizze links zu identifizieren, wäre sie nicht Teil des Materials zum Bahnhof Stadelhofen. Calatrava stellt sich Menschen in bestimmten Bereichen des fertigen Bauwerks vor, ehe noch der erste Beton gegossen ist.

Il pourrait être difficile d'identifier le croquis à gauche s'il ne faisait partie du projet de la gare de Stadelhofen. L'architecte imagine les usagers dans des zones précises de l'œuvre achevée, bien avant que le premier béton ne soit coulé.

For this expansion and redefinition of an existing station, intended as an inner-city node for a rapid transit system, Santiago Calatrava participated in the competition with the architect Arnold Amsler and the landscape architect Werner Rüeger. As a 1981 graduate of Zurich's highly reputed ETH school, Calatrava was familiar with the city, but the establishment of his offices there was due in part to his victory in this competition. Located against a curved, green embankment near the Bellevueplatz and not far from the Theaterstrasse, the Stadelhofen Railway Station is close to the city center, and to Lake Zurich. Although the station stretches 270 meters (with a width of 40 meters), it reveals its structure only as the traveler reaches the train tracks. A transparent glass canopy covers the entire length of the platform, giving it a great deal of natural light in spite of the fairly enclosed site. By proposing to undercut and redefine the existing hillside while maintaining its slope, the architects obviated the need for a tunnel, a solution readily accepted by the client, who put a premium on the rapidity of the work to be done. Approached through a series of pedestrian streets, the first visible sign of the station is a 19th-century building, preserved because of its value in terms of the local context. A cable trellis creates a "transparent green canopy that softens the station's intrusion into its environment." Below ground, a parallel shopping area, whose ribbed concrete design may appear to be anthropomorphic, follows the curve of the tracks themselves. Mouthlike hatches or doorways intended to permit the evening closure of the facility lead downwards toward this commercial zone. Santiago Calatrava's drawings typically reveal such practical inspiration as the form of the human hand that he adopted for the inclined columns.

In this early work, Santiago Calatrava has inserted a repetitive, yet wholly unexpected, structural system into the tight, curved site. Working within the constraints imposed by the location, the requirements of the railway, and passenger access and comfort, he nonetheless succeeds in going far beyond a standardized solution.

Bei diesem Frühwerk fügte Calatrava ein sich wiederholendes, aber gänzlich unerwartetes konstruktives System in das enge, gebogene Baugelände ein. Trotz der Beschränkungen durch Standort, Auflagen der Eisenbahn, Erreichbarkeit und Komfort gelang es ihm, weit mehr als eine Standardlösung anzubieten.

Dans cette réalisation de ses débuts, Calatrava a inséré un système structurel répétitif mais totalement inattendu dans un site aussi étroit et incurvé. Tout en respectant les contraintes du lieu, des voies de chemin de fer, et les impératifs d'accès et de confort des voyageurs, il réussit à établir des propositions bien au-delà des solutions standard.

Mit dem Architekten Arnold Amsler und dem Landschaftsarchitekten Werner Rüeger beteiligte sich Santiago Calatrava am Wettbewerb um die Erweiterung und Neustrukturierung eines vorhandenen Bahnhofs, der als innerstädtischer Knotenpunkt in einem Schnellnahverkehrssystem vorgesehen war. Als Absolvent der renommierten Zürcher ETH war Calatrava mit der Stadt vertraut, aber die Eröffnung seines Büros dort ist größtenteils seiner erfolgreichen Teilnahme an diesem Wettbewerb zu verdanken. Der Bahnhof Stadelhofen liegt in der Nähe des Stadtzentrums und des Zürichsees an einer begrünten bogenförmigen Böschung nahe dem Bellevueplatz und unweit der Theaterstrasse. Obgleich sich der 40 m tiefe Bahnhof über eine Länge von 270 m erstreckt, kann der Reisende seine Bauart erst erfassen, wenn er die Bahngleise erreicht. Ein transparentes Vordach aus Glas überdeckt die gesamte Länge des Bahnsteigs und sorgt trotz des recht eng bebauten Geländes für sehr viel Tageslicht. Der Vorschlag der Architekten, bei Erhaltung des Gefälles den unteren Teil des vorhandenen Abhangs abzutragen und umzugestalten, machte einen Tunnel überflüssig, eine Lösung, die der Auftraggeber begrüßte, da es ihm auf eine schnelle Durchführung der anstehenden Arbeiten ankam. Wer sich dem Bahnhof durch einige Fußgängerstraßen nähert, sieht zunächst einen Bau aus dem 19. Jahrhundert, der wegen seiner Bedeutung für das unmittelbare Umfeld denkmalgeschützt ist. Ein Gitter aus gespannten Seilen erzeugt ein „transparentes grünes Vordach, das den Bahnhof in seinem Kontext weniger als Fremdkörper erscheinen lässt". Unterirdisch folgt eine parallel angelegte Ladengalerie, deren geripptes Betondesign zoomorph wirken mag, der Kurve der Gleise. An Münder gemahnende Öffnungen, die sich abends verschließen lassen, führen nach unten zu den Geschäften. Santiago Calatravas Zeichnungen zeigen, dass er sich bei den geneigten Stützen von der Form der menschlichen Hand inspirieren ließ.

topografia
ciudad

À l'occasion du concours organisé pour la restructuration et l'extension d'une gare existante destinée à devenir la plate-forme d'échanges du système de transports locaux, Santiago Calatrava a collaboré avec l'architecte Arnold Amsler et l'architecte paysagiste Werner Rüeger. Diplômé en 1981 de la prestigieuse ETH, Calatrava connaissait très bien la ville, mais la décision d'y implanter son agence est due en partie à cette commande. Située le long d'un talus incurvé et boisé près de la Bellevueplatz et non loin de la Theaterstrasse, la gare de Stadelhofen est proche du centre-ville et du lac. Bien qu'elle s'étende sur 270 mètres (pour 40 mètres de large), elle ne révèle au voyageur l'importance de sa structure qu'au moment où il atteint les quais. Un auvent en verre transparent couvre la totalité de ceux-ci et leur assure un éclairage généreux malgré le relatif encaissement du site. En proposant de remodeler et de découper le flanc de la colline tout en conservant sa pente, les architectes ont évité de creuser un tunnel, solution appréciée par le client pour lequel la courte durée du chantier était un élément essentiel. Le premier signe visible de cette gare, que l'on atteint au débouché de rues piétonnes, est un bâtiment du XIXe siècle conservé pour sa valeur historique locale. Un treillis de câbles crée un « auvent vert transparent qui adoucit l'effet de l'insertion de la gare dans son environnement ». En sous-sol, un espace commercial, dont la structure en béton aux impressionnantes nervures peut sembler d'inspiration anthropomorphique, épouse la courbe des voies. Des demi-portes en forme de bouches qui permettent de fermer les installations le soir donnent accès à cette partie commerciale. Le dessin de Calatrava montre à sa manière caractéristique une inspiration formelle tirée du corps humain comme, par exemple, dans le profil de mains des colonnes inclinées.

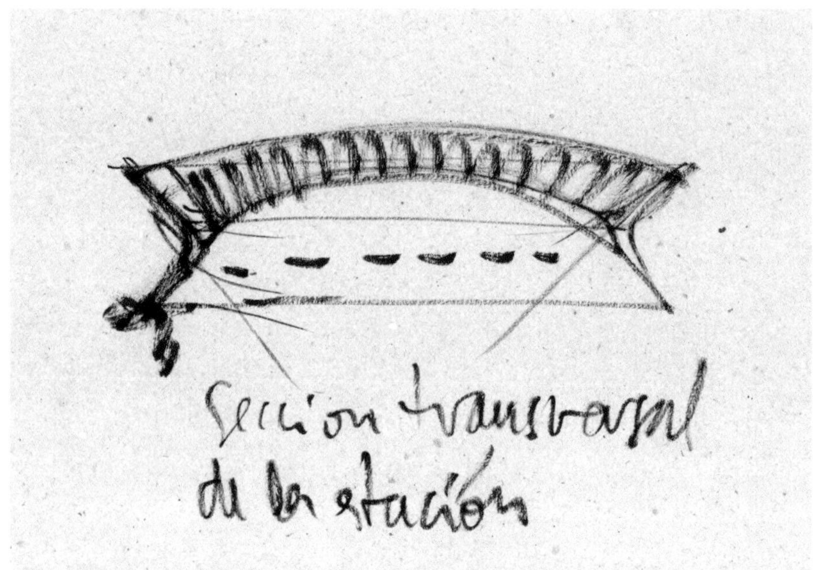

The ribbed concrete designs of the areas below the station platforms might evoke a dinosaur skeleton, but they are certainly an original and effective solution to the space requirements of the facility.

Zwar mag das gerippte Betondesign der Bereiche unterhalb der Bahnsteige an ein Dinosaurierskelett erinnern, doch sind sie zweifellos eine originelle und effektive Lösung für die Raumbedürfnisse der Anlage.

Les nervures en béton des zones situées sous les quais de la gare évoquent certes un squelette de dinosaure, mais sont avant tout une réponse originale et efficace aux exigences du programme en termes d'espace.

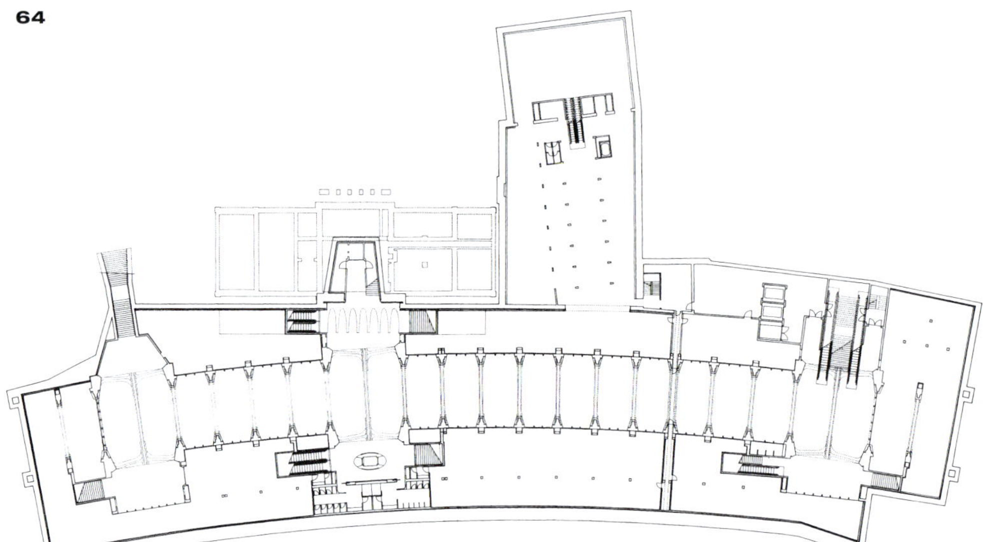

Where architects are often obliged to conceive just the outer shell of their buildings, Calatrava has succeeded here in carrying through his aesthetic and functional ideas throughout the interiors, giving a coherent and consistent appearance and feeling to the whole.

Wo Architekten häufig gezwungen sind, nur die äußere Hülle ihrer Bauten zu gestalten, gelang es Calatrava hier, seine ästhetischen und funktionalen Ideen auch im Inneren umzusetzen und so dem Gesamtprojekt ein kohärentes, stimmiges Erscheinungsbild zu geben.

Alors que les architectes doivent souvent se cantonner à l'extérieur des bâtiments, Calatrava a réussi à développer ses conceptions esthétiques et fonctionnelles à l'intérieur, pour donner une vraie cohérence à l'ensemble.

BACH DE RODA-
FELIPE II BRIDGE

Barcelona, Spain. 1984–1987.

Project

BACH DE RODA-FELIPE II BRIDGE

Location

BARCELONA, SPAIN

Length

128 METERS

Calatrava's education as an engineer, and the specific nature of bridge design led him to reduce his formal expression to the strict minimum that is necessary. The real measure of his talent is that he finds new ways to solve age-old problems.

Calatravas Ausbildung als Ingenieur und der spezifische Charakter seiner Brückenentwürfe brachten ihn dazu, seinen formalen Ausdruck auf das absolut notwendige Minimum zu reduzieren. Sein wahres Talent ist, neue Lösungen für uralte Probleme zu finden.

La formation d'ingénieur de Calatrava et la nature spécifique des problèmes de la conception de ponts l'ont conduit à réduire l'expression formelle au strict nécessaire. Son vrai talent consiste à apporter des solutions révolutionnaires à des problèmes très anciens.

With its overall length of 128 meters and its twin inclined and split arches, this bridge was one of the first to contribute to the reputation of Santiago Calatrava. Indeed, the 60-degree inclination of the lateral steel arches appears almost like a stylistic signature of the architect-engineer, not so much because he has repeated it on other occasions but because of the willful appearance of imbalance, or "frozen motion," that suffuses this bridge as well as his other work. Crossing a kind of no-man's-land originally created by the existence of railway lines, the bridge links the Bach de Roda and Felipe II streets, reconnecting a large section of the city to the sea. Its recognizable form is a testimony to the accuracy of the theory of Calatrava that peripheral urban areas can indeed be regenerated by such a symbolic intervention. Combining powerful concrete supports, monolithic granite columns and a steel arch structure which grows progressively lighter as it rises, the Bach de Roda-Felipe II Bridge also demonstrates Calatrava's adherence to a hierarchy of materials and forms, chosen in relation to their distance from the ground. Despite its very different structural nature, the Lyon-Saint-Exupéry Station (see page 104) employs a similar hierarchy.

Mit ihrer Gesamtlänge von 128 m und ihrem Paar zweigeteilter, gekippter Bögen war diese Brücke eine der ersten, die den Ruf Santiago Calatravas begründete. In der Tat erscheint die 60-Grad-Neigung der seitlichen Stahlbögen beinahe wie eine stilistische Signatur des Ingenieurarchitekten, nicht so sehr, weil er sie an anderer Stelle wiederholte, sondern wegen des Eindrucks gewollten Ungleichgewichts oder „eingefrorener Bewegung", die diese Brücke ebenso wie sein übriges Werk kennzeichnet. Die Brücke, die eine Art Niemandsland mit Bahnanlagen überquert, verbindet die Bach-de-Roda- mit der Felipe-II-Straße und stellt damit den Zugang eines großen Teils der Stadt zum Meer wieder her. Ihre markante Form ist Beleg für Calatravas Theorie, dass sich städtische Randbezirke durch solch symbolische Intervention tatsächlich wiederbeleben lassen. Die Brücke, für deren Bau mächtige Betonstützen, monolithische Granitpfeiler sowie eine mit zunehmender Höhe leichter werdende Stahlbogenkonstruktion kombiniert wurden, veranschaulicht darüber hinaus Calatravas Festhalten an einer Hierarchie der Materialien und Formen, die in Relation zu ihrer Distanz zum Erdboden verwendet werden. Ungeachtet ihres höchst unterschiedlichen konstruktiven Charakters kommt beim Bahnhof Lyon-Saint-Exupéry (siehe Seite 104) eine ähnliche Hierarchisierung zur Anwendung.

D'une longueur totale de 128 mètres et doté d'arches jumelles inclinées qui se répondent, ce pont fut l'un des premiers à asseoir la réputation de Santiago Calatrava. L'inclinaison à 60 degrés des arcs latéraux en acier semble être devenue la signature stylistique de l'architecte-ingénieur, non pas tant parce qu'il l'a répétée dans d'autres occasions, mais à cause de cet audacieux déséquilibre donnant l'impression d'un « mouvement figé » que dégagent ses ponts autant que ses autres réalisations. Franchissant une sorte de *no man's land* jadis occupé par des voies de chemin de fer, le pont qui relie les rues Bach de Roda et Felipe II connecte de nouveau une grande partie de la ville à la mer. Sa forme si identifiable témoigne de la pertinence de la théorie de Calatrava, pour lequel les zones urbaines périphériques peuvent être régénérées par ce type d'intervention symbolique. En associant de puissants supports en béton, des colonnes monolithiques en granit et une structure d'arcs en acier qui s'allège en s'élevant, cet ouvrage illustre par ailleurs la hiérarchie de matériaux et de formes voulue par l'architecte, qui les choisit en fonction de leur distance par rapport au sol. Malgré sa nature structurelle très différente, la gare de Lyon-Saint-Exupéry (voir page 104) applique une hiérarchie similaire.

The design of bridges often appears to be subjected to a kind of paralysis, with just three or four basic types dominating the world over. Time and again, Santiago Calatrava has shown that this is not some fatality born of the rules of engineering, but rather a lack of a pertinent combination of knowledge and aesthetic sense. Calatrava's bridges do what they are meant to do while exploring new forms.

Da nur drei oder vier Grundtypen von Brücken weltweit vorherrschen, hat es den Anschein, als befiele die Architekten bei der Planung eine Art Blockade. Santiago Calatrava hat immer wieder bewiesen, dass es sich dabei nicht um einen durch die Regeln des Ingenieurwesens bedingten schicksalhaften Verlauf handelt, sondern um den Mangel einer passenden Kombination von Kenntnis und ästhetischem Gespür. Calatravas Brücken erfüllen ihren Zweck und sondieren dabei neue Formen.

La conception de ponts est souvent victime d'une sorte de paralysie : trois ou quatre types seulement semblent dominer partout dans le monde.
À chaque fois, Santiago Calatrava a montré qu'il ne s'agit pas là d'une fatalité née des lois de l'ingénierie mais plutôt d'un déficit du lien indispensable entre connaissances techniques et sens esthétique. Ses ponts répondent à leur fonction tout en explorant de nouvelles formes.

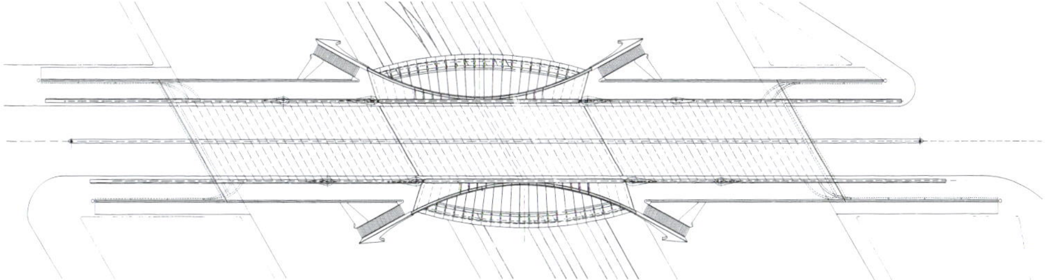

The thin bed and simple, dynamic arches of the bridge give it a forward-looking, modern appearance that may well withstand the judgment of time.

Die dünne Tafel und die einfachen, dynamischen Bögen der Brücke verleihen ihr ein zukunftsorientiertes, modernes Erscheinungsbild, das sich sehr wohl als zeitlos erweisen könnte.

Le mince tablier et les arches simples et dynamiques du pont lui donnent un aspect moderne et presque futuriste qui supportera sans doute le verdict du temps.

Galeria en Toronto
Cerrado
En la posicion
cerrada la venta
determina un pla
con los muros
de ladrillo que

BCE PLACE: GALLERIA AND HERITAGE SQUARE

Toronto, Canada. 1987–1992.

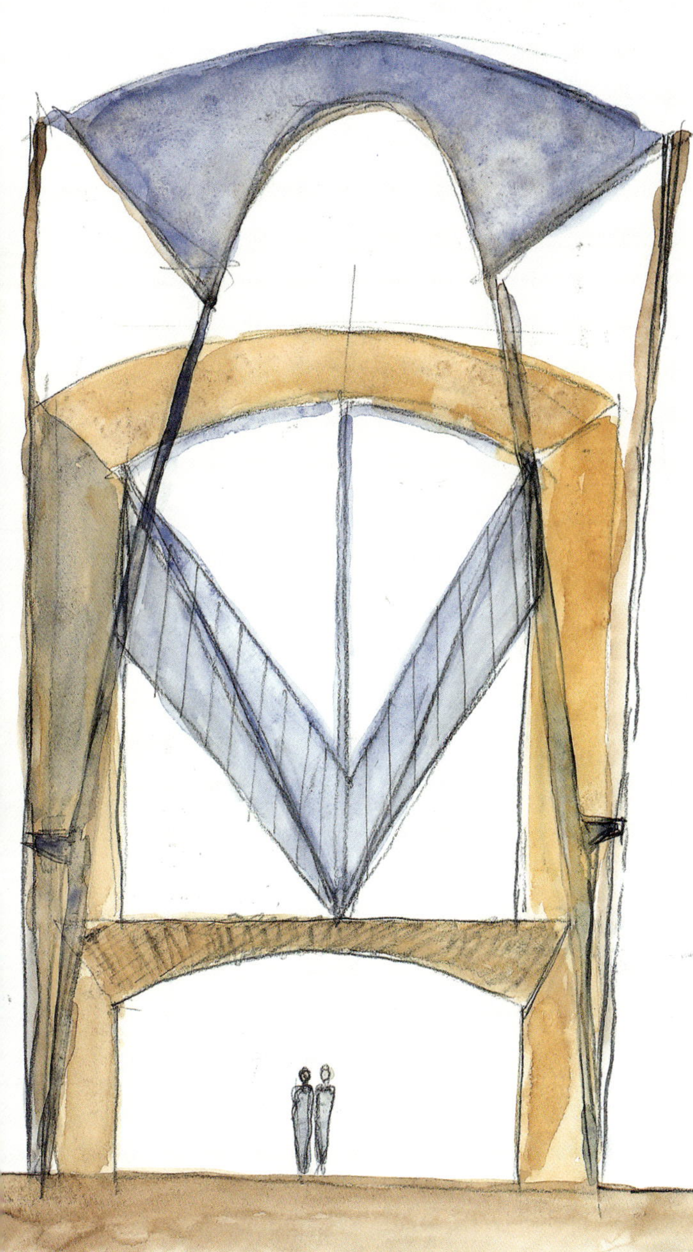

Al final de la galería en el vínculo entre galería y plaza aparece una ventana de grandes dimensiones capaz de optimizar la apertura entre galería y plaza en el tramo superior

este elemento que se descompone en dos segmentos y que es capaz de pivotar al rededor de su diagonal principal crea una apertura que permanece ligada al carácter de la arquitectura metálica del edificio, enmarcado por el arco y las jambas de ladrillo y toma un carácter escultural explícito

Project

BCE PLACE: GALLERIA AND HERITAGE SQUARE

Location

TORONTO, CANADA

Client

BROOKFIELD DEVELOPMENT CORPORATION, TORONTO

Length / Height / Width

130 METERS / 27 METERS / 14 METERS

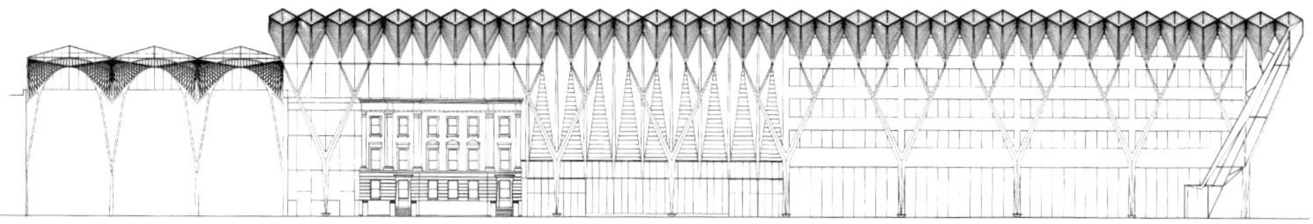

What would otherwise be a dull, uninteresting space between large buildings becomes a focal point for the city in the hands of the architect. Soaring volumes may not serve a purpose in the most rigorous utilitarian sense, but it is this extra space that generates the success of the project.

Ein ansonsten öder, reizloser Ort zwischen hohen Gebäuden wird in den Händen des Architekten zu einem urbanen Brennpunkt. Hoch aufragende Baukörper mögen im strikt utilitaristischen Sinn keinen Zweck erfüllen, aber es ist dieser zusätzliche Raum, der den Erfolg des Projekts generiert.

Entre les mains de l'architecte, ce qui aurait pu n'être qu'un volume sans intérêt entre deux grands immeubles est devenu un lieu d'attraction pour la ville. Ses volumes élancés ne sont peut-être pas fonctionnels au sens utilitariste du terme, mais cet espace généreux a assuré le succès du projet.

The structural typology of the tree, present in projects as diverse as the Oriente Station in Lisbon, the Science Museum in Valencia and the St. John the Divine proposal, is also at the heart of the Bell Canada Enterprises Place: Galleria and Heritage Square in Toronto. Here, Calatrava worked with the New York office of corporate architects Skidmore, Owings & Merrill to create a six-story, 130-meter-long, 14-meter-wide, and 27-meter-high gallery connecting two towers with a white painted, welded steel and glass passageway. As *The New York Times* said: "This gallery is nothing if not Gaudí-esque." With this design, Calatrava reaches back to some of the roots of Western architecture, in an almost literal sense, using the image of the tree to create a great urban space with links to the Gothic tradition as well as to that of more modern figures like Gaudí. The transition from Calatrava's Galleria to Heritage Square is marked by two large, rotating glass panels or "wings" that take the place of more elaborate folding doors originally proposed by the architect. A circular fountain designed by Calatrava, and made of steel tubes that open like a flower, is placed in the square itself. There is also a link in this proposal, which far exceeded the original competition program, to covered spaces that can be found in Europe, such as the Galleria Vittorio Emanuele II in Milan, although in typical, radical fashion, the architect conceived his project as a freestanding element between existing buildings. As the architect's project description says: "It appears as a new typology for weather-protected precincts. In this case, it is also a focal point for an entrance to Toronto's subterranean, central pedestrian network. A space-defining function has thus been created that imposes a new point of orientation upon these otherwise disparate structures."

Die Struktur des Baums, die in so unterschiedlichen Projekten wie dem Bahnhof Oriente in Lissabon, dem Wissenschaftsmuseum in Valencia und dem Entwurf für St. John the Divine deutlich wird, liegt auch der Galerie und dem Heritage Square des Bell Canada Enterprises Place in Toronto zugrunde. Hier arbeitete Calatrava mit dem New Yorker Architekturbüro Skidmore, Owings & Merrill an der Konzeption einer sechsgeschossigen, 130 m langen, 14 m breiten und 27 m hohen Galerie zusammen, die zwei Türme durch einen weiß gestrichenen Durchgang aus geschweißtem Stahl und Glas verbindet. Der Kommentar der *New York Times* dazu lautete: „Diese Galerie erinnert stark an Gaudí." Calatrava griff hier auf bestimmte Wurzeln der westlichen Architektur zurück, die er fast wörtlich zitiert. Er verwendete das Bild des Baums, um einen bedeutenden urbanen Raum zu schaffen, der Verbindungen zur gotischen Tradition, aber auch zu modernen Baumeistern wie Gaudí aufweist. Der Übergang von Calatravas Galerie zum Heritage Square wird von zwei großflächigen, sich drehenden Glasscheiben oder „Flügeln" hervorgehoben anstelle der ursprünglich vom Architekten geplanten kunstvolleren Falttüren. Auf dem Platz selbst befindet sich ein von Calatrava entworfener kreisrunder Brunnen aus Stahlröhren, die sich einer Blüte gleich entfalten. Darüber hinaus gibt es bei diesem Projekt eine Verbindung, die weit über die Wettbewerbsausschreibung hinausgeht, und zwar zu den überdachten urbanen Räumen Europas, wie die Galleria Vittorio Emanuele II in Mailand, wiewohl der Architekt in typisch radikaler Manier sein Projekt als freistehendes Element zwischen vorhandenen Gebäuden konzipierte. In der Beschreibung des Architekten heißt es dazu: „Es erscheint als neues Modell für witterungsgeschützte Bereiche. Hier signalisiert es außerdem einen Eingang zu Torontos unterirdischem, zentralem Wegenetz für Fußgänger. So entstand eine raumbegrenzende Funktion, die diesen ansonsten disparaten Bauten zu einem neuen Orientierungspunkt verhilft."

La typologie arborescente, présente dans des projets aussi divers que la gare de l'Orient à Lisbonne, le musée des Sciences à Valence et le projet pour la cathédrale Saint John the Divine à New York, est au cœur de cette réalisation. Calatrava a travaillé avec l'agence new-yorkaise d'architecture institutionnelle Skidmore, Owings & Merrill pour créer cette galerie en acier laqué blanc et verre de 130 mètres de long, 14 mètres de large et 27 mètres de haut qui réunit au niveau du sol deux tours d'assez grande hauteur. Comme l'écrivit le *New York Times*, « Cette galerie est pour le moins gaudíesque. » Calatrava se rapproche de certaines racines (au sens quasi littéral du terme) de l'architecture occidentale en utilisant l'image de l'arbre pour créer un vaste espace urbain lié à la tradition gothique ou à des interventions plus modernes comme celles de Gaudí. La transition entre la galerie et l'Heritage Square est marquée par deux grands pans de verre pivotants ou « ailes » qui remplacent les portes articulées plus élaborées proposées à l'origine par l'architecte. Également dessinée par Calatrava, une fontaine circulaire en tubes d'acier qui s'ouvre comme une fleur est installée sur la place même. On pourrait également voir ici un lien avec d'autres espaces couverts européens, comme la Galleria Vittorio Emanuele II à Milan, bien qu'à sa façon caractéristique et radicale, l'architecte ait conçu un projet indépendant des bâtiments qu'il relie. Comme le descriptif de l'agence le note : « [Ce projet] invente une nouvelle typologie d'espace protégé des intempéries. Ici, il constitue également un signal pour l'une des entrées du réseau souterrain piétonnier du centre de Toronto. Une fonction de définition de l'espace a ainsi été créée, qui impose un nouveau point d'orientation au milieu de ces structures par ailleurs disparates. »

The fundamentally repetitive use of treelike forms on a large scale creates much greater spatial variety than might be expected because of the complexity of the structure, but also because of the variations in light and shadow that it introduces to the space.

Die grundsätzlich repetitive Verwendung baumartiger Formen in großem Maßstab schafft eine unerwartete räumliche Vielfalt durch die Komplexität der Struktur, aber auch durch das abwechslungsreiche Licht- und Schattenspiel, mit dem sie den Raum füllt.

Le recours répétitif à des piliers arboriformes à grande échelle crée une diversité spatiale beaucoup plus importante que l'on pouvait s'y attendre, du fait de la complexité de la structure mais aussi à cause des variations d'ombre et de lumière qu'ils introduisent dans l'espace.

ALAMILLO BRIDGE AND LA CARTUJA VIADUCT

Seville, Spain. 1987–1992.

Project
ALAMILLO BRIDGE AND LA CARTUJA VIADUCT

Location
SEVILLE, SPAIN

Client
REGIONAL GOVERNMENT OF ANDALUSIA, SEVILLE

Span
200 METERS

Pylon height
142 METERS

Even if the Seville Expo itself left less of a mark than its organizers might have hoped, Calatrava's bridge with its dramatic angled tower remains. Might it be that bridges are less ephemeral than buildings?

Selbst wenn die Expo in Sevilla weniger Spuren hinterließ, als ihre Organisatoren gehofft haben mögen, bleibt Calatravas Brücke mit ihrem spektakulär geneigten Turm erhalten. Könnte es sein, dass Brücken weniger kurzlebig sind als Gebäude?

Même si l'Expo de Séville n'a pas laissé une empreinte aussi marquante que ses organisateurs l'avaient espéré, le pont de Calatrava et son pylône à l'inclinaison spectaculaire demeurent. Les ponts seraient-ils moins éphémères que les bâtiments ?

Part of a plan initiated by the government of the region of Andalusia on the occasion of Expo '92, this bridge has a 200-meter span over the Meandro de San Jerónimo, a shallow branch of the Guadalquivir River. Its most striking feature is a 142-meter-high pylon, inclined at an angle of 58 degrees, the same as that of the Pyramid of Cheops. Filled with cement, this tower is sufficiently massive to counterbalance the bridge deck, obviating the need for backstays, and allowing the bridge to be held up with just 13 pairs of cables. Santiago Calatrava's personal research on the Alamillo Bridge involved a 1986 sculpture called *Running Torso* made of cubes of marble held in equilibrium at an angle by a wire under tension. His drawings of running figures also come to mind. He originally proposed a second bridge, located 1.5 kilometers from the first one, with a mirror image pylon at the point where the road crosses the same river again, but the client opted instead for the 526-meter-long Puente de La Cartuja Viaduct, with its two 10-meter-wide lanes, which was used as the northern entrance to the Expo '92 site. Conceptually speaking the Alamillo Bridge is clearly innovative, simplifying basic bridge design and allowing for the use of only half the normal number of cable stays. The double bridge concept would have created an enormous, partially imaginary triangle, with its point high in the sky above the Expo site. Frequently imitated by other engineers and architects, the inclined pylon of the Alamillo Bridge stands out as a symbol of modern Seville. Without suggesting any specific influence, it can be noted that the Dutch architect Ben van Berkel, author of the Erasmus Bridge in Rotterdam (inaugurated in 1996), worked in 1988 in the office of Santiago Calatrava just before creating his own firm, UN Studio, with Caroline Bos.

Die Alamillo-Brücke, die mit einer Spannweite von 200 m den Meandro San Jeronimo, einen flachen Seitenarm des Guadalquivir, überquert, ist Teil einer von der Regierung der Region Andalusien anlässlich der Expo '92 initiierten Planung. Ihr markantestes Merkmal ist der 142 m hohe Brückenpfeiler, der in einem Winkel von 58 Grad, dem der Cheopspyramide entsprechend, geneigt ist. Der mit Zement gefüllte Turm ist wuchtig genug, um als Gegengewicht zur Brückentafel zu dienen; er macht rückseitige Verankerungen überflüssig und ermöglicht, dass die Brücke von nur 13 Seilpaaren gehalten wird. Zu Santiago Calatravas persönlichen Studien zur Alamillo-Brücke gehört die 1986 entstandene Skulptur *Running Torso*. Sie besteht aus Marmorkuben, die von einem gespannten Draht in Schräglage im Gleichgewicht gehalten werden. Auch seine Zeichnungen von laufenden Figuren fallen einem dazu ein. Ursprünglich hatte er im Abstand von 1,5 km eine zweite Brücke über den Guadalquivir vorgeschlagen, die spiegelbildlich positioniert werden sollte, aber der Auftraggeber entschied sich stattdessen für das 526 m lange La-Cartuja-Viadukt mit seinen zwei 10 m breiten Fahrspuren, das als nördlicher Eingang zum Gelände der Expo '92 dient. In konzeptueller Hinsicht ist die Alamillo-Brücke innovativ, da sie den grundlegenden Brückenbau vereinfacht und mit der Hälfte der üblicherweise nötigen Seilverankerungen auskommt. Die Planung mit der doppelten Brücke hätte ein riesiges, teilweise imaginäres Dreieck geschaffen, dessen Spitze hoch oben im Himmel über dem Expo-Gelände gelegen hätte. Der von anderen Ingenieuren und Architekten häufig nachgeahmte geneigte Pylon der Alamillo-Brücke fällt als Symbol des modernen Sevilla ins Auge. Ohne spezifische Einflüsse andeuten zu wollen, bleibt festzuhalten, dass der Niederländer Ben van Berkel, Architekt der 1996 eingeweihten Erasmusbrücke in Rotterdam, kurz vor Gründung seiner eigenen Firma UN Studio mit Caroline Bos, 1988 im Büro von Santiago Calatrava tätig war.

Though the sketch of a human figure by Calatrava on the left is not specifically related to this bridge project, it does illustrate the architect's fascination with movement and tension, two elements that inform the Alamillo Bridge design.

Obgleich Calatravas Skizze einer menschlichen Figur (links) nicht speziell mit diesem Brückenprojekt in Zusammenhang steht, veranschaulicht sie, wie sehr der Architekt von Bewegung und Spannung fasziniert ist, zwei Faktoren, ohne die die Alamillo-Brücke nicht denkbar wäre.

Bien que le croquis d'une figure humaine par Calatrava (à gauche) ne soit pas spécifiquement relié à ce projet, il illustre sans aucun doute la fascination de l'architecte pour le mouvement et la tension, deux éléments qui nourrissent le dessin du pont Alamillo.

Construit dans le cadre d'un plan initié par le Gouvernement de la région d'Andalousie à l'occasion d'Expo '92, ce pont de 200 mètres de portée franchit le Meandro San Jeronimo, un bras peu profond du Guadalquivir. Sa caractéristique la plus spectaculaire est un pylône de 142 mètres de haut incliné à 58° (le même angle que la pyramide de Khéops). Le poids de cette tour remplie de ciment suffit à contrebalancer celui du tablier, éliminant le recours à des haubans arrière et permettant que treize paires de câbles seulement soutiennent l'ouvrage. Les recherches personnelles de Santiago Calatrava sur ce projet ont débuté en 1986 à partir d'une de ses sculptures, *Running Torso*, faite de cubes de marbre inclinés, maintenus en équilibre par un fil de fer en tension. On pense également à ses dessins de figures en train de courir. À l'origine il avait proposé un second pont, à 1,5 kilomètre du premier, doté d'un pylône identique incliné dans le sens inverse, mais le client préféra la solution du viaduc de La Cartuja. Long de 526 mètres avec deux voies de 10 mètres de large, ce dernier est utilisé pour desservir l'entrée nord d'Expo '92. Sur le plan conceptuel, le pont Alamillo est novateur par la simplification qu'apporte sa conception et l'utilisation de la moitié seulement des haubans normalement nécessaires. Le double pont aurait créé un énorme triangle « chapeautant » le site de l'Expo. Fréquemment imité par d'autres ingénieurs et architectes, ce pylône incliné est aujourd'hui l'un des symboles de la Séville moderne. Sans pour autant suggérer une influence, on peut noter que l'architecte néerlandais Ben Van Berkel, auteur du pont Erasmus à Rotterdam (inauguré en 1996), travaillait en 1988 chez Calatrava, juste avant de fonder sa propre agence, UN Studio, avec Caroline Bos.

MONTJUïC COMMUNICATIONS TOWER

Barcelona, Spain. 1989–1992.

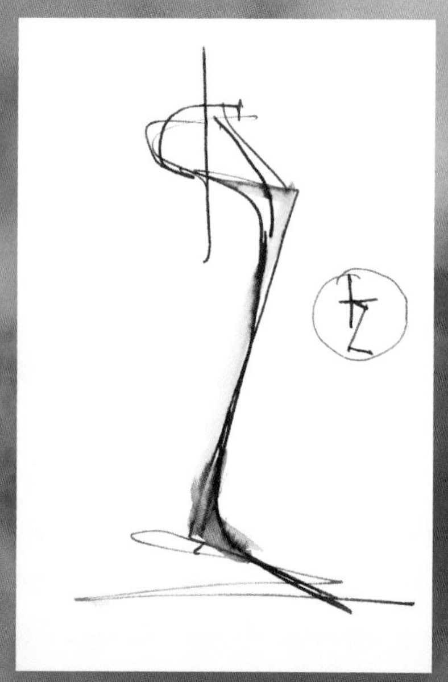

Project

MONTJUÏC COMMUNICATIONS TOWER

Location

BARCELONA, SPAIN

Client

TELEFONICA S. A.

Height

136 METERS

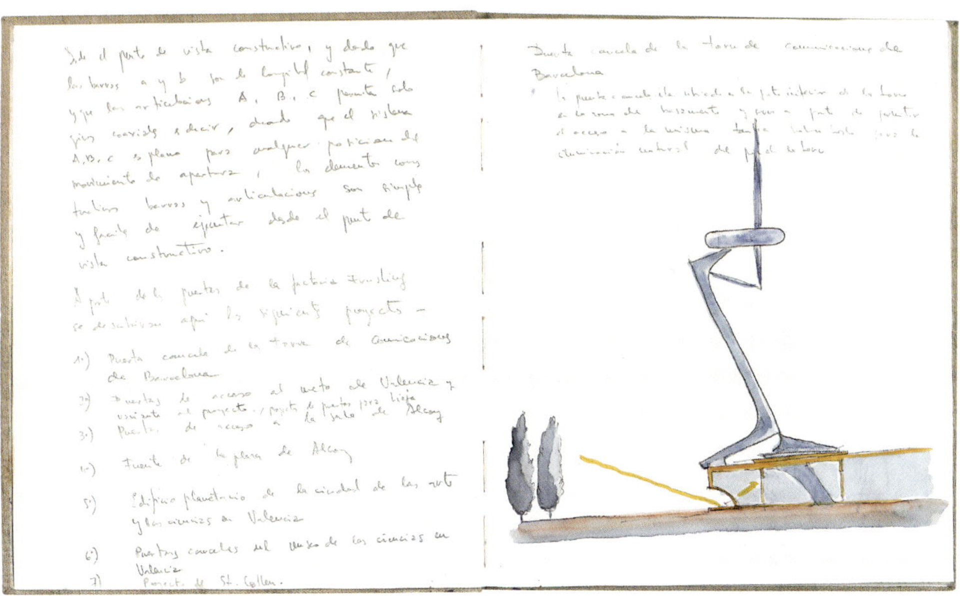

The page of sketches above shows the Montjuïc Communications Tower with a relatively high degree of accuracy as compared to the completed structure, seen on the left. This fact underlines the interest and importance of Calatrava's sketches.

Der Vergleich einer recht detaillierten Skizze des Montjuïc-Fernmeldeturms (oben) mit dem fertigen Gebäude (links) unterstreicht den Wert und die Bedeutung der Skizzen Calatravas.

Cette page de croquis montre la tour de télécommunications de Montjuïc avec un degré de précision relativement avancé par rapport à la réalisation de la structure, vue ici à gauche. Elle souligne l'intérêt et l'importance des croquis de l'architecte.

The spectacular form of the tower and its base are closely related to Calatrava's fascination with the human eye. Although its shape is not as simple as that of his earlier Collserola project, the angled tower is a monument to the art of the engineer.

Die fulminante Form des Turms und seines Sockels stehen in engem Zusammenhang mit Calatravas Interesse am menschlichen Auge. Wenngleich seine Form nicht so schlicht ist wie die seines früheren Collserola-Projekts, ist der geneigte Turm ein Denkmal für die Kunst des Ingenieurs.

La forme spectaculaire de la tour et de sa base est étroitement liée à la fascination de Calatrava pour l'œil humain. Bien qu'elle ne soit pas aussi simple que celle du projet antérieur pour Collserola, cette tour inclinée est un monument à l'art de l'ingénieur.

Located near the Palau Sant Jordi designed by the Japanese architect Arata Isozaki, the Montjuïc Communications Tower is 136 meters high. Built like its neighbor for the 1992 Olympic Games, it is based on an inclined trunk with an annular element containing the actual antennas above. Although, because of its angle and its pointed tip, it may recall a javelin, the tower is based on Calatrava's own drawings of a kneeling figure making an offering. This image might well be appropriate to the original Olympic context of the site. The three-point base of the structure may also bring to mind ancient object design. The base, closed by a door formed by metal blades, is related to his studies of the human eye. This door was developed along similar lines to the loading bay doors at Ernsting's Warehouse in Coesfeld-Lette, Germany (see page 36). Acting like a sundial, the trunk projects a shadow onto the circular platform. The platform at the base, a brick drum containing the communications equipment imposed at the time of the competition, is covered in broken tiles, evoking the Park Güell by Antoni Gaudí. Related at once to the geographic and solar locations of the site, the Montjuïc Tower is at once a symbol of the Olympic Games, but also of the progressive, artistically oriented history of Barcelona itself. Calatrava's sense of drama and suspended equilibrium is just as evident in this tower as it is in any of his bridges. The structure is by no means anthropomorphic, but it is sufficiently related to the body and its movement to somehow generate a sentiment of familiarity in the minds of viewers.

In der Nähe des von dem japanischen Architekten Arata Isozaki errichteten Palau Sant Jordi steht der 136 m hohe Montjuïc-Fernmeldeturm. Wie sein Nachbar für die Olympischen Spiele 1992 konzipiert, besteht der Turm aus einem geneigten Schaft mit einem ringförmigen Element, in dem die eigentlichen Antennen untergebracht sind. Obwohl der Turm aufgrund seiner Neigung und der zugespitzten Form an einen Speer erinnert, fußt er doch auf Calatravas Zeichnungen einer ein Opfer darbringenden, knienden Figur. Dieses Bild entspräche dem olympischen Kontext des Ortes. Der auf drei Punkten ruhende Unterbau des Turms könnte ebenfalls an antike Objektgestaltung erinnern. Der Sockel, der mit einem aus Metallblättern bestehenden Tor verschlossen wird, steht in Zusammenhang mit Calatravas Studien des menschlichen Auges. Dieses Tor wurde nach ähnlichen Richtlinien entwickelt wie die Tore der Laderampen von Ernsting's Lagerhaus in Coesfeld-Lette (siehe Seite 36).

Der wie der Zeiger einer Sonnenuhr wirkende Schaft wirft einen Schatten auf das kreisförmige Podium. Das aus Backsteinen gemauerte runde Podium, das die zur Zeit des Wettbewerbs geforderte Fernmeldetechnik enthält, ist mit Ziegelscherben bedeckt, die an den Parque Güell von Antoni Gaudí denken lassen. Der ebenso auf die geografischen wie solaren Bedingungen des Geländes bezogene Torre de Montjuïc gilt gleichermaßen als Symbol der Olympischen Spiele wie der fortschrittlichen, künstlerisch ausgerichteten Geschichte Barcelonas. Calatravas Gespür für Dramatik und zeitweilig aufgehobenes Gleichgewicht ist in diesem Turm ebenso augenfällig wie in seinen Brücken. Der Bau ist keineswegs anthropomorph, aber er ist hinreichend auf den Körper und seine Bewegungen bezogen, um bei den Betrachtern ein Gefühl der Vertrautheit hervorzurufen.

Située près du Palau Sant Jordi conçu par l'architecte japonais Arata Isozaki, cette tour mesure 136 mètres de haut. Construite, comme son voisin, à l'occasion des Jeux olympiques de 1992, elle est constituée d'un fût incliné soutenant en partie supérieure un élément annulaire contenant les antennes. Si elle peut évoquer l'image d'un javelot, elle est issue d'un dessin de l'architecte représentant un personnage agenouillé en position d'offrande, situation peut-être appropriée dans le contexte olympique. Le socle tripode peut également rappeler un objet ancien. Sa porte en ailettes métalliques est issue des études de Calatrava sur le thème de l'œil humain et rappelle celles des sas de chargement de l'entrepôt Ernsting's en Allemagne (voir page 36). Jouant le rôle du style d'un cadran solaire, le fût projette son ombre sur la plate-forme circulaire. Celle-ci, en forme de tambour de brique, contient les équipements de communications prévus au cahier des charges de l'époque, et est habillée de tesselles de carrelage, dans l'esprit des bancs du parc Güell d'Antoni Gaudí. Par ce lien avec la géographie et la course du soleil, la tour de Montjuïc est devenue un symbole des Jeux, mais aussi celui d'une capitale catalane progressiste et ouverte sur l'art. Le sens du spectaculaire de Calatrava manifesté dans cet équilibre en suspension est aussi évident dans cette tour que dans ses ponts. Elle n'est en rien anthropomorphique, mais cependant assez liée au corps et à ses mouvements pour générer un sentiment de familiarité.

As is most often the case, the architect's sketches reveal many of the ideas that are at the origin of his projects. A kneeling figure, who might be imagined to hold the Olympic flame, or an athlete balanced in motion like the *Discobolus* by Myron are the sublimated references here.

Wie so häufig offenbaren die Skizzen des Architekten viele der Ideen, die am Anfang seiner Projekte stehen. In diesem Fall sind die sublimierten Bezugspunkte eine kniende Figur, von der man sich vorstellen kann, sie hielte die olympische Flamme, oder ein in Bewegung erstarrter Athlet, wie der *Diskobol* des Myron.

Comme la plupart du temps, les croquis de l'architecte illustrent les multiples pistes qui sont à l'origine de ses projets. Une silhouette agenouillée, qui pourrait tenir la flamme olympique, ou un athlète saisi dans l'équilibre de son geste, comme le *Discobole* de Myron, sont les références spirituelles de ces dessins.

Informed by the knowledge of the engineer, the drawings of the architect might resemble those of an artist. The difference of course is that the pure artist is freed from the constraints of practicality, while Calatrava integrates them in ways that are obvious only to him.

Erfüllt vom Wissen des Ingenieurs, könnten die Zeichnungen des Architekten denen eines Künstlers ähneln. Natürlich ist Letzterer frei von den Zwängen der Funktionalität, während Calatrava ihnen mit Methoden gerecht wird, die sich nur ihm alleine erschließen.

Nourris des connaissances de l'ingénieur, les dessins de l'architecte peuvent aussi ressembler à ceux d'un artiste. La différence est que l'artiste est libre des contraintes de la réalité tandis que Calatrava les intègre d'une façon qui n'est évidente que pour lui.

ZURICH UNIVERSITY LAW FACULTY

Zurich, Switzerland. 1989–2004.

Project
ZURICH UNIVERSITY LAW FACULTY

Location
ZURICH, SWITZERLAND

Client
CANTON OF ZURICH

Cost
$ 30 MILLION

The Faculty of Law of the University of Zurich had been divided into eight different buildings. The facilities for the faculty and the library, including the second largest rare law book collection in Switzerland, were housed in a building designed in 1908 by Hermann Fietz as a high school and laboratory. Santiago Calatrava was asked in 1989 to study additions to two wings added to this structure in 1930 in order to modernize and enlarge them. Rather than filling in the existing courtyard with floor space, Calatrava proposed to create an atrium in place of the courtyard. In the final design, Calatrava created workspaces for the students, with direct access to the library and seminar spaces. A series of seven oval reading levels are hung within the atrium, "staggered on each level so that it is no longer the floor area that increases as they approach the roof but the space they circumscribe." This design allows natural light to penetrate deeper into the heart of the structure and its reading area. To support the cascade of galleries, eight attachment points have been created within or against the walls of the existing façade. As the architect describes the design: "The basic structure of each gallery is formed by a steel torsion tube, from which T-shaped, tapering steel beams cantilever in a regular rhythm. Each gallery is braced by balustrades, which have been designed as load-bearing trusses. By channeling the forces away from the center of the atrium, this design also leaves the basement areas free of obstruction." He goes on to say that "an important aspect of the design is the complete independence of old and new. The reading room, the two new stories and the roof are treated as separate from the existing building, both architectonically and with regard to materials." Ever a master of spectacular shapes, Santiago Calatrava has created what is in good part a library that is at once practical for its users and architecturally inspiring. As is the case in many of Calatrava's projects, this structure evolved and matured over a relatively long period. It might be ventured that the ovoid form of the library may also echo that of the female sex, source of life, much as the library is the source of knowledge. Calatrava's own admitted sources do not include this type of reference, but the observer may be excused for thinking along lines inspired by his long fascination with the human body.

Inserted into an existing courtyard, the new law library, whose central space is visible to the left, shows to what extent the architect is capable of occupying a space and making it his own, even within the relatively tight constraints of this project.

Die in einen vorhandenen Hof eingefügte neue Juristische Bibliothek, deren zentraler Raum links zu sehen ist, zeigt, in welchem Maß der Architekt fähig ist, Raum zu besetzen und sich zu eigen zu machen, selbst bei den eher beschränkten Verhältnissen dieses Projekts.

Insérée dans une cour existante, la nouvelle bibliothèque de droit dont le volume central est visible ici à gauche, montre à quel point l'architecte sait occuper un espace et se l'approprier, même dans le cadre des contraintes relativement fortes d'un projet tel que celui-ci.

Die Rechtswissenschaftliche Fakultät der Universität Zürich war auf acht Standorte verteilt. Die Einrichtungen für die Fakultät und die Bibliothek, darunter die zweitgrößte Sammlung seltener juristischer Bücher in der Schweiz, waren in einem 1908 von Hermann Fietz als Schule und Labor entworfenen Gebäude untergebracht. Santiago Calatrava wurde 1989 aufgefordert, sich Gedanken über Anbauten an zwei 1930 ergänzte Flügel zu machen, mit dem Ziel, diese Gebäude zu modernisieren und zu vergrößern. Statt den bestehenden Innenhof in Nutzfläche umzuwandeln, schlug Calatrava vor, dort ein Atrium zu schaffen. Im endgültigen Entwurf plante Calatrava hier Arbeitsplätze für die Studenten mit direktem Zugang zur Bibliothek und zu den Seminarräumen. Innerhalb des Atriums wurden sieben ovale Leseebenen aufgehängt, „auf jeder Ebene versetzt angeordnet, sodass nicht die Bodenfläche, sondern der von ihnen umschriebene Raum zunimmt, je näher sie dem Dach kommen". Diese Bauweise lässt Tageslicht tiefer in das Gebäudeinnere und die Lesezonen eindringen. Um diese Kaskade von Galerien abzustützen, wurden acht Befestigungspunkte innerhalb oder an den Wänden der vorhandenen Fassade geschaffen. Der Architekt beschreibt seinen Entwurf so: „Die grundlegende Konstruktion jeder Empore besteht aus einer Torsionsröhre aus Stahl, von der T-förmige, sich verjüngende Stahlträger in regelmäßigen Abständen vorkragen. Jede Empore wird von Brüstungen versteift, die als tragende Fachwerkbinder konzipiert wurden. Da die Kräfte vom Zentrum des Atriums abgelenkt werden, erlaubt diese Planung ein stützenfreies Untergeschoss.“ Er führt weiter aus: „Ein wichtiger Aspekt des Entwurfs ist die völlige Autonomie von Alt und Neu. Der Lesesaal, die beiden neuen Geschosse und das Dach werden sowohl architektonisch als auch hinsichtlich der Materialien als getrennt vom bestehenden Gebäude behandelt.“ Stets ein Meister spektakulärer Formgebung, hat Santiago Calatrava eine Bibliothek geschaffen, die gleichermaßen zweckdienlich für ihre Benutzer wie architektonisch inspirierend ist. Wie bei vielen Projekten Calatravas reifte auch dieser Entwurf über einen relativ langen Zeitraum. Man könnte so weit gehen anzunehmen, die Eiform des Bibliotheksbaus solle auf das weibliche Geschlecht als Ursprung des Lebens anspielen, ebenso wie die Bibliothek als Quelle des Wissens gilt. Calatrava bekennt sich nirgends zu dieser Art von Bezug, jedoch sei es dem Betrachter gestattet, derartige Überlegungen anzustellen angesichts Calatravas Faszination für den menschlichen Körper.

La Faculté de droit de l’Université de Zurich répartit ses activités entre huit immeubles. Les installations pour le corps professoral et la bibliothèque, qui contient la seconde plus vaste collection helvétique de livres rares de droit, se trouvent dans un bâtiment conçu en 1908 par Hermann Fietz pour accueillir un collège et des laboratoires. En 1989, Santiago Calatrava reçut commande d’une étude pour agrandir et moderniser deux ailes ajoutées dans les années 1930. Plutôt que de combler la cour existante, il proposa de remplacer celle-ci par un atrium. Dans son projet final, il créa des espaces de travail supplémentaires pour les étudiants avec un accès direct à la bibliothèque et aux salles de séminaire. Sept espaces de lecture de forme ovale sont ainsi suspendus dans l’atrium, « décalés de niveau en niveau, de telle façon que ce n’est plus la surface au sol qui s’accroît au fur et à mesure que l’on monte vers la toiture mais l’espace qu’ils circonscrivent ». Cette disposition permet à la lumière naturelle de mieux pénétrer au cœur même de la structure et des zones de lecture. Pour soutenir cette cascade de galeries, huit points d’attache ont été créés à l’intérieur ou contre les murs de la façade existante. Comme l’explique l’architecte : « La structure de base de chaque galerie est constituée d’un tube en acier en torsion d’où partent en porte-à-faux, selon un rythme régulier, des poutres d’acier en T effilé. Chaque galerie est entretoisée par des balustrades qui sont en fait des fermes porteuses. En canalisant la charge au-delà du centre de l’atrium, cette conception libère en même temps le rez-de-chaussée de toute obstruction. » Il poursuit : « Un aspect important du projet est la totale indépendance du nouveau par rapport à l’ancien. La salle de lecture, les deux étages neufs et la toiture sont traités séparément des bâtiments existants, aussi bien architectoniquement qu’en termes de matériaux. » Grand maître des formes spectaculaires, Santiago Calatrava a ainsi créé une bibliothèque qui est à la fois pratique pour ses usagers et d’une architecture inspirée. Cette structure aussi a évolué et mûri sur une assez longue période. On pourrait avancer que sa forme ovoïde fait écho à celle d’un sexe féminin, source de vie comme la bibliothèque est source de savoir. Calatrava ne reconnaît pas ce type de référence, mais l’observateur peut se prendre au jeu de sa fascination durable pour le corps humain.

Rather than creating closed reading rooms, the architect chose a much more surprising solution, cantilevered platforms that run around the elliptical, or rather ocular, central atrium of the library.

Anstelle abgeschlossener Lesesäle entschied sich der Architekt für eine weit ausgefallenere Lösung: vorkragende Podien, die um das elliptische oder augenförmige zentrale Atrium der Bibliothek verlaufen.

Plutôt que de créer des salles de lecture fermées, l'architecte a préféré une solution beaucoup plus surprenante : des plateaux en porte-à-faux qui rayonnent à partir de l'atrium central en ellipse, ou en forme d'œil, de la bibliothèque.

de la escultura a la realidad Arquitectónica

LYON-SAINT-EXUPÉRY AIRPORT RAILWAY STATION

Colombier-Saugnieu, France. 1989–1994.

Procedimiento de ventilación del hall de acceso a los deambulatorios

La disposición de las ventanas laterales permite el aprovechamiento de las corrientes convectivas para la ventilación del hall de viajeros.

La disposición de las alas del techo del hall de viajeros al lado sur permite que durante los meses de verano haya sombra al interior del hall.

Project

LYON-SAINT-EXUPÉRY AIRPORT RAILWAY STATION

Location

COLOMBIER-SAUGNIEU, FRANCE

Client

RHÔNE-ALPES REGIONAL GOVERNMENT AND SNCF

Floor area

5600 m²

Cost

600 MILLION FRANCS (1994 VALUE)

Calatrava's sketches show his interest not only in overall form, but also in such factors as the movement of air through the completed structure, and the way, in this instance, in which it reacts to the problem of solar heat gain.

Calatravas Skizzen belegen, dass sein Interesse nicht nur der Gesamtform gilt, sondern auch Faktoren wie der Luftzirkulation im fertigen Bauwerk und der Art, wie sie in diesem Fall das Problem des Sonnenwärmegewinns bewältigt.

Les croquis de Calatrava montrent son intérêt non seulement pour la forme d'ensemble mais aussi pour des facteurs comme le mouvement de l'air à travers la structure achevée et la manière dont elle réagira à la chaleur due à l'ensoleillement.

Originally called the Lyon Satolas Station, this project is surely one of Calatrava's best-known works. The architect was the winner of a competition organized by the Rhône-Alpes Region and Lyon Chamber of Commerce and Industry (CCIL). The competition brief called for a building that would provide smooth passenger flow while creating an exciting and symbolic "gateway to the region." Despite its obvious similarity to a sort of prehistoric bird, the shape of this 5600-square-meter facility, which was designed for the French national railway company (SNCF) serving to connect the high-speed train network (TGV) to the formerly called Lyon Satolas Airport, is more closely related to Calatrava's sculptures than to any animal. The winged design may recall Eero Saarinen's TWA Terminal at Kennedy Airport (1957–62), but its function and aspects, such as the 500-meter-long covered platform for the trains, differentiate it from its predecessor in a decisive manner. Built at a total cost of 600 million francs in three phases, the station accommodates six tracks, with the middle two encased in a concrete shell for trains that pass through at high speed (300 km/h) without stopping. A 180-meter-long steel connecting bridge linking the facility to the airport terminal itself gives the plan a shape which might bring to mind a stingray as much as a bird. Its essential feature remains the main hall with its 1300-ton roof, measuring 120 x 100 meters, with a maximum height of 40 meters and a span of 53 meters. Largely cast-in-place concrete using local white sand was used, giving the building a "natural" muted color.

la Estación de Lyon Satolas

vista lateral de la estación sección por el eje medio

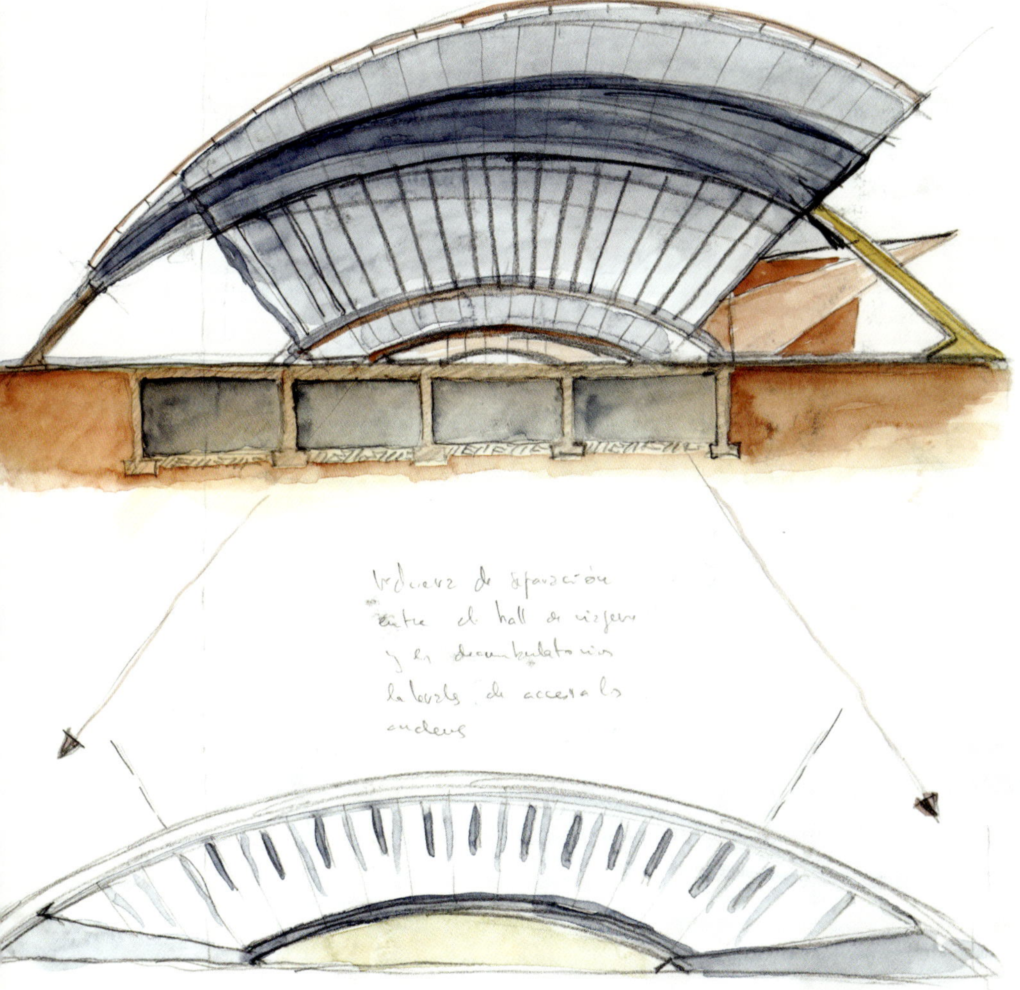

Calatrava's design for Lyon has been compared to a prehistoric bird, with its swooping beak planted in the earth. The dramatic angling of its surfaces and its ample glazing make it a functional and spectacular facility.

Calatravas Entwurf für Lyon wurde mit einem prähistorischen Vogel verglichen, dessen Schnabel zur Erde herabstößt. Die eminente Verkantung seiner Oberflächen und deren großflächige Verglasung machen den Bau ebenso imposant wie funktional.

Le projet de Calatrava pour Lyon a été comparé à un oiseau préhistorique au bec planté dans le sol. Ses angles impressionnants et ses vitrages généreux en font une gare à la fois spectaculaire et fonctionnelle.

Dieses anfänglich Bahnhof Lyon-Satolas genannte Projekt zählt sicherlich zu Calatravas bekanntesten Bauten. Er konnte einen von der Region Rhône-Alpes und der Lyoner Handels- und Industriekammer (CCIL) ausgeschriebenen Wettbewerb für sich entscheiden. In der Ausschreibung wurde ein Gebäude verlangt, das einen reibungslosen Passagierverkehr gewährleisten und darüber hinaus als reizvolles symbolisches „Tor zur Region“ fungieren sollte. Das für die Nationale Gesellschaft der französischen Eisenbahnen (SNCF) konzipierte Gebäude, das den ehemaligen Flughafen Lyon-Satolas an das Netz der Hochgeschwindigkeitszüge (TGV) anbinden sollte, ist ungeachtet seiner augenfälligen Ähnlichkeit mit einer Art prähistorischem Vogel enger mit Calatravas Skulpturen als mit irgendeinem Tier verwandt. Der „geflügelte“ Bau mag an Eero Saarinens TWA-Terminal (1957–62) am Kennedy Airport in New York erinnern, aber seine Funktion und Teilaspekte wie der 500 m lange überdachte Bahnsteig unterscheiden ihn deutlich von seinem Vorgänger. Der für Gesamtkosten in Höhe von umgerechnet 91,5 Millionen Euro in drei Bauabschnitten errichtete Bahnhof verfügt über sechs Gleisanlagen, wobei die zwei mittleren in einer Betonröhre verlaufen und durchfahrenden Hochgeschwindigkeitszügen (300 km/h) vorbehalten sind. Eine 180 m lange Stahlbrücke, die den Bahnhof mit dem Flughafenterminal verbindet, gibt dem Grundriss eine Form, die an einen Stachelrochen oder einen Vogel erinnert. Der maßgebliche Bauteil ist jedoch die Haupthalle mit ihren Abmessungen von 120 x 100 m, einer maximalen Höhe von 40 m und einer Spannweite von 53 m unter dem 1300 t schweren Dach. Es kam in erster Linie vor Ort gegossener Beton zum Einsatz, für den heimischer weißer Sand verwendet wurde, der dem Gebäude eine „natürliche“ gedämpfte Farbe verleiht.

As he did in his Zurich Stadelhofen Station, Calatrava succeeds in carrying over the themes of the exterior of the terminal in its soaring interiors. Lyon-Saint-Exupéry is one of the first stations in France to reverse the long trend toward anonymous and ugly railway facilities.

Wie schon bei seinem Zürcher Bahnhof Stadelhofen gelang es Calatrava, die Attribute des Außenbaus in die himmelhohen Innenräume zu übertragen. Lyon-Saint-Exupéry ist einer der ersten Bahnhöfe Frankreichs, der den seit Langem bestehenden Trend zu gesichtslosen, hässlichen Bahngebäuden umkehrt.

Comme pour la gare de Stadelhofen à Zurich, Calatrava réussit ici à transférer la thématique visuelle de l'extérieur à l'intérieur. Lyon-Saint-Exupéry est l'une des premières réalisations en France à contrarier la tendance habituelle à construire des gares aussi laides qu'anonymes.

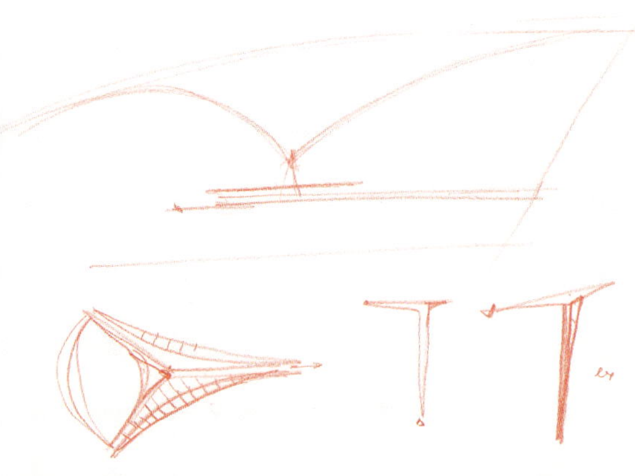

Ce projet – qui s'appelait à l'origine gare de Lyon-Satolas – fruit d'un concours organisé par la région Rhône-Alpes et la Chambre de commerce et d'industrie de Lyon, est certainement l'une des œuvres plus célèbres de Calatrava. Il s'agissait d'un bâtiment destiné à faciliter les déplacements des voyageurs et à faire en même temps office de « porte » symbolique de la région. Malgré son évidente ressemblance avec quelque oiseau préhistorique, cet ensemble de 5 600 mètres carrés conçu pour la SNCF afin de relier une ligne de TGV à l'aérogare Saint-Exupéry est en fait plus apparenté aux sculptures de Calatrava qu'à un quelconque animal. Le dessin en ailes peut rappeler le terminal TWA d'Eero Saarinen pour l'aéroport Kennedy à New York (1957–62), mais sa fonction et divers éléments comme ses 500 mètres de quais couverts le différencient radicalement de ce prédécesseur. Construite en trois phases pour un budget de 600 millions de francs, la gare est desservie par six voies, les deux du centre, réservées aux trains qui la traversent à 300 km/h sans s'arrêter, étant enfermées dans une coque en béton. La passerelle en acier de 180 mètres de long qui connecte directement les quais au terminal de l'aéroport donne au plan une allure de raie manta ou d'oiseau. L'élément le plus caractéristique de la gare reste le grand hall dont la couverture de 1 300 tonnes mesure 120 x 100 mètres pour une hauteur maximale de 40 mètres et une portée de 53 mètres. Le béton, en grande partie coulé sur place à partir de sable blanc local, donne à l'ensemble une couleur neutre, « naturelle ».

Trains au Départ
Train Departures
Départ Destination
Porte RHONE

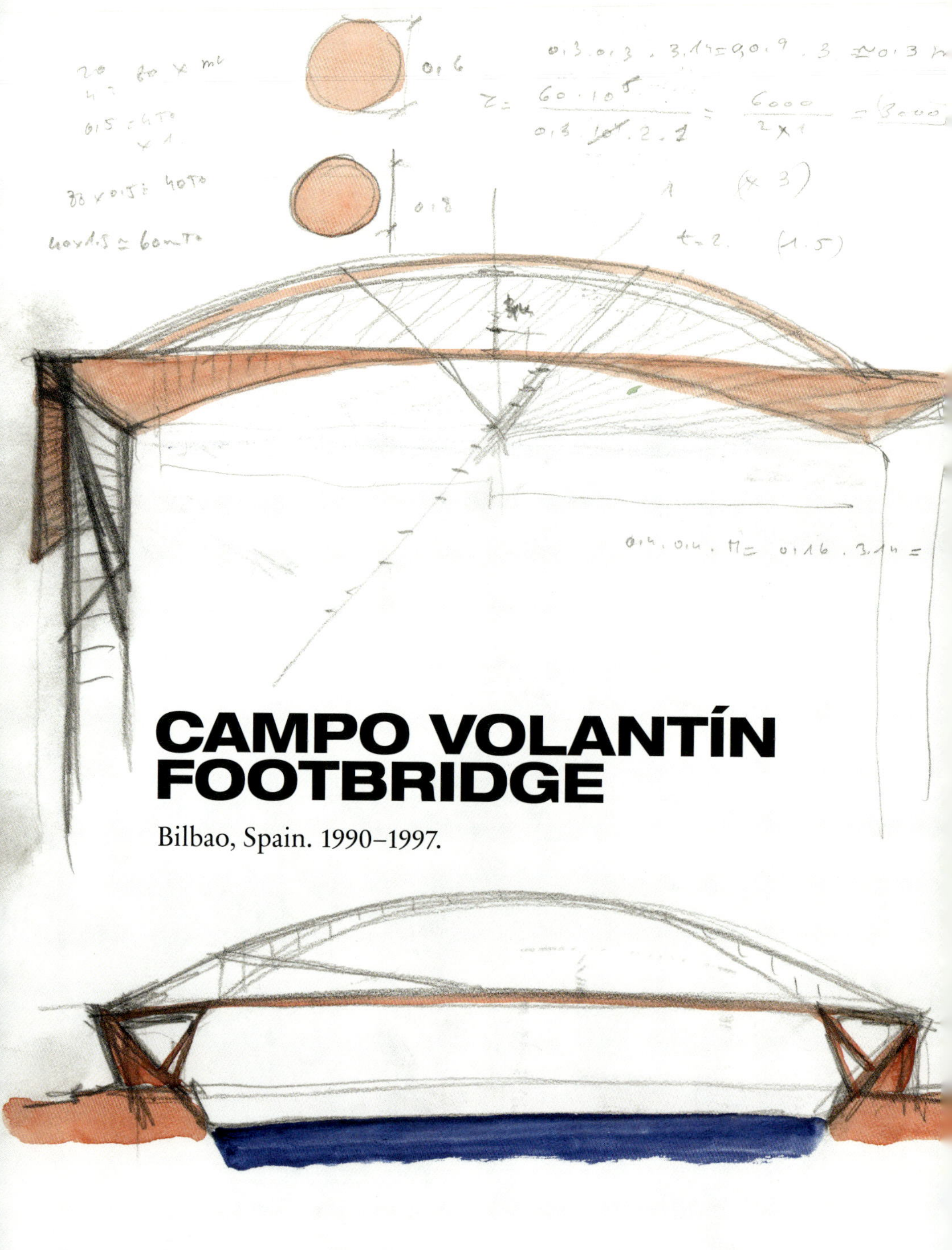

CAMPO VOLANTÍN FOOTBRIDGE

Bilbao, Spain. 1990–1997.

1,20
160
160

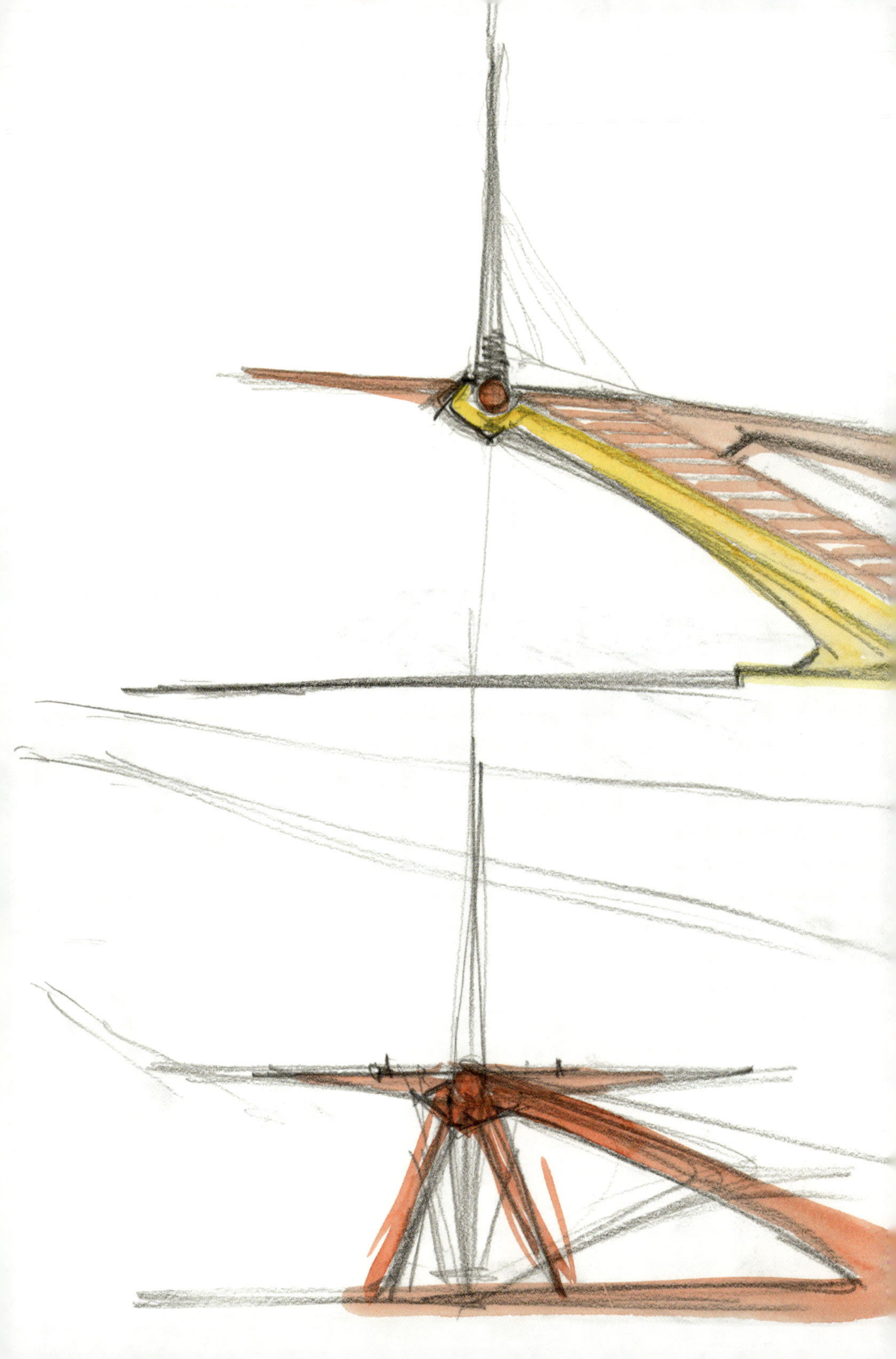

Project

CAMPO VOLANTÍN FOOTBRIDGE

Location

BILBAO, SPAIN

Length and maximum span

75 METERS

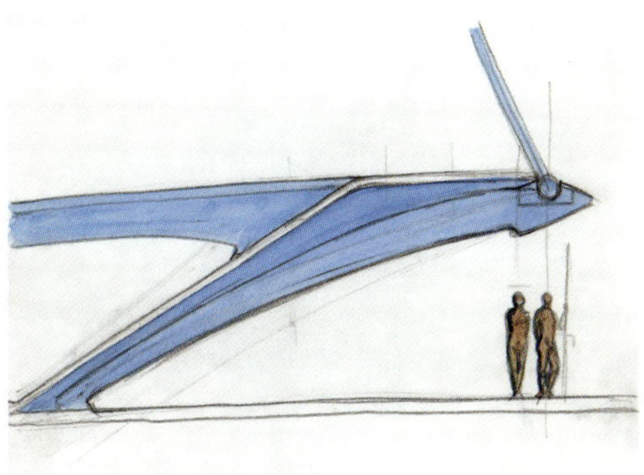

Cantilevered or suspended, the shapes imagined by the architect-engineer always show the forces that play on them in a dynamic way, almost giving the impression that they are about to take flight or run forward.

Gleich ob auskragend oder hängend, die von dem Ingenieurarchitekten erdachten Formen zeigen stets die auf sie einwirkenden Kräfte in dynamischer Weise und erwecken fast den Eindruck, als seien sie im Abheben oder Weglaufen begriffen.

En porte-à-faux ou suspendues, les formes imaginées par l'architecte-ingénieur montrent toujours les forces en jeu de façon dynamique, donnant presque l'impression qu'elles vont prendre leur envol ou s'enfuir.

This inclined parabolic arch structure has a total span of 75 meters. Serving to link a rundown commercial area called Uribitarte with the city of Bilbao across the Nervion River, the Campo Volantín Footbridge is one aspect of a vast campaign of urban renewal, which includes Frank Gehry's Guggenheim Bilbao Museum, subway stations by Lord Norman Foster, and Calatrava's own Sondica Airport project (see page 130). As in many other designs by Santiago Calatrava, an apparent disequilibrium, or rather a sense of frozen movement, is heightened by the lightness of the structure and the steel uprights that run from the arch to the deck of the bridge every 5.7 meters. Its spectacular night lighting and its glass-surfaced deck emphasize the symbolic importance of the bridge, which may indeed have participated in urban renewal. As the architect explains, this project actually came to be realized in two distinct episodes. In 1990, Calatrava created a design for what was then known as the Uribitarte Bridge site, on behalf of a client engaged in an exchange of land with the municipality. The second design was commissioned by local authorities, who were sympathetic to the original idea of making an urban statement but wanted to avoid any association with the project's previous incarnation. The bridge now takes its name not from the Uribitarte, but from the Campo de Volantín, a street on the opposite bank.

Die Brücke mit einem geneigten Parabelbogen hat eine Gesamtspannweite von 75 m. Sie verbindet das heruntergekommene Geschäftsviertel Uribitarte mit der auf der anderen Seite des Nervión bzw. der Ría de Bilbao gelegenen Innenstadt und ist Teil einer groß angelegten Sanierungsmaßnahme der Stadt. Dazu gehören ferner Frank Gehrys Guggenheim-Museum, U-Bahn-Stationen von Lord Norman Foster sowie Calatravas Flughafen Sondica (siehe Seite 130). Wie bei zahlreichen anderen Entwürfen Santiago Calatravas wird ein scheinbares Ungleichgewicht oder vielmehr der Eindruck einer „angehaltenen Bewegung“ durch die Leichtigkeit des Bauwerks mit den Stahlstützen verstärkt, die sich jeweils im Abstand von 5,7 m zwischen Bogen und Brückentafel erheben. Die spektakuläre nächtliche Beleuchtung sowie die mit Glas belegte Brückentafel unterstreichen die symbolische Bedeutung der Brücke, die Anteil an der Stadtsanierung hat. Dem Architekten zufolge wurde dieses Projekt in zwei getrennten Schritten realisiert. 1990 fertigte Calatrava im Auftrag eines Bauherrn, der in einen Grundstückstausch mit der Kommune involviert war, einen Entwurf für die damals als Standort der Uribitarte-Brücke bekannte Örtlichkeit an. Der zweite Entwurf wurde von den örtlichen Behörden in Auftrag gegeben, die die ursprüngliche Idee eines städtebaulichen Impulses aufgreifen, aber jegliche Assoziation an die Vorgeschichte des Projekts vermeiden wollten. Die Brücke wurde nun nicht nach Uribitarte benannt, sondern erhielt ihren Namen vom Campo de Volantín, einer Straße am gegenüberliegenden Ufer.

Cette structure en arc parabolique d'une portée totale de 75 mètres reliant une zone commerciale en déshérence appelée Uribitarte à la ville de Bilbao, de l'autre côté du fleuve Nervión, fait partie d'un vaste programme de rénovation urbaine comprenant le musée Guggenheim de Frank Gehry, les stations de métro de Norman Foster et le projet pour l'aéroport de Sondica par Calatrava (voir page 130). Comme dans plusieurs de ses précédents travaux, le déséquilibre apparent, ou plutôt le sentiment de mouvement figé, est mis en valeur par la légèreté de la structure et les montants verticaux en acier qui descendent de l'arc vers le tablier tous les 5,7 mètres. Un éclairage nocturne spectaculaire et un tablier en verre renforcent l'impact symbolique de ce pont qui a joué un rôle actif dans la rénovation du centre de la ville. Comme l'explique l'architecte, ce projet a été réalisé en deux phases. En 1990, il avait dessiné des plans pour ce qui était alors le site du pont d'Uribitarte, à la demande d'un client qui échangeait des terrains avec la municipalité. Le second projet fut commandité par la municipalité elle-même qui appréciait l'idée originale mais voulait éviter toute association avec la première approche. Le pont a aujourd'hui abandonné le nom d'Uribitarte pour celui de Campo Volantín, une rue située sur la rive opposée.

Located just up the river from Gehry's Bilbao Guggenheim, the Campo Volantín Footbridge participates in the astonishing renovation of the dull, industrial city by a few significant works of architecture. Its simplicity and lightness contrasts with the otherwise gray surroundings.

Die unweit von Gehrys Guggenheim-Museum gelegene Campo-Volantín-Fußgängerbrücke ist Teil einer erstaunlichen Auffrischung dieser öden Industriestadt durch einige wenige bedeutsame Bauwerke. Schlichtheit und Leichtigkeit stehen in Kontrast zur ansonsten grauen Umgebung.

Un peu en amont du Guggenheim Bilbao de Frank Gehry, la passerelle de Campo Volantín participe à l'étonnante rénovation de cette ville industrielle grâce à quelques interventions architecturales. Sa simplicité et sa légèreté contrastent avec l'environnement grisâtre.

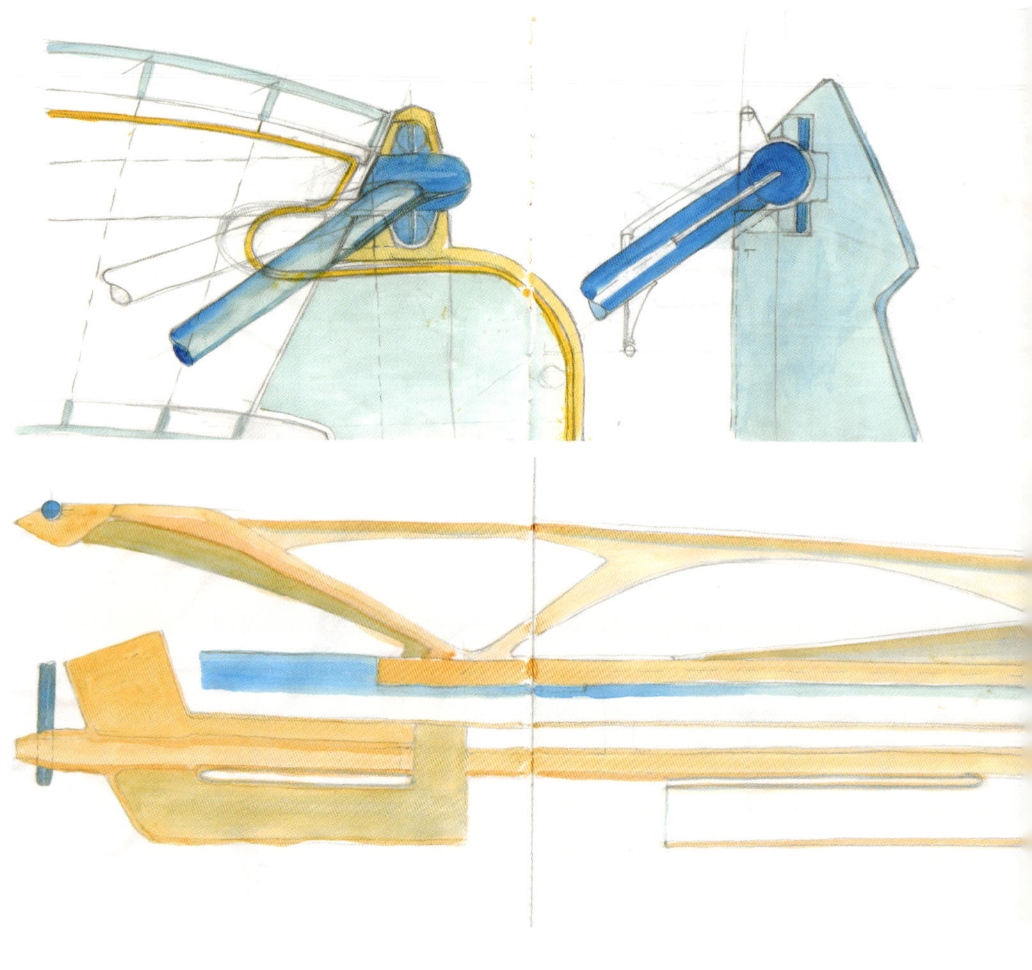

The architect's sketches reveal the integration of carefully thought-out details of structure with the overall effect he seeks in the profile of the bridge. These are not two different processes but part of a unified approach.

Die Skizzen des Architekten offenbaren die Einbeziehung sorgfältig durchdachter baulicher Details in die Gesamtwirkung, die er mit dem Profil der Brücke anstrebt. Dabei handelt es sich um zwei verschiedene Arbeitsgänge, die gleichwohl Teil einer einheitlichen Auffassung sind.

Les croquis de l'architecte montrent l'intégration de détails de la structure mûrement réfléchis dans l'effet d'ensemble qu'il recherche à travers le profil du pont. Ce ne sont pas deux processus distincts, mais les composantes d'une approche globale.

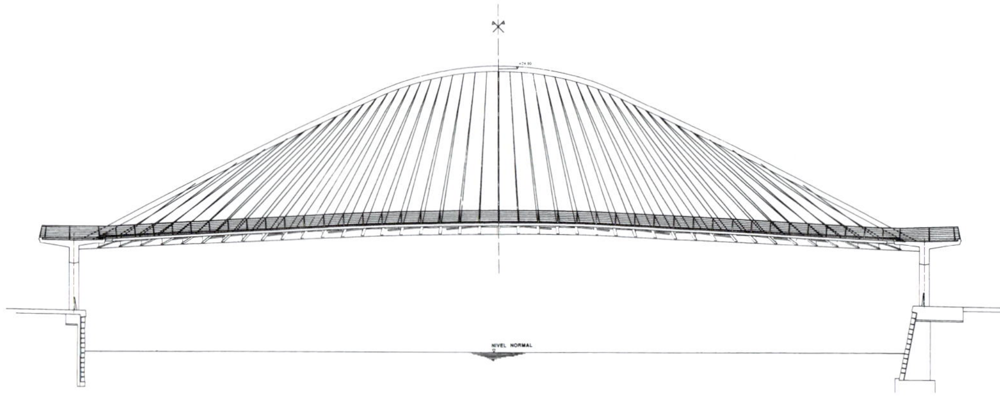

Although the curvature of the bridge seems simple and elegant, it of course complicates the engineering, a fact that Calatrava in no way reveals in his design.

Die scheinbar einfache, elegante Krümmung der Brücke verkompliziert natürlich die technische Planung, ein Umstand, den Calatravas Entwurf in keiner Weise offenbart.

Même si la courbe du pont paraît simple et élégante, sa conception est bien évidemment complexe, ce que Calatrava ne révèle absolument pas dans ses esquisses.

SONDICA AIRPORT AND CONTROL TOWER

Bilbao, Spain. 1990–2000.

Aeropuerto de Bilbao.-

Vista lateral

Bilbao

Project

SONDICA AIRPORT AND CONTROL TOWER

Location

BILBAO, SPAIN

Client

AEROPUERTOS ESPAÑOLES Y NAVEGACIÓN AÉREA

Height of control tower

42 METERS

Terminal floor area

29 000 m²

After having been asked in 1990 to design a new four-gate airport facility for the Basque city of Bilbao, Santiago Calatrava was commissioned four years later to double the size of the terminal, located 10 kilometers north of the city. The architect responded with a triangular plan, amply glazed structure whose roof sweeps upward in the direction of the landing field. Where glass is not used, the concrete structure is treated with a unifying aluminum cladding. Recalling an eyelid in elevation, and perhaps a steel-ribbed ray in plan, the structure can simultaneously handle the arrival and departure of eight aircraft through lateral wings that are intended for possible future expansion. Like Frank Gehry's Guggenheim Bilbao, this project underlines the will of Bilbao to compete in architectural and cultural terms with southern Spanish cities such as Barcelona. Departures are located on the upper floor, and arrivals below. Able to handle two million passengers a year as of 2000, Sondica Airport was conceived to eventually receive up to five times more travelers. Parking facilities for 1500 vehicles are connected to the terminal via a 100-meter underground passageway and are clearly integrated into the plan both visually and in terms of function. The architect's overall plan for the airport also provided for future facilities such as hotels. Santiago Calatrava's design for the new Bilbao Airport facilities included the construction of a 42-meter-high control tower, located 270 meters from the terminal building (1993–96). Calatrava was selected on the basis of a separate limited competition and for reasons of airport function the control tower was given priority in the construction schedule over the other buildings. Inverting the normal typology for such structures, the tower is designed to have a progressively larger volume as it rises, culminating in a control deck with 360-degree visibility. Originally, the architect proposed that a single, central concrete pillar support the roof of the air traffic control room, but this idea was rejected by the client in favor of a steel support located along the edges of the space. Built of reinforced concrete with some aluminum cladding, the tower has become the symbol of the airport itself.

Nachdem Calatrava 1990 beauftragt worden war, für die baskische Stadt Bilbao einen neuen Flughafen mit vier Gates zu entwerfen, erhielt er vier Jahre später den Auftrag, die Größe der 10 km nördlich der Stadt gelegenen Terminals zu verdoppeln. Der Architekt antwortete mit einem dreieckigen Grundriss und einem großzügig verglasten Bau, dessen Dach in Richtung des Landefeldes aufwärtsstrebt. Wo kein Glas verwendet wird, erhielt der Betonbau eine harmonisierende Aluminiumverkleidung. Der Bau, der an ein sich öffnendes Augenlid oder im Grundriss vielleicht an die Umrisse eines Rochens mit stählernen Rippen erinnert, kann dank der für einen künftigen Ausbau gedachten Seitenflügel gleichzeitig den An- und Abflug von acht Flugzeugen abwickeln. Ebenso wie Frank Gehrys Guggenheim-Museum unterstreicht dieses Projekt die Absicht Bilbaos, sich in architektonischer und kultureller Hinsicht mit anderen spanischen Städten wie Barcelona zu messen. Abfliegende Passagiere werden über die obere Ebene, ankommende über die untere abgefertigt. Der Flughafen Sondica, der seit dem Jahr 2000 jährlich zwei Millionen Passagiere abfertigt, ist letzten Endes auf die fünffache Zahl von Fluggästen ausgelegt. Parkmöglichkeiten für 1500 Fahrzeuge sind mit dem Terminal durch eine 100 m lange unterirdische Passage verbunden und in die Anlage visuell wie funktionell klar integriert. Der Gesamtplan des Architekten für den Flughafen sieht auch künftige Einrichtungen wie Hotels vor. Ebenfalls zum Projekt gehört ein 42 m hoher Kontrollturm, der 270 m vom Terminal (1993–96) entfernt steht. Calatrava wurde hierfür im Rahmen eines separaten geschlossenen Wettbewerbs ausgewählt, und um den Flughafen funktionsfähig zu halten, entstand der Tower vor den übrigen Gebäuden. In Umkehrung der üblichen Form derartiger Bauten vergrößert der Turm mit zunehmender Höhe sein Volumen und endet in einer Kontrollebene mit ungehinderter Rundumsicht. Ursprünglich hatte der Architekt einen einzelnen zentralen Betonpfeiler vorgesehen, der das Dach des Kontrollraums stützen sollte, aber die Idee wurde vom Auftraggeber abgelehnt zugunsten von Stahlstützen entlang der Ränder des Raumes. Der aus Stahlbeton errichtete Turm ist teilweise mit Aluminium verkleidet und mittlerweile das Symbol des ganzen Flughafens.

Après la commande, en 1990, d'une nouvelle aérogare à quatre passerelles d'embarquement implantée à dix kilomètres au nord de la ville basque espagnole de Bilbao, Santiago Calatrava se vit confier quatre ans plus tard le doublement du premier projet. Le bâtiment de plan triangulaire et généreusement vitré, se caractérise par une couverture qui s'élève vers le ciel dans l'axe des pistes. Les parties en béton sont unifiées par un habillage en aluminium. Rappelant une paupière (en élévation) voire une raie (sur plan), la structure peut traiter simultanément l'arrivée et le départ de huit appareils grâce à des passerelles latérales conçues pour permettre une future extension. Comme le musée Guggenheim de Frank Gehry, ce projet exprime la volonté de la ville de Bilbao de rivaliser, en termes d'architecture et de culture, avec d'autres villes espagnoles, notamment Barcelone. Les départs s'effectuent au niveau supérieur, et les arrivées à celui des pistes. Cet aéroport, d'une capacité de trafic de deux millions de passagers par an en 2000, pourra un jour en recevoir dix millions. Les parkings pour 1 500 véhicules sont raccordés au terminal par un passage souterrain de 100 mètres de long et totalement intégrés au plan, aussi bien visuellement que fonctionnellement. Le plan masse de l'aéroport prévoit également l'implantation d'équipements futurs tels que des hôtels. Ce projet comprenait par ailleurs la construction d'une tour de contrôle de 42 mètres de haut, à 270 mètres du terminal (1993–96). Calatrava a été choisi lors d'un concours sur invitation et, pour des raisons de fonctionnement, la tour a eu la priorité sur les autres constructions. Inversant la typologie habituelle de ce genre de structure, elle se présente sous forme d'un volume en cornet qui s'élargit peu à peu avant de culminer dans une plate-forme offrant une visibilité à 360 degrés. À l'origine, l'architecte avait proposé qu'un pilier central unique en béton soutienne la salle de contrôle du trafic aérien, mais cette idée a été refusée par le client, qui a préféré des piliers en acier à la périphérie de la salle. Édifiée en béton armé et partiellement habillée d'aluminium, la tour est devenue le symbole de l'aéroport.

The raylike form seen elsewhere in Calatrava's oeuvre is visible in the sketch below. The photo of the site and new building above emphasizes the metaphor of flight implicit in the overall design.

Die aus Calatravas Werken bekannte Rochenform ist in der Skizze unten wiederzuerkennen. Das Foto der Baustelle und des neuen Gebäudes (oben) verdeutlicht die Metapher des Fliegens, die den gesamten Entwurf prägt.

La forme de raie, déjà vue dans l'œuvre de Calatrava, réapparaît dans le croquis de gauche. Les photos du site et du nouveau bâtiment, ci-dessus, mettent en évidence la métaphore du vol implicite dans le projet d'ensemble.

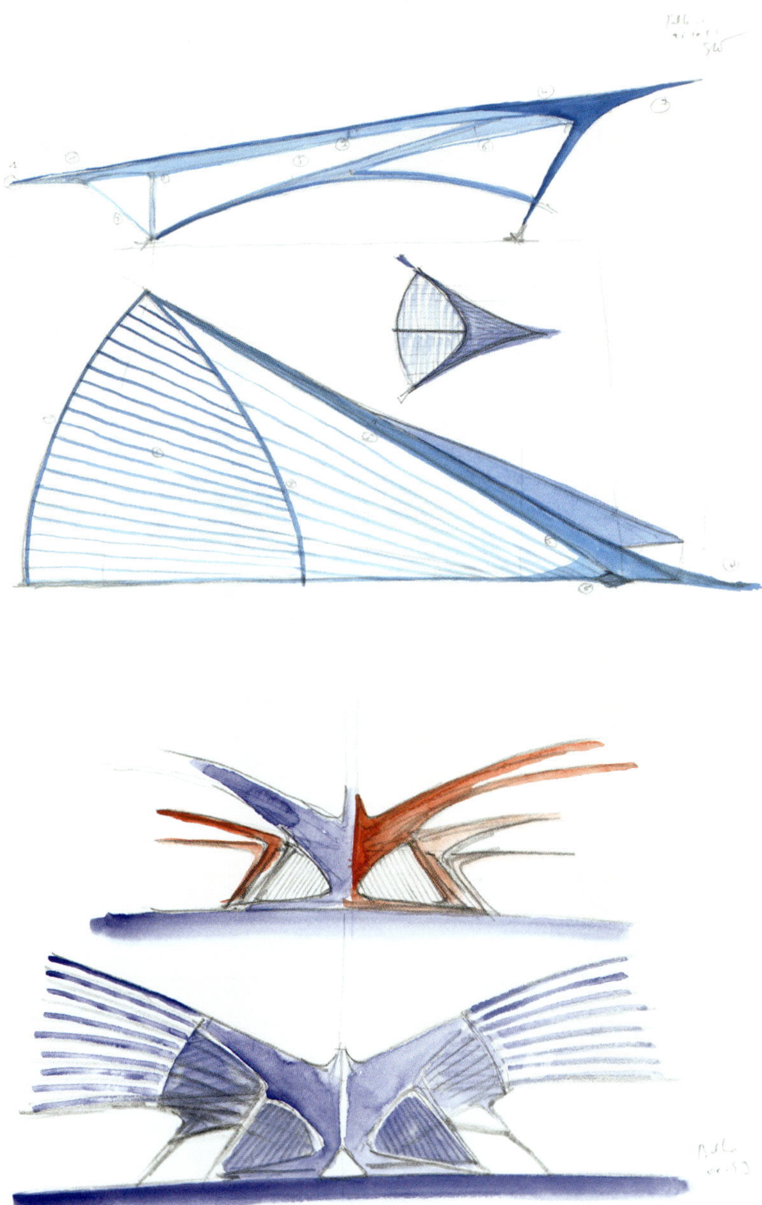

Fascinated by the idea of movement in architecture, if not specifically with flight, Calatrava nonetheless frequently calls on an apparently aviary vocabulary, most clearly visible in the sketches reproduced above.

Fasziniert von der Idee der Bewegung in der Architektur, wenn auch nicht speziell vom Fliegen, verweist Calatrava dennoch oft auf vogelähnliche Formen, deutlich erkennbar an seinen oben abgebildeten Skizzen.

Fasciné par l'idée de mouvement en architecture, si ce n'est spécifiquement par le vol, Calatrava fait souvent appel à un vocabulaire formel qui évoque l'oiseau, comme le montrent les croquis reproduits ci-dessus.

The raking cantilevered roof and forms of the airport carry an obvious relation to Calatrava's work on bridges, appearing to defy gravity but based in a natural comprehension of the engineering involved.

Das stark geneigte vorkragende Dach und die Formen des Flughafens lassen eine offensichtliche Verbindung zu Calatravas Brückenentwürfen erkennen, die der Schwerkraft zu trotzen scheinen und sich doch auf ein natürliches Verständnis der beteiligten Technik stützen.

Le profil du toit et l'inclinaison des éléments en porte-à-faux de l'aéroport montrent une relation évidente avec les recherches de Calatrava sur les ponts, semblant défier la gravité mais s'appuyant sur une compréhension intuitive de l'ingénierie.

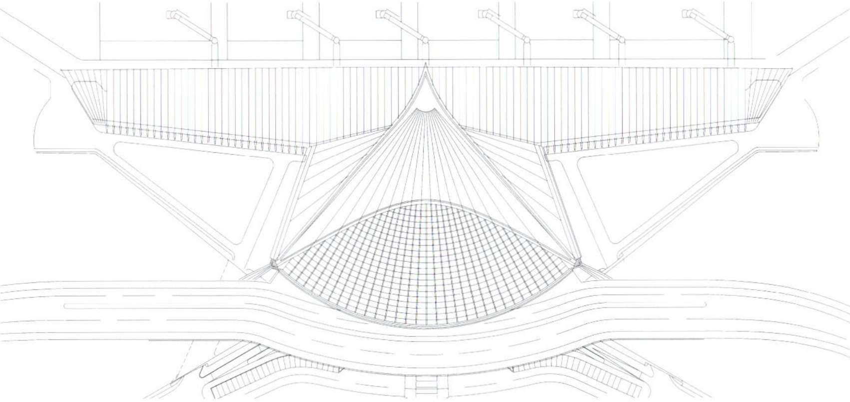

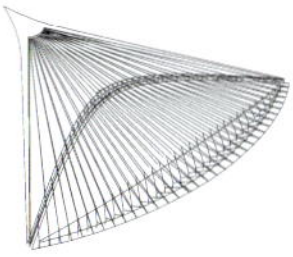

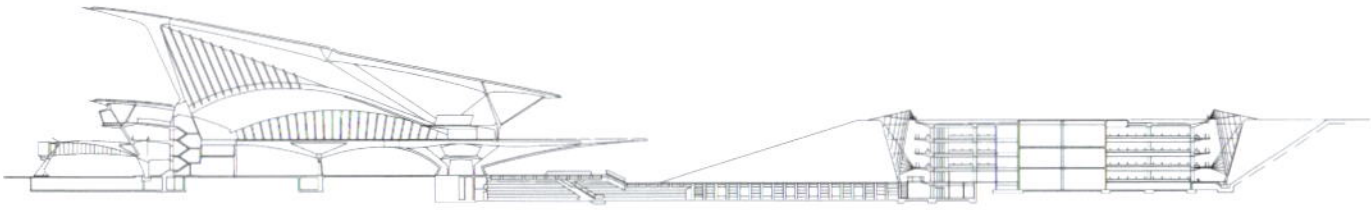

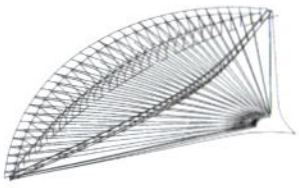

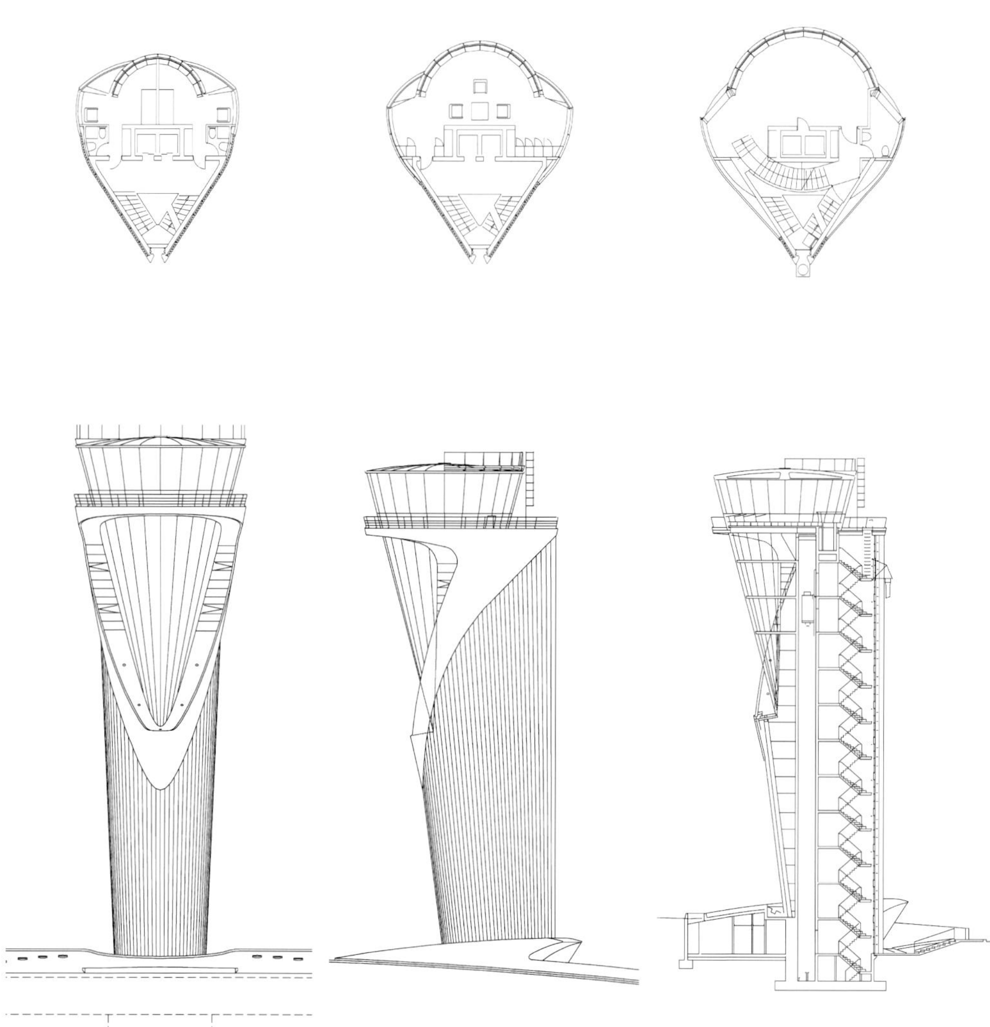

Much as he does with bridges, here Calatrava has taken a basic form, that of the airport control tower, usually subject to very little aesthetic effort, and turned it into a sculptural object that nonetheless is fully capable of its intended functions.

Ähnlich wie bei Brücken nahm sich Calatrava hier einer Grundform an, eines Flughafentowers, dem gewöhnlich wenig ästhetische Überlegung zuteilwird. Er verwandelte ihn in ein plastisches Objekt, das seiner vorgesehenen Funktion zur Gänze gerecht wird.

En grande partie comme pour ses ponts, Calatrava se saisit ici d'une forme de base, celle de la tour de contrôle, généralement un peu négligée sur le plan esthétique, pour en faire un objet sculptural qui n'en remplit pas moins parfaitement sa fonction première.

The cantilevered or ribbed forms seen in the Zurich Stadelhofen or Lyon-Saint-Exupéry Stations are again present here with variations and an apparent effort to simplify forms, or to render them more pure.

Die bei den Bahnhöfen Zürich-Stadelhofen und Lyon-Saint-Exupéry auskragenden oder gerippten Formen kommen auch hier vor, jedoch abgewandelt und in dem offensichtlichen Bemühen, sie zu vereinfachen oder unverfälschter wiederzugeben.

Les formes nervurées ou en porte-à-faux déjà vues dans la gare de Stadelhofen, à Zurich, ou dans celle de Lyon-Saint-Exupéry réapparaissent ici, mais dans une variante et une tentative de simplification qui les rend encore plus pures.

TENERIFE AUDITORIUM

Santa Cruz de Tenerife, Spain. 1991–2003.

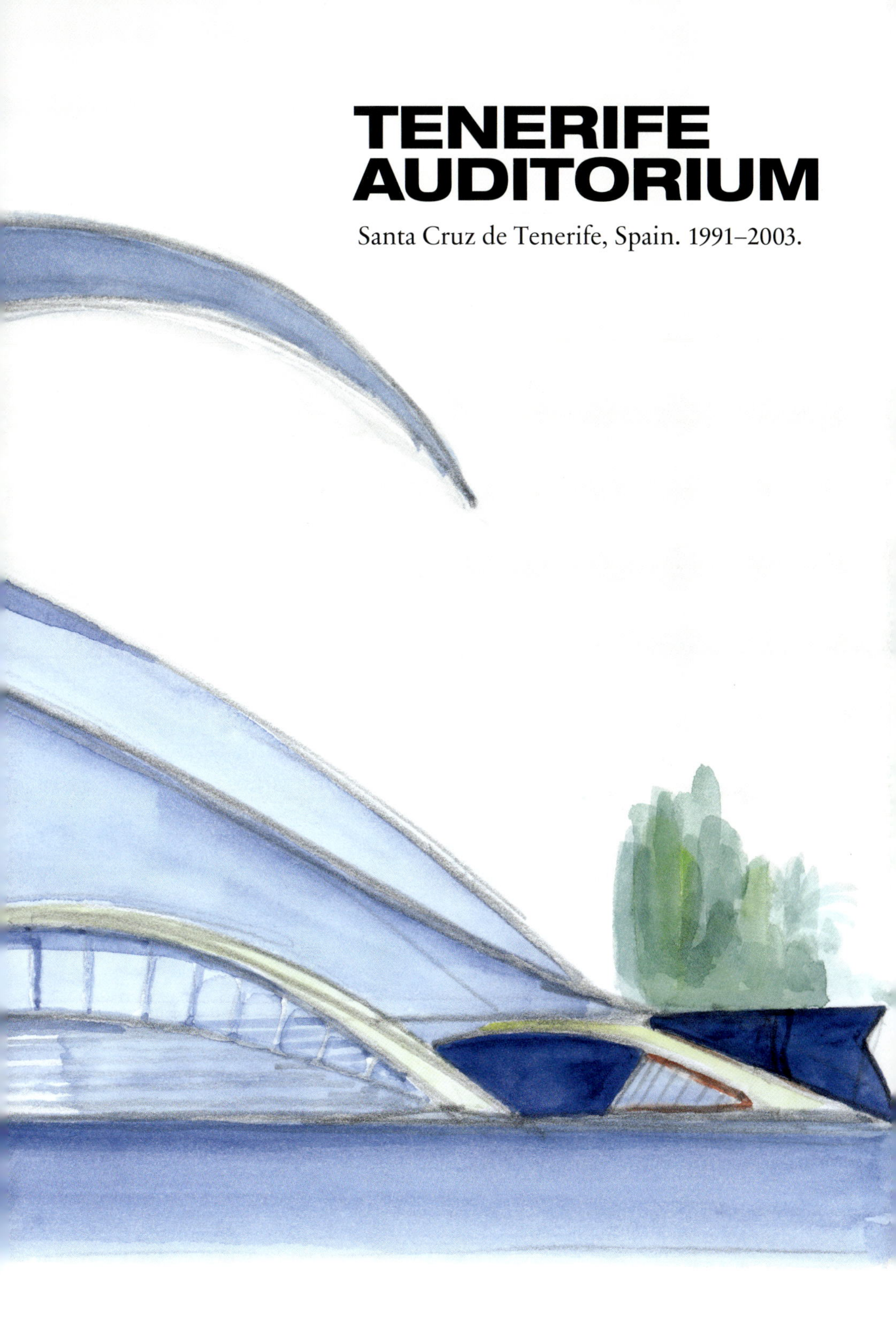

Project
TENERIFE AUDITORIUM

Location
SANTA CRUZ DE TENERIFE, CANARY ISLANDS, SPAIN

Client
TENERIFE TOWN COUNCIL

Capacity
1558 SEATS (MAIN CONCERT HALL) 428 SEATS (CHAMBER MUSIC HALL)

Cost
$ 82 MILLION

On an unprecedented scale in his oeuvre, the Tenerife building carries some of Calatrava's familiar preoccupations to new heights. An eye, or perhaps even forms inspired by female anatomy, inform the architecture without becoming explicit.

In einem Ausmaß, das in Calatravas Œuvre beispiellos ist, steigert das Opernhaus von Teneriffa einige seiner bekannten Lieblingsmotive zu neuen Höhen. Ein Auge oder vielleicht sogar von der weiblichen Anatomie inspirierte Formen beseelen die Architektur, ohne jedoch offenkundig zu werden.

D'une échelle sans précédent dans son œuvre, le projet de Tenerife illustre certaines des préoccupations familières de Calatrava, poussées ici vers de nouveaux sommets. Un œil, ou peut-être des formes inspirées de l'anatomie féminine, sont présents sans être pour autant évidents.

Completed in 2003, this 1558-seat capacity concert hall is located at the intersection of the Tres de Mayo Avenue and Maritima Avenue in the city of Santa Cruz de Tenerife. The facility also includes a chamber music hall with seating for 428. On this site in the harbor, the city expressed "a desire for a dynamic, monumental building that would not only be a place for music and culture but would also create a focal point for the area." With its distinctive concrete shell roof, in a curved triangular form culminating 60 meters above the plaza surrounding the building, this concert hall is one of the most visually spectacular structures designed by Calatrava. Beyond the basic functions of the project, the hall clearly takes on a symbolic value by the very nature of its appearance, in a way that might recall Jørn Utzon's Sydney Opera House. Located on a 154 x 100-meter rectangular site that has the particularity of including a 60-meter change in levels, the concert hall is set on a stepped platform or plinth that contains technical facilities and changing rooms. As the architect says of the actual concert space: "To fine-tune the acoustics, the wood paneling of the interior takes on a crystalline form, which also contributes to the drama of the space. These fittings were determined by investigations on models at 1:10. The placing of sound reflectors was determined by laser tests, which also helped define the dimensions of the vaulted interior. Instead of having stage curtains, the auditorium is provided with a concertina screen of vertical aluminum slats, which, upon opening, lift up into the auditorium to act as a sound-reflector above the orchestra pit." The roof of the shell of the structure is clad in broken tile, while local volcanic basalt is used for much of the paving and the cladding of the plinth. A 50-meter-high dome covers the main hall, recalling a number of Santiago Calatrava's studies of the human eye and its lid.

Diese 2003 fertiggestellte Konzerthalle mit 1558 Sitzplätzen liegt an der Kreuzung der Avenida Tres de Mayo mit der Avenida Maritima in der Stadt Santa Cruz de Tenerife. Der Bau umfasst außerdem einen Kammermusiksaal mit 428 Plätzen. An dieser Stelle im Hafen wünschte sich die Stadt „ein dynamisches, monumentales Bauwerk, das nicht nur ein Ort für Musik und Kultur sein sollte, sondern auch ein Wahrzeichen für die Gegend". Mit ihrem charakteristischen Betonschalendach, das sich in gebogener Dreiecksform 60 m über die das Gebäude umgebende Plaza aufschwingt, stellt die Konzerthalle in visueller Hinsicht einen der ungewöhnlichsten Bauten Calatravas dar. Über seine Funktionalität hinaus erhält das Projekt allein durch sein Aussehen eine symbolische Wertigkeit, die an Jørn Utzons Opernhaus von Sydney denken lässt. Das 154 x 100 m große, rechteckige Gelände der Konzerthalle weist einen Höhenunterschied von 60 m auf. Die Halle selbst wurde auf einem abgetreppten Sockel errichtet, in dem technische Einrichtungen und Umkleideräume untergebracht sind. Zum eigentlichen Konzertraum sagt der Architekt: „Um die Akustik genau abzustimmen, erhielt die Holzverkleidung des Innenraums eine kristalline Formgebung, die außerdem zur Dramatik des Raumes beiträgt. Über diese Einbauten wurde nach Versuchen mit einem Modell im Maßstab 1:10 entschieden. Die Platzierung von Klangreflektoren wurde durch Lasertests bestimmt, die auch halfen, die Abmessungen des gewölbten Innenraums festzulegen. Anstelle von Bühnenvorhängen ist das Auditorium mit einem Ziehharmonikaschirm aus vertikalen Aluminiumlamellen ausgerüstet, der sich beim Öffnen in das Auditorium hinein erhebt und über dem Orchestergraben als Klangreflektor fungiert." Die Decke der Schalenkonstruktion des Gebäudes ist mit Kachelscherben ausgekleidet, während für einen Großteil der Pflasterung und die Sockelverkleidung heimischer vulkanischer Basalt verwendet wurde. Der Hauptsaal ist von einer 50 m hohen Kuppel überwölbt, die an einige Studien Calatravas zum menschlichen Auge und Augenlid erinnert.

Achevé en 2003, ce complexe réunissant une salle de concerts de 1 558 places et une salle pour musique de chambre de 428 places est situé à l'angle des avenues Tres de Mayo et Maritima à Santa Cruz de Tenerife. Pour ce terrain jouxtant le port, la ville avait exprimé « le désir d'un bâtiment monumental et dynamique qui serait non seulement un lieu destiné à la musique et à la culture mais également un centre d'attraction pour toute cette zone ». Avec son toit extrêmement original en coque de béton dessinant un triangle incurvé et culminant à 60 mètres au-dessus d'une place, cette salle de concerts est l'un des projets les plus spectaculaires de Calatrava. La valeur symbolique et la nature même de cette présence prennent le pas sur les fonctions basiques de l'équipement, comme dans le cas de l'Opéra de Jørn Utzon à Sydney. Construite sur un terrain rectangulaire de 154 x 100 mètres qui a la particularité de présenter une différence de niveaux de 60 mètres, la salle est posée sur un terre-plein, un socle en gradins dont la base contient les équipements techniques et les loges des artistes. Comme l'architecte l'explique, pour la grande salle, « C'est pour des raisons d'acoustique que nous avons donné au lambrissage en bois de l'intérieur ce relief facetté, cristallin, qui contribue également à l'aspect spectaculaire du volume. Ces équipements ont été élaborés à l'aide d'études menées sur des maquettes au 1/10. Les emplacements des réflecteurs sonores ont été déterminés par des tests au laser qui ont également permis de définir les dimensions de la voûte intérieure. Au lieu d'un rideau de scène, l'auditorium est équipé d'un écran de lattes d'aluminium verticales qui s'élève dans les cintres et sert de réflecteur sonore au-dessus de la fosse d'orchestre. » La coque est revêtue de tesselles de carrelage et un basalte local a été retenu pour le pavage de la plupart des sols et l'habillage du socle. La coupole de 50 mètres de haut qui couvre l'entrée principale rappelle un certain nombre d'études de Santiago Calatrava sur l'œil et la paupière.

As is most usually the case, Calatrava's relatively simple sketches outline both the final form of the building and its essential structural reality. This sort of combination of aesthetics and the hard facts of engineering and construction is almost unique in contemporary architecture.

Wie beinahe immer geben Calatravas eher simple Skizzen sowohl die endgültige Form des Bauwerks als auch seine wesentliche konstruktive Realität wieder. Diese Kombination aus Ästhetik und den harten technischen und baulichen Fakten ist in der zeitgenössischen Architektur fast beispiellos.

Comme très souvent, les croquis relativement simples de Calatrava font ressortir à la fois la forme finale du projet et sa réalité structurelle essentielle. Cette façon de conjuguer l'esthétique et avec l'aspect pratique et technique de la construction est quasi unique dans l'architecture contemporaine.

Interior volumes are in complete harmony with the exterior shapes of the building as can be seen in this confrontation of images. Light and shadow animate the forms in ways that are also part of Calatrava's thought process.

Wie an dieser Gegenüberstellung von Bildern zu sehen, harmonieren die Innenräume aufs Beste mit den äußeren Formen des Gebäudes. Licht und Schatten beleben sie in einer Weise, die auch Teil von Calatravas Überlegungen ist.

Les volumes internes sont en complète harmonie avec les formes extérieures, comme le montre cette confrontation d'images. L'ombre et la lumière animent les formes dans une approche spécifique qui fait partie du processus de pensée de Calatrava.

The challenge in this instance may well be to generate usable and indeed astonishing interior spaces given the overtly sculptural nature of the exterior design. A theater of course does not pose the same problems as a museum, and here the architect gives free rein to his imagination.

Angesichts des skulpturalen Charakters des Außenbaus könnte die Herausforderung in diesem Fall darin bestanden haben, nutzbare und wirklich überraschende Innenräume zu schaffen. Naturgemäß stellen sich bei einem Theater nicht dieselben Probleme wie bei einem Museum, und hier lässt der Architekt seiner Fantasie freien Lauf.

Le défi était peut-être ici de créer des espaces intérieurs pratiques mais étonnants, en relation avec la nature ouvertement sculpturale de l'extérieur. Un théâtre ne pose pas les mêmes problèmes qu'un musée et l'architecte a pu laisser libre cours à son imagination.

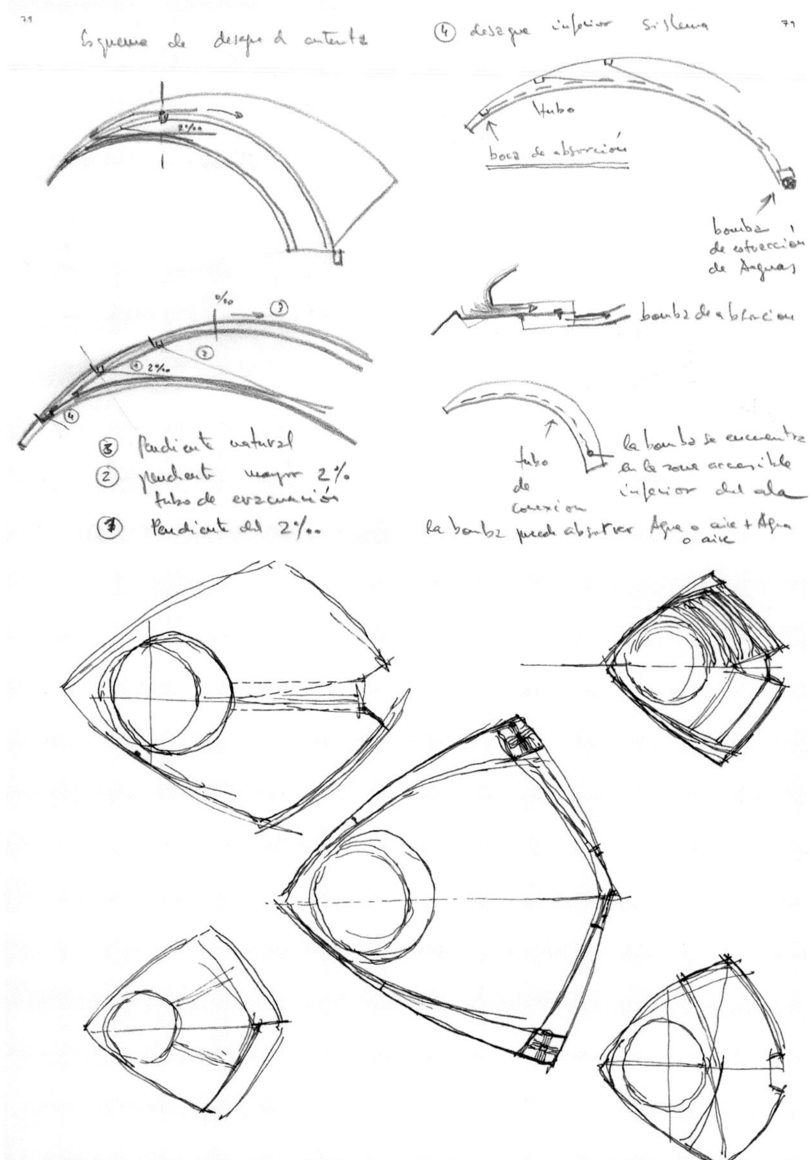

Night lighting completes the dramatic presence of the building, while the sketches above hint at inspiration from natural forms that might include a ray, a shape also seen in the Lyon-Saint-Exupéry Airport Railway Station.

Die nächtliche Beleuchtung betont die eindrucksvolle Präsenz des Gebäudes, während die Skizzen oben Inspiration aus der Natur andeuten, beispielsweise den Rochen – eine Form, die auch beim Bahnhof Lyon-Saint Exupéry erkennbar ist.

L'éclairage nocturne affirme la présence spectaculaire du bâtiment. Les croquis ci-dessus montrent une inspiration tirée de formes naturelles comme celle de la raie, déjà repérable dans la gare de Lyon-Saint-Exupéry.

Dealing here with both acoustics and aesthetics, the radiating sunlike form seen in the auditorium to the right confirms that the natural world is a source of inspiration as it is for the exterior forms. There is an almost mystical power in this architecture, criticized by some for its apparent extravagance.

Die einer strahlenden Sonne ähnelnde Form im Inneren des Auditoriums (rechts) wird ästhetischen und akustischen Anforderungen gerecht und bestätigt, dass die Natur nicht nur Inspirationsquelle für die Außengestaltung ist. Die von einigen wegen ihrer offenkundigen Extravaganz gescholtene Architektur Calatravas verfügt über eine fast mystische Kraft.

Liée à l'acoustique et à l'esthétique, la forme de l'auditorium, semblable à un soleil rayonnant (à droite), confirme que le monde naturel est une source d'inspiration à l'intérieur comme à l'extérieur du bâtiment. Cette architecture, critiquée par certains pour son apparente extravagance, dégage une puissance quasi mystique.

Sweeping curves, large openings, and carefully calculated lighting characterize these interior views, where anthropomorphic inspiration seems present without delving into overt imitation or quotation.

Diese Innenansichten, in denen anthropomorphe Einflüsse präsent scheinen, ohne in offenkundige Nachahmung oder Anführung zu verfallen, sind geprägt von schwungvollen Linien, großen Öffnungen und sorgfältig geplanter Beleuchtung.

Des courbes généreuses, de vastes ouvertures et un éclairage soigneusement calculé caractérisent ces vues de l'intérieur. L'inspiration anthropomorphique semble présente sans tomber dans l'imitation ni la citation.

CITY OF ARTS AND SCIENCES

Valencia, Spain. 1991–2000/1996–2005/2005–2009.

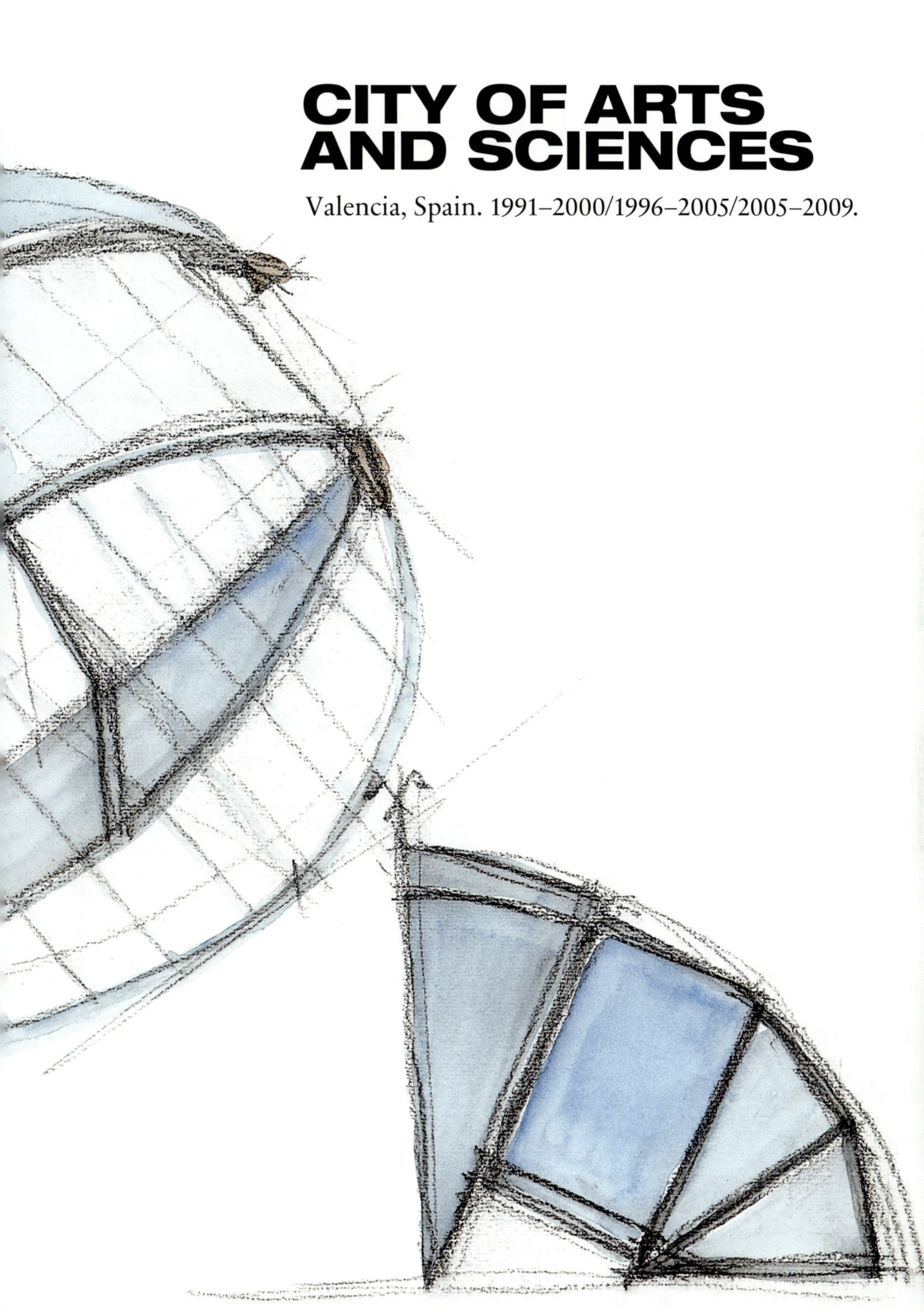

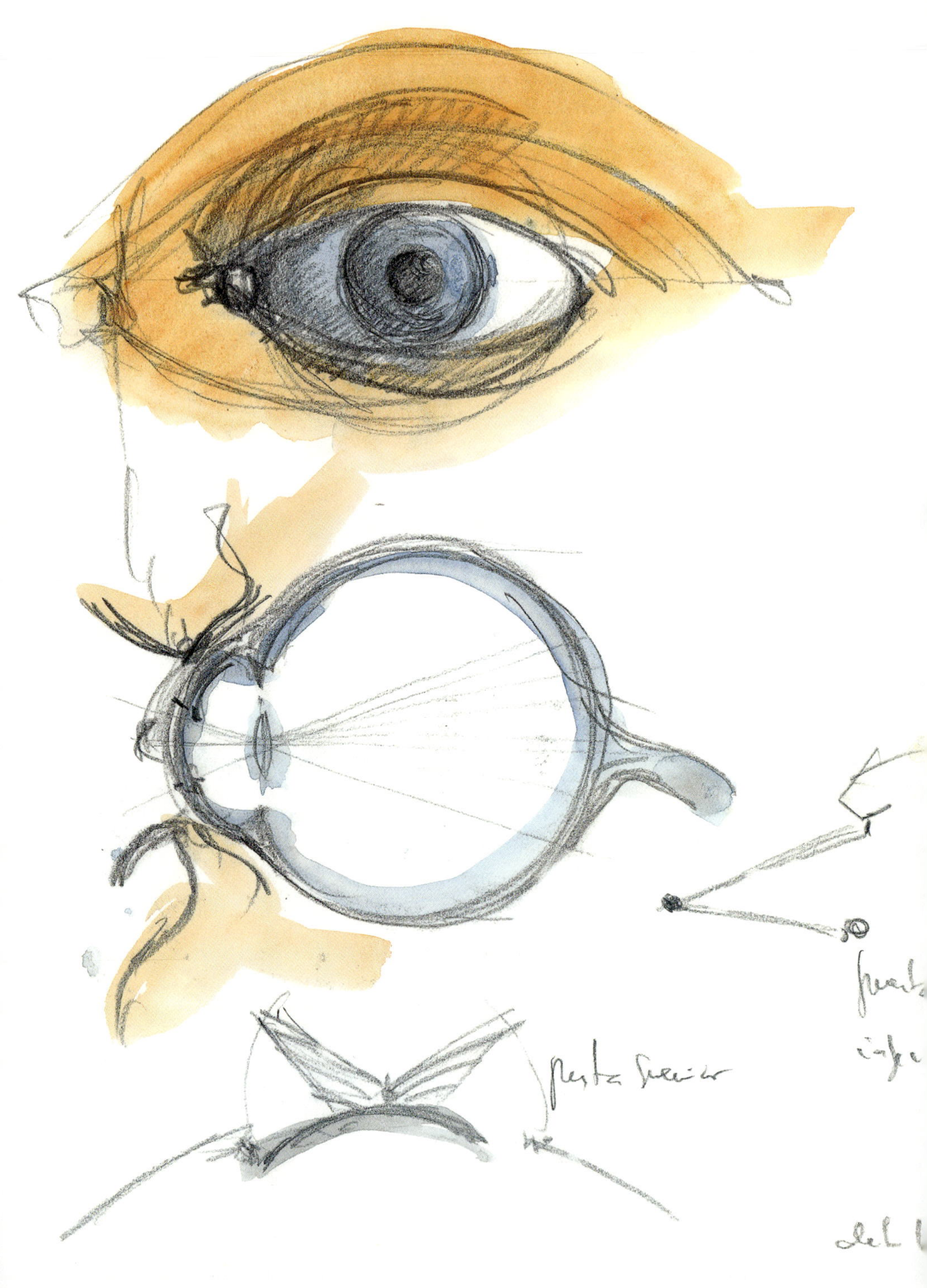

Project

PLANETARIUM, SCIENCE MUSEUM, AND L'UMBRACLE

Location

VALENCIA, SPAIN

Client

GENERALITAT VALENCIANA, CITY OF ARTS AND SCIENCES S. A.

Though the metaphor of an eye—the architect's eye—is frequently present in the work of Calatrava, the sketches opposite and on the previous page show the particular attention he pays to the actual realization of such forms on a large scale, a more complex task than it might seem at first glance.

Obgleich die Metapher des Auges – das des Architekten – im Werk Calatravas häufig vorkommt, belegen die Skizzen links und auf der vorangegangenen Seite die besondere Aufmerksamkeit, die er der tatsächlichen Umsetzung solcher Formen in großem Maßstab widmet, eine komplexere Aufgabe, als es auf den ersten Blick scheint.

Bien que la métaphore de l'œil – celui de l'architecte – soit fréquente dans l'œuvre de Calatrava, les croquis à gauche et sur la page précédente montrent l'attention particulière qu'il porte à la réalisation concrète de ces formes à grande échelle, tâche beaucoup plus complexe qu'il pourrait sembler au premier abord.

Part of a long-standing effort on the part of the government of Valencia to rehabilitate a 35-hectare area at the eastern periphery of the city, lodged between a large highway and the Turia River, Calatrava's City of Arts and Sciences took almost 20 years to be completed. A native of Valencia, he won a 1991 competition for the project that included a telecommunications tower sitting on three elongated feet. This tower would have been the most visible element of the complex, rising to a height of 327 meters. A change in city government led to a replacement of the tower in 1996 by a music center, the Palau de les Arts, or Opera House, completed by Calatrava in 2006. The Planetarium, an IMAX theater, with its elliptical, or rather eye-shaped plan and hemispheric dome with movable ribbed covering and an area of almost 2600 square meters, was built between 1995 and 1998. As Calatrava's sketches for this structure show clearly, he was inspired by the shape of an eye for the design. Indeed the eye (of the architect) is a frequent theme in his work. The 241-meter-long, 41 530-square-meter Príncipe Felipe Science Museum is based on an asymmetrical repetition of tree and riblike forms filled with glass to admit ample daylight. A structure known as L'Umbracle is a promenade and parking garage, built within an open arcade that is intended as "a contemporary reinvention of the winter garden." With its spectacular domed Planetarium this complex is visually arresting, but for reasons independent of the architect's design, detailing of the project was not handled as skillfully as it might have been. The Opera House (see page 198) completed this ambitious composition.

Bis zur Fertigstellung von Calatravas Ciudad de las Ciencias sollten mehr als 20 Jahre vergehen; sie ist Teil des langjährigen Bemühens der Stadtregierung von Valencia, ein 35 ha großes Gebiet am Ostrand der Stadt zu sanieren, das eingezwängt zwischen einer viel befahrenen Straße und dem Fluss Turia liegt. Der nahe Valencia geborene Calatrava konnte einen 1991 ausgeschriebenen Wettbewerb für das Projekt, zu dem ein auf drei hoch aufragenden Stützen stehender Fernmeldeturm gehörte, für sich entscheiden. Dieser 327 m hohe Turm wäre das auffälligste Element des Komplexes gewesen. Ein Wechsel in der Stadtregierung führte 1996 zu einem Austausch des Turmes gegen ein Musikzentrum, den 2006 von Calatrava fertiggestellten Palau de les Arts. Zwischen 1995 und 1998 entstanden das Planetarium und ein IMAX-Kino mit elliptischem oder vielmehr augenförmigem Grundriss, einer Halbkuppel mit beweglicher Rippenabdeckung und einer nahezu 2600 m² großen Fläche. Wie Calatravas Skizzen für dieses Gebäude deutlich zeigen, bezog er die Anregung für diesen Entwurf unmittelbar von der Form des Auges. Tatsächlich wird das Auge (des Architekten) in seinem Werk häufig thematisiert. Das 241 m lange, 41 530 m² umfassende Wissenschaftsmuseum Príncipe Felipe fußt auf der asymmetrischen Wiederholung baum- und rippenartiger Formen, die mit Glas ausgefacht wurden, um reichlich Tageslicht einfallen zu lassen. Dieser Komplex mit dem markanten überkuppelten Planetarium fällt ins Auge, wenngleich aus Gründen, für die der Architekt nicht verantwortlich zeichnet, da die bauliche Durchbildung des Projekts nicht so geschickt wie eigentlich möglich umgesetzt wurde. Das Opernhaus (siehe Seite 198) komplettiert dieses ehrgeizige Projekt.

Dans le cadre d'un programme à long terme mené par la municipalité de Valence pour la réhabilitation d'une zone de trente-cinq hectares en périphérie orientale de la ville, entre une autoroute et le fleuve Turia, le chantier de la Cité des sciences conçue par Calatrava aura duré presque vingt ans. Né à Valence, l'architecte avait remporté, en 1991, le concours pour ce projet qui comprenait également une tour de télécommunications reposant sur trois longs pieds. Cette tour de 327 mètres en aurait été l'élément le plus visible. Un changement de municipalité a conduit, en 1996, au remplacement de la tour par une Cité de la musique, le Palau de les Arts, achevé en 2006. Le planétarium et la salle IMAX de plan elliptique dotée d'une coupole hémisphérique mobile (de 2 600 mètres carrés) à couverture nervurée ont été construits entre 1995 et 1998. Comme le montrent clairement ses croquis préparatoires, Santiago Calatrava s'est directement inspiré de la forme d'un œil, thème récurrent dans son œuvre. Le Musée des sciences Príncipe Felipe se déploie sur 241 mètres de long pour une surface de 41 530 mètres carrés et utilise la répétition asymétrique de formes de nervures et « d'arbres » largement vitrées. La construction appelée « l'Umbracle » consiste en une promenade et un parking aménagés à l'intérieur d'une galerie en arcade ouverte qui est « une relecture contemporaine du jardin d'hiver ». Avec son planétarium au dôme spectaculaire, ce complexe est visuellement très surprenant, mais pour des raisons indépendantes du projet fourni par l'architecte, sa mise en œuvre n'a pas été aussi habile qu'elle aurait dû l'être. Le Palau de les Arts (l'Opéra, voir page 198) a parachevé cette ambitieuse composition.

The Planetarium of the Valencia City of Sciences may be Calatrava's most explicit reference to the human eye (compare page 173), and his sketches for the project make this link clear. The movable sunshade on the structure further heightens this expression of his fascination with vision.

Das Planetarium der Ciudad de las Sciencias in Valencia ist vielleicht Calatravas deutlichster Verweis auf das menschliche Auge (vergleiche Seite 173), und die Projektskizzen verdeutlichen diese Verbindung. Noch verstärkt wird seine Faszination für das Sehen durch den beweglichen Sonnenschutz.

Le planétarium de la Cité des sciences de Valence est peut-être la référence la plus explicite de Calatrava à l'œil humain (cf. page 173), comme le montrent clairement ses croquis. L'auvent mobile renforce cette expression de sa fascination pour la vision.

El planetario de la ciudad de las ciencias de Valencia

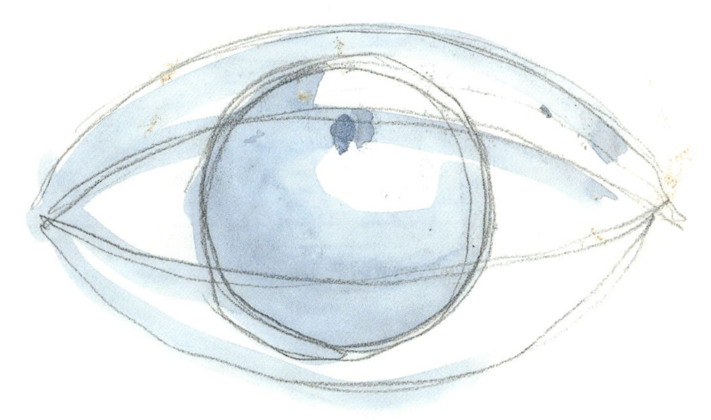

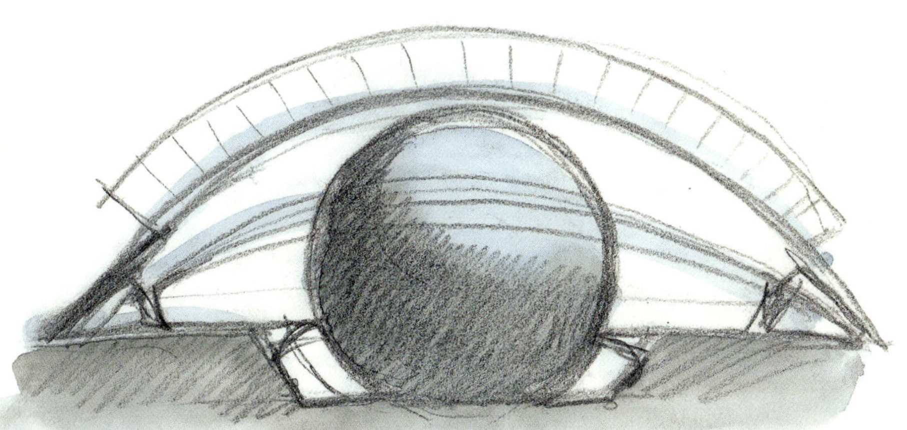

idea del ojo para la introspección del mundo
visión interna idea de proyección hacia el interior

The swooping anchor of the structure may bring to mind that of the Lyon-Saint-Exupéry Airport Railway Station, but here there is a fundamental symmetry that is not part of the French design.

Die abgesenkte Spitze des Gebäudes könnte an den Bahnhof Lyon-Saint Exupéry erinnern, wenn hier nicht eine Symmetrie herrschen würde, die dem französischen Projekt fehlt.

L'ancrage rabattu de la structure peut rappeler la gare de Lyon-Saint-Exupéry, mais traitée ici dans une symétrie qui n'existe pas dans le projet français.

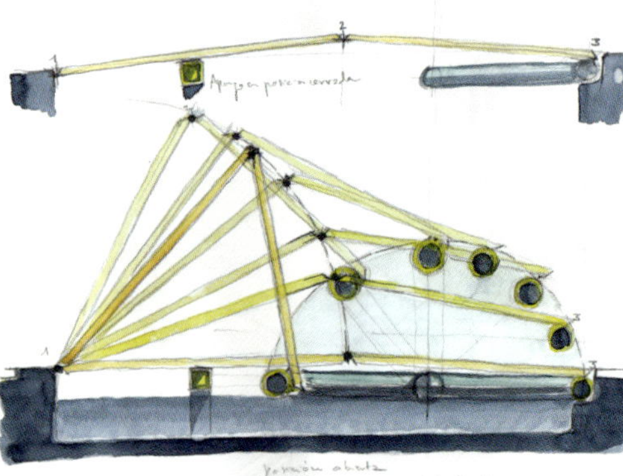

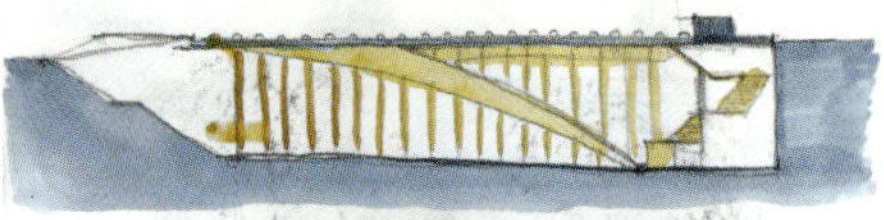

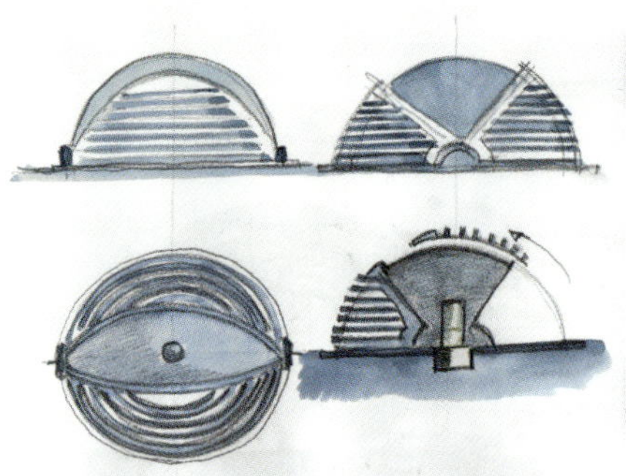

Calatrava frequently draws human figures in his designs, underlining both his own analysis of proportions and the relation of the human body to the architecture.

Calatrava zeichnet häufig menschliche Figuren auf seine Entwürfe und unterstreicht damit seine eigene Analyse der Proportionen sowie den Bezug des menschlichen Körpers zur Architektur.

Calatrava dessine fréquemment des silhouettes humaines dans ses projets pour éclairer à la fois son analyse des proportions et la relation entre le corps humain et l'architecture.

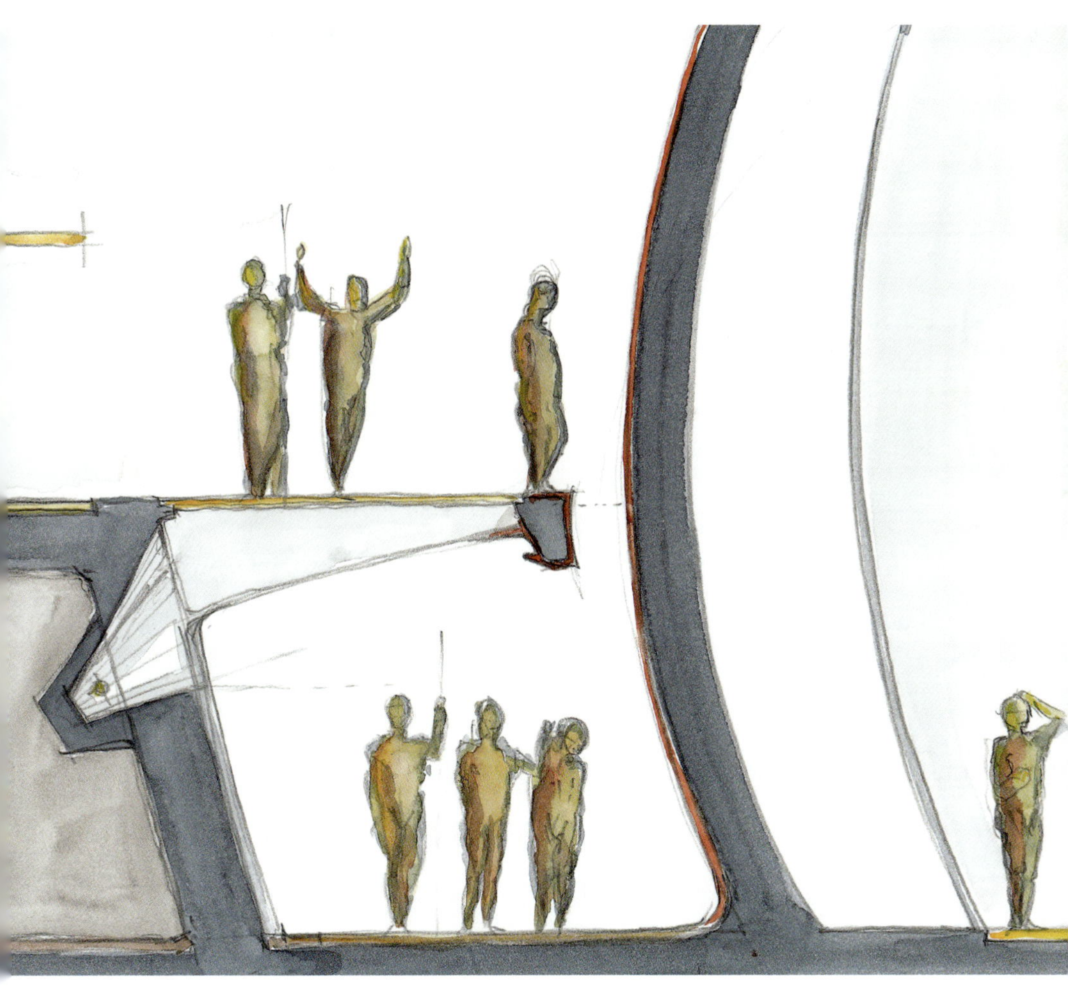

The half sphere necessary for the projection of IMAX movies is the kind of geometric form that stimulates the imagination of Calatrava; it represents the human eye, but also the spheres of the cosmos.

Die für das Vorführen von IMAX-Filmen nötige Halbkugel ist die Art geometrischer Form, die Calatravas Fantasie anregt; sie stellt das menschliche Auge, aber auch die Himmelskörper dar.

La demi-sphère nécessaire à la projection des films au format Imax est le type de forme géométrique qui stimule l'imagination de l'architecte. Elle représente l'œil humain mais aussi les sphères du cosmos.

Calatrava's drawings for this project, in particular the one in the middle (left) bring to mind those of Étienne-Louis Boullée for Newton's Cenotaph.

Calatravas Zeichnungen zu diesem Projekt (links), insbesondere die in der Mitte, rufen jene Étienne-Louis Boullées für Newtons Kenotaph in Erinnerung.

Les dessins de Calatrava pour ce projet (à gauche), en particulier celui du centre, font penser à ceux d'Étienne-Louis Boullée pour le cénotaphe de Newton.

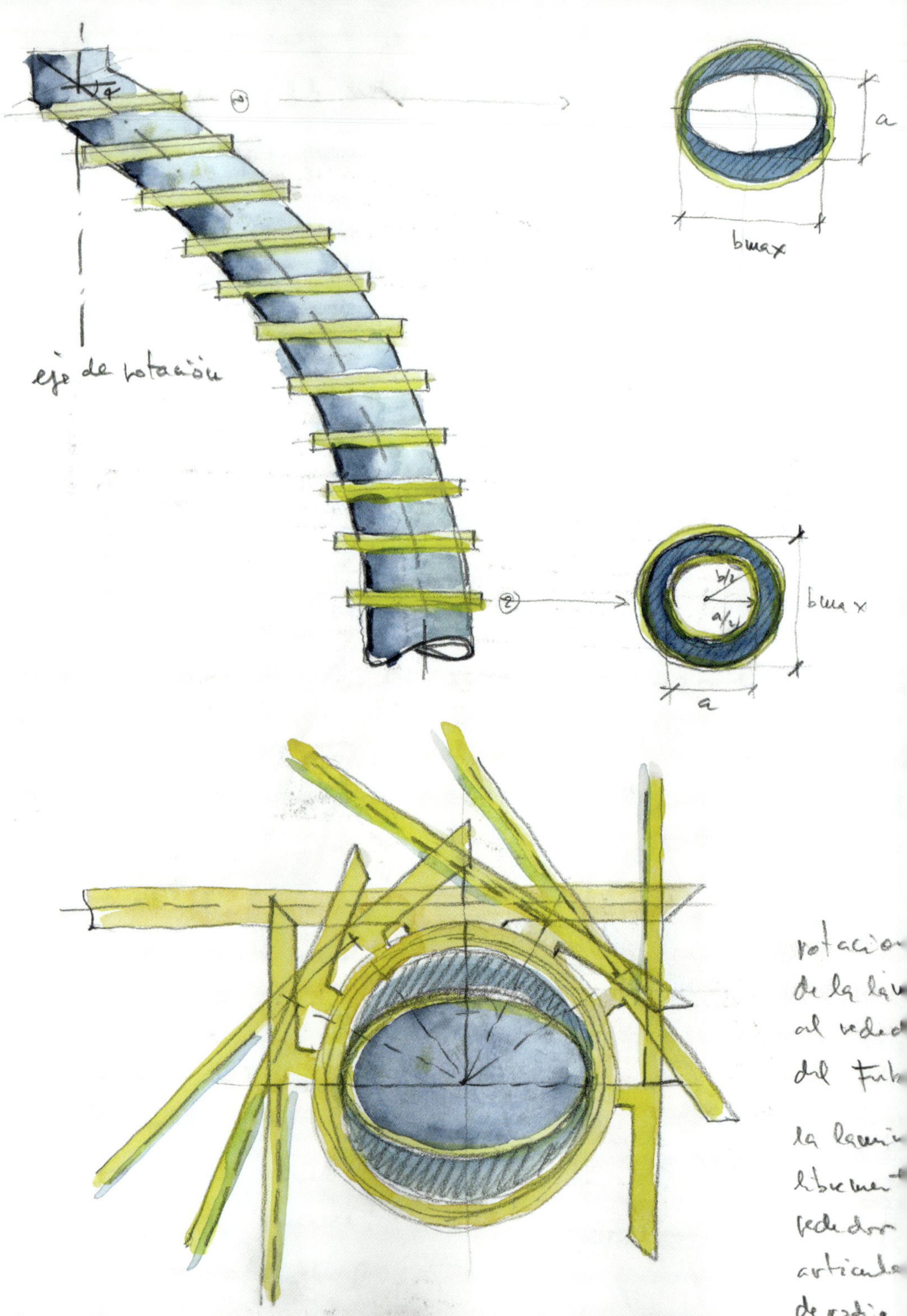
eje de rotación
bmax
a
b/2
a/2
bmax
a

posicion cerrada
posición abierta

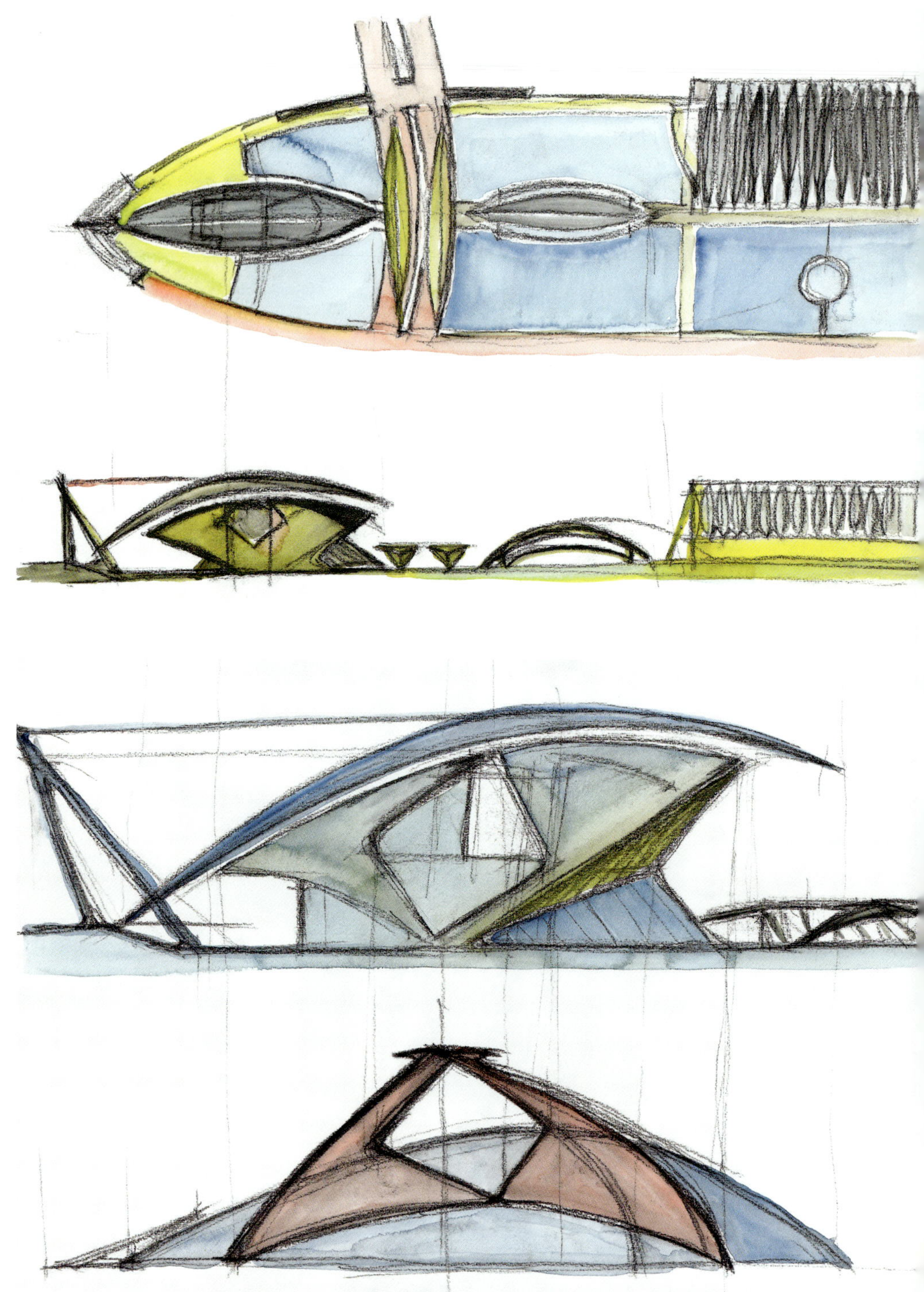

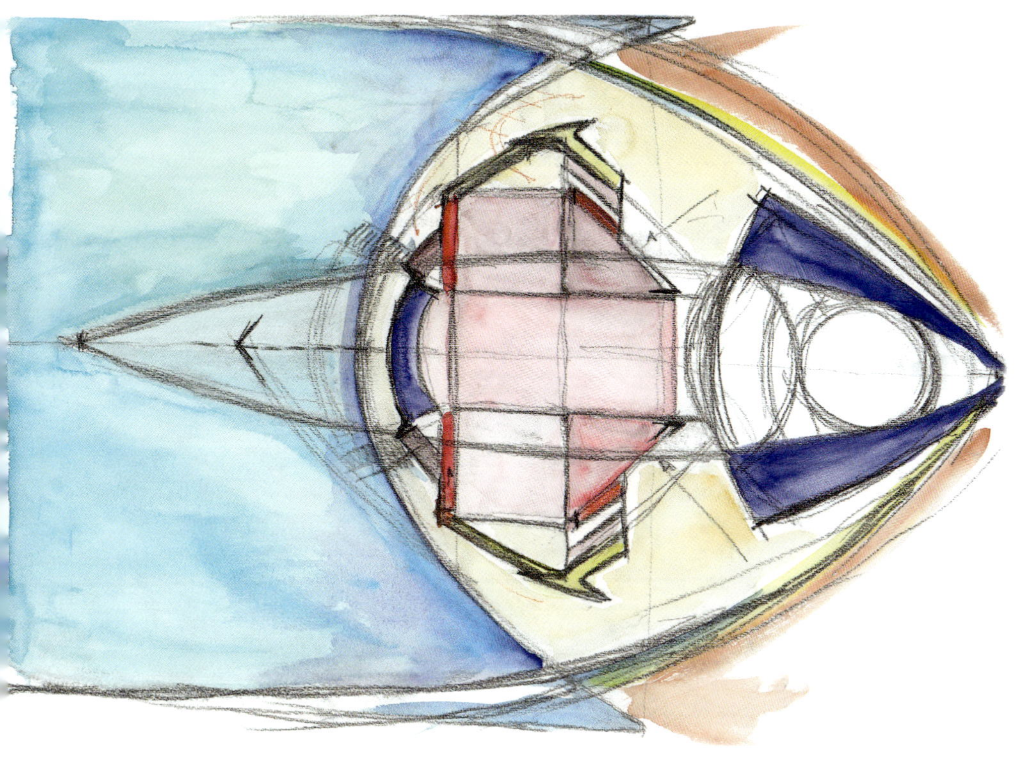

In these sketches, Calatrava outlines the succession of forms that constitute his City of Sciences, with the Planetarium in the center (above, left). His cantilevered or slanting forms consistently bring to mind the idea of motion.

Auf diesen Skizzen stellt Calatrava die Abfolge der Formen dar, aus denen sich seine Ciudad de las Sciencias mit dem Planetarium in der Mitte (oben, links) zusammensetzt. Die auskragenden oder geneigten Formen lassen durchgehend an Bewegung denken.

Dans ces croquis, Calatrava esquisse la série de formes qui constituent sa Cité des sciences avec, au centre, le planétarium (ci-dessus, à gauche). Ces formes inclinées ou en porte-à-faux font que l'on a toujours en tête l'idée de mouvement.

Throughout the oeuvre of Calatrava, forms are rendered more dynamic by the use of large glazed surfaces. Lit from within at night, they are the source of the continuous variation of interior lighting during the day.

In Calatravas Œuvre werden Formen durch den Einsatz großer Glasflächen dynamischer gestaltet. Nachts von innen beleuchtet, sind sie die Quelle ständig wechselnder Innenbeleuchtung tagsüber.

Dans l'œuvre de Calatrava, les formes tirent un dynamisme du recours à de larges surfaces vitrées. Éclairées de l'intérieur pendant la nuit, elles sont à la source des variations permanentes de la luminosité pendant la journée.

The ribbed shapes used by the architect are not unlike those that appear in earlier works, but here, his effort to simplify and render even more powerful this vocabulary is evident. The natural world is never far removed from his design process.

Die von Calatrava hier verwendeten Rippenformen ähneln jenen früherer Projekte. Vorliegend ist jedoch das Bemühen, diese Formensprache zu vereinfachen und noch ausdrucksvoller zu gestalten, offenkundig. Die Natur ist während des Gestaltungsprozesses stets präsent.

Ces formes nervurées ne sont pas sans rapport avec celles vues dans des œuvres antérieures, mais ici, l'effort de simplification de ce vocabulaire pour lui donner encore plus de force est évident. Le monde naturel n'est jamais très loin du processus de conception.

The architect solves design problems in a continuous process that leads from his knowledge of engineering to that of architecture and materials, and is rooted in his own profound aesthetic sense.

Der Architekt löst Entwurfsprobleme in einem kontinuierlichen Prozess, der von seinem technischen Verständnis zu seinen Kenntnissen von Architektur und Materialien führt und in seinem profunden ästhetischen Empfinden wurzelt.

L'architecte résout les problèmes de conception en un processus continu qui passe par sa connaissance de l'ingénierie, de l'architecture et des matériaux, mais qui prend sa source dans une authentique sensibilité esthétique.

Though it may bring to mind the atrium of BCE Place, Calatrava's work in Valencia is reaching for an even higher dimension, both literally and figuratively. This is an architecture of a soaring spirit.

Wenngleich dieses Projekt an den BCE Place erinnern mag, ist Calatravas Anspruch hier in Valencia sowohl im Wort- als auch im übertragenen Sinn ein noch höherer. Dies ist die Architektur eines hochfliegenden Geistes.

Bien que l'on puisse penser à l'atrium de BCE Place, cette intervention de Calatrava à Valence atteint une dimension encore supérieure, aussi bien littéralement que figurativement. Cette architecture tient de l'élévation spirituelle.

Project
OPERA HOUSE

Location
VALENCIA, SPAIN

Client
GENERALITAT VALENCIANA, CITY OF ARTS AND SCIENCES S. A.

Building area
44 100 m²

Site area Opera House
3.3 HECTARES

Usually quite intent on the use of white in his buildings, Calatrava here delves into a surprising composition with a dark blue fragmented surface. This abstract image is indicative of the power that his buildings embody, without ever becoming overtly monumental.

Calatrava, der üblicherweise Weiß bevorzugt, überascht hier mit einer Komposition aus dunkelblau fragmentierten Flächen. Dieses abstrakte Bild zeigt die Kraft seiner Bauten, nie monumental wirken.

Généralement plutôt attaché à l'utilisation du blanc, Calatrava surprend ici par une composition de surface fragmentée bleu foncé. Cette image abstraite est révélatrice de la force qu'incarne cet édifice sans qu'il soit pour autant lourdement monumental.

Conceived as the final element in the City of Arts and Sciences complex (see page 168), rising to a height of 75 meters on its western edge, the Valencia Opera House was "designed as a series of apparently random volumes, which become unified through their enclosure within two symmetrical, cutaway concrete shells. These forms are crowned by a steel sheath, which projects axially from the entrance concourse out over the uppermost contours of the curvilinear envelope. The structure that results defines the identity of the opera house, enhancing its symbolic and dynamic effect within the landscape, while offering protection to the terraces and facilities beneath." Calatrava defines the design as being akin to a "monumental sculpture." The central volume of the complex is occupied by the 1706-seat auditorium as well as the equipment required for the stage settings. A smaller auditorium, conceived mainly for chamber music, seats 380, while a large auditorium to the east, partially covered by the open shell, can seat 1520 people. The first concert was held on October 8, 2005, but the opera house was actually completed late in 2006. The architect created two large murals for the main auditorium and restaurant and two low relief sculptures. Located adjacent to the main building is a 400-seat auditorium for experimental theater and dance, with gallery space for art exhibitions. The five structures of the complex are linked by gardens and bodies of water.

Als abschließendes Element der Stadt der Künste und Wissenschaft (siehe Seite 168) konzipiert, entstand das am Westrand der Anlage erbaute, 75 m hohe Opernhaus als „Reihe scheinbar zufälliger Baukörper, die durch zwei symmetrische, ausgeschnittene Betonschalen zusammengeschlossen werden. Diese Formen werden von einer stählernen Scheide bekrönt, die vom Eingangsvorplatz in axialer Richtung über den höchsten Punkt der gebogenen Umhüllung reicht. Dieses Element bestimmt die Identität des Opernhauses und steigert seine symbolische und dynamische Wirkung in der Landschaft, während es gleichzeitig den Terrassen und darunterliegenden Einrichtungen Schutz bietet." Calatrava zufolge ähnelt dieser Entwurf einer „monumentalen Skulptur". Der zentrale Raum des Komplexes enthält das Auditorium mit 1706 Sitzplätzen sowie die für die Bühnenbilder erforderlichen Vorrichtungen. Ein in erster Linie für Kammermusik vorgesehenes Auditorium bietet 380 Plätze, während in einer größeren, nach Osten gelegenen Halle 1520 Personen Platz finden; sie ist teilweise von der offenen Betonschale überdeckt. Das erste Konzert fand am 8. Oktober 2005 statt, während das Opernhaus erst Ende 2006 fertiggestellt wurde. Für den Hauptsaal und das Restaurant schuf der Architekt zwei großflächige Wandbilder sowie zwei Reliefs. Neben dem Hauptgebäude befindet sich ein Auditorium mit 400 Sitzplätzen für experimentelles Theater und Tanz sowie einem Galerieraum für Kunstausstellungen. Zwischen den fünf Baukörpern des Komplexes befinden sich verbindende Grünanlagen und Wasserflächen.

Élément final implanté à l'ouest du complexe de la Cité des arts et des sciences (voir page 168), l'Opéra de Valence a été « conçu comme une série de volumes apparemment aléatoires, unifiés par leur réunion en deux coques de béton symétriques découpées. Ces formes culminant à 75 mètres sont couronnées par un fourreau d'acier, qui jaillit dans l'axe du hall d'entrée au-dessus des contours les plus élevés de l'enveloppe curviligne. La structure qui en résulte définit avec force l'identité de cet Opéra et met en valeur son aspect symbolique et dynamique au cœur du paysage, tout en offrant une protection aux terrasses et installations qu'elle surplombe. » Calatrava dit de ce projet qu'il est analogue à une « sculpture monumentale ». Le volume central est occupé par une salle de 1 706 places et par les équipements de scène. Une salle plus petite, dévolue à la musique de chambre, peut accueillir 380 auditeurs et une seconde grande salle à l'est, en partie protégée par une coque ouverte, 1 520 personnes. Le premier concert s'est déroulé le 8 octobre 2005 mais l'Opéra n'a été vraiment achevé qu'en 2006. L'architecte a créé deux grandes œuvres murales dans la salle principale et le restaurant et deux sculptures en bas-relief. À proximité du bâtiment principal, se trouve également une salle de 400 places consacrée au théâtre expérimental et à la danse, dotée d'une galerie d'expositions. Les cinq constructions sont reliées par des jardins et des bassins.

A helmet, a snake's head, or a craft from a distant world. All of these images might be applied to these forms, and yet none of them are accurate. Like his compatriot Salvador Dalí, Santiago Calatrava has an extraordinarily fertile imagination from which his architecture emerges. His buildings are an incontestable expression of his mind.

Ein Helm, ein Schlangenkopf oder einn Gefährt aus einer fernen Welt. All diese Bilder könnten auf diese Formen angewendet werden und sind dennoch nicht zutreffend. Wie sein Landsmann Salvador Dalí verfügt Santiago Calatrava über eine außerordentlich schöpferische Fantasie, aus der seine Architektur entsteht. Seine Bauten veranschaulichen zweifelsfrei sein Denken.

Un casque, une tête de serpent ou un engin venu d'un autre monde – toutes ces images peuvent s'appliquer à ces formes sans qu'aucune soit exactement la bonne. Comme son compatriote Salvador Dalí, Santiago Calatrava possède une imagination extraordinairement fertile, d'où naissent ses formes architecturales. Ses réalisations sont incontestablement l'expression de sa pensée.

Though the image to the left may bring to mind Calatrava's Tenerife Auditorium, he ventures here into different territory, approaching an almost Surrealist range of shapes.

Obgleich die Abbildung links an Calatravas Auditorium auf Teneriffa erinnern mag, betritt er hier Neuland und nähert sich einer nahezu surrealistischen Formenskala.

Si l'image de gauche peut rappeler l'auditorium de Tenerife, Calatrava se risque ici sur un territoire différent, abordant une gamme de formes quasi surréalistes.

The overlapping and varied design of curved surfaces in the building reveals the inventiveness of the architect and his originality.

Das sich überlappende und abwechslungsreiche Design der gekrümmten Oberflächen des Gebäudes zeugt von Calatravas Kreativität und Originalität.

Le design varié et superposé des surfaces courbes du bâtiment révèle l'inventivité et l'originalité de l'architecte.

Where the repetition of identical forms in Modernist architecture led often to a kind of inherent boredom, Calatrava makes repetition the source of variety and movement by introducing curves, or fanlike shapes, as is the case in these images.

Wo in der architektonischen Moderne die Wiederholung identischer Formen häufig eher öde wirkt, lässt Calatrava aus Wiederholung Vielfalt und Bewegung entstehen, indem er Biegungen oder fächerförmige Elemente einbringt, wie auf diesen Abbildungen zu sehen.

Alors que la répétition de formes identiques a, dans l'architecture moderniste, souvent conduit à un ennui intrinsèque, Calatrava en fait une source de variété et de mouvement en introduisant des courbes ou des motifs en éventail, comme le montrent ces images.

While some contemporary architects, who shall remain unnamed, seek innovation in extravagant but often unusable forms, the vocabulary of Calatrava is rooted in a sense of design and engineering which proceeds more from within than from an imposed and dysfunctional artistic ambition.

Während einige zeitgenössische Architekten, die ungenannt bleiben sollen, Innovation in überspannten, oft unbrauchbaren Formen suchen, fußt die Formensprache Calatravas auf einem Gespür für Gestaltung und Technik, das eher aus seinem Inneren handelt als aus aufgesetztem künstlerischen Ehrgeiz.

Tandis que certains architectes contemporains (dont nous tairons le nom) recherchent l'innovation dans des formes extravagantes mais parfois inutilisables, le vocabulaire de Calatrava s'enracine dans une approche de conception et d'ingénierie qui part de l'intérieur plutôt que d'une abusive et problématique ambition artistique.

Comparación de structuras móviles con la naturaleza

ARBOLES BAUSCHANZLI

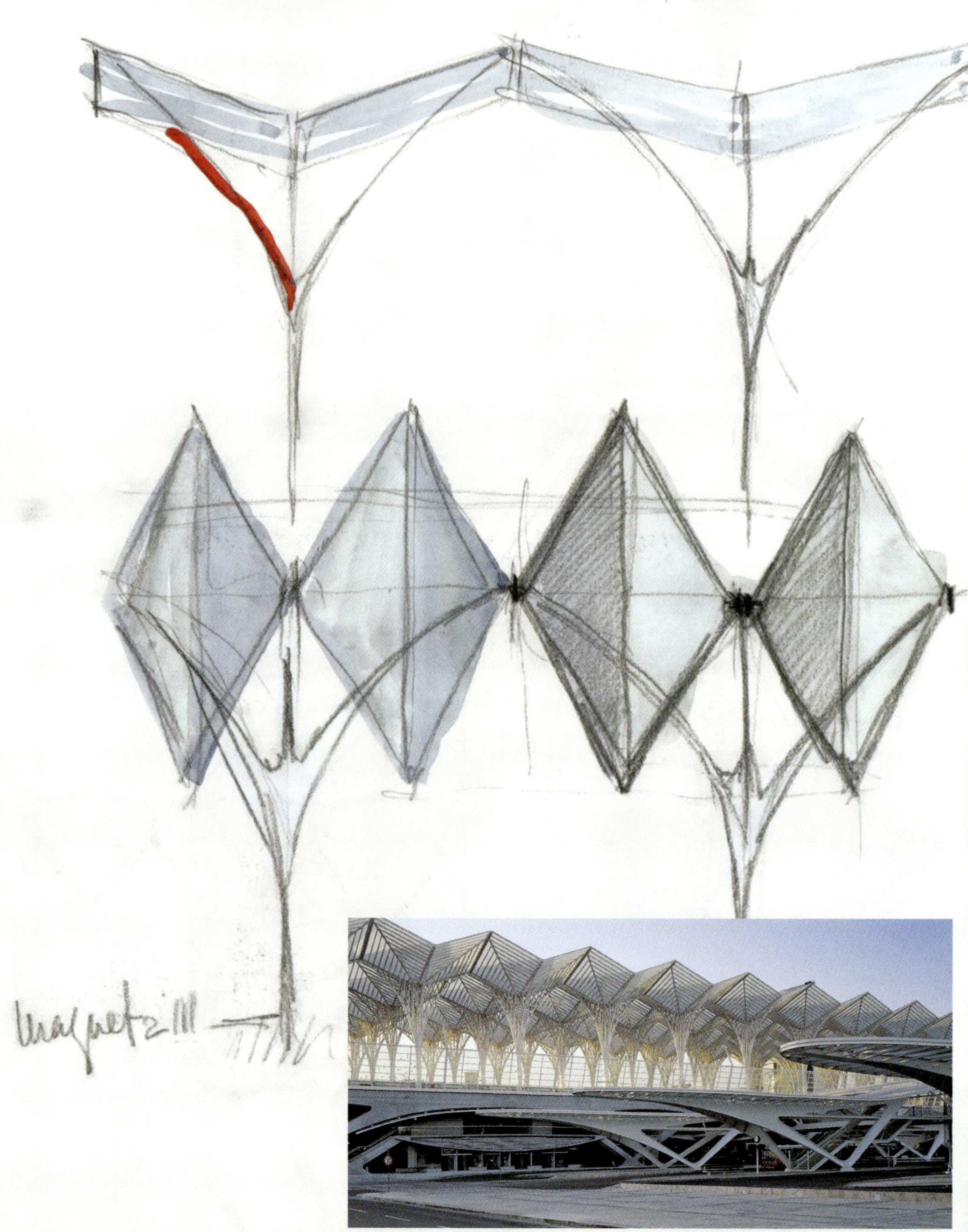

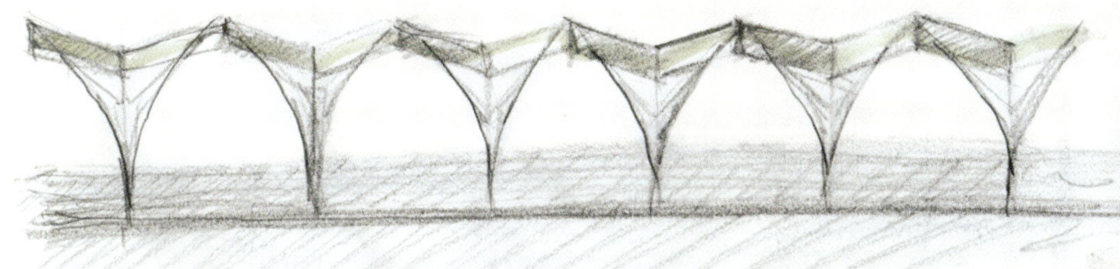

ORIENTE STATION

Lisbon, Portugal. 1993–1998.

Project

ORIENTE STATION

Location

LISBON, PORTUGAL

Client

G.I.L. EXPO '98

In aligning his treelike forms on the top of the elevated railway platform, the architect makes reference to a poem by Fernando Pessoa, but also to his own spontaneous thought that such a hillside, whether natural or artificial, should be covered with trees.

Indem er seine baumartigen Formen auf dem erhöhten Bahnsteig in Reih und Glied ausrichtet, nimmt er Bezug auf ein Gedicht Fernando Pessoas, und auch auf einen eigenen Gedanken: ein Hang, natürlich oder künstlich, sollte mit Bäumen bepflanzt sein.

En alignant ces silhouettes ressemblant à des arbres au sommet des quais surélevés de la gare, l'architecte se réfère à un poème de Fernando Pessoa, mais aussi à sa propre réflexion : un flanc de colline, artificielle ou naturelle, doit être planté d'arbres.

Part of an ambitious plan concerning the Universal Exposition of 1998 that was held in the Portuguese capital, this new train station is located in a former industrial zone about five kilometers from the historic center of Lisbon, not far from the broad Tagus River. The most spectacular aspect of the project is undoubtedly the 78 x 238-meter covering over the eight raised railway tracks whose typology might recall that of a forest. The architect, winner of an invited competition, was obliged to make do with the existing tracks, set up on a nine-meter-high embankment. Rather than emphasizing the break between the city and the river implied by the station, Calatrava has sought, here as elsewhere, to open passageways and reestablish links. Prior to the station's construction, the railway tracks had marked a distinct barrier between the residential and industrial parts of the city. The new complex includes two large glass and steel awnings over the openings, measuring no less than 112 meters in length and 11 meters in width. There is a bus station and car park, a metro station below, and a longitudinal gallery including commercial spaces included in Calatrava's brief. Ticketing and service facilities are located five meters below the tracks, with an atrium marking the longitudinal gallery five meters lower, and the opening on the river side intended as the main access point, serving the area that has developed subsequent to the 1998 event. As the architect concludes: "Conceived as the Expo's primary transport connection, Oriente Station has proven to be the main component in the transformation of the area. It has become one of Europe's most comprehensive transport nodes: an important interchange for high-speed intercity trains, rapid regional transport, standard rail services, and tram and metro networks."

Dieser neue Bahnhof ist Teil einer ambitionierten Planung im Zusammenhang mit der Weltausstellung 1998, die in der portugiesischen Hauptstadt stattfand. Er liegt in einem ehemaligen Industriegebiet etwa 5 km vom historischen Zentrum Lissabons entfernt unweit des breiten Flusses Tejo. Der eindrucksvollste Teil des Projekts ist zweifellos die 78 x 238 m große Überdachung über den acht erhöhten Bahngleisen, die mit ihren filigranen Verzweigungen an ein Wäldchen erinnert. Calatrava, der einen geschlossenen Wettbewerb gewonnen hatte, musste mit den vorhandenen, auf einer 9 m hohen Böschung verlaufenden Gleisanlagen arbeiten. Anstatt nun die von den Bahnanlagen hervorgerufene Trennung zwischen Stadt und Fluss zu unterstreichen, war er hier wie anderswo bestrebt, Durchgänge zu öffnen und Verbindungen wiederherzustellen. Vor der Erbauung des Bahnhofs hatten die Bahngleise eine deutliche Barriere zwischen den Wohngebieten und dem industriell genutzten Teil der Stadt dargestellt. Der neue Komplex umfasst zwei großflächige Schutzdächer aus Stahl und Glas über den Zugängen, die beide nicht weniger als 112 m lang und 11 m breit sind. Zu Calatravas Auftrag gehörten außerdem ein Busbahnhof und ein Parkhaus mit darunterliegender U-Bahn-Station sowie eine lang gestreckte Galerie, die auch Ladengeschäfte umfasst. Die Einrichtungen für Ticketverkauf und Service befinden sich 5 m unter den Gleisen, mit einem Atrium, das die weitere 5 m tiefer gelegene Galerie markiert, und dem Eingang auf der Flussseite, der als Hauptzugangspunkt dient und das Gebiet versorgt, das sich hier seit der Expo 1998 entwickelt hat. Abschließend äußert sich der Architekt: „Konzipiert als Hauptverkehrsknotenpunkt der Expo, erwies sich der Bahnhof Oriente als wichtigste Komponente bei der Umgestaltung der Gegend. Er wurde zu einem der bedeutendsten Verkehrsknotenpunkte Europas für Hochgeschwindigkeitszüge, die zwischen Großstädten verkehren, für schnelle Regionalzüge, normale Eisenbahndienste sowie Straßen- und U-Bahnen."

Élément d'un vaste programme lié à l'Exposition mondiale de Lisbonne (1998), cette nouvelle gare ferroviaire est située dans une ancienne zone industrielle, à cinq kilomètres environ du centre historique de la capitale, à proximité du Tage. L'aspect le plus spectaculaire de ce projet est sans aucun doute la couverture (238 x 78 mètres) des huit voies surélevées dont la typologie peut évoquer une forêt. L'architecte, qui a remporté le concours restreint, devait tenir compte des voies existantes passant sur un talus de neuf mètres de haut qui constituait une barrière entre la partie résidentielle de la ville et les rives du Tage. Plutôt que d'accentuer cette rupture entre la ville et le fleuve, Calatrava a cherché ici, comme souvent, à ouvrir des passages et à rétablir des liens. Le nouveau complexe comprend deux immenses auvents de verre et d'acier de 112 x 11 mètres suspendus au-dessus des entrées. Le cahier des charges incluait également une gare routière, un parking, une station de métro et une galerie commerciale souterraine tout en longueur. Les guichets sont situés à cinq mètres sous les quais, ainsi qu'un atrium signalant la galerie commerciale cinq mètres plus bas. L'ouverture côté fleuve, principal point d'accès, dessert la zone qui a connu un fort développement depuis l'Exposition. Comme l'explique l'architecte : « Conçue comme le principal site de correspondances de transports de l'Expo, la gare de l'Orient est devenue un facteur essentiel de la transformation de ce secteur, l'une des plates-formes d'échanges entre les trains à grande vitesse, les transports rapides régionaux, les trains classiques, le tram et le réseau de métro, les plus complètes d'Europe. »

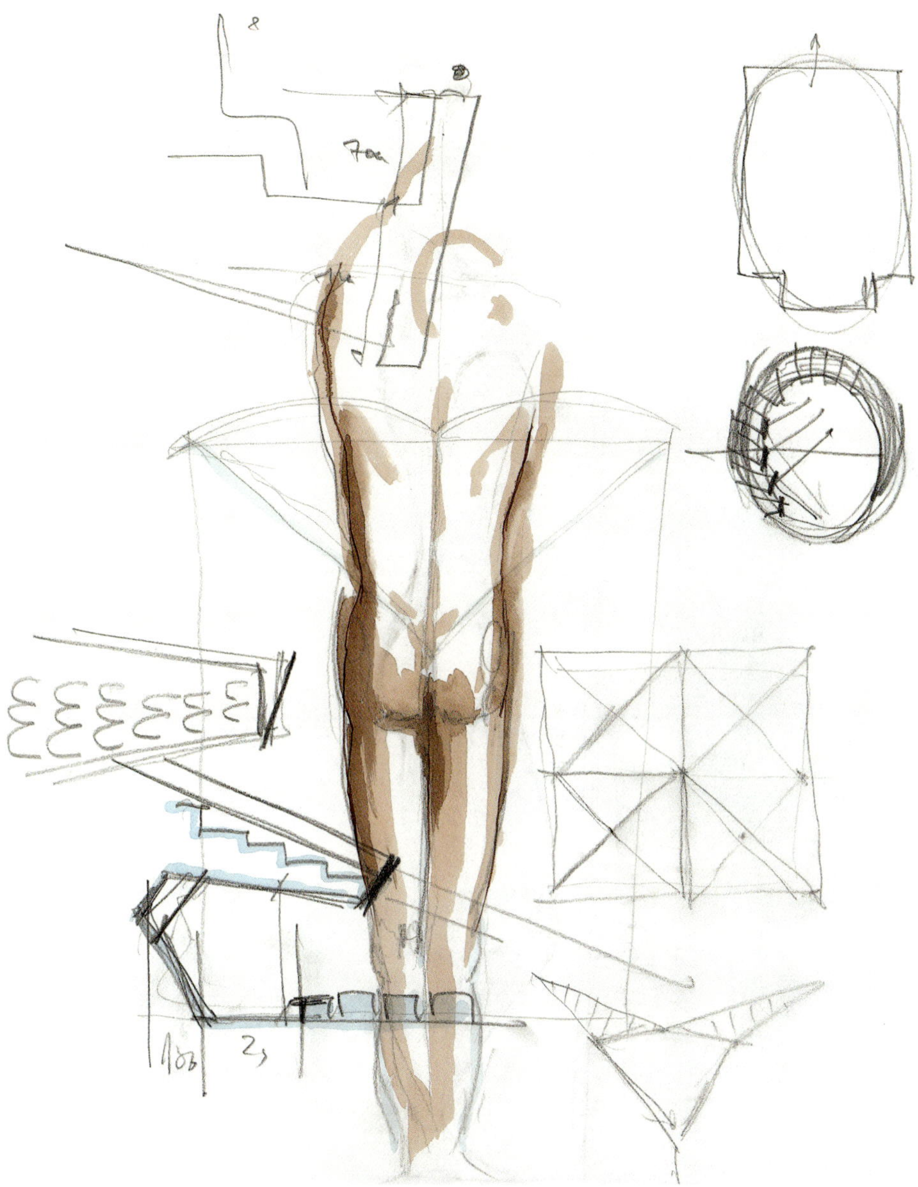

The surprising sketches here relate some of Calatrava's structural designs to the human figure, as well as to forms of engineering and architectural history that are familiar to the architect. These references and others are sublimated while somehow remaining present enough to elicit the viewer's adhesion.

Diese interessanten Skizzen verbinden einige von Calatravas strukturellen Entwürfen mit der menschlichen Figur und mit Formen der Ingenieurs- sowie Architekturgeschichte, die dem Architekten vertraut sind. Diese Bezüge sind auf eine höhere Ebene verlagert, wenngleich sie präsent genug bleiben, um die Aufmerksamkeit des Betrachters zu fesseln.

Les croquis surprenants présentés ici associent certaines des conceptions structurelles de Calatrava à la figure humaine et à des formes issues de l'histoire de l'ingénierie et de l'architecture, familières à l'architecte. Ces références, et d'autres, sont sublimées tout en restant d'une certaine façon assez présentes pour emporter l'adhésion du spectateur.

In the sketch above, the architect shows an almost idyllic vision of the new station, which today stands in a much denser urban environment. He addresses the difference in level caused by the elevated tracks in the sketches on the right-hand side.

Auf der Skizze oben zeigt der Architekt eine beinahe arkadische Vision des neuen Bahnhofs, der heute in weitaus dichterer Bebauung steht. Den Niveauunterschied erhöht verlaufender Gleise thematisiert er auf den Skizzen der rechten Seite.

Dans le croquis ci-dessus, l'architecte offre une vision presque arcadienne d'un site urbain qui va pourtant subir une forte densification. Il thématise la différence de niveau due aux voies surélevées dans les croquis de la page de droite.

Estação do Oriente

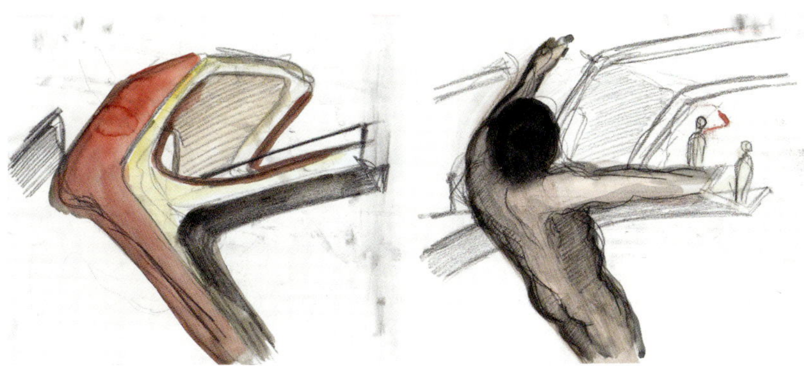

The sharply angled supports of the station inevitably give it a sensation of movement, but Calatrava's own sketch (above) highlights a kind of human movement that might not have immediately come to mind. Once seen, this sketch is difficult to forget when viewing the architecture.

Die geneigten Stützen des Bahnhofs verleihen ihm eine bewegte Anmutung, aber Calatravas Skizze (oben) hebt eine Art menschlicher Bewegung heraus, die vielleicht nicht sofort offenkundig wäre. Einmal gesehen, fällt es allerdings schwer, diese Skizze beim Anblick des Gebäudes zu vergessen.

Les supports fortement inclinés de la gare créent inévitablement un sentiment de mouvement, mais le croquis de Calatrava (ci-dessus) met l'accent sur une sorte de mouvement humain dont la perception n'était pas évidente au premier coup d'œil. Ce croquis est difficile à oublier voyant le projet achevé.

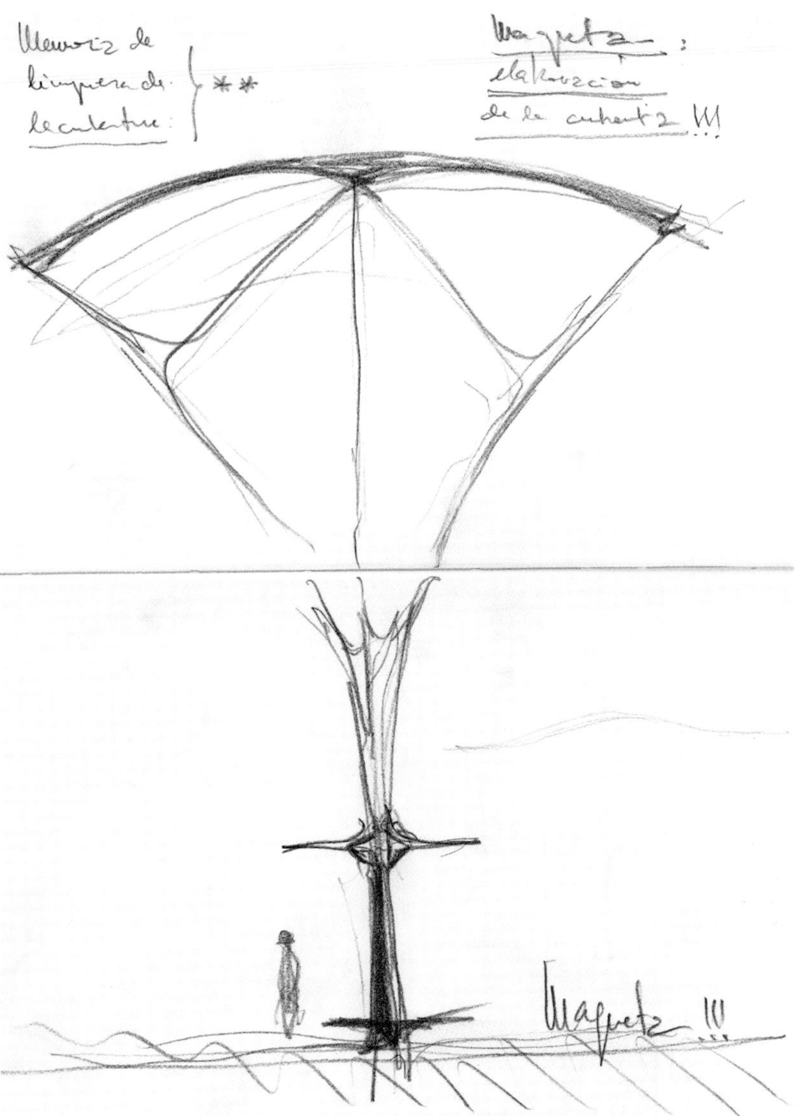

The tree columns of the station platform might be more complex than they really need to be, but this complexity lends itself to the play of light and variety of visual experiences offered to the everyday commuter.

Die baumartigen Pfeiler des Bahnsteigs mögen vertrackter als nötig sein, aber ihr komplexer Aufbau sorgt für das Spiel des Lichts und die Vielfalt visueller Erfahrungen, die der Berufspendler dort erleben kann.

Les colonnes en forme d'arbres du quai de la gare sont peut-être plus complexes que nécessaires, mais cette complexité se prête au jeu de la lumière et offre une diversité d'effets visuels au voyageur quotidien.

6 A
5 A

Successive ribs, like those seen in numerous other Calatrava projects, cover the Oriente Station galleries (right). Offering large, column-free spaces under structures designed to accept the very considerable weight of trains, the architect makes engineering seem effortless.

Aufeinanderfolgende Rippen, wie in zahlreichen anderen Projekten Calatravas zu sehen, überdecken die Galerien des Bahnhofs Oriente. Mit großen, stützenfreien Räumen unter Strukturen, die darauf ausgelegt sind, das erhebliche Gewicht von Zügen zu tragen, lässt der Architekt die Konstruktion mühelos erscheinen.

Des successions de nervures, comme dans de nombreux autres projets de l'architecte, recouvrent les galeries de la gare de l'Orient (à droite). En créant ces vastes volumes sans colonne sous une structure conçue pour supporter le poids considérable des trains, l'architecte semble effacer toute notion d'effort.

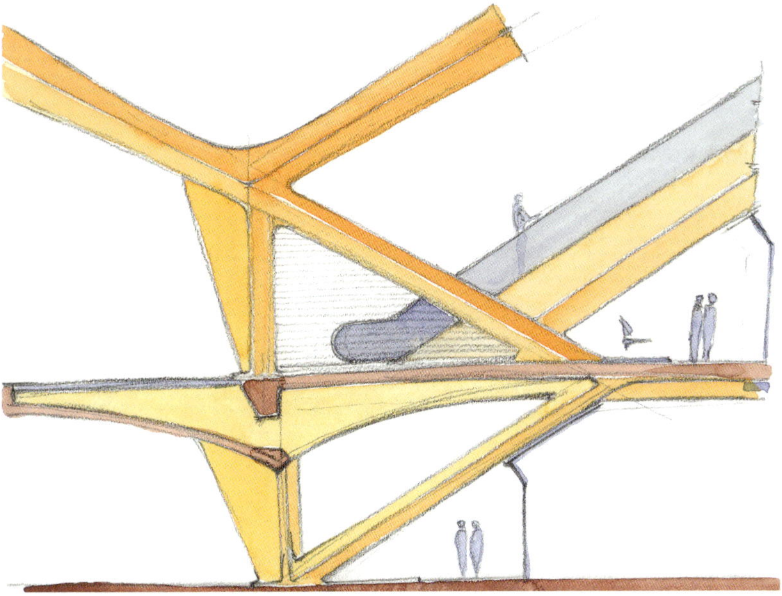

Where a few ugly, thick columns might have done the trick, Calatrava skews his supports and gives his entire design an apparent disequilibrium that never seems threatening.

Wo ein paar hässliche, plumpe Säulen ausgereicht hätten, neigt Calatrava seine Stützen und verleiht dem gesamten Bau ein scheinbares Ungleichgewicht, das jedoch nie bedrohlich wirkt.

Alors que quelques grosses colonnes épaisses auraient pu faire l'affaire, Calatrava effile ses supports et confère à son projet une impression de déséquilibre qui n'est jamais menaçant.

MILWAUKEE ART MUSEUM

Milwaukee, Wisconsin, USA. 1994–2001.

Project
MILWAUKEE ART MUSEUM

Location
MILWAUKEE, WISCONSIN, USA

Client
MILWAUKEE ART MUSEUM

Floor area
13 200 m²

The forms imagined by Santiago Calatrava are so original that it is difficult to classify him in any established trend in contemporary architecture. This is undoubtedly because he synthesizes parallel interests in architecture, art, and engineering.

Die von Calatrava erdachten Formen sind so ursprünglich, dass es schwerfällt, ihn irgendeinem etablierten Trend in der zeitgenössischen Architektur zuzuordnen. Dies liegt zweifellos daran, dass er seine parallelen Interessen an Architektur, Kunst und Technik miteinander verbindet.

Les formes imaginées par l'architecte sont si originales qu'il est difficile de le ranger dans une quelconque catégorie de l'architecture contemporaine. C'est sans doute parce qu'elles illustrent la synthèse de ses intérêts parallèles pour l'architecture, l'art et l'ingénierie.

The Milwaukee Art Museum was housed in a 1957 structure designed by Eero Saarinen as a War Memorial overlooking Lake Michigan. The architect David Kahler added a large slab structure to the museum in 1975. In 1994, the Trustees of the Milwaukee Art Museum considered a total of 77 architects for a "new grand entrance, a point of orientation for visitors, and a redefinition of the museum's identity through the creation of a strong image." Santiago Calatrava won the competition with his proposal for a 27-meter-high glass and steel reception hall shaded by a movable sunscreen (baptized the "Burke Brise Soleil"). Made of steel plates welded and stiffened inside, the 115-ton brise soleil consists of two equal wing elements formed by 36 fins whose lengths range between 32 and eight meters. A computerized system automatically overrides the manual control of the structure when wind speed exceeds 40 miles per hour. As the architect explains the overall project: "The design adds 13 200 square meters to the existing 14 900 square meters, including a linear wing (made of glass and stainless steel, with lamella roof) that is set at a right angle to Saarinen's structure. The design allows for future expansion, offset from but symmetrical to the exhibition facilities, on the other side of the Kahler building. At shore level, the expansion houses: the atrium; 1500 square meters of gallery space for temporary exhibitions; an education center with 300-seat lecture hall; and a gift shop. The 100-seat restaurant, which is placed at the focal point of the pavilion, commands panoramic views onto the lake." Although Calatrava generally denies specific biomorphic inspiration in his work, the Quadracci Pavilion has a decidedly birdlike quality to it, especially when the "wings" of the brise soleil are open. Calatrava is also responsible for the Reiman Bridge, a suspended pedestrian link between downtown and the lakefront. Public gardens for the complex were designed by the noted landscape architect Dan Kiley.

Das Kunstmuseum von Milwaukee war in einem 1957 von Eero Saarinen als Kriegsgedenkstätte errichteten Bau mit Blick auf den Lake Michigan untergebracht. 1975 ergänzte der Architekt David Kahler das Museum um einen großen Plattenbau. 1994 zogen die Treuhänder des Kunstmuseums von Milwaukee insgesamt 77 Architekten in Betracht für die Schaffung eines „neuen, imposanten Eingangs, eines Orientierungspunktes für Besucher und einer Neubestimmung der Identität des Museums durch ein neu zu schaffendes, starkes Image". Santiago Calatrava gewann den Wettbewerb mit seinem Entwurf einer 27 m hohen Empfangshalle aus Glas und Stahl, die mittels eines beweglichen Sonnensegels (Spitzname „Burke Brise Soleil") beschattet werden kann. Die aus geschweißten, innen versteiften Stahlplatten zusammengesetzte, 115 t schwere Sonnenblende besteht aus zwei gleich großen Flügeln aus 36 Rippen, deren Länge zwischen 32 und 8 m variiert. Wenn die Windgeschwindigkeit 65 km/h übersteigt, hebt ein Computersystem die manuelle Steuerung der Anlage auf. Mit den folgenden Worten erläutert der Architekt das gesamte Projekt: „Der Entwurf ergänzt die vorhandenen 14 900 m² um 13 200 m², darunter ein aus Glas und Edelstahl bestehender linearer Flügel mit Lamellendach, der im rechten Winkel zu Saarinens Bau steht. Die Planung ermöglicht künftige Erweiterungen, die, zwar abgesetzt von den Ausstellungsräumen, aber symmetrisch zu ihnen stehend, auf der anderen Seite des Gebäudes von Kahler errichtet werden könnten. In dem auf Höhe des Sees liegenden Erweiterungsbau sind das Atrium, 1500 m² Galerieräume für Wechselausstellungen, ein Lernzentrum mit einem Vortragssaal mit 300 Plätzen und ein Museumsladen untergebracht. Von dem im Zentrum des Pavillons liegenden Restaurant mit 100 Plätzen bieten sich weiträumige Ausblicke auf Lake Michigan." Obgleich Calatrava im Allgemeinen von spezifischen biomorphen Anklängen in seinem Werk nichts wissen will, erinnert der Quadracci-Pavillon doch stark an einen Vogel, insbesondere wenn die „Flügel" der Sonnenblende geöffnet sind. Calatrava zeichnet darüber hinaus auch für die Reiman Bridge verantwortlich, eine Hängebrücke für Passanten, die Innenstadt und Seeufer verbindet. Die öffentlichen Gartenanlagen des Komplexes gestaltete der renommierte Landschaftsarchitekt Dan Kiley.

Le Milwaukee Art Museum occupait un bâtiment d'Eero Saarinen de 1957 donnant sur le lac Michigan et conçu pour être un mémorial de guerre. L'architecte David Kahler y avait ajouté, en 1975, une importante construction en barre, et, en 1994, les administrateurs du musée consultèrent soixante-dix-sept architectes pour créer « une nouvelle entrée de prestige, un centre d'orientation pour les visiteurs » et pour « redéfinir l'identité du musée par une image forte ». Santiago Calatrava remporta le concours grâce à sa proposition d'un hall d'accueil de 27 mètres de haut, en verre et en acier, protégé par un écran solaire mobile (appelé « Burke Brise Soleil »). Ce brise-soleil de 115 tonnes en plaques d'acier soudées et armées de raidisseurs se compose de deux ailes constituées de trente-six ailettes de 8 à 32 mètres de longueur. Un ordinateur prend le relais des commandes manuelles lorsque la vitesse du vent dépasse 65 km/h. Comme l'explique l'architecte : « Le projet ajoute 13 200 mètres carrés aux 14 900 mètres carrés existants. Cette extension comprend une aile rectiligne (en verre et acier à toit en lames), implantée à angle droit du bâtiment de Saarinen. Une extension future est prévue, symétrique aux salles d'expositions, de l'autre côté de l'immeuble de Kahler. Au niveau du lac se trouvent une cour intérieure, 1 500 mètres carrés d'espaces pour expositions temporaires, un centre éducatif avec une salle de conférences de 300 places et une boutique de cadeaux. Le restaurant de cent couverts, situé au centre du pavillon, bénéficie de vues panoramiques sur le lac. » Bien que Calatrava réfute généralement l'idée d'une inspiration biomorphique, le Quadracci Pavilion n'en fait pas moins penser à un oiseau, en particulier lorsque les « ailes » du brise-soleil sont ouvertes. Il est également l'auteur du pont Reiman, une passerelle piétonnière suspendue entre le centre-ville et les bords du lac. Les jardins du complexe ont été réalisés par le célèbre architecte paysagiste Dan Kiley.

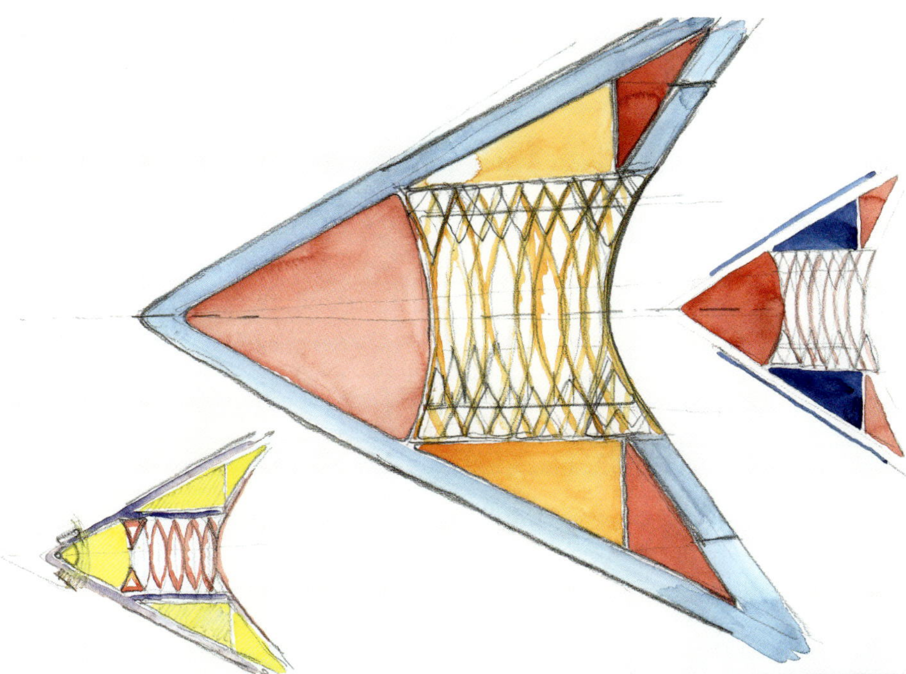

The raylike form seen in other Calatrava plans reappears here, but, typically, the architect has altered it both to fit the circumstances and because as a matter of method he refines his ideas over considerable periods of time.

Die von anderen Plänen Calatravas bekannte Rochenform taucht hier wieder auf, wenngleich sie der Architekt in typischer Manier verändert hat, zum einen, um sie den Gegebenheiten anzupassen, zum anderen, weil er methodisch seine Ideen über beträchtliche Zeiträume weiterentwickelt.

La forme d'une raie, déjà observée dans d'autres projets de Calatrava, réapparaît ici, mais à sa façon caractéristique, l'architecte l'a modifiée, non seulement pour l'adapter au contexte mais aussi parce qu'il perfectionne systématiquement ses idées, sur des périodes de temps considérables.

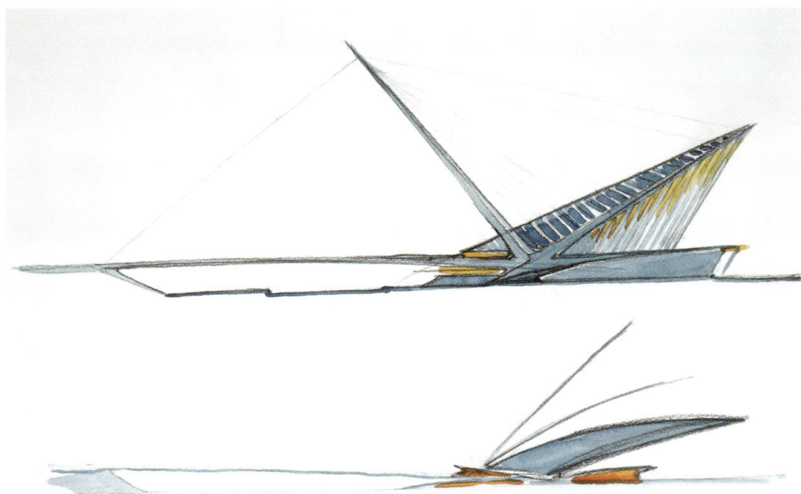

Seen from the city with its "wings" spread, Calatrava's building stands out in any circumstances, breaking the stolid geometric rhythm of the aligned office buildings, soaring up and out toward the lake.

Mit ausgebreiteten „Flügeln" von der Stadt aus gesehen, fällt Calatravas Bau in jedem Fall ins Auge, indem er den geometrischen Rhythmus der in gerader Linie ausgerichteten Bürobauten unterbricht und sich über und auf den See hinaus erhebt.

Vu depuis la ville et avec les « ailes » déployées, le bâtiment se détache avec force. Il rompt le rythme géométrique massif de l'alignement d'immeubles de bureaux en s'élevant au-dessus et vers le lac.

This multiple-exposure photography (above) shows the winglike positions of the Burke Brise Soleil, surely one of the largest examples of Calatrava's continual efforts to bring actual movement into his architecture and sculpture.

Eine Mehrfachbelichtung (oben) zeigt die flügelgleichen Positionen des Sonnensegels, sicherlich eines der stattlichsten Beispiele für Calatravas ständige Bemühungen, Bewegung in seine Bauten und Skulpturen zu bringen.

La photographie à expositions multiples (ci-dessus) montre les positions successives du Burke Brise Soleil, sans doute l'un des plus importants exemples des efforts continuels de l'architecte pour insuffler du mouvement à ses architectures et à ses sculptures.

As the sketches show, Calatrava has integrated a bridge directly into the design, using the angled spike support both to hold the bridge and to anchor the actual museum structure.

Wie die Skizzen zeigen, integrierte Calatrava eine Brücke direkt in das Design, wobei die schräge Maststütze sowohl zur Halterung der Brücke als auch zur Verankerung des eigentlichen Museumsbaus dient.

Comme le montrent les croquis, Calatrava a d'emblée intégré le pont dans son projet, utilisant le pylône incliné à la fois pour soutenir ce dernier et pour ancrer le bâtiment du musée.

The folded "wings" of the Brise Soleil assume a compact, simple form (left). Above, sketches show the relationship between the pedestrian bridge and the museum structure, forming a continuous composition.

Die zusammengelegten „Flügel“ des Sonnensegels ergeben eine kompakte, einfache Form (links). Die Skizzen oben zeigen die Beziehung zwischen Fußgängerbrücke und Museumsbau, die eine zusammenhängende Komposition ergeben.

Repliées, les « ailes » du brise-soleil prennent une forme simple et compacte (à gauche). Les croquis ci-dessus montrent la relation entre la passerelle piétonnière et le musée, qui dessinent une composition continue.

As surprising as the cantilevered platforms designed by Calatrava may appear, they are clearly thought-out in terms of scale and location to offer spectacular views, and to allow visitors to better participate in the architecture itself, seeing it from different angles.

So frappant die von Calatrava konzipierten auskragenden Plattformen erscheinen mögen, im Hinblick auf Maßstäblichkeit und Standort sind sie doch eindeutig durchdacht. Von ihnen bieten sich fulminante Ausblicke, und sie gestatten den Besuchern, die Architektur von verschiedenen Blickwinkeln aus besser zu erfahren.

Aussi surprenantes puissent-elles paraître, ces plates-formes en porte-à-faux sont clairement conçues, dans leur échelle et leur implantation, pour offrir des vues spectaculaires et permettre aux visiteurs de mieux apprécier l'architecture en la voyant sous différents angles.

The architect's sketches regularly place human figures in their context, but Calatrava's purpose is not as calculated as that of Le Corbusier's Modulor for example.

Auf den Skizzen des Architekten erscheinen immer wieder menschliche Figuren, wenngleich Calatrava, anders als beispielsweise Le Corbusier mit seinem Modulor, keinen bestimmten Zweck mit ihnen verfolgt.

Les croquis de l'architecte comprennent régulièrement des figures humaines, mais l'objectif de Calatrava n'est pas aussi utilitaire que celui de Le Corbusier avec son Modulor, par exemple.

The unexpected shapes of openings and passageways give a variety to the architecture which is consistently designed with respect to the exteriors of the building. These interiors thus seem to have a natural rapport with the outside of the structure.

Die überraschenden Formen von Öffnungen und Durchgängen lassen die Architektur, die im Hinblick auf das Äußere des Gebäudes konsequent gestaltet wurde, vielfältig erscheinen. Diese Innenräume scheinen folglich ein natürliches Verhältnis zum Außenbau zu unterhalten.

Les formes inattendues des ouvertures et des passages confèrent à l'architecture un aspect diversifié toujours conçu dans le respect de l'extérieur des bâtiments. Les intérieurs semblent entretenir un rapport naturel avec l'extérieur de la structure.

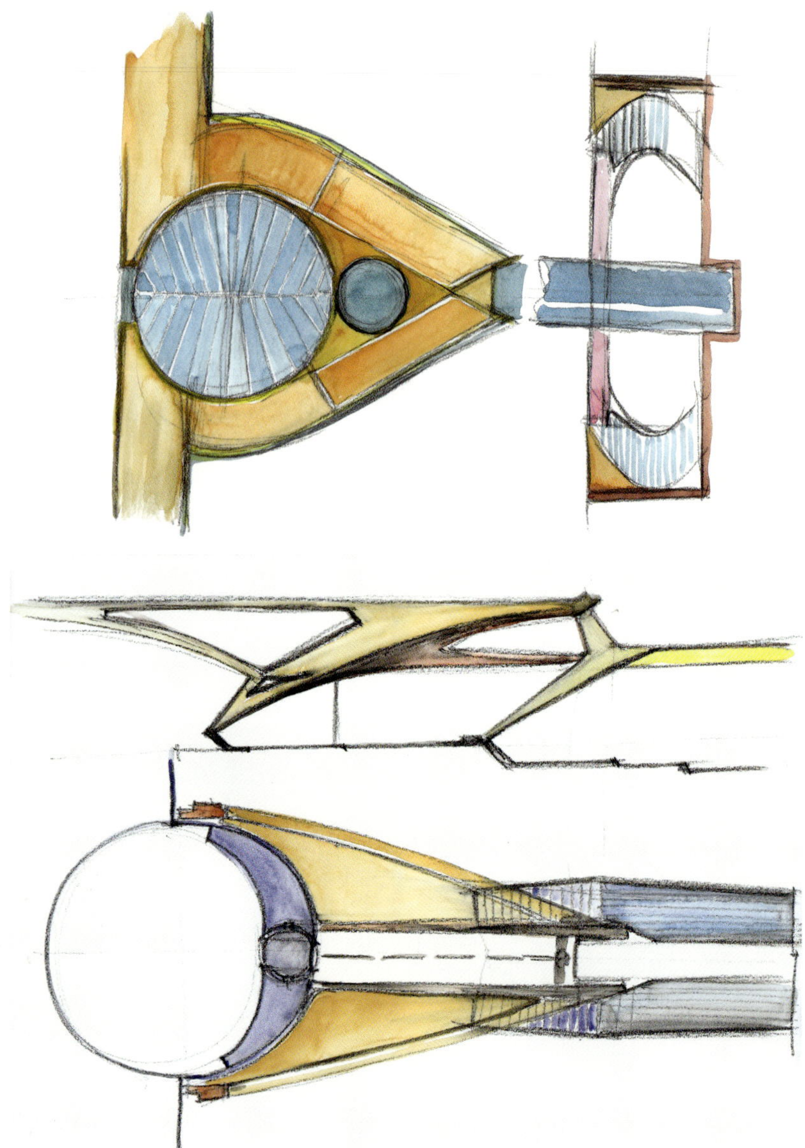

A number of Calatrava's sketches may bring to mind those of da Vinci. The structure of the eye linked to the optic nerve might be evoked in the drawings above. The actual architecture, as seen to the right, is not specifically anthropomorphic however.

Eine Reihe von Calatravas Skizzen mögen an die da Vincis erinnern. So könnte in den Zeichnungen oben die Verbindung des Auges mit dem Sehnerv angedeutet sein. Die tatsächliche Architektur (rechts) ist jedoch nicht explizit anthropomorph.

Plusieurs croquis de Calatrava peuvent évoquer ceux de Vinci. La structure de l'œil et du nerf optique sont reconnaissables dans le dessin ci-dessus. La réalisation architecturale, à droite, n'est cependant pas spécifiquement anthropomorphique.

TICKET POINT
14/09–23/11/2008
OUT THERE
ARCHITECTURE BEYOND BUILDING

FOURTH BRIDGE ON THE CANAL GRANDE

Venice, Italy. 1999–2008.

Project

FOURTH BRIDGE ON THE CANAL GRANDE

Location

VENICE, ITALY

Client

MUNICIPALITY OF VENICE

Cost

€ 6.7 MILLION

The bridge is located close to the busy central railway station of Venice, relatively far from the entrance to the Grand Canal at Saint Mark's Square.

Die Brücke liegt unweit des geschäftigen Hauptbahnhofs von Venedig und damit relativ weit entfernt von der Mündung des Canal Grande am Markusplatz.

Le pont se trouve à proximité de la très animée gare de Venise, relativement éloigné de l'embouchure du Grand Canal à la place Saint-Marc.

The aptly named Quarto Ponte sul Canal Grande pedestrian bridge is only the fourth to be built over Venice's Grand Canal since the 16th century. It was first spanned by the Rialto Bridge, built in 1588–91. Suggested as early as 1488, the Accademia Bridge was not built until 1854. The original steel structure, designed by Alfred Neville, was demolished and replaced by a wooden bridge in 1934. This second bridge, in bad condition, was razed and replaced by the present identical bridge in 1985. Designed by Eugenio Miozzi, the Scalzi Bridge replaced an older iron bridge in 1934 and connects the sestieri of Santa Croce and Cannaregio near the Santa Lucia Railway Station. Calatrava's new bridge, for which he was selected by a public commissioning process in 1999, connects the Piazzale Roma Bus Station to the railway station. His design was approved in February 2001 and the project approved in April 2002, with a budget of 6.7 million euros. Conscious of the high visibility of this location and its historical significance, Calatrava says: "Care has been taken to integrate the bridge with the quays on either side. The steps and ramps are designed to add vitality to both sides of the canal, while the abutments (which are crescent-shaped) leave pedestrians free access to the quays. The areas at either end act as extensions of the bridge, creating new celebratory spaces for Venice. On the south side, the design also provides a new passage between Piazzale Roma and the mooring platforms for the ACTV water transport." The bridge is 101 meters long, with a central span of 80 meters. Its width varies, from 5.39 meters (at either foot) to 9.38 meters at the midpoint. The bridge rises from a height of 3.2 meters at the foot to 9.28 meters at midpoint. The all-steel structural element consists of a central arch of very large radius (180 meters), with two side arches and two lower arches.

Wie der Name sagt, ist die Fußgängerbrücke seit dem 16. Jahrhundert erst das vierte Bauwerk dieser Art, das über den Canal Grande errichtet wurde. Das erste war die 1588–91 erbaute Rialto-Brücke. Erst 1854 wurde die bereits 1488 erwähnte Accademia-Brücke realisiert. Baufällig geworden, wurde diese zweite Brücke abgerissen und 1985 durch die heutige identische Brücke ersetzt. Die Scalzi-Brücke von Eugenio Miozzi löste 1934 eine ältere Eisenbrücke ab und verbindet die Stadtteile Santa Croce und Cannaregio in der Nähe des Bahnhofs Santa Lucia. Calatravas neue Brücke, für die er 1999 durch ein öffentliches Auftragsverfahren ausgewählt wurde, verbindet den Busbahnhof an der Roma mit dem Bahnhof. Sein Entwurf wurde im Februar 2001, das Projekt mit einem Budget von 6,7 Millionen Euro im April 2002 genehmigt. Eingedenk des öffentlichkeitswirksamen Standorts und seiner historischen Bedeutung sagt Calatrava: „Wir haben uns bemüht, die Brücke in die Kaianlagen auf beiden Seiten einzugliedern. Die Treppen und Rampen sollen beide Seiten des Kanals optisch beleben, während die halbmondförmigen Widerlager den Passanten freien Zugang zu den Kaianlagen gewähren. Die Areale an beiden Enden fungieren als Erweiterungen des Brückenraums und bieten Venedig Festplätze. Auf der Südseite entsteht außerdem ein neuer Durchgang zwischen der Piazzale Roma und den Anlegestellen des ACTV." Die Brücke misst 101 m mit einer zentralen Spannweite von 80 m. Die Breite variiert von 5,39 m am Fuß bis auf 9,38 m im Scheitelpunkt, die Brücke erhebt sich von 3,2 m Höhe am Fuß zu 9,28 m in der Mitte. Das zur Gänze aus Stahl gefertigte Tragwerk besteht aus einem mittleren Bogen mit dem sehr großen Radius von 180 m und wird auf beiden Seiten von zwei weiteren, flacheren Bögen eingefasst.

Ce pont est le quatrième seulement que l'on ait construit depuis le XVIe siècle sur le Grand Canal de Venise. Le premier fut le pont du Rialto (1588–91), le second le pont de l'Accademia, envisagé en 1488 mais édifié en acier en 1854 seulement par Alfred Neville, puis remplacé par un ouvrage en bois en 1934 (lui-même reconstruit à l'identique en 1985). Enfin, le pont des Scalzi, conçu par Eugenio Miozzi, avait supplanté un ancien pont de fer en 1934 pour relier les quartiers de Santa Croce et de Cannaregio, près de la gare de Santa Lucia. Le pont de Santiago Calatrava, qui a fait l'objet d'une commande publique en 1999, connecte la gare routière de la Piazzale Roma à la gare de chemin de fer. Son plan a été approuvé en février 2001 et le budget de 6,7 millions d'euros en avril 2002. Conscient de la haute visibilité du site et de la signification historique de l'ouvrage, Calatrava commente : « Nous avons pris soin d'intégrer le pont au quai à ses deux extrémités. Les marches et les rampes sont conçues pour donner plus de vitalité aux deux rives du canal, tandis que les culées (en croissant) laissent libre accès aux quais. Les deux rives ont été traitées en nouveaux espaces publics pour Venise. Au sud, le projet prévoit également un nouvel ouvrage entre la Piazzale Roma et les plates-formes d'amarrage des *vaporetti.* » Le pont mesure 101 mètres de long et sa portée centrale 80 mètres. Sa largeur varie de 5,39 mètres au départ à 9,38 mètres au centre. Il s'élève de 3,20 mètres à la base jusqu'à 9,28 mètres en partie centrale. La construction entièrement en acier consiste en une arche de très grand rayon (180 mètres), deux arches latérales et deux arches inférieures.

Sketches by Santiago Calatrava and a night lighting scheme give more color to the bridge than it has during the day. Its simple handrails and glass protection contribute to the overall impression of elegance and economy of means.

Auf Skizzen Calatravas und bei nächtlicher Beleuchtung gibt sich die Brücke farbiger als tagsüber. Die schlichten Handläufe und Glasgeländer tragen zum eleganten Gesamtbild bei und zeugen vom reduzierten Materialeinsatz.

Les croquis de Calatrava et l'éclairage nocturne donnent une impression beaucoup plus colorée du pont qu'en journée. La simplicité du traitement des garde-corps contribue au sentiment général d'élégance et d'économie de moyens.

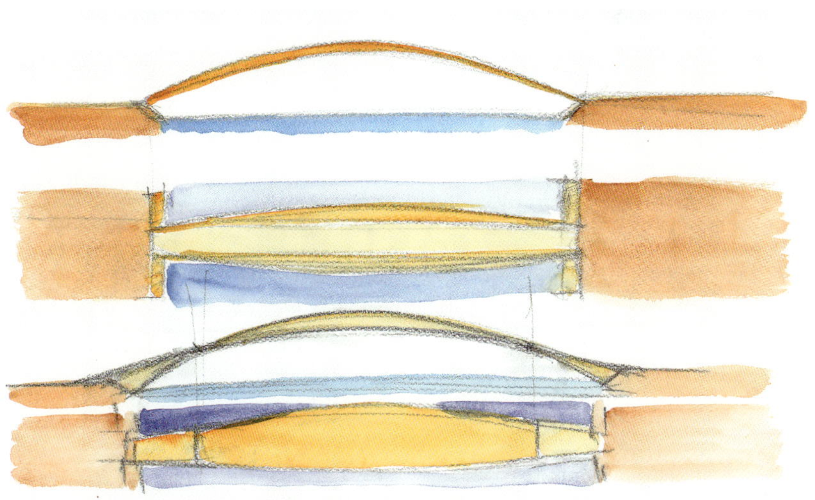

LIÈGE-GUILLEMINS RAILWAY STATION

Liège, Belgium. 1996–2009.

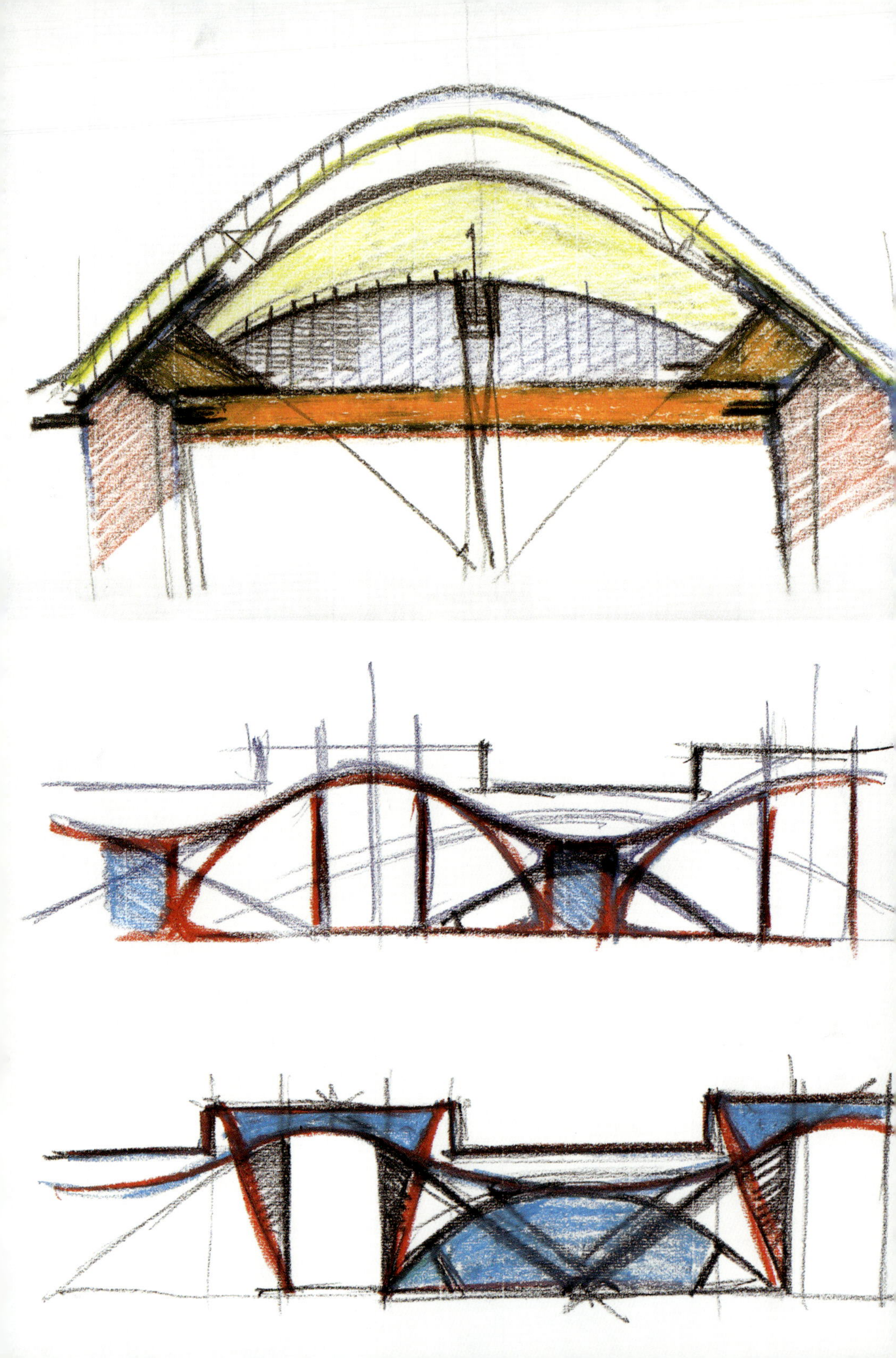

Project

LIÈGE-GUILLEMINS RAILWAY STATION

Location

LIÈGE, BELGIUM

Client

SNCB-HOLDING/INFRABEL/ EURO LIÈGE TGV

Santiago Calatrava's sketches render the wavelike form of the station roof explicit and show the relative simplicity of the engineering solutions chosen.

In den Skizzen Calatravas wird die wellenartige Form des Bahnhofsdachs augenfällig. Zugleich veranschaulichen sie die hier gewählten, vergleichsweise einfachen bautechnischen Lösungen.

Les croquis de Santiago Calatrava explicitent la forme en vague de la couverture de la gare et illustrent la simplicité relative des solutions techniques retenues.

For a number of years, the French rapid trains (TGV) bound for Cologne in Germany passed through the Belgian city of Liège at a pace that recalled the 19th century more than the 21st. Along with the inevitable modernization of the train lines concerned, it was also necessary to update the stations along the line from Brussels to Germany. Santiago Calatrava received the commission to design the new Liège-Guillemins Station, largely because of his experience in the field, in projects such as Lyon-Saint-Exupéry and the Oriente Station in Lisbon (see pages 104 and 212). Much as he had in Lisbon, he conceived the station as a link between two distinct areas of the city of Liège, which previously had been separated by the railroad tracks. On the north side of the site is a rundown urban area, laid out in a typical 19th-century scheme. On the south side, on the slopes of the Cointe Hill, is a less dense, landscaped residential area. Calatrava's design bridges these two areas with a 200-meter passenger terminal, built symmetrically along a northwest-southeast axis. The arched roof of the terminal building extends over the five platforms for another impressive 145 meters. A monumental vault made of glass and steel allows the station to be completely open to the city. Pedestrian bridges and a walkway under the tracks allow for fluid communication between the two sides of the station. Particular attention was paid to the architectural detailing of these spaces. Basing his design on the open transition from interior to exterior, Calatrava resolutely rejected the monumental façade that has traditionally characterized railway stations, at least until they became underground rabbit warrens in the image of New York's Penn Station. Given the need to keep the station functioning throughout construction, techniques learned from building bridges were employed to install the main elements at night.

Viele Jahre lang passierten die französischen Hochgeschwindigkeitszüge auf dem Weg nach Köln die belgische Stadt Lüttich mit einer Geschwindigkeit, die eher an das 19. als an das 21. Jahrhundert gemahnte. Neben der fälligen Instandsetzung der betroffenen Gleisanlagen war es auch notwendig, die Bahnhöfe entlang der Verbindung von Brüssel nach Deutschland zu modernisieren. Santiago Calatrava erhielt den Auftrag, den neuen Bahnhof Liège-Guillemins zu entwerfen, in erster Linie aufgrund seiner Erfahrung auf diesem Gebiet mit Projekten wie dem Bahnhof Lyon-Saint-Exupéry und dem Lissaboner Bahnhof Oriente (siehe Seiten 104 und 212). Ähnlich wie in Lissabon konzipierte er auch hier den Bahnhof als Bindeglied zwischen zwei verschiedenartigen Stadtteilen von Lüttich, die zuvor durch die Gleise getrennt gewesen waren. Im Norden des Geländes befindet sich ein in typischer Manier des 19. Jahrhunderts angelegtes, vernachlässigtes städtisches Areal. Auf der Südseite liegt auf den Hängen des Cointe ein weniger dicht besiedeltes, begrüntes Wohngebiet. Calatrava verband diese beiden Areale mit einem 200 m langen Passagierterminal, das symmetrisch entlang einer von Nordwest nach Südost verlaufenden Achse entstand. Das gewölbte Dach des Terminals überspannt mit eindrucksvollen 145 m fünf Bahnsteige. Dank eines monumentalen Bogens aus Glas und Stahl kann der Bahnhof zur Stadt hin vollständig offen bleiben. Fußgängerbrücken sowie ein Laufgang unter dem Gleiskörper ermöglichen einen ungestörten Verkehr zwischen den beiden Bahnhofsseiten. Der architektonischen Ausgestaltung dieser Räume wurde besondere Aufmerksamkeit gewidmet. Calatrava, dessen Entwurf auf dem offenen Übergang zwischen Innen- und Außenraum fußt, lehnte die monumentale Fassade ab, wie sie traditionellerweise für Bahnhöfe typisch war, ehe sie in der Art der New Yorker Penn Station zu unterirdischen Maulwurfsbauten wurden. Da der Bahnhof während der gesamten Bauzeit in Betrieb bleiben musste, kamen beim Brückenbau erprobte Techniken zur Anwendung, und die Hauptelemente wurden nachts installiert.

Pendant un certain nombre d'années, les TGV Paris-Cologne traversaient Liège à une allure qui évoquait plus le XIXe siècle que le XXIe. Il était nécessaire de moderniser non seulement les voies, mais aussi les gares entre Bruxelles et l'Allemagne. Santiago Calatrava reçut commande de la gare de Liège-Guillemins en grande partie grâce à son expérience dans ce domaine, illustrée par des projets comme la gare de Lyon-Saint-Exupéry ou celle de l'Orient à Lisbonne (voir pages 104 et 212). Comme il le fit au Portugal, il a conçu ici une gare qui fait lien entre deux zones distinctes de la ville jusqu'alors séparées par les voies ferrées : au nord, une zone urbaine délabrée typique de l'urbanisme du XIXe siècle ; au sud, sur les flancs de la colline de Cointe, une zone résidentielle paysagée, moins dense. Le projet de Calatrava jette un pont entre ces deux quartiers, avec un terminal pour passagers de 200 mètres de long de part et d'autre d'un axe nord-ouest/sud-est. La couverture voûtée du bâtiment se prolonge au-dessus des cinq quais par un impressionnant auvent de 145 mètres de long. La voûte monumentale en acier et en verre donne l'impression que la gare est complètement ouverte sur la ville. Des passerelles pour piétons et un passage sous les voies fluidifient la circulation entre les deux côtés de la gare. Une attention particulière a été portée à la qualité de réalisation architecturale de ces espaces. En misant sur une transition ouverte entre l'intérieur et l'extérieur, Calatrava a résolument rejeté le principe de façade monumentale qui a si longtemps caractérisé les gares, du moins jusqu'à ce qu'elles disparaissent sous terre, comme Penn Station à New York. Étant donné la nécessité de maintenir la gare en activité pendant le chantier, des techniques empruntées à la construction de ponts ont été utilisées pour poser les principaux composants en nocturne.

The broad, bright arch over the tracks imagined by the architect is an ode to movement and a modern vision of rail transport.

Der vom Architekten gestaltete weite, leuchtende Bogen über den Gleisen ist ein Lobgesang auf die Bewegung und eine moderne Vision vom Schienentransport.

Dans une vision contemporaine du transport ferroviaire, l'immense arche éclatante de lumière qui protège les quais est comme une ode au mouvement.

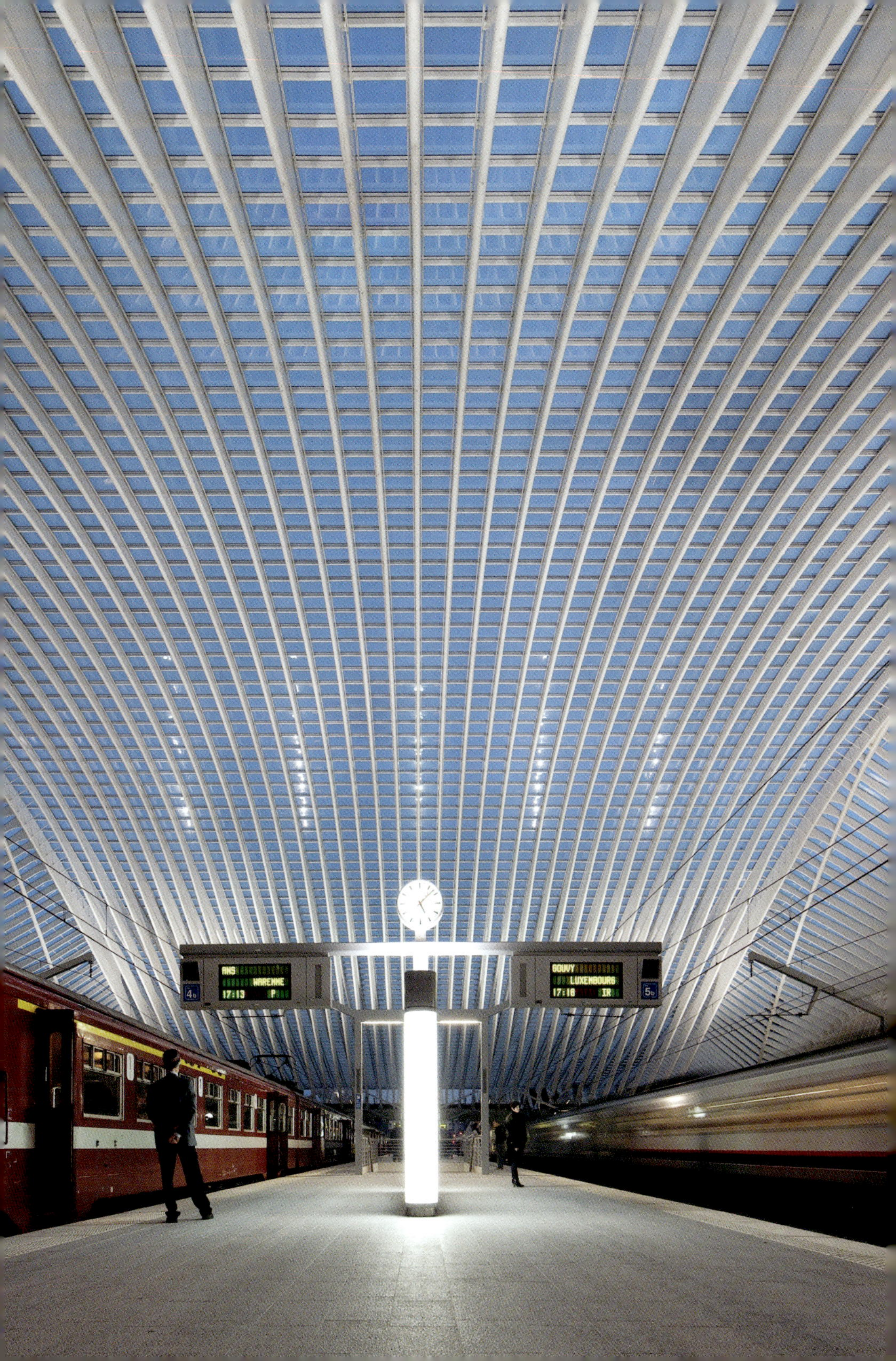

4b
ANS
WAREMME
17:13
P
GOUVY
LUXEMBOURG
17:18
IR
5b

A sketch by the architect, right, shows the relation of the station to the city, with the square in the foreground and the great central arch of the building visible. Far right, the vast open space covered by the arch seen in the sketch.

Eine Skizze des Architekten (rechts) zeigt das Verhältnis des Bahnhofs zur Stadt: , außerdem die monumentale, zentrale bogenförmige Aufwerfung des Baus. Ganz rechts: ein Foto des offenen, vom Bogen überspannten Bereichs.

Un croquis de l'architecte, à droite, montre la relation entre la gare, la place qui lui fait face et le grand arc décrit par la couverture de la gare. Tout à fait à droite, vue de l'intérieur de l'ample espace protégé par l'arche.

A sketch by the architect (right) echoes the ribbed, soaring design of the canopy and roof structure seen in completed form on page 259.

Eine Skizze des Architekten (rechts) deutet das rippenartige, hoch auffliegende Vordach und die Dachkonstruktion an, die auf Seite 259 als fertiger Bau zu sehen sind.

Un croquis de l'architecte (à droite) illustre la forme nervurée en projection de l'auvent et la structure de la toiture, que l'on aperçoit achevés à la page 259.

Interior views of the station show the continuity with much earlier work like the Zurich Stadelhofen Station (see page 52) and with slightly later projects such as the Milwaukee Art Museum (see page 232). The architect seems to be moving toward ever lighter, more aerial designs.

Innenansichten des Bahnhofs belegen die Kontinuität zu wesentlich früheren Arbeiten wie dem Bahnhof Zürich-Stadelhofen (siehe Seite 52) sowie zu wenig später realisierten Projekten, etwa dem Milwaukee Art Museum (siehe Seite 232). Der Architekt scheint sich immer stärker auf lichtere, durchlässigere Entwürfe hinzubewegen.

Ces vues intérieures de la gare montrent une continuité avec une réalisation beaucoup plus ancienne – la gare de Stadelhofen à Zurich (voir page 52) –, mais aussi avec des projets plus récents comme le Musée d'art de Milwaukee (voir page 232). L'architecte semble s'orienter vers des réalisations encore plus légères et aériennes.

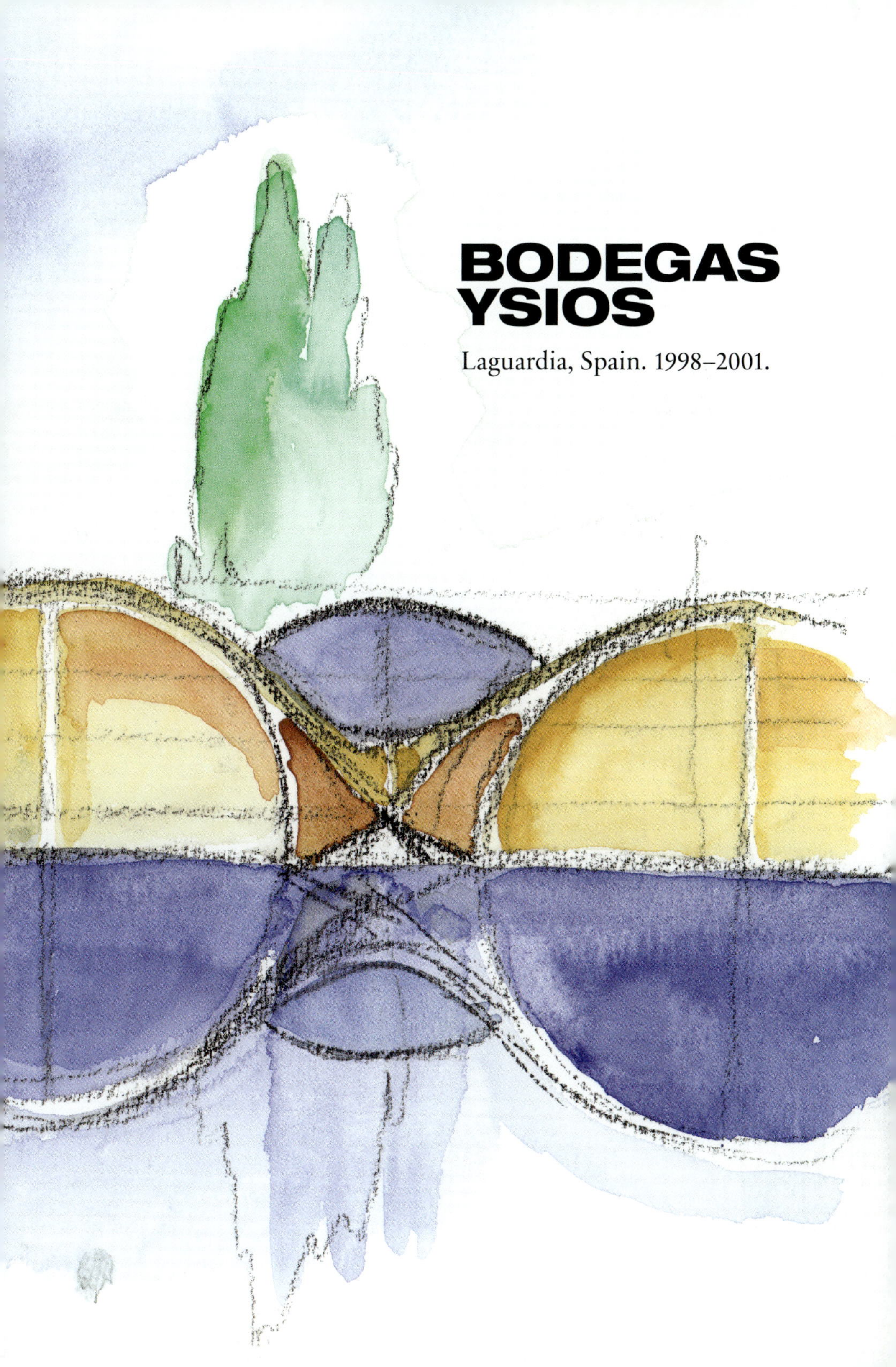

BODEGAS YSIOS

Laguardia, Spain. 1998–2001.

YSIOS

Project
BODEGAS YSIOS

Location
LAGUARDIA, ÁLAVA, SPAIN

Client
BODEGAS & BEBIDAS GROUP

Floor area
8000 m²

Cost
$ 10 MILLION

The strong undulating roof of the building defines its overall form. The sketch above relates its height to those of trees.

Das stark gewellte Dach des Gebäudes bestimmt die Gesamtform. In der Skizze oben ist seine Höhe im Verhältnis zu Bäumen dargestellt.

La forte ondulation du toit définit sa forme d'ensemble. Le croquis ci-dessus montre le rapport d'échelle avec la hauteur des arbres.

The Bodegas & Bebidas Group wanted a building that would be an icon for its prestigious new Rioja Alavesa wine. They called on architect Santiago Calatrava to design an 8000-square-meter winery complex, a building that had to be designed to make, store, and sell wine. Vineyards occupy half of the rectangular site. A difference in height of 10 meters from the north to the south of the site complicated the design. The linear program of the winemaking process dictated that the structure should be rectangular and it was set along an east-west axis. Two longitudinal concrete load-bearing walls, separated from each other by 26 meters, trace a 196-meter-long sinusoidal shape in plan and in elevation. These walls are covered with wooden planks, which are mirrored in a reflecting pool and "evoke the image of a row of wine barrels." The roof, composed of a series of laminated wood beams, is designed as a continuation of the façades. The result is a "ruled surface wave," which combines concave and convex surfaces as it evolves along the longitudinal axis. The roof is clad in aluminum, creating a contrast with the warmth of the wooden façades and yet continuing their design. A visitor's center conceived as a "balcony that overlooks the winery and the vineyard" is situated in the center of the structure.

Die Gruppe Bodegas & Bebidas wünschte ein Gebäude, das als Signum für ihren prestigeträchtigen neuen Rioja-Alavesa-Wein dienen konnte. Sie wandte sich an Santiago Calatrava, der eine 8000 m² große Anlage gestalten sollte, in der Wein hergestellt, gelagert und verkauft werden kann. Die Hälfte des rechtwinkligen Geländes wird von Rebstöcken eingenommen. Ein zwischen dem nördlichen und südlichen Teil des Standorts bestehender Höhenunterschied von 10 m erschwerte die Aufgabe. Der lineare Ablauf der Weinherstellung gab die Rechtwinkligkeit des Gebäudes vor, das entlang einer Ost-West-Achse errichtet wurde. Zwei längs verlaufende tragende Betonwände im Abstand von 26 m folgen in Grund- und Aufriss einer Wellenform. Diese Wände sind mit Holzbohlen verschalt, die sich in einem Wasserbecken spiegeln und „das Bild einer Reihe von Weinfässern hervorrufen“. Das aus aneinandergereihten Schichtholzbalken bestehende Dach ist als Fortführung der Fassade konzipiert. Entlang der Längsachse entsteht so eine regelmäßig gewellte Oberfläche, bei der konkave und konvexe Flächen kombiniert sind. Das mit Aluminium verkleidete Dach kontrastiert mit der Wärme der Holzfassaden, führt deren Formgebung jedoch weiter. Ein als „Balkon, der Kellerei und Rebstöcke überschaut“, gestaltetes Besucherzentrum, befindet sich in der Mitte des Gebäudes.

Le groupe Bodegas & Bebidas souhaitait construire un bâtiment qui symbolisât son prestigieux Rioja Alavesa. Il fit appel à Santiago Calatrava pour ce chai de 8 000 mètres carrés dédié à l’élaboration, la conservation et la commercialisation de ce nouveau vin. Une dénivellation de dix mètres entre la partie nord et la partie sud compliquait l’aménagement de ce terrain rectangulaire occupé pour moitié par des vignes. Le processus linéaire de fabrication du vin exigeait un bâtiment rectangulaire, qui fut implanté est-ouest. Deux murs porteurs en béton, séparés de 26 mètres, dessinent une forme sinusoïdale de 196 mètres de long, en plan comme en élévation. Ils sont habillés d’un bardage de bois qui se reflète dans un bassin et « évoquent un alignement de barriques ». Le toit, réalisé en poutres

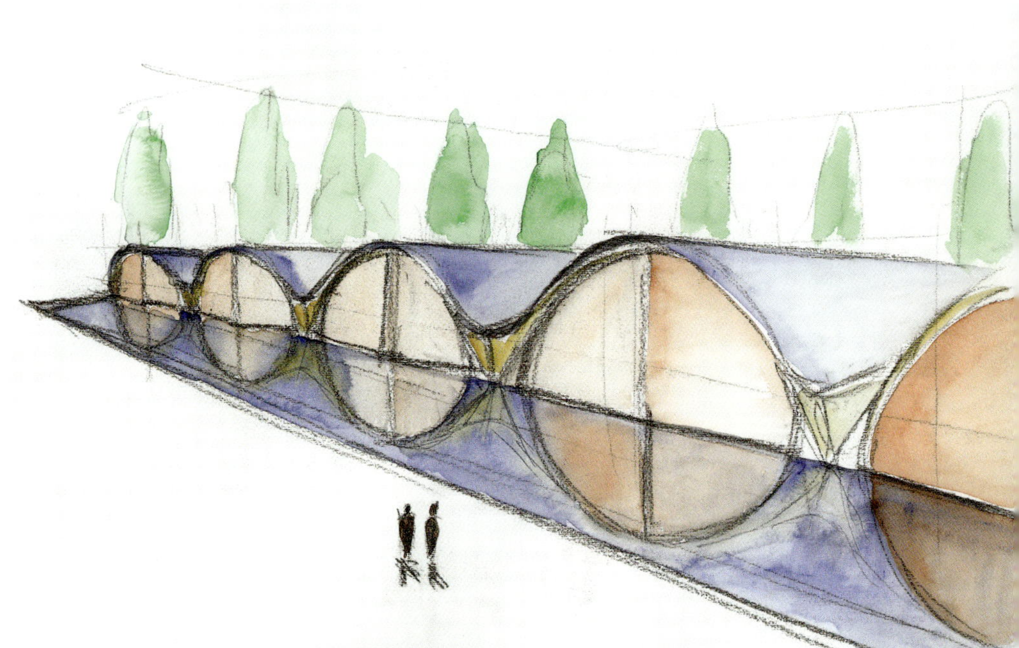

de bois lamellé, est dans le prolongement des façades. Il en résulte un effet de « vagues » alternant surfaces convexes et concaves tout au long de l'axe longitudinal. L'aluminium qui habille la toiture contraste avec le bois chaleureux des façades. Au centre des installations est implanté le centre d'accueil des visiteurs, conçu comme « un balcon dominant le chai et le vignoble ».

The undulating form of the roof of the building again recalls that of a human eye when it is reflected in the sketch on the left. Calatrava renews the traditional architecture of the vineyard with this structure.

Die gewellte Form des Daches erinnert in der Skizze links – wenn sie gespiegelt wird – wieder an jene des menschlichen Auges. Calatrava erneuert mit diesem Bau die traditionelle Architektur der Weinberge.

La ligne ondulée du toit, avec ses reflets, rappelle un œil humain comme le souligne le croquis à gauche. Avec ce projet, Calatrava renouvelle l'architecture traditionnelle des installations viticoles.

Despite their apparent simplicity, Calatrava's sketches (above) offer a very accurate vision of the completed structure, as the roof detail to the right demonstrates.

Trotz ihrer scheinbaren Einfachheit geben Calatravas Skizzen (oben) eine sehr genaue Ansicht des fertigen Gebäudes wieder, wie der Dachausschnitt rechts veranschaulicht.

Malgré leur simplicité apparente, les croquis de Calatrava (ci-dessus) offrent une vision très précise de la structure achevée, comme le prouve ce détail du toit (à droite).

Unlike some very well-known architects who consistently privilege exterior appearance in their work, Calatrava can be recognized almost immediately by his mastery of interior spaces, conceived in harmony with the outer shell of the building.

Anders als einige bekannte Architekten, die oft das äußere Erscheinungsbild ihrer Werke betonen, zeichnet sich Calatrava durch die meisterhafte Gestaltung von Innenräumen aus, die in Harmonie mit der äußeren Form des Gebäudes stehen.

Contrairement à certains architectes célèbres qui, dans leurs travaux, privilégient systématiquement l'aspect extérieur, ceux de Calatrava sont immédiatement reconnaissables à la maîtrise des volumes intérieurs conçus en harmonie avec l'enveloppe extérieure du bâtiment.

TURNING TORSO

Malmö, Sweden. 1999–2004.

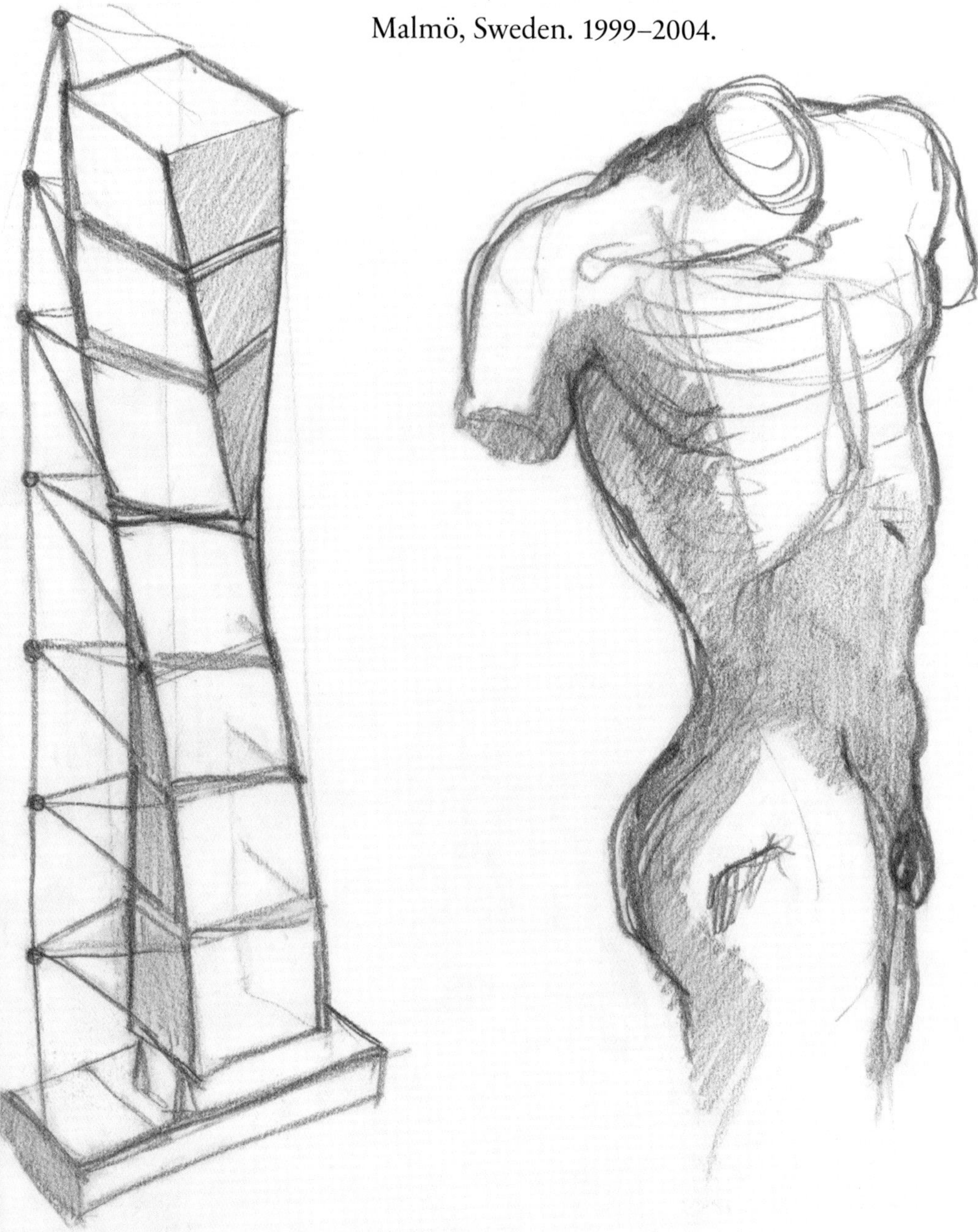

ultura (4) Vanizzati al torso. 5bis

a

b

Project
TURNING TORSO

Location
MALMÖ, SWEDEN

Client
HSB, MALMÖ

Height
190 METERS

The twisting design of the tower is readily comprehensible in the sketch to the left. The similarity with a number of Calatrava's sculptures, some dating back more than 20 years, is also clear.

Der gedrehte Entwurf des Turms ist auf der Skizze links ohne Weiteres verständlich. Auch ist die Ähnlichkeit mit einigen zum Teil vor über 20 Jahren entstandenen Skulpturen Calatravas deutlich.

La forme en torsion de la tour est mise en lumière par le croquis de gauche. La similarité avec plusieurs sculptures de l'architecte, dont certaines datent de plus de vingt ans, est évidente.

Calatrava's Turning Torso building in Malmö, Sweden (1999–2004), is the result of his intense interest in sculpture, an art he often treats as a study in statics. Calatrava first created a sculpture in which "seven cubes are set around a steel support to produce a spiral structure, which resembles a twisting human spine." His tower in Malmö was designed for a prominent site in the city on the occasion of the 2001 European Housing Expo there. Malmö was selected amongst Swedish cities after a competition to host "Bo01, the European Housing Expo 2001," which was intended to "start a debate on how we wish to live in the city of tomorrow." The "City of Tomorrow" exhibition theme was examined from a variety of angles: ecological, social, technical, and human sustainability. Calatrava's project was one of 44 building and art projects carried out, mostly by local and Scandinavian architects, in the city's Western Harbor area. Santiago Calatrava does not hesitate to refer to the "sculptural presence" of the completed building, which is 190 meters tall and twists a total of 90 degrees from base to top. Malmö is the third largest city in Sweden, situated in the southernmost province of Skåne, near Copenhagen, Denmark. It has about 270 000 inhabitants, and nearly 600 000 in the metropolitan area. Malmö was one of the earliest industrial cities of Scandinavia, but has in recent decades been struggling to adapt to a postindustrial economy. As the architect explains the relationship of the tower to the sculpture: "In the Turning Torso building, the spiraling tower is composed of nine box units, each of five floors. The equivalent in the tower of the sculpture's steel support is the nucleus of internal elevators and stairs, through which the box units communicate." The cubes of the original sculpture are replaced by "sub-buildings" each of which has a floor area of approximately 2200 square meters, with each floor within these boxes accommodating from one to five residence units around the vertical nucleus. Areas in the "spine" are reserved for common facilities such as meeting rooms or a gym. As is often the case, the engineering used by Calatrava simplified and accelerated construction greatly, relying on prefabricated elements for the exterior steel structure and façade for example.

Calatravas 1999–2004 erbautes Hochhaus Turning Torso in Malmö ist das Ergebnis seines leidenschaftlichen Interesses an Skulptur, einer Kunstform, die er häufig als Studie zur Statik behandelt. Calatrava schuf zu Anfang eine Skulptur, bei der „sieben Kuben um eine Stahlstütze herum angeordnet wurden, die eine an ein gedrehtes menschliches Rückgrat erinnernde Spiralkonstruktion bilden". Sein Turm in Malmö wurde anlässlich der dort stattfindenden European Housing Expo 2001 für einen markanten Standort in der Stadt entworfen. Unter mehreren schwedischen Städten fiel die Wahl auf Malmö als gastgebende Stadt dieser Ausstellung, bei der „eine Diskussion darüber beginnen sollte, wie wir in der Stadt von morgen leben wollen". Das Ausstellungsthema, „Die Stadt von morgen", wurde aus einer Vielzahl von Blickwinkeln betrachtet, so ging es um ökologische, soziale, technische und menschliche Nachhaltigkeit. Calatravas Projekt war eines von 44 Gebäuden und Kunstprojekten, die vorrangig von heimischen und skandinavischen Architekten im westlichen Hafengebiet der Stadt realisiert wurden. Calatrava zögert nicht, von der „plastischen Präsenz" des fertiggestellten Gebäudes zu sprechen, das bei einer Höhe von 190 m zwischen Basis und Spitze eine Drehung von 90 Grad vollzieht. Malmö ist die drittgrößte Stadt Schwedens und liegt in der südlichsten Provinz Skåne, nahe Kopenhagen, Dänemark. Sie hat etwa 270 000 Einwohner und fast 600 000 im Großraum. Malmö gehörte zu den frühesten Industriestädten Skandinaviens, kämpft aber in jüngerer Zeit darum, eine postindustrielle Ökonomie zu entwickeln. Die Beziehung des Turms zur Skulptur erläutert der Architekt wie folgt: „Bei dem Gebäude Turning Torso ist der gedrehte Turm aus neun Kastenelementen zusammengesetzt, die jeweils fünf Geschosse umfassen. Das Äquivalent zum Stahlstützgerüst der Skulptur ist der Turmkern aus internen Aufzügen und Treppen, über die die Kasteneinheiten miteinander verbunden sind." An die Stelle der Kuben der Skulptur traten „Subgebäude", von denen jedes etwa 2200 m² umfasst. Innerhalb dieser Kästen gruppieren sich auf jedem Geschoss zwischen ein und fünf Wohneinheiten um den vertikalen Kern. Flächen im „Rückgrat" sind Gemeinschaftseinrichtungen wie Versammlungsräumen oder einem Fitnesszentrum vorbehalten. Wie so oft vereinfachte und beschleunigte die von Calatrava verwendete Technik die Bauarbeiten erheblich, da er beispielsweise bei der außen liegenden Stahlkonstruktion und der Fassade auf vorgefertigte Elemente zurückgriff.

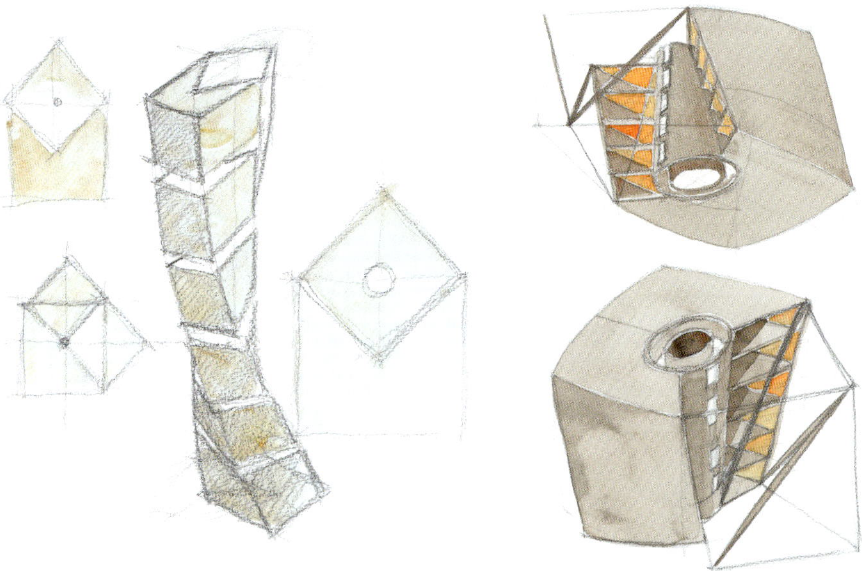

La Turning Torso de Calatrava, construite en 1999–2004 à Malmö, est l'aboutissement de son intérêt permanent pour la sculpture, art qu'il traite souvent comme une étude de statique. Il s'agissait à l'origine d'une pièce dans laquelle « sept cubes empilés sur un support en acier créaient une structure en spirale ressemblant à une colonne vertébrale vrillée ». La tour éponyme a été conçue pour un site très visible de Malmö, la troisième ville de Suède (270 000 habitants, près de 600 000 pour son agglomération), située dans la province méridionale de Scanie en face de Copenhague, la capitale danoise. C'est l'un des premiers centres industriels scandinaves, mais elle se bat depuis de longues années pour s'adapter à l'économie post-industrielle. En 2001, s'y tint « BoO1, Exposition européenne sur le logement 2001 » qui se proposait de « lancer un débat sur la façon dont nous souhaitons vivre dans la ville de demain ». Le thème de l'exposition, « La Cité de Demain », était analysé sous divers angles : écologique, social, technique et développement durable. La proposition de Calatrava fut l'un des quarante-quatre projets d'art et d'architecture réalisés dans la zone ouest du port, confiés pour la plupart à des architectes locaux ou scandinaves. L'architecte insiste sur la « présence sculpturale » de cet immeuble qui mesure 190 mètres de haut et pivote de 90 degrés entre sa base et son sommet. Il explique le lien entre la sculpture et la tour Turning Torso en ces termes : « La tour en spirale est composée de neuf boîtes de cinq étages. L'équivalent du support en acier de la sculpture est le noyau d'escaliers et d'ascenseurs par lequel les boîtes communiquent. » Les cubes de la sculpture sont ici des « sous-immeubles » de 2 200 mètres carrés environ, dont chaque niveau accueille de un à cinq appartements. Certains espaces ont été réservés à des équipements collectifs, notamment des salles de réunion et de gymnastique. Comme souvent, l'ingénierie de Calatrava a grandement simplifié et accéléré le processus de construction, par exemple en utilisant des éléments préfabriqués pour la structure extérieure en acier ou la façade.

Clearly related to Calatrava's sculptures that place blocks of granite in a tensioned spiral, these sketches also establish the link he imagines to the male torso.

Diese Skizzen, eindeutig verwandt mit Calatravas Skulpturen, bei denen er Granitblöcke in einer gespannten Spirale anordnet, stellen darüber hinaus die von ihm gedachte Verbindung zum männlichen Torso her.

Clairement liés aux sculptures de Calatrava réalisées à partir de blocs de granit superposés en spirale, ces croquis montrent également le lien qu'il entrevoit avec l'image d'un torse masculin.

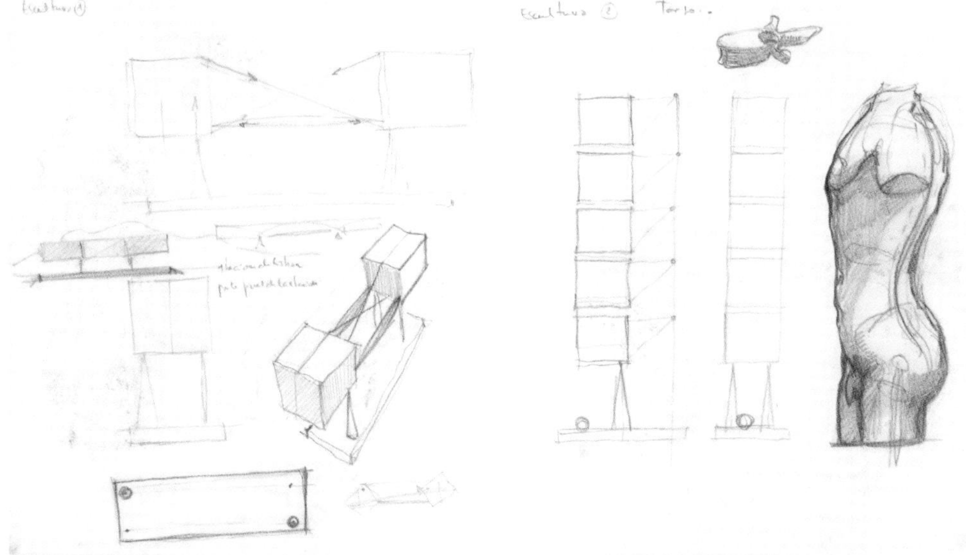

The relation of the completed building to a human figure is rendered explicit in the title "Turning Torso," but, in any case, the architect pursues his fascination with the idea of motion, real or implied in architecture.

Die Beziehung des fertigen Bauwerks zum menschlichen Körper ist im Titel „Turning Torso" explizit enthalten; in jedem Fall jedoch geht der Architekt der ihn faszinierenden Vorstellung von realer oder implizierter Bewegung iin der Architektur nach.

La relation entre l'immeuble achevé et la figure humaine est rendue explicite par son nom de « Turning Torso ». L'architecte retrouve ici sa fascination pour l'idée du mouvement en architecture, qu'il soit réel ou implicite.

Although the sketch below does not specifically correspond to the completed tower in Sweden, its fundamental idea of rotated, piled cubes is that of the actual building.

Obgleich die Skizze unten nicht genau mit dem fertigen Turm in Schweden übereinstimmt, entspricht ihr Grundgedanke von rotierenden, gestapelten Würfeln jenem des tatsächlichen Gebäudes.

Bien que le croquis ci-dessous ne corresponde pas spécifiquement à la tour réalisée en Suède, l'idée fondamentale de cubes empilés en une colonne vrillée subsiste.

Where engineering of tall buildings has tended to take the most obvious approach, by stacking each story in a pile and reducing floor area as the building rises, Calatrava uses his knowledge of the analysis of loads (force, movement, torque) on a physical system in static equilibrium to produce a surprising solution.

Während im Hochbau oft einfach jede Etage auf die nächste gestapelt wird und die Fläche mit zunehmender Höhe abnimmt, wendet Calatrava sein Wissen über die Lastanalyse (Kraft, Bewegung, Drehmoment) auf ein physisches System im statischen Gleichgewicht an, um eine unerwartete Lösung zu erzielen.

Alors que l'ingénierie des immeubles de grande hauteur a tendance à adopter l'approche la plus facile consistant à empiler des niveaux de surface dégressive au fur et à mesure qu'ils s'élèvent, Calatrava utilise ses connaissances en analyse des charges (force, mouvement, couple) pour imaginer un système physique en équilibre statique qui débouche sur une solution surprenante.

THE NEW YORK TIMES CAPSULE

New York, USA. 1999–2001.

Project

THE NEW YORK TIMES CAPSULE

Location

THE AMERICAN MUSEUM OF NATURAL HISTORY, NEW YORK, USA

Client

THE NEW YORK TIMES COMPANY FOUNDATION

Calatrava's simple sketch on page 290 on the right corresponds directly to the shape of the completed capsule seen to the left.

Die auf Seite 290 rechts abgebildete einfache Skizze Calatravas scheint direkt der Form der fertigen Kapsel, links, zu entsprechen.

Le petit croquis de Calatrava à droite à la page 290 correspond exactement à la forme de la capsule achevée (à gauche).

In 1999, *The New York Times Magazine* organized an international competition to design a capsule, which would contain objects documenting life on earth in the 20th century, and which would be sealed until January 1, 3000. Santiago Calatrava's design was selected from 50 competition entries submitted from 15 countries. The artifacts were selected by *The New York Times*, based on suggestions made by visitors to an exhibition at the Museum of Natural History, and through the newspaper's Web site. The chosen objects were treated with preservatives and specially packed. On March 28, 2001, the artifacts were placed inside *The New York Times Capsule*, and the capsule was welded shut. The capsule, made of polished stainless steel, measures 1.5 meters in diameter, weighs 600 kilos, and contains 1.4 cubic meters of storage space. Its form, resembling a flower, was derived from a series of sculptures by Calatrava that explores the properties of folded spherical frames. His ongoing interest in sculpture despite a heavy schedule of architectural work shows the importance that Santiago Calatrava gives this aspect of his activity, which is in many senses at the origin of his architecture. The challenge of designing an object intended to last 1000 years or more also surely spoke to his sense of the permanence of the forms that animate all of his work.

Das *New York Times Magazine* organisierte 1999 einen internationalen Wettbewerb für die Gestaltung einer Kapsel, die bestimmte Objekte zur Dokumentation des Lebens auf der Erde im 20. Jahrhundert aufnehmen und bis zum 1. Januar 3000 versiegelt bleiben sollte. Aus 15 Ländern wurden 50 Wettbewerbsbeiträge eingereicht, unter denen man sich für Santiago Calatravas Entwurf entschied. Die Objekte waren von der *New York Times* ausgewählt worden, basierend auf Vorschlägen, die Besucher einer Ausstellung im Museum of Natural History abgegeben oder über die Website der Zeitung eingereicht hatten. Die Objekte wurden mit Konservierungsmitteln behandelt und speziell verpackt. Am 28. März 2001 wurden sie in die *New York Times Capsule* eingelegt und diese zugeschweißt. Die aus poliertem Edelstahl bestehende Kapsel hat einen Durchmesser von 1,5 m, wiegt 600 kg und umfasst 1,4 m^3 Rauminhalt. Die einer Blüte ähnelnde Form entstammt einer Reihe von Skulpturen Calatravas, die die Eigenschaften gefalteter sphärischer Gehäuse ausloten. Sein Interesse an Skulptur, das ungeachtet eines mit Architekturaufträgen angefüllten Terminplans anhält, zeugt von der Bedeutung, die Calatrava jenem Teil seiner Arbeit beimisst, der in vieler Hinsicht als Ausgangspunkt seiner Architektur gelten kann. Die Herausforderung, ein Objekt zu entwerfen, das 1000 Jahre oder länger bestehen soll, sprach darüber hinaus gewiss sein Empfinden für die Dauerhaftigkeit der Formen an, die sein gesamtes Œuvre inspiriert.

En 1999, le *New York Times Magazine* organisa un concours international pour une capsule devant contenir des artefacts illustrant la vie sur la planète Terre au XXe siècle et qui resterait scellée jusqu'au 1er janvier 3000. La proposition de Santiago Calatrava fut sélectionnée parmi cinquante participations venues de quinze pays. Les artefacts furent choisis par le journal à partir des suggestions des visiteurs d'une exposition organisée au Museum of Natural History et de celles d'internautes. Les objets furent spécialement conditionnés pour leur conservation et emballés puis, le 28 mars 2001, déposés dans la Capsule que l'on souda hermétiquement. Faite d'acier inoxydable, elle mesure 1,5 mètre de diamètre et pèse 600 kilos pour un volume intérieur de 1,4 mètre cube. Sa forme de fleur est inspirée d'une série de sculptures de l'architecte explorant les propriétés des ossatures sphériques pliées. Malgré l'ampleur et le nombre de ses projets architecturaux, Calatrava accorde toujours beaucoup d'importance à ces recherches sculpturales qui sont, à de nombreux égards, à l'origine de son architecture. Le défi qui consistait à concevoir un objet destiné à perdurer un millier d'années illustre également le sens de la permanence des formes qui anime l'ensemble de son œuvre.

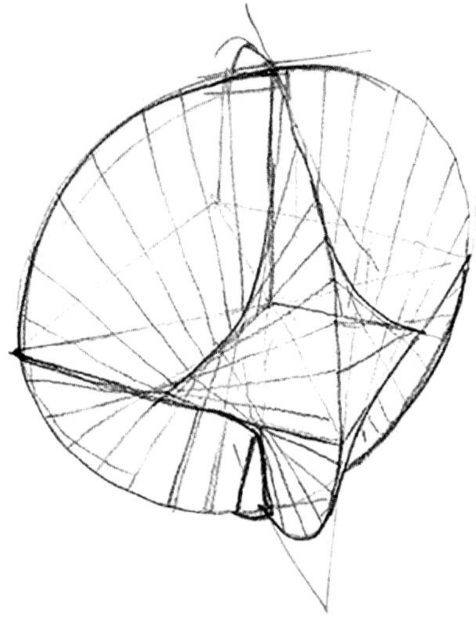

Intended to last for 1000 years, *The New York Times Capsule* adopts a seemingly inviolable form made of polished stainless steel. Though it resembles a flower or a seed pod, the shape is derived from the architect's study of spheres.

Für die *New York Times Capsule*, die einen Zeitraum von 1000 Jahren überdauern soll, wählte Calatrava eine anscheinend unzerstörbare Form aus poliertem Edelstahl. Obgleich sie einer Blume oder einer Samenkapsel ähnelt, ist ihre Form den Kugelstudien des Architekten entnommen.

Prévue pour durer mille ans, la capsule en acier inoxydable poli du *New York Times* a adopté une forme qui paraît inviolable. Bien qu'elle ressemble à une fleur ou à une gousse végétale, elle est issue d'une recherche de l'architecte sur les sphères.

OLYMPIC SPORTS COMPLEX

Athens, Greece. 2001–2004.

Project
OLYMPIC SPORTS COMPLEX

Location
ATHENS, GREECE

Client
MINISTRY OF CULTURE OF GREECE

Site area
199 000 m² OF PLAZAS
94 000 m² OF PATHWAYS
61 000 m² OF GREEN AREAS
29 000 m² OF WATER ELEMENTS
130 000 m² OF SERVICE FACILITIES
178 000 m² OF PARKING LOTS AND ROADS

Calatrava's design was intended to deal with the facilities of the existing Athens Olympic Sports Complex (OAKA, located in Marousi, a suburb north of Athens) as well as their infrastructure and access network (subway, commuter rail, highways). As he explains: "The design aimed to meet all the functional requirements of the Olympic and Paralympic Games; to integrate the OAKA's elements aesthetically by providing a common identity through a combination of built and natural elements; to accommodate people with special needs; and to respect the environment through the use of autochthonous plantings (such as olive trees and cypresses), provision of efficient solutions to waste management, and other elements of ecologically sensitive design." The principal architectural interventions were: a new roof for the Olympic Stadium; a new roof and refurbishing of the Velodrome; the creation of entrance plazas and entrance canopies for the complex as a whole; the creation of a central Olympic Icon (a movable steel sculpture in the form of a 110-meter-high spindle); the design of a sculptural *Nations Wall* (a 250-meter-long, 20-meter-high tubular steel sculpture); provision of new warm-up areas for athletes; improvement of pedestrian bridges and connections to public transportation; provision of parking areas and bus terminals; and design of the installations and infrastructure for all elements. The most spectacular element is the roof of the Olympic Stadium, covering a surface of 25 000 square meters, with two "bent leaf" structures made of tubular steel and spanning 304 meters each. The structures were designed so that they could be prefabricated off-site to the greatest extent possible, reducing the need for on-site personnel and equipment and minimizing interference with other construction work on the existing buildings. Though Calatrava's intervention was rendered difficult by local working conditions, and perhaps overshadowed by the Olympic Games themselves, his intervention in Athens will remain as one of the major, symbolic encounters between architecture, engineering, and sports.

Calatravas Konzeption sollte sich der Einrichtungen der vorhandenen Olympischen Sportanlagen (OAKA) in Marousi, einem nördlichen Vorort Athens, sowie deren Infrastruktur und Verkehrsanbindung mittels Untergrundbahn, Nahverkehrszügen und Schnellstraßen annehmen. Calatrava erläutert: „Das Design zielte darauf ab, alle funktionalen Anforderungen der Olympischen und Paralympischen Spiele zu erfüllen; die Elemente des OAKA ästhetisch zu integrieren, indem eine gemeinsame Identität durch eine Kombination aus gebauten und natürlichen Elementen geschaffen wurde; Menschen mit besonderen Bedürfnissen gerecht zu werden; sowie die Umwelt durch einheimische Pflanzen (wie Olivenbäume und Zypressen), effiziente Abfallmanagementlösungen und andere umweltgerechte Elemente zu respektieren.“ Die hauptsächlichen architektonischen Maßnahmen umfassten: ein neues Dach für das Olympiastadion, ein neues Dach und die Modernisierung des Velodroms, die Schaffung von Vorplätzen und Vordächern für die gesamte Anlage, die Gestaltung eines zentralen olympischen Symbols (eine bewegliche Stahlskulptur in Form einer 110 m hohen Spirale), die Gestaltung einer skulpturalen Wand der Nationen *(Nations Wall)* (eine 250 m lange, 20 m hohe Stahlrohrplastik), die Schaffung neuer Aufwärmplätze für Sportler, die Instandsetzung von Fußgängerbrücken und die Anbindung an den öffentlichen Nahverkehr, die Schaffung von Parkplätzen und Busterminals sowie die Planung der Installationen und Infrastruktur für sämtliche Bereiche. Das 25 000 m² große Dach des Olympiastadions mit zwei „gebogenen Blattformen“ aus Stahlrohr, die jeweils 304 m überspannen, ist zweifellos das markanteste Element. Die Planung der Bauten sah vor, sie weitestgehend andernorts vorzufertigen, um den Bedarf an Personal und Ausrüstung vor Ort zu reduzieren und Störungen der Bauarbeiten an den bestehenden Gebäuden zu minimieren. Obwohl Calatravas Intervention durch die Arbeitsbedingungen vor Ort erschwert und vielleicht von den Olympischen Spielen selbst überschattet wurde, wird sein Wirken in Athen als eine der großen, symbolischen Begegnungen zwischen Architektur, Ingenieurwesen und Sport in Erinnerung bleiben.

Le projet de Calatrava pour le Complexe des Sports olympiques d'Athènes, situé à Marousi dans la banlieue nord de la capitale, portait sur des équipements spécifiques, leurs infrastructures et leur réseau d'accès (métro, trains de banlieue, autoroutes). « Le projet avait pour but de répondre aux besoins fonctionnels de l'organisation des Jeux olympiques et paralympiques et d'intégrer esthétiquement les éléments de l'OAKA en leur assurant une identité commune par la combinaison d'éléments construits et d'éléments naturels, de répondre aux besoins des personnes handicapées, de respecter l'environnement par l'utilisation de plantes locales (oliviers et cyprès par exemple), de prévoir des solutions efficaces de gestion des déchets et des eaux usées et autres éléments écologiquement sensibles. » Les principales interventions architecturales furent un nouveau toit pour le stade olympique, un autre pour le vélodrome qui était également à rénover, la création de places et d'auvents devant les entrées, une « icône » olympique (sculpture mobile en acier en forme de navette de 110 mètres de haut), la conception d'un *Mur des Nations* (sculpture en tube d'acier de 250 mètres de long et 20 mètres de haut), des aires d'entraînement pour les athlètes, l'amélioration des passerelles piétonnières et des connexions avec les transports publics, des parkings et des gares routières et toutes les infrastructures indispensables. La création la plus spectaculaire est le toit du stade olympique dont la structure en « feuilles recourbées » de tubes d'acier de 304 mètres de portée chacun recouvre une surface de 25 000 mètres carrés. Les éléments ont été conçus de façon à être préfabriqués le plus souvent possible, afin de réduire les besoins en personnel et équipements de chantier et de limiter les interférences avec les travaux menés en parallèle sur les constructions. Si l'intervention de Calatrava a été compliquée par les conditions de travail locales et peut-être éclipsée par les Jeux olympiques eux-mêmes, elle restera comme l'une des rencontres symboliques majeures entre l'architecture, l'ingénierie et le sport.

The series of sketches seen on this page put the human body through unexpected contorsions. It is as though Calatrava's interest focuses not on ordinary movements, but rather on those of dance or certain sports that might entail jumping or falling through space, as in the pole vault, long jump or in diving.

Die Skizzenserie auf dieser Seite zeigt den menschlichen Körper in unvermuteten Verdrehungen. Es ist, als gelte Calatravas Interesse nicht alltäglichen Bewegungen, sondern denen des Tanzes oder bestimmter Sportarten, wie Stabhochsprung, Weitsprung oder Turmspringen, die Sprünge oder das Fallen mit sich bringen.

La série de croquis de cette page montre le corps humain dans des contorsions inattendues, comme si l'intérêt de Calatrava se concentrait non sur des mouvements ordinaires mais sur ceux de danseurs ou d'athlètes en saut à la perche, saut en longueur, ou plongée.

The relation of Calatrava's architectural compositions in studies of the human body in motion, such as the sketches below, seems particularly significant in the context of the curving roof of the Olympic Stadium.

Der Bezug von Calatravas Architektur zu Studien des menschlichen Körpers in Bewegung – wie bei den unten stehenden Skizzen – erscheint im Kontext der gebogenen Dachform des Olympiastadions besonders bezeichnend.

La relation entre les compositions de Calatrava et ses études sur le corps humain en mouvement (tels les croquis ci-dessous), semble particulièrement claire dans le contexte de la couverture en courbe du stade olympique.

The sketch above of a fallen warrior seems directly related to a pedimental sculpture from the Temple of Aphaia in Aegina (c. 500–480 b.c., Munich, Glyptothek), an appropriate reference for this Olympic Stadium in Athens.

Zwischen der oben stehenden Skizze eines gefallenen Kriegers und einer Skulptur vom Giebel des Aphaia-Tempels in Ägina (ca. 500–480 v. Chr., Glyptothek, München) besteht augenscheinlich ein direkter Zusammenhang, eine passende Geste für das Olympiastadion in Athen.

Le croquis (ci-dessus) d'un guerrier à terre semble être une référence directe à une sculpture du fronton du temple d'Aphaia à Égine (vers 500–480 av. J.-C., Munich, Glyptothèque), référence tout à fait appropriée s'agissant du stade olympique d'Athènes.

The actual structures tend to be more complex than the drawings. Numerous devices seen in other contexts—the suspended spire present in the upper part of the Montjuïc Tower (in the middle) or the angled arches (on both sides) and seen in many Calatrava bridges—here serve other functions.

Die realisierten Bauten sind in der Regel komplexer als Calatravas Zeichnungen. Viele Einfälle aus anderen Zusammenhängen – die hängende Spitze vom oberen Teil des Torre de Montjuïc (mittig) oder die geneigten Bögen (seitlich), wie bei vielen Brücken Calatravas – übernehmen hier andere Funktionen.

Les projets réalisés sont en général plus complexes que les dessins. De nombreux procédés vus dans d'autres contextes – l'antenne suspendue de la partie supérieure de la tour de Montjuïc (au milieu) ou les arcs inclinés (sur les côtés) et présents dans de nombreux ponts de l'architecte –, servent ici d'autres desseins.

The volumetric expression of Calatrava's drawings tends toward simplicity, the essential play of forces and forms that explain his architecture.

Der volumetrische Ausdruck von Calatravas Zeichnungen strebt nach Einfachheit und zeigt das seiner Architektur zugrunde liegende essenzielle Spiel der Kräfte und Formen.

L'expression volumétrique des dessins de Calatrava tend à la simplicité, mettant en valeur le jeu essentiel des forces et des formes qui nourrissent son architecture.

The spectacular empty space of the Athens Olympic Stadium seen to the right or the array of fountains leading to one of the arches (above) speak with the eloquence of forms designed by an engineer, and yet they are also imbued with an aesthetic sense, one that sets Calatrava apart from his contemporaries.

Der bezwingende leere Innenraum des Athener Olympiastadions (rechts) oder die Phalanx der zu einem der Bögen hinführenden Brunnen (oben) sprechen mit der Eloquenz der von einem Ingenieur erdachten Formen und sind doch darüber hinaus von einem ästhetischen Empfinden erfüllt, das Calatrava von seinen Zeitgenossen abhebt.

Le spectaculaire espace vide du stade olympique d'Athènes (à droite) ou le majestueux ensemble de fontaines menant à l'une des arches (ci-dessus) expriment avec éloquence les idées d'un ingénieur et dégagent, dans le même temps, ce « plus » esthétique qui place Calatrava à part dans l'univers de ses contemporains.

Even Calatrava's critics cannot deny that images such as the one above give an impression of dynamism and modernity, even if it is difficult to classify the architect in any movement in particular. He started in the footsteps of engineers like the Italian, Pier Luigi, Nervi, and he has gone on to trace his own path.

Selbst Calatravas Kritiker können nicht leugnen, dass Bilder wie das oben gezeigte den Eindruck von Dynamik und Modernität vermitteln, auch wenn es schwierig ist, den Architekten einem bestimmten Stil zuzuordnen. Er begann in den Fußstapfen italienischer Ingenieure wie Pler Luigi Nervi und verfolgte dann seinen eigenen Weg.

Même les critiques de Calatrava ne peuvent nier que des images comme celle du haut donnent une impression de dynamisme et de modernité, même s'il est difficile de classifier l'architecte dans un mouvement particulier. Après avoir mis ses pas dans ceux d'ingénieurs comme l'Italien Pier Luigi Nervi, il a su se tracer sa propre voie.

The elegance and simplicity of the Velodrome, seen in the detail above and in the overall, covered image, is an indication of the efficiency of the architect's intervention. He brings daylight into the space and renews it.

Die Eleganz und Schlichtheit des Velodroms, erkennbar in den Details und im gesamten überdachten Bereich, zeugt von der effizienten Gestaltung des Architekten. Er bringt Tageslicht in den Raum und verleiht ihm neues Leben.

L'élégance et la simplicité du vélodrome, visibles dans le détail ci-dessus et dans la vue d'ensemble, illustrent l'efficacité des interventions de l'architecte. En apportant la lumière naturelle dans ce volume, il le renouvelle.

Like the soaring canopies of the Oriente Station in Lisbon (see page 212), the arched entrance seen left and above sets the tone for the Olympic facilities—great open spans associated with fundamental lightness, and not the slightest hint of pomposity.

Ähnlich den schwebenden Überdachungen des Oriente-Bahnhofs in Lissabon (siehe Seite 212) prägt der gewölbte Eingang (links und oben) den Charakter der olympischen Anlagen: weite, offene Spannweiten, die eine elementare Leichtigkeit ausstrahlen ohne den geringsten Hauch von Pomp.

Comme dans le cas des auvents suspendus de la gare de l'Orient à Lisbonne (voir page 212), l'entrée en arc (photos de gauche et ci-dessus) donne le ton de cet équipement olympique : de grandes portées ouvertes associées à une légèreté de construction sans la moindre trace de pompe.

Designs like the architect's broken tile doves above blend with the airy lightness of the entrance sequence seen below.

Details wie die aus Fliesenscherben zusammengesetzten Tauben passen zur luftigen Schwerelosigkeit der Eingangssequenz unten.

Des motifs comme les colombes en tesselles de faïence (en haut) s'allient à la légèreté aérienne des arches de l'entrée (ci-dessous).

Despite being located in the congested Greek capital, the Olympic facilities allow for bucolic views with olive trees such as the one on the right—a kind of reminiscence of the shining city that was ancient Athens.

Trotz ihrer Lage in der belebten griechischen Hauptstadt bieten die olympischen Anlagen idyllische Ausblicke mit Olivenbäumen (rechts) – gewissermaßen eine Reminiszenz an das strahlende Athen der Antike.

Bien que situées dans la capitale grecque congestionnée, les installations olympiques peuvent offrir des vues bucoliques avec par exemple des oliviers, comme à droite, façon de rappeler quelle brillante cité fut l'Athènes antique.

Three views of the *Nations Wall* show its movement and a lightness that seems to defy gravity. As he did in Valencia, Calatrava shows a talent for composing architectural elements in a unified whole, leading to the Olympic Stadium.

Die drei Ansichten der *Nations Wall* zeigen ihre Schwingung und ihre sich über die Schwerkraft anscheinend hinwegsetzende Leichtigkeit. Wie bereits in Valencia stellt Calatrava seine Begabung zur Komposition architektonischer Elemente zu einem organischen Ganzen unter Beweis mit dem Olympiastadion als Höhepunkt.

Ces trois vues du *Mur de la Nation* montrent à la fois son mouvement et une légèreté qui semble défier la pesanteur. Comme à Valence, Calatrava démontre ici son talent à réunir des éléments architecturaux divers en un tout harmonieux, aboutissant au stade olympique.

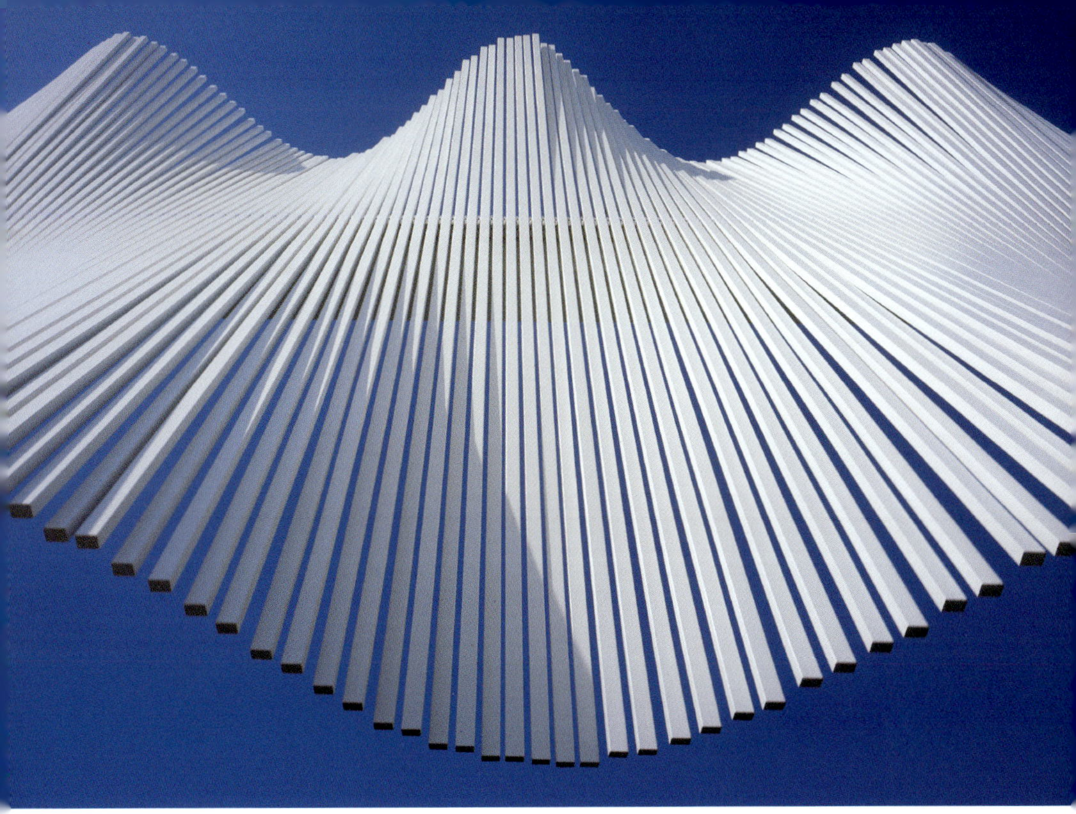

WORLD TRADE CENTER TRANSPORTATION HUB

New York, USA. 2003–2016.

Project

WORLD TRADE CENTER TRANSPORTATION HUB

Location

NEW YORK, USA

Client

PORT AUTHORITY OF NEW YORK & NEW JERSEY

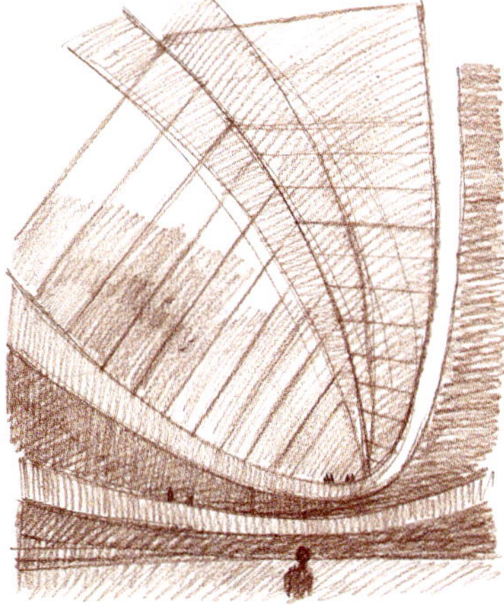

Left page, a bird in flight in front of the ribbed structure of the Transportation Hub. Previous double page, a general view of the site as seen from the National September 11 Memorial.

Linke Seite: Ein Vogel im Flug vor der gerippten Struktur des Bahnhofs. Vorhergehende Doppelseite: Das gesamte Bauwerk vom Mahnmal für den Anschlag des 11. September aus gesehen.

Oiseau en vol sur le fond des nervures de la structure de la plateforme de transports. Double page précédente : vue d'ensemble du site, prise du mémorial national du 11-Septembre.

As might be expected given the circumstances, the plans to rebuild the area around the former World Trade Center in New York were wracked by disagreements and changes. One of the few projects that advanced as originally planned is that of Santiago Calatrava for a new, permanent transportation hub, designed to serve riders of the Port Authority Trans-Hudson (PATH) commuter trains, New York city subway trains (1/9, E and N/R lines), and a potential rail link to John F. Kennedy International Airport. Set directly to the east of the footprint of the Twin Towers, now the 9/11 Memorial called *Reflecting Absence* (architect, Michael Arad), work on the Hub was carried out with DMJM + Harris as well as the STV Group. It is next to Four World Trade Center by Fumihiko Maki. As is almost always the case in Calatrava's work, the Transportation Hub has a spectacular element—a freestanding structure made of glass and steel bringing forth the image of "a bird released from a child's hands" and measuring about 107 meters long, 35 meters across at its widest point, and 49 meters high from the lower concourse to the apex of the skylight. As the architect explains: "The steel ribs that support this structure extend upward into a pair of canopies, which resemble outspread wings and rise to a maximum height of 51 meters." The main concourse of the hub is located about 10 meters below street level, and the PATH train platforms eight meters lower. In good weather and on each September 11, the roof can be opened to the sky. Both the birdlike form and the possibility to open the roof are typical gestures of Calatrava, and yet, in this instance, both take on a particularly poignant and appropriate meaning. Calatrava's ability to deal with the considerable local, state, city, and business bureaucracies involved in each step of the design is a testament to his capacity to overcome substantial obstacles to obtain what he wants.

Wie unter den gegebenen Umständen zu erwarten, fielen viele Pläne für den Wiederaufbau des Gebiets um das frühere World Trade Center in New York Unstimmigkeiten und Änderungswünschen zum Opfer. Eines der wenigen Projekte, die wie ursprünglich vorgesehen realisiert wurden, ist der neue Verkehrsknotenpunkt von Santiago Calatrava für die Fahrgäste der Port Authority Trans-Hudson (PATH), der New York City Subway (Linien 1/9, E und N/R) und einer potenziellen Bahnverbindung zum John F. Kennedy International Airport. Der Bau unmittelbar östlich vom früheren Standort der Twin Towers, wo sich jetzt die 9/11-Gedenkstätte namens *Reflecting Absence* (Architekt: Michael Arad) befindet, wurde von der Firma DMJM + Harris sowie der STV Group ausgeführt. Daneben steht das Four World Trade Center von Fumihiko Maki. Wie fast alle Bauten von Calatrava zeichnet sich auch der Transportation Hub durch ein spektakuläres Element aus – eine frei stehende Konstruktion aus Glas und Stahl, die an das Bild „eines Vogels" erinnert, „der aus einer Kinderhand aufsteigt". Sie misst etwa 107 m in der Länge, 35 m an ihrer breitesten Stelle und ist von der unterirdischen Halle bis zu ihrem Scheitelpunkt 49 m hoch. Der Architekt erläutert: „Die stählernen Rippen, welche dieses Bauwerk tragen, ragen aufwärts zu zwei Baldachinen, die ausgebreiteten Flügeln gleichen und sich bis zu einer maximalen Höhe von 51 m erheben." Die große Halle des Bahnhofs befindet sich etwa 10 m unter Straßenniveau; die Gleise der PATH-Züge liegen noch einmal 8 m darunter. Bei gutem Wetter und an jedem 11. September lässt sich das Dach öffnen. Sowohl die vogelähnliche Form als auch die Möglichkeit, das Dach zu öffnen, sind zwar typische Elemente in Calatravas Architektur, erhalten aber in diesem Falle noch eine besonders prägnante und dem Ort angemessene Bedeutung. Calatravas Fähigkeit, sich bei jedem Planungsschritt mit der nicht unerheblichen Bürokratie auf örtlicher, staatlicher und kommunaler Ebene sowie mit finanziellen Belangen auseinanderzusetzen, zeigt wieder einmal, dass er beachtliche Hindernisse zu überwinden vermag, um seine Ziele zu erreichen.

Comme on avait pu s'y attendre dans ce contexte, les plans de reconstruction de la zone de l'ancien World Trade Center à New York ont été marqués par des controverses et des changements. L'un des rares projets à progresser comme prévu à l'origine est celui de Santiago Calatrava pour la nouvelle plateforme de transports destinée aux utilisateurs des trains de banlieue de la Port Authority Trans-Hudson (PATH), du métro new-yorkais (lignes 1/9, E et N/R) et d'une future liaison prévue avec l'aéroport international John F. Kennedy. Implanté directement à proximité du Four World Trade Center de Fumihiko Maki et à l'est de l'ancienne empreinte des Tours jumelles, aujourd'hui Mémorial 9/11 appelé *Reflecting Absence* (architecte Michael Arad), ses travaux ont été menés avec DMJM + Harris et le STV Group. Comme c'est presque toujours le cas chez Calatrava, ce hub s'exprime à travers un élément spectaculaire, une structure autoporteuse en verre et acier à l'image « d'un oiseau s'échappant des mains d'un enfant », mesurant environ 107 mètres de long, 35 dans sa plus grande largeur et 49 de hauteur du hall inférieur à son sommet. Comme l'explique l'architecte : « Les nervures d'acier qui composent la structure se développent vers le haut en forme de deux auvents, qui ressemblent à des ailes déployées s'élevant à une hauteur maximum de 51 mètres. » Le hall principal de la plateforme est situé à 10 mètres au-dessous du niveau du sol et les quais du PATH huit mètres plus bas. Par beau temps, et chaque 11 septembre, le toit peut s'ouvrir vers le ciel. La forme en ailes d'oiseau et cette possibilité d'ouverture de la toiture sont des gestes typiques de Calatrava, mais qui prennent néanmoins ici tous deux un sens particulièrement poignant et approprié. L'habileté de Calatrava à traiter avec les lourdes bureaucraties locales, d'État, municipales et des promoteurs impliqués dans chaque étape du projet témoigne de sa capacité à surmonter les obstacles les plus importants pour obtenir ce qu'il veut.

The ribs are angled and spaced in such a way so as to provide very different perspectives according to the location of the visitor and the time of day.

Die Rippen sind so geneigt und angeordnet, dass sie je nach Standort des Besuchers und Tageszeit immer neue Perspektiven eröffnen.

Les nervures, inclinées et espacées, offrent des perspectives très différentes selon l'endroit où se trouve le visiteur et l'heure de la journée.

Bennett
sugarfina

Left, a sketch of the structure by Santiago Calatrava. Above, as seen from street level the soaring wings of the building resemble a bird taking flight. Right page, detail images of the ribbed design.

Links: eine Zeichnung des Bauwerks von Santiago Calatrava. Oben: Von der Straße gesehen, ähnelt das Gebäude den Flügeln eines emporfliegenden Vogels. Rechte Seite: Detailaufnahmen der Rippenstruktur.

À gauche : croquis de la structure par Santiago Calatrava. Au-dessus : vues prises au niveau de la rue. Les deux ailes déployées du bâtiment font penser à un oiseau prenant son envol. Page de droite : détails des nervures d'acier.

The Oculus is the central space of the World Trade Center Transportation Hub. It is approximately 107 meters long, 35 meters across at its widest point, and rises from the lower concourse to a height of 49 meters at the apex of the skylight.

Der Oculus bildet den zentralen Bereich des World Trade Center Transportation Hub. Er ist etwa 107 m lang, an seiner weitesten Stelle 35 m breit und erreicht von der unterirdischen Halle bis zum Scheitelpunkt eine Höhe von 49 m.

L'Oculus est l'espace central du World Trade Center Transportation Hub. D'environ 107 mètres de long par 35 au point le plus large, il s'élève à 49 mètres de hauteur du hall inférieur à son sommet.

Six of the many drawings prepared by Santiago Calatrava that give the client a clear idea of the vast interior of the building.

Sechs der vielen Zeichnungen, mit denen Santiago Calatrava dem Bauherrn einen guten Eindruck vom großzügigen Innenraum des Bauwerks vermittelte.

Six des nombreux dessins préparatoires de Santiago Calatrava qui ont donné au client une idée précise du vaste volume intérieur du bâtiment.

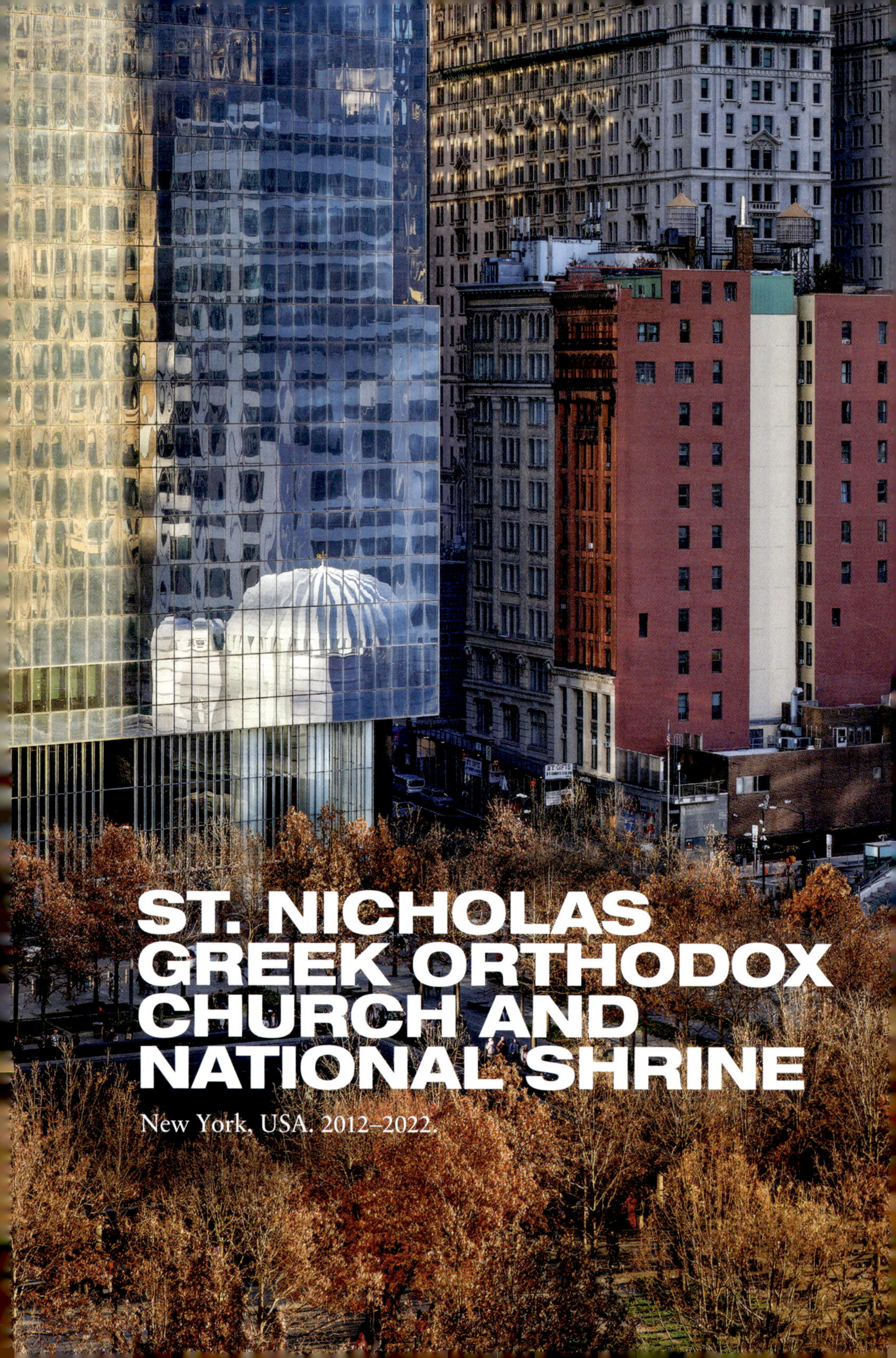

ST. NICHOLAS GREEK ORTHODOX CHURCH AND NATIONAL SHRINE

New York, USA. 2012–2022.

Project

ST. NICHOLAS GREEK ORTHODOX CHURCH AND NATIONAL SHRINE

Location

NEW YORK, USA

Client

GREEK ORTHODOX ARCHDIOCESE OF AMERICA

Height

15.96 METERS

Building area

1068 m² (ABOVE PLAZA LEVEL)

Calatrava's design was chosen over a dozen other schemes and was influenced in its form by Hagia Sophia and the Church of the Holy Savior in Chora, both in Istanbul. Here the church glows from within at nightfall.

Calatravas Entwurf wurde aus einem Dutzend anderer Vorschläge ausgewählt und zeigt Einflüsse der Hagia Sophia und der Erlöserkirche in Chora, beide in Istanbul. Hier leuchtet die Kirche bei Einbruch der Dunkelheit von innen.

Le projet de Calatrava a été choisi parmi plus de douze autres. Sa forme rappelle la basilique Sainte-Sophie et l'église du Saint-Sauveur-in-Chora, à stanbul. L'église est illuminée à la nuit tombée.

Eight years after its cornerstone was laid in 2014, Calatrava's first religious building, the St. Nicholas Greek Orthodox Church and National Shrine opened in 2022 next to the World Trade Center Memorial in Manhattan. An earlier Greek Orthodox church, located at 155 Cedar Street, near the South Tower of the former World Trade Center, was the only religious structure destroyed on September 11, 2001. In 2008, the Port Authority of New York purchased the land on which the church had stood, and committed to providing a new site, three times larger and less than 50 meters to the east, on the elevated platform of Liberty Park. Santiago Calatrava was selected as the architect and he carefully studied Byzantine architecture and art finding inspiration in a mosaic representing the Virgin Mary on "The Throne of Wisdom" in Hagia Sophia in Istanbul, which was originally built as a Greek Orthodox church. Although Calatrava was involved in the interiors, the paintings now in place were executed by a priest-monk at the Monastery of Xenophontos on Mount Athos and brought to New York before the opening. Both the layout of the church and these paintings are inscribed along the traditional lines of Orthodox liturgy, which church officials were careful to preserve. As Santiago Calatrava stated to the author: "I wanted to create a space that directly addresses the traditional Greek Orthodox liturgy while honoring the church's connection to the greater World Trade Center Memorial site, which is why the mosaic in Hagia Sophia was fundamental in defining the shape of the St. Nicholas Greek Orthodox Church. Building the church with Pentelic marble adds another level of symbolism, as the Parthenon in Greece was made of the same material, and I consider Hagia Sophia the Parthenon of Orthodoxy. Creating the dome out of thin stone and glass that are illuminated from within is also meant to invoke the feeling of being a beacon of hope amid the night."

Acht Jahre nach der Grundsteinlegung 2014 wurde mit der St. Nicholas Greek Orthodox Church and National Shrine 2022 neben Manhattans World Trade Center Memorial Calatravas erstes sakralbauliches Projekt eingeweiht. Die frühere griechisch-orthodoxe Kirche in 155 Cedar Street nahe dem Südturm des ehemaligen World Trade Center, war das einzige religiöse Gebäude, das am 11. September 2001 zerstört worden war. 2008 erwarb die New Yorker Hafenbehörde das Grundstück dieser Kirche und verpflichtete sich, einen neuen, dreimal größeren Standort weniger als 50 m östlich auf der Anhöhe des Liberty Park bereitzustellen. Santiago Calatrava wurde als Architekt ausgewählt und ließ sich von der byzantinischen Architektur und Kunst inspirieren, insbesondere von einem Mosaik der Jungfrau Maria auf dem „Thron der Weisheit" in der einst als griechisch-orthodoxe Kirche erbauten Hagia Sophia in Istanbul. Obwohl Calatrava bei den Innenräumen mitwirkte, wurden die Gemälde von einem Priestermönch im Kloster Xenophontos auf dem Berg Athos ausgeführt und vor der Eröffnung nach New York gebracht. Sowohl der Grundriss der Kirche als auch diese Gemälde folgen den traditionellen Linien der orthodoxen Liturgie, deren Bewahrung den Kirchenverantwortlichen wichtig war. „Ich wollte einen Raum schaffen, der die traditionelle griechisch-orthodoxe Liturgie direkt anspricht und gleichzeitig die Verbindung der Kirche zur größeren Gedenkstätte des World Trade Center ehrt", erklärte Calatrava dem Autor, „weshalb das Mosaik in der Hagia Sophia entscheidend für die Gestaltung der St. Nicholas Greek Orthodox Church war. Der Bau der Kirche aus pentelischem Marmor fügt eine weitere symbolische Ebene hinzu, da der Parthenon in Griechenland aus demselben Material besteht und ich die Hagia Sophia als den Parthenon der Orthodoxie betrachte. Auch die von innen beleuchtete Kuppel aus dünnem Stein und Glas soll das Gefühl vermitteln, ein Leuchtfeuer der Hoffnung inmitten der Nacht zu sein."

Huit ans après la pose de la première pierre en 2014, le premier édifice religieux construit par Calatrava, l'église grecque orthodoxe St. Nicolas et sanctuaire national de Manhattan, a ouvert ses portes en 2022 à côté du mémorial du World Trade Center. La première église grecque-orthodoxe du 155 Cedar Street, près de la tour sud de l'ancien World Trade Center, est le seul bâtiment religieux à avoir été détruit le 11 septembre 2001. En 2008, les autorités portuaires de New York acquièrent le terrain où elle se trouvait et lui attribuent un nouvel emplacement, trois fois plus grand, à moins de 50 mètres à l'est, sur la plate-forme surélevée de Liberty Park. Santiago Calatrava est sélectionné pour être l'architecte de la nouvelle église, il étudie de près l'architecture et l'art byzantins et trouve l'inspiration dans une mosaïque de la Vierge Marie sur « le trône de la sagesse » de la mosquée Hagia Sophia, à Istanbul, ancienne église grecque-orthodoxe. Il a travaillé à l'intérieur de l'église, mais les peintures qui s'y trouvent sont l'œuvre d'un moine et prêtre du monastère de Xénophon, sur le mont Athos. Elles ont été transférées à New York avant l'ouverture. La forme générale de l'église et ces peintures s'inscrivent dans la tradition de la liturgie orthodoxe que les autorités ecclésiastiques tenaient à préserver. Santiago Calatrava nous a expliqué : « J'ai voulu créer un espace destiné directement à la liturgie grecque-orthodoxe traditionnelle, tout en rendant hommage au lien entre l'église et le mémorial plus important du World Trade Center, c'est pourquoi la mosaïque de Sainte-Sophie a été essentielle pour définir la forme de l'église St. Nicolas. De même, construire l'église en marbre du Pentélique a ajouté un niveau de symbolisme puisque c'est le marbre utilisé pour le Parthénon et que je considère Hagia Sophia comme le Parthénon de l'orthodoxie. Enfin, le dôme de pierre fine et de verre éclairé de l'intérieur doit donner le sentiment que donne une lueur d'espoir dans la nuit. »

A sketch by the architect shows the plan of the church, which seems to recall both traditional Greek Orthodox church design and other preoccupations of the architect, such as the shape of the human eye.

Eine Zeichnung des Architekten zeigt den Grundriss der Kirche, der sowohl an die traditionelle griechisch-orthodoxe Kirchenarchitektur wie auch an andere typische Bezüge des Architekten, etwa die Form des menschlichen Auges, erinnert.

Un croquis de l'architecte montre le plan au sol de l'église, qui semble rappeler à la fois ceux des églises orthodoxes grecques et d'autres préoccupations de l'architecte comme la forme de l'œil humain.

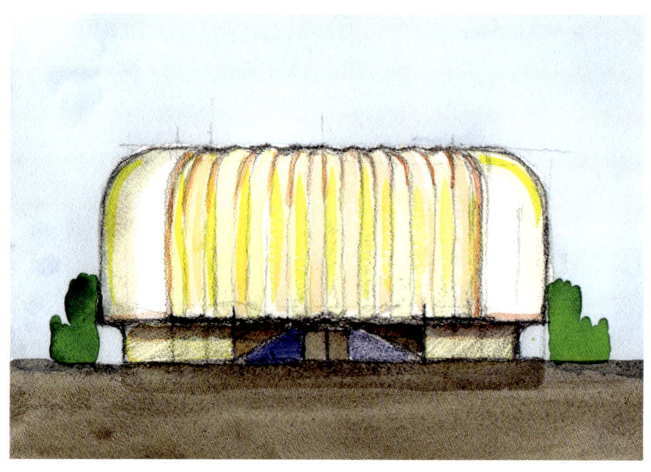

Calatrava's watercolor sketches give an idea of his interest in light and space as it is expressed in this religious structure.

Calatravas Aquarelle geben eine Vorstellung von seinem Interesse für Licht und Raum, das auch dieses religiöse Bauwerk prägt.

Les croquis à l'aquarelle de Calatrava donnent une idée de son intérêt pour la lumière et l'espace, comme exprimé dans cet édifice religieux.

The site of the church posed considerable constraints of size and orientation. A model and photograph (right and below) show the church and its immediate environment near the World Trade Center Memorial fountains.

Der Standort brachte beträchtliche Einschränkungen hinsichtlich Größe und Ausrichtung der Kirche mit sich. Modell und Foto (rechts und unten) zeigen sie in ihrer unmittelbaren Umgebung der Gedenkbrunnen des World Trade Centers.

Un croquis de l'architecte montre le plan de l'église, qui semble rappeler à la fois ceux des églises orthodoxes grecques et d'autres préoccupations de l'architecte comme la forme de l'œil humain.

SAINT NICHOLAS

IC
XC
ΕΙΡΗΝΗ ΥΜΙΝ ΕΓΩ ΕΙΜΙ
ΤΟ ΦΩΣ ΤΟΥ ΚΟΣΜΟΥ

Calatrava's drawings of the Virgin and Child, above, show the influence of this form on the new church. Left, the interior cupola, and, below, another drawing by the architect. The interior paintings are by a Greek Orthodox monk.

Calatravas Zeichnungen der Jungfrau mit Kind (oben) zeigen den Einfluss dieser Form auf die neue Kirche. Links: die Innenkuppel. Unten: eine weitere Zeichnung des Architekten. Die Innenmalereien stammen von einem griechisch-orthodoxen Mönch.

Ces dessins par Calatrava d'une Vierge à l'enfant, en haut, montrent l'influence de cette forme sur la nouvelle église. À gauche, on voit l'intérieur de la coupole, et ci-dessous, un autre dessin de l'architecte. Les peintures de l'intérieur sont l'œuvre d'un moine orthodoxe grec.

CHICAGO SPIRE

Chicago, Illinois, USA. 2005 (design).

Project
CHICAGO SPIRE

Location
CHICAGO, ILLINOIS, USA

Client
SHELBOURNE DEVELOPMENT

Height
610 METERS

Floor area
278 700 m²

Calatrava's drawings cannot always be specifically related to a project or a detail of a project, and yet the movement of the human body, or of animals, appears to constantly inform his research into new forms.

Calatravas Zeichnungen lassen sich nicht immer bestimmten Projekten oder Projektdetails zuordnen, doch scheinen Körper in Bewegung, menschliche ebenso wie die von Tieren, seine Suche nach neuen Formen zu beeinflussen.

Les dessins de Calatrava ne peuvent pas être systématiquement reliés à un projet précis ou au détail d'un projet et cependant le mouvement du corps humain, ou celui des animaux, réapparaît constamment dans sa recherche de formes nouvelles.

Located on North Water Street at Lake Shore Drive, this 150-story condominium structure will be the tallest building in the United States, as well might seem appropriate in a city that long held the record for the tallest building in the world. Located on a one-hectare site, the tower was originally to have a footprint of just 1300 square meters and a gross floor area of 85 500 square meters. Enlarged to include as many as 1300 condominiums, the new design is broader than the original and has a much higher floor area as well. As the architect's office describes the design: "Based on a sculpture by Santiago Calatrava, the building is a tall, slender elegant form whose glass façade seems to ripple downward in waves, like the folds of a cloak swirling around a figure. This effect is achieved by means of a structural innovation. Each floor unit of the tower is built out from the central core like a separate box, with gently curving, concave sides. As these boxes are stacked up, each is rotated by a little more than two degrees from the one below. In this way, the floors turn 270 degrees around the core as they rise, giving the façade an impression of movement." Floor-to-ceiling windows and column-free floor plans will allow both hotel and condominium residents to have breathtaking views. Calatrava specifically links his design proposal, in its rippling aspect, to his sculptures such as the MoMA *Shadow Machine* or the SMU *Wave*, as well as architectural works like the Brise Soleil at the Milwaukee Art Museum (see page 232) or the curving roof of the Bodegas Ysios (see page 264). The idea of cantilevered geometric modules suspended from a central core is of course explored both in the Turning Torso (see page 276) and 80 South Street Tower. In his capacity as an engineer, Calatrava has also carefully examined the strength of the structural core of the tower and its ample emergency exits. He further advances that its twisting form will reduce the lateral force of wind gusts on the structure.

Das in der North Water Street am Lake Michigan geplante, 150-geschossige Hochhaus mit Eigentumswohnungen wird das höchste Gebäude der Vereinigten Staaten sein, durchaus passend für eine Stadt, die lange den Rekord für das höchste Bauwerk der Welt innehatte. Der Turm, der auf einem 1 ha großen Baugelände errichtet wird, sollte sich auf einer Grundfläche von nur 1300 m² erheben und eine Bruttogeschossfläche von 85 500 m² haben. Das neue Design ist nun breiter als ursprünglich geplant und bietet mehr Grundfläche und Raum für insgesamt 1300 Apartments. Das Büro des Architekten beschreibt den Entwurf so: „Das auf einer Skulptur von Santiago Calatrava basierende Gebäude zeichnet sich durch eine hoch aufragende, schlanke, elegante Form aus, deren Glasfassade wellenförmig nach unten fließt wie die Falten eines Umhangs, der um eine Figur schwingt. Dieser Effekt entsteht durch eine bauliche Neuerung. Jede Geschosseinheit wird vom zentralen Kern aus nach außen gebaut wie ein autarker Kasten mit sanft gebogenen, konkaven Seiten. Beim Stapeln dieser Kästen wird jeder um etwas mehr als 2° über dem darunterliegenden verschoben. Auf diese Art vollziehen die Geschosse mit zunehmender Höhe um den Kern herum eine Drehung von 270° und lassen die Fassade bewegt erscheinen.“ Deckenhohe Fenster und stützenfreie Grundrisse ermöglichen Hotelgästen wie Bewohnern überwältigende Ausblicke. Calatrava setzt seinen Entwurf wegen des Welleneffekts in Bezug zu seinen Skulpturen *Shadow Machine* im MoMA oder *Wave* im Meadows Museum und zu architektonischen Werken wie der Sonnenblende am Kunstmuseum Milwaukee (siehe Seite 232) oder dem geschwungenen Dach der Bodegas Ysios (siehe Seite 264). Die Idee, einen zentralen Kern mit auskragenden, geometrischen Modulen zu bestücken, wurde auch beim Turning Torso (siehe Seite 276) und dem South Street Tower verwirklicht. In seiner Eigenschaft als Bauingenieur hat Calatrava die Stärke des tragenden Turmkerns wie auch die zahlreichen Notausgänge einer sorgfältigen Prüfung unterzogen. Er führt ferner aus, dass die gedrehte Form des Gebäudes die seitliche Kraft der Windböen verringern wird.

Située North Water Street près de Lake Shore Drive, cette tour de 150 étages prévue pour des appartements sera l'immeuble le plus haut des États-Unis, ce qui convient à une ville qui a longtemps détenu le record du plus haut immeuble du monde. Édifiée sur un terrain d'un hectare, elle devait n'occuper à l'origine qu'une emprise au sol de 1 300 mètres carrés pour une surface utile totale de 85 500 mètres carrés. Agrandi pour offrir 1 300 appartements, le nouveau design est plus vaste. Selon la description de l'agence : « Inspiré d'une sculpture de Santiago Calatrava, l'immeuble présente une forme élégante et élancée dont la façade de verre semble ondoyer en vagues descendantes, comme les plis d'un manteau. Cet effet est dû à une innovation structurelle. Chaque appartement est construit à partir du noyau central comme une boîte indépendante à faces délicatement incurvées. En s'emplilant les unes sur les autres, ces boîtes pivotent chacune d'un peu plus de deux degrés par rapport à la boîte inférieure. De cette façon, les niveaux tournent de 270 degrés autour de l'axe central, ce qui crée une impression de mouvement. » Des baies du sol au plafond et des espaces ouverts dénués de piliers permettront aux clients de l'hôtel comme aux résidents de bénéficier de vues à couper le souffle. Calatrava relie spécifiquement cet aspect ondoyant à certaines de ses sculptures, comme la *Shadow Machine* du MoMA, la *Wave* du Meadows Museum des réalisations architecturales comme le brise-soleil du Milwaukee Art Museum (voir page 232) ou le toit ondulé des Bodegas Ysios (voir page 264). L'idée de modules géométriques en porte-à-faux accrochés à un noyau central est par ailleurs explorée dans les tours du Turning Torso (voir page 276) et de South Street. En tant qu'ingénieur, Calatrava a également étudié avec soin la résistance du noyau structurel de la tour et les questions de sécurité ; il pense que cette forme en torsion réduira les forces latérales du vent sur la tour.

As his sketches show, Calatrava wishes to impart a dynamic twisting movement to this very high tower—a structure that will be subjected to the high winds typical of Chicago's lakefront.

Wie seine Skizzen zeigen, möchte Calatrava diesem sehr hohen Turm eine dynamische Drehbewegung verleihen – einem Bauwerk, das dem für Chicago typischen Wind vom Michigansee ausgesetzt sein wird.

Comme le montrent ses croquis, Calatrava souhaite insuffler un mouvement de torsion dynamique à cette très haute tour, structure qui sera soumise aux vents violents caractéristiques de Chicago.

Even when compared with such very large buildings as the Willis Tower or John Hancock Center, the tower soars higher still while retaining the lightness that is one of Calatrava's trademarks.

Der Turm übertrifft mit seiner Höhe selbst Gebäude wie den Willis Tower oder das John Hancock Center und bewahrt gleichwohl die für Calatrava charakteristische Leichtigkeit.

Comparée à des tours aussi importantes que la Willis Tower ou le John Hancock Center, la « Chicago Spire » s'élève encore plus haut, tout en conservant la légèreté qui caractérise les œuvres de Calatrava.

CONSTELLATION

River Point Park, Chicago, Illinois, USA. 2020.

Project
CONSTELLATION

Location
RIVER POINT PARK, CHICAGO, ILLINOIS, USA

Client
RIVERPOINT PARTNERS IVANHOÉ CAMBRIDGE, HINES AND LEVY FAMILY PARTNER

Height
8.8 METERS

Left, the sculpture and its reflection seen in front of the parabolic arch that marks the entrance to River Point Tower (not designed by Calatrava).

Links: die Skulptur und ihre Spiegelung vor dem parabolischen Bogen, der den Eingang des River Point Tower markiert (nicht von Calatrava entworfen).

À gauche, la sculpture et son reflet devant l'arche parabolique qui marque l'entrée de la River Point Tower (qui n'a pas été créée par Calatrava).

Constellation is a bright-red, spiraling, welded-aluminum sculpture installed in front of the 52-story River Point Tower (architect: Pickard Chilton) in the Fulton River District of Chicago, at the northern edge of the Loop. The work by Santiago Calatrava was commissioned and financed by the developers of River Point, Ivanhoé Cambridge, Hines, and Levy Family Partners. It is set on a steel pedestal anchored in a circular concrete base that is covered by a grass mound. The work is 8.8-meters high and equally wide, and it echoes the parabolic arch that fronts the River Point Tower. Its spiraling form assumes different aspects depending on the angle of view. According to Hines: "Calatrava's intention in this sculpture is for it to simply grow from the ground. Within each figure, an internal logic of autonomy delivers lyrical forms and implies a sense of elevation and spiritual uplifting, reflecting the building's mirrored architectural arch." Revealed in 2018, the work was delayed by approximately a year because the Cleveland firm in charge of its fabrication had to give priority to the repair of faulty fuel tanks made for NASA. Other works of public art nearby include Olafur Eliasson's *Atmospheric Wave Wall*, Alexander Calder's *Flamingo* in Federal Plaza, and Anish Kapoor's *Cloud Gate* in Millennium Park.

Diese leuchtend rote spiralförmige Skulptur aus geschweißtem Aluminium steht im Chicagoer Fulton River District nördlich des Loop vor dem 52-stöckigen River Point Tower (Architekt: Pickard Chilton). In Auftrag gegeben und finanziert wurde sie von den Bauherren und Eigentümern des River Point Towers: Ivanhoé Cambridge, Hines und Levy Family Partners. Ihr Stahlsockel ist in einem runden, von einem Grashügel bedeckten Betonfundament verankert. Das Kunstwerk von je 8,8 m Höhe und Breite stellt das Gegenstück zum parabolischen Bogen der River-Point-Tower-Fassade dar. Je nach Blickwinkel offenbart seine spiralförmige Form unterschiedliche Eindrücke und Facetten. „Calatrava schuf diese Skulptur, indem er sie schlicht aus dem Boden emporwachsen ließ", so Hines. „Die innere Logik jedes ihrer Elemente schafft ihre eigenen lyrischen Formen. Das Werk erweckt ein erhebendes Gefühl spirituellen Aufstiegs und spiegelt damit den architektonischen Bogen des Gebäudes wider." Die für 2017 geplante Enthüllung der Skulptur verzögerte sich um etwa ein Jahr, da die mit der Herstellung beauftragte Firma aus Cleveland der Reparatur fehlerhafter NASA-Treibstofftanks Vorrang einräumen musste. In der Nähe befinden sich weitere öffentliche Kunstwerke, darunter Olafur Eliassons *Atmospheric Wave Wall*, Alexander Calders *Flamingo* auf der Federal Plaza und Anish Kapoors *Cloud Gate* im Millennium Park.

Constellation est une sculpture faite d'une spirale d'aluminium soudé rouge vif, elle a été placée devant le gratte-ciel River Point de 52 étages (architecte : Pickard Chilton) dans le Fulton River District de Chicago, à l'extrémité nord du Loop. L'œuvre de Santiago Calatrava a été commandée et financée par les développeurs du River Point, Ivanhoé Cambridge, Hines et Levy Family Partners. Elle est posée sur un socle en acier moulé dans une base circulaire en béton qui est elle-même recouverte d'un monticule herbeux. Sa hauteur est de 8,8 mètres, de même que sa largeur, et elle fait écho à l'arche parabolique à l'avant de l'immeuble. Sa forme en spirale change d'aspect selon l'angle sous lequel elle est vue. Pour Hines : « Calatrava veut simplement que cette sculpture donne l'impression de s'élever à partir du sol. Chaque motif comporte sa propre logique dont découlent des formes lyriques et un sentiment d'élévation et d'envol spirituel reflétant l'arche architecturale de l'immeuble. » Révélée en 2018, la réalisation de l'œuvre a été retardée de presque un an car l'entreprise de Cleveland qui en était chargée a dû réparer en priorité des réservoirs défectueux de carburant pour la NASA. D'autres œuvres d'art ornent l'espace public à proximité, parmi lesquelles *Atmospheric Wave Wall* d'Olafur Eliasson, *Flamingo* d'Alexander Calder sur Federal Plaza et *Cloud Gate* d'Anish Kapoor dans le Millennium Park.

The photograph and drawings show the scale of the sculpture which is perched on a single point, almost seeming to defy gravity.

Das Foto und die Zeichnungen verdeutlichen die Größe der Skulptur, die auf einem einzigen Punkt balanciert und fast der Schwerkraft zu trotzen scheint.

La photographie et le schéma ci-dessous montrent l'échelle de la sculpture posée sur un seul point, comme pour défier les lois de la gravité.

ERNST & YOUNG

MARGARET HUNT HILL BRIDGE

Dallas, Texas, USA. 2010–2012.

Project
MARGARET HUNT HILL BRIDGE

Location
DALLAS, TEXAS, USA

Client
CITY OF DALLAS

Height / length / width
136 x 418.5 x 36.7 METERS

Maximum span
209.25 METERS

Cost
$ 44 MILLION

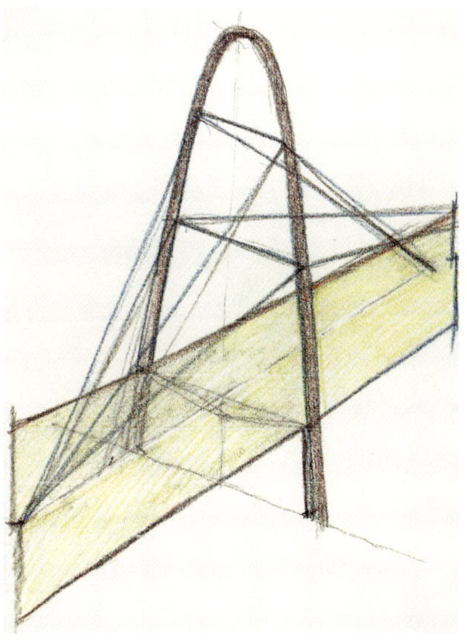

The high arch of this bridge and its night lighting, as seen to the left, make it appear like a great sculpture. The relatively simple drawing to the above and the completed work are very similar.

Der hohe Bogen dieser Brücke und ihre nächtliche Beleuchtung (wie links zu sehen) lassen sie wie eine große Skulptur erscheinen. Die relativ einfache Zeichnung oben und das ausgeführte Bauwerk ähneln sich sehr.

La grande arche du pont et son éclairage nocturne (à gauche) en font une sorte de sculpture. Le croquis relativement simple (ci-dessus) et le pont achevé sont très similaires.

This cable-stayed steel bridge with a white parabolic pylon located in Dallas is seen as a major step in revitalizing the city, connecting the downtown area to West Dallas. The bridge carries six lanes of traffic across the Trinity River and is 418.5 meters long, 36.7 meters wide, and spans 209.25 meters. The central support pylon is 136 meters high, giving the bridge a considerable presence in the city. The 58 cables, with diameters ranging from 127 to 165 millimeters and lengths ranging from 119 to 196 meters, distribute the loads of the structure through the slender and spectacular arched pylon. The actual pylon is a closed steel tube with internal diaphragms, stiffeners, and anchors for the cables. The Margaret Hunt Hill Bridge was the first of a series of bridges designed by Santiago Calatrava to span the Trinity River and also Calatrava's first vehicular bridge in the United States.

Diese stählerne Schrägseilbrücke mit einem weißen, parabolischen Pylon in Dallas, die die Innenstadt mit dem westlichen Stadtbereich verbindet, gilt als wichtige Maßnahme zur Stadterneuerung. Sie führt mit sechs Verkehrsspuren über den Trinity River und ist 418,5 m lang, 36,7 m breit und hat eine Spannweite von 209,25 m. Der zentrale Pylon ist 136 m hoch und verleiht der Brücke eine beachtliche Präsenz in der Stadt. Die 58 Stahlseile mit Durchmessern von 127 bis 165 mm und Längen von 119 bis 196 m verteilen die Lasten der Konstruktion über den schlanken und spektakulär gebogenen Pylon. Dieser besteht aus einem geschlossenen Stahlrohr und enthält Zwischenwände, Aussteifungen und Verankerungen für die Stahlseile. Diese Brücke war die erste von mehreren, die Santiago Calatrava über den Trinity River geplant hat, und auch seine erste Fahrzeugbrücke in den Vereinigten Staaten.

Ce pont en acier à haubans et pylône parabolique blanc est considéré comme une avancée majeure de la revitalisation urbaine de Dallas dont il relie le centre aux quartiers ouest. Son tablier à six voies de 36,7 mètres de large et de 418,5 mètres de portée surplombe la Trinity River. Le pylône central de 136 mètres de haut lui assure une présence monumentale. Les 58 câbles, de diamètres de 127 à 165 mm et de longueurs allant de 119 à 196 mètres, distribuent les charges structurelles vers ce fin et spectaculaire pylône en forme d'arc. Il est constitué d'un tube d'acier fermé à diaphragmes, raidisseurs et système d'ancrage des câbles intégrés. Ce pont est le premier d'une série d'ouvrages conçus par Santiago Calatrava sur la Trinity River, et aussi le premier destiné à la circulation automobile conçu par l'architecte aux États-Unis.

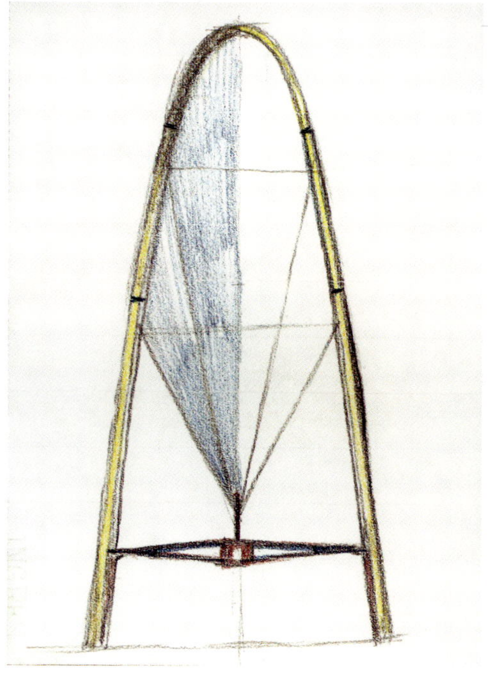

In this instance, Calatrava's drawing of a man seems almost more earthbound than the forms he sketches for the bridge, which is willfully conceived according to the rules of nature.

In diesem Fall wirkt Calatravas Zeichnung eines Mannes fast erdverbundener als seine Skizzen für die Brücke, die er bewusst nach den Gesetzen der Natur konzipierte.

Dans ce cas précis, le dessin de l'homme semble d'esprit descriptif plus réaliste que les formes du pont vues dans le croquis, conçues délibérément selon les règles de la nature.

Right page, another sketch by Santiago Calatrava emphasizes the movement of several figures, tracing lines of force in space. Again, the bridge seems airy in comparison.

Rechts: Eine weitere Zeichnung von Santiago Calatrava zeigt die Bewegung einiger Figuren, die den Kraftlinien im Raum folgen. Im Vergleich wirkt die Brücke wiederum leicht.

Page de droite : un autre croquis de l'architecte met scène plusieurs figures traçant des lignes de force dans l'espace. Par comparaison, le pont semble d'une légèreté aérienne.

The light structure of the bridge stands out against the heavier architectural environment of the city, while emphasizing an upward movement shared by the skyscrapers.

Die leichte Struktur der Brücke hebt sich von der massiveren Architektur der Stadt ab und betont gleichzeitig die Aufwärtsbewegung der Wolkenkratzer.

Légère, la structure se détache de l'environnement des tours du centre-ville, tout en reprenant le mouvement vers le haut partagé par les gratte-ciel.

REGGIO EMILIA AV – MEDIOPADANA STATION

Reggio Emilia, Italy. 2010–2014.

Project

REGGIO EMILIA AV – MEDIOPADANA STATION

Location

REGGIO EMILIA, ITALY

Client

COMUNE DI REGGIO EMILIA AND TRENO AD ALTA VELOCITÀ SPA (TAV)

Site area

150 000 m²

Floor area

30 000 m²

Total length

495 METERS

Cost

€ 70 MILLION ESTIMATED

A fan-shaped canopy marks the entrance to the station and echoes the design of the building visible behind it.

Das fächerförmige Vordach markiert den Eingang zum Bahnhof und greift die Gestaltung des dahinter sichtbaren Gebäudes auf.

L'auvent en éventail qui marque l'entrée de la gare rappelle en écho le dessin du bâtiment, visible en arrière-plan.

This station was conceived for Reggio Emilia as a new northern gateway to the city. The program includes not only the high-speed train station, but also a comprehensive master plan with bridges, a highway toll station, and other infrastructure intended to facilitate access to the city. The three new bridges were inaugurated in 2007. Located four kilometers north of the city center, the Mediopadana Station is the only local stop on the Milan–Bologna high-speed railway line. Visible from the nearby A1 highway, the station is recognizable as a new landmark. The design brief called for the canopy of the station and the platforms to be built independently from an existing viaduct. The architect explains: "The repetition of a 25.4-meter-long module consists of a succession of 25 steel portals spaced approximately one meter apart. The repetition of the sequence reaches the total length of 495 meters, which creates a dynamic wave effect. The wave lines on both the floor plan and elevation give rise to a three-dimensional sinusoidal volume. The glass canopy and façade, realized by placing the laminated glass between the portals by means of an aluminum frame, cover the entire length of the platforms." Set on a 15-hectare site, the structure itself occupies three hectares and is 50 meters wide. It went into service on June 8, 2013. The main entrance in Reggio Emilia is marked by a projecting canopy, opening onto a landscaped piazza and 300 parking spaces.

Dieser Bahnhof in Reggio Emilia wurde als nördliches Tor zur Stadt geplant. Das Programm beinhaltete nicht nur den Bahnhof für Hochgeschwindigkeitszüge, sondern auch einen umfassenden Masterplan mit Brücken, einer Autobahnmautstation und weiteren Infrastruktureinrichtungen, die den Zugang zur Stadt erleichtern sollen. Die drei neuen Brücken wurden 2007 eingeweiht. Der 4 km nördlich vom Stadtzentrum gelegene Bahnhof Mediopadana ist der einzige Halt auf der Hochgeschwindigkeitsstrecke von Mailand nach Bologna. Das von der nahe gelegenen Autobahn A1 sichtbare Gebäude ist zu einem neuen Wahrzeichen geworden. Die Ausschreibung forderte, das Dach des Bahnhofs und die Bahnsteige unabhängig von einem bestehenden Viadukt zu errichten. Der Architekt erläutert: „Ein 25,4 m langes Modul aus 25 stählernen Portalen, die jeweils etwa 1 m auseinanderstehen, wird auf einer Gesamtlänge von etwa 495 m mehrfach hintereinandergesetzt, wodurch eine dynamische Wellenwirkung entsteht. Diese Wellenlinien erzeugen auf dem Grundriss wie auch auf der Ansicht ein dreidimensionales, sinusförmiges Volumen. Das Dach und die Fassade aus Glas, für die das Verbundglas in Aluminiumrahmen zwischen die Portale gesetzt wurde, finden sich entlang der gesamten Bahnsteiglänge." Das Bauwerk auf einem 15 ha großen Gelände nimmt 3 ha ein und hat eine Breite von 50 m. Es ist seit dem 8. Juni 2013 in Betrieb. Der Haupteingang in Reggio Emilia zeichnet sich durch ein vorspringendes Vordach aus, das auf eine begrünte Piazza und 300 Parkplätze führt.

Cette nouvelle gare pour Reggio Emilia a été conçue comme une porte d'entrée de la ville par le nord. Le programme portait à la fois sur une gare pour les trains à grande vitesse et un plan directeur comprenant des ponts, une station de péage autoroutier et diverses infrastructures destinées à faciliter l'accès à la ville. Les trois nouveaux ponts ont été inaugurés en 2007. Située à quatre kilomètres au nord du centre-ville, la gare Mediopadana est le seul arrêt sur la ligne à grande vitesse Milan-Bologne. Visible de l'autoroute A1 toute proche, elle présente une forte dimension monumentale. L'appel d'offres prévoyait que la verrière recouvrant la gare et les quais soit indépendante d'un viaduc existant. « La répétition d'un module de 25,4 mètres de long forme une succession de 25 portails en acier espacés d'environ un mètre chacun, explique Calatrava. Cette séquence répétitive se poursuit sur une longueur totale de 495 mètres en créant un effet dynamique de vague. Les lignes de ces vagues, tant en plan qu'en élévation, définissent un volume sinusoïdal en trois dimensions. La verrière et la façade à panneaux de verre feuilleté posés dans un cadre en aluminium entre les portiques, protègent les quais sur toute leur longueur. » Implantée sur un site de 15 hectares, la structure en occupe trois sur 50 mètres de large. Elle est entrée en service le 8 juin 2013. L'entrée principale est signalée par un auvent qui se projette vers une place paysagée et un parking de 300 places.

The angled, undulating, ribbed, and folded forms proceed from a regular and repetitive pattern, but their disposition and juxtaposition create an impression of considerable freedom and autonomy.

Die angeschrägten, wellenförmigen, gerippten und gefalteten Formen folgen einem regelmäßigen , fortlaufenden Muster, doch ihre Anordnung und Gegenüberstellung schaffen den Eindruck bemerkenswerter Freiheit und Autonomie.

Les formes inclinées, ondulées, nervurées et pliées procèdent d'une motif répétitif régulier, mais leur disposition et leur juxtaposition laissent néanmoins une forte impression de liberté et d'autonomie.

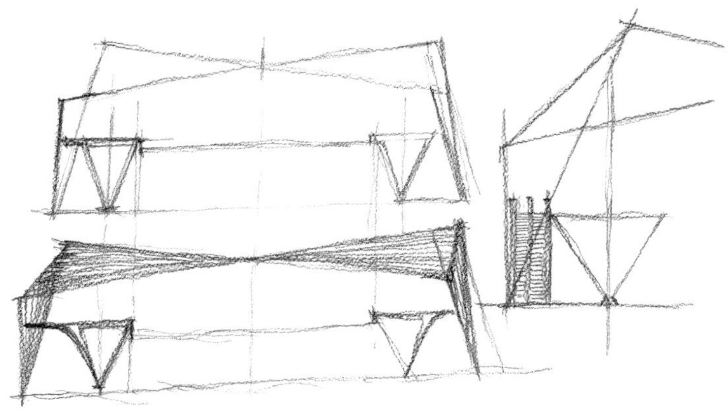

Uscita Exit

A relatively simple sketch by Calatrava (below) shows the tiers of the undulating design that resembles a bridge at the lower level. Train tracks, seen on the left page, are covered by a roof that admits ample natural light.

Eine recht einfache Skizze von Calatrava (unten) zeigt die Lagen des wellenförmigen Entwurfs, der auf der unteren Ebene einer Brücke ähnelt. Die links abgebildeten Gleise sind von einem Dach bedeckt, das reichlich Tageslicht einlässt.

Le croquis relativement simple de Calatrava (ci-dessous) montre les différents niveaux du projet traité en ondulations, qui fait penser à un pont en partie inférieure. Les voies ferrées (page de gauche) sont protégées par une toiture qui laisse filtrer un généreux éclairage naturel.

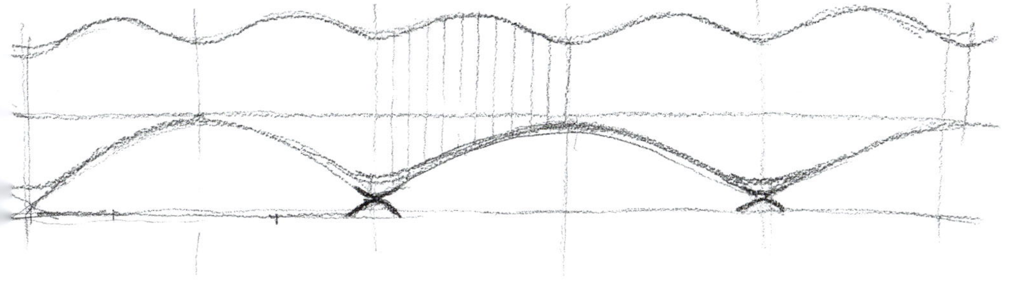

MONS STATION

Mons, Belgium. 2004–2024.

Project

MONS STATION

Location

MONS, BELGIUM

Client

SOCIÉTÉ NATIONALE DES CHEMINS DE FER BELGES (SNCB)

Length

200 METERS (GALLERY)
350 METERS (PLATFORM ROOFS)

Site area / Construction area

37 850 m² / 42 500 m²

Cost

€ 125 MILLION ESTIMATED

Angles and curves dominate the design, which has a decidedly futuristic aspect (see previous spread). Diagonals give a dynamic aspect to the spaces.

Schrägen und Kurven beherrschen den Entwurf, der auf dem Bild von Seite 378–379 entschieden futuristische Aspekte aufweist. Die Diagonalen verleihen den Räumen einen dynamischen Charakter.

Courbes et inclinaisons dominent ce projet d'aspect résolument futuriste, voir l'illustration page 378–379. L'utilisation d'éléments en diagonale confère à ces espaces un aspect dynamique.

Calatrava was commissioned to design a new multi-modal railway station and its surrounding urban landscape after winning a design competition in 2004. The station's gallery forms a bridge over the tracks and platforms, linking two formerly disconnected and distinct areas of the city: a residential area to the north and the historic city to the south. Five hundred underground parking spaces are to be located at the station's south entrance. To the north of the station, an underground structure with utility rooms and 350 parking spots is being created beneath the new Place de Congrès. Speaking at the start of the project, Santiago Calatrava explains: "Mons was the European Capital of Culture 2015 and one might compare the station we've designed there to a 'library' as opposed to the cathedral-like volume of the Liège-Guillemins Station (see page 254). In the case of the University Library in Zurich (Law Faculty, Zurich, 1989–2004, see page 96), I used wood and steel, an idea applied here to create a much more intimate atmosphere than in a larger station. The exterior of the station is in glass, but the interior is made with a steel frame and a great deal of wood. The skylight of the central gallery will be movable to allow natural ventilation."

Nachdem Calatrava 2004 einen Wettbewerb gewonnen hatte, wurde er mit der Planung eines neuen, multimodalen Bahnhofs einschließlich dazugehöriger Infrastruktur beauftragt. Die Galerie des Bahnhofsgebäudes bildet eine Brücke über den Bahnsteigen und Gleisen, die zwei bisher getrennte Stadtviertel miteinander verbindet: ein Wohngebiet im Norden und die historische Altstadt im Süden. Unter dem Südausgang soll eine Tiefgarage mit 500 Parkplätzen angelegt werden. Nördlich vom Bahnhof entsteht unter der neuen Place de Congrès unterirdisch ein Bau mit Versorgungseinrichtungen und 350 Parkplätzen. Zu Beginn des Projekts erklärte Calatrava: „Mons war die europäische Kulturhauptstadt 2015, und der von uns entworfene Bahnhof ließe sich mit einer Bibliothek vergleichen, im Gegensatz zur kathedralenartigen Baumasse des Bahnhofs Liège-Guillemins (siehe Seite 254). Für die Universitätsbibliothek in Zürich (Juristische Fakultät, Zürich, 1989–2004, siehe Seite 96) verwendete ich Holz und Stahl – hier griff ich diese Idee auf, um eine intimere Atmosphäre als in einem größeren Bahnhof zu schaffen. Das Äußere des Gebäudes besteht aus Glas, aber das Innere ist mit einem Stahlrahmen und viel Holz gestaltet, unter Berücksichtigung der ökologischen Anliegen der Stadt. Das bewegliche Oberlicht der zentralen Galerie ermöglicht eine natürliche Belüftung."

Calatrava a reçu commande de cette nouvelle gare multimodale et de diverses installations d'accompagnement à l'issue d'un concours organisé en 2004. Une galerie en forme de pont, qui franchit les voies et les quais, relie deux quartiers de la ville jusque-là séparés : une zone résidentielle au nord et la ville historique au sud. Les 500 places du parking souterrain sont accessibles de l'entrée sud. Au nord, une structure également en sous-sol regroupant diverses installations techniques et 350 places de parking est en cours de construction sous la nouvelle place de Congrès. À l'époque, pour Santiago Calatrava : « Mons était la Capitale européenne de la Culture 2015 et l'on peut rapprocher la gare que nous avons conçue ici de l'esprit d'une bibliothèque, comparativement au volume de cathédrale de celle de Liège-Guillemins (voir page 254). Dans le cas de la bibliothèque universitaire de Zurich (Faculté de droit, Zurich, 1989–2004, voir page 96), j'ai utilisé le bois et l'acier, idée retenue ici pour créer une atmosphère nettement plus intime que dans une gare plus importante. L'extérieur est en verre, mais l'intérieur à ossature d'acier utilise beaucoup de bois, pour prendre en considération les préoccupations écologiques de la ville. Les puits de lumière de la galerie centrale sont conçus mobiles pour permettre une ventilation naturelle. »

Calatrava's vocabulary of forms frees interior space to a point where the great railway architecture of the past is evoked in terms of grandeur.

Calatravas Formenvokabular befreit den Innenraum in einem Maße, das an die großartige Eisenbahnarchitektur der Vergangenheit erinnert.

Le vocabulaire des formes de Calatrava lui permet de libérer l'espace intérieur au point d'évoquer la grandeur de l'architecture des gares du passé.

Human figures drawn to scale make it clear that the architect is not thinking only of his soaring forms, but also of the users of the station.

Die maßstäblich wiedergegebenen menschlichen Figuren verdeutlichen, dass der Architekt nicht nur seine aufragenden Formen im Sinn hat, sondern ebenso die Nutzer des Bahnhofs.

Les figures humaines représentées à l'échelle montrent clairement que l'architecte ne réfléchit pas seulement à la beauté formelle de ses créations, mais qu'il y intègre aussi les besoins des futurs usagers de la gare.

UNIVERSITY OF SOUTH FLORIDA POLYTECHNIC CAMPUS MASTER PLAN

Lakeland, Florida, USA. 2009–2014.

Project
UNIVERSITY OF SOUTH FLORIDA POLYTECHNIC CAMPUS MASTER PLAN

Location
LAKELAND, FLORIDA, USA

Location
FLORIDA POLYTECHNIC UNIVERSITY (FPU)

Gross / net building area
18 580 m² / 11 148 m²

Height
25 METERS (LOUVERS CLOSED)
39 METERS (LOUVERS OPEN)

Cost
$ 60 MILLION

Left, a multiple-exposure photography of the operable brise-soleils on top of the Innovation, Science and Technology Building, shows the complete change in the outline of the structure.

Links: Die Mehrfachbelichtung zeigt die verstellbaren Brises-soleil auf dem Innovation, Science and Technology Building, die das Erscheinungsbild des Gebäudes vollkommen verändern.

À gauche, photographie à expositions multiples montre le déploiement des brise-soleil mobiles de la toiture du Bâtiment de l'innovation, de la science et de la technologie, qui modifie complètement ses contours.

In 2009, Santiago Calatrava was selected to create the master plan for the new campus of Florida Polytechnic, and to design the first building. The master plan placed a good deal of importance on landscaping, vehicular and pedestrian traffic, and the creation of "an iconic structure marking the campus within the larger local and regional context." Calatrava designed the Innovation, Science and Technology Building (2009–13) as the "centerpiece and anchor of the University." It is located to the north of a lake and at the end of the central axis of the campus. Science and research labs are located in the interior of the building with non-technical teaching labs around the periphery. The two-story corridors have clerestory glazing, while faculty offices are on the second floor, surrounding a large multiuse hall lit by a central skylight. Given its role as the first building, the structure was conceived as a "miniature campus." A light steel trellis or pergola surrounds the building, reducing solar gain by as much as 30%. The architect explains: "The operable roof consists of a series of hydraulically activated brise-soleils that provide shading to the commons' skylight. The louvers are individually controlled and can be programmed to follow the course of the sun throughout the day. In the next stage of development, the brise-soleils will be outfitted with solar panels creating a 1860-square-meter solar array."

2009 wurde Santiago Calatrava mit der Erarbeitung des Masterplans und der Planung des ersten Gebäudes für den neuen Campus der technischen Hochschule Florida Polytechnic beauftragt. Der Masterplan sollte besonderen Wert auf die Landschaftsgestaltung legen, auf den Auto- und Fußgängerverkehr sowie auf die Errichtung „eines ikonischen Bauwerks, das den Campus aus dem größeren lokalen und regionalen Kontext hervorhebt". Calatrava entwarf den Neubau, das Innovation, Science and Technology Building (2009–2013), als „Herzstück und Anker der Universität". Es liegt nördlich vom See und am Ende der zentralen Achse, die über den Campus führt. Wissenschaftliche Arbeitsräume und Forschungslaboratorien befinden sich im Inneren des Gebäudes, die nichttechnischen Lehrsäle sind an der Peripherie angeordnet. Die zweigeschossigen Korridore sind von oben natürlich belichtet; die Fakultätsbüros liegen im zweiten Geschoss rund um einen großen Mehrzwecksaal, der durch ein zentrales Oberlicht Tageslicht erhält. Als erstes Gebäude auf dem Gelände wurde der Bau als „Miniaturcampus" konzipiert. Umgeben ist er von einem leichten Stahlgitter, einer Art Pergola, die den Sonneneinfall um bis zu 30 % reduziert. Der Architekt erklärt: „Das verstellbare Dach besteht aus einer Reihe hydraulisch angetriebener Sonnenschutzelemente, die das Oberlicht beschatten. Diese Blenden können einzeln kontrolliert und nach dem jeweiligen Sonnenstand programmiert werden. In der nächsten Entwicklungsstufe sollen sie mit Solarzellen ausgestattet werden, die eine 1860 m^2 große Fläche bilden."

C'est en 2009 que Santiago Calatrava a été choisi pour concevoir le plan directeur du nouveau campus de Florida Polytechnic et en dessiner le premier bâtiment. Le plan directeur accordait beaucoup d'importance au traitement du paysage, à la circulation des piétons et des véhicules et à la création d'une « structure iconique identifiant le campus dans son contexte local et régional ». Calatrava a conçu le Bâtiment de l'innovation, de la science et de la technologie (2009–13) comme « l'élément central, le point d'ancrage de l'université ». Il est implanté au bord d'un lac, à l'extrémité de l'axe central du campus. Les laboratoires des sciences et de la recherche sont installés à l'intérieur du bâtiment, ceux des enseignements non techniques étant répartis en périphérie. Les corridors à deux niveaux sont éclairés par des ouvertures hautes, et les bureaux des enseignants sont situés au second niveau autour d'un vaste hall multifonction, éclairé par une verrière zénithale centrale. Étant donné qu'elle est le premier bâtiment construit, cette structure a été conçue comme un « campus miniature ». Un treillis léger en acier — sorte de pergola —, entoure l'immeuble et permet de réduire le gain solaire de près de 30 pour cent. « Le toit transformable, explique l'architecte, consiste en une série de brise-soleil à commande hydraulique qui assurent la protection nécessaire des verrières. Chaque volet est contrôlé individuellement et l'ensemble programmé pour suivre la courbe du soleil. Dans une prochaine étape de développement, ces brise-soleil seront dotés de panneaux solaires, ce qui créera une petite installation photovoltaïque de 1 860 mètres carrés.

To the right, interior space that has all the hallmarks of a Calatrava design—the arched ribs and curving, generous forms that he is known for.

Rechts: Der Innenbereich zeigt alle Merkmale eines Calatrava-Entwurfs – die gebogenen Rippen und die gekrümmten, großzügigen Formen, für die der Architekt bekannt ist.

À droite, l'espace intérieur est caractéristique du style Calatrava : arcs, courbes et générosité des volumes.

The successive ribs seen in these interior spaces are evocative of the natural world (skeletons) but cannot be specifically related to any living organism.

Die aufeinanderfolgenden Rippen in diesen Innenräumen erinnern an die Welt der Natur (Skelette), lassen sich aber keinem spezifischen lebenden Organismus zuschreiben.

Les arcs successifs de ces volumes intérieurs évoquent le monde naturel (squelettes), mais ne se rattachent à aucun organisme vivant en particulier.

MUSEUM OF TOMORROW

Rio de Janeiro, Brazil. 2010–2015.

Project
MUSEUM OF TOMORROW

Location
RIO DE JANEIRO, BRAZIL

Client
FUNDAÇÃO ROBERTO MARINHO, RIO DE JANEIRO, BRAZIL

Floor area
12 600 m²

Length
340 METERS

As is often the case, Calatrava integrates a human form in his watercolor sketches but is subtle in revealing the specific relationship between the person and the architectural design.

Wie so oft fügt Calatrava auch hier eine menschliche Form in seine Aquarellskizzen ein, ohne aber eine direkte Beziehung zwischen der Person und dem Architekturentwurf herzustellen.

Comme souvent, Calatrava intègre une forme humaine dans ses croquis à l'aquarelle, tout en sachant rester subtil dans la démonstration de cette relation particulière entre l'individu et la conception architecturale.

Located at Rio de Janeiro's Mauá Harbor Pier, the Museum of Tomorrow played a central role in the city's urban revitalization plans for the 2016 Olympic and Paralympic Games. The program provided for 5000 square meters of exhibition space, as well as an auditorium, observatory, administrative offices, archives, and technical areas for a total of nearly 12 500 square meters. The two-story structure is 18 meters high, allowing for 10-meter ceilings on the upper exhibition floor but low enough to respect nearby historic landmarks. Below the exhibition area are offices, educational and commercial facilities, research rooms, a cafe, a theater, the lobby, the archive, and the storage and delivery zones. The cantilevered roof and façade structure with operable wings stretches almost the entire length of the pier. A landscaped strip occupies the southern length of the pier, and a large reflecting pool marks the northern side. The pool, which uses water pumped in from the bay to cool the structure, gives visitors the impression that the museum is floating. Filtered water is returned to the bay after use. The building has a north–south orientation and is off-center from the pier's longitudinal east–west axis, "maximizing a continuous landscaping feature containing beautiful gardens, paths, and leisure areas along the southern length of the pier."

Das auf der Landungsbrücke des Hafens Mauá in Rio de Janeiro gelegene Museum von Morgen spielte eine wichtige Rolle bei der Stadterneuerungsplanung für die Olympischen und Paralympischen Spiele von 2016. Sein Programm sah 5000 m² Ausstellungsfläche und eine Veranstaltungshalle vor, ein Observatorium, Verwaltungsbüros, Archivräume sowie technische Einrichtungen für eine Gesamtanlage von fast 12 500 m². Das zweigeschossige Bauwerk ist 18 m hoch und bietet eine Deckenhöhe von 10 m im oberen Ausstellungsgeschoss, ist aber auch niedrig genug, um die benachbarten historischen Gebäude nicht zu beeinträchtigen. Unter dem Ausstellungsbereich befinden sich Büros, Bildungseinrichtungen, Geschäfte, Forschungsräume, ein Café, ein Theater, die Eingangshalle, das Archiv, das Lager sowie der Anlieferungsbereich. Die auskragende Dach- und Fassadenkonstruktion mit verstellbaren Flügeln erstreckt sich fast über die gesamte Länge des Piers, dessen südlichen Teil ein Grünstreifen einnimmt. Ein großer, reflektierender Pool kennzeichnet die Nordseite. Er nutzt Wasser, das aus der Bucht gepumpt wird, um das Gebäude zu kühlen, und vermittelt den Besuchern den Eindruck, das Museum schwebe. Das gefilterte Wasser wird danach zurück ins Meer geleitet. Das Gebäude ist nord-süd-orientiert und von der ost-westlichen Längsachse des Piers seitlich versetzt, wodurch es dem „durchgehenden Grünbereich mit seinen schönen Gärten, Fußwegen und Freizeitflächen entlang der Südseite des Piers" mehr Raum gewährt.

Implanté sur la jetée du port de Mauá à Rio de Janeiro, le Musée de demain a joué un rôle central dans les plans de revitalisation de la ville mis en œuvre pour les Jeux olympiques et paralympiques de 2016. Son programme comprenait un auditorium, un observatoire, 5 000 mètres carrés d'espaces d'exposition, des bureaux administratifs, des locaux d'archives et des équipements techniques pour un total d'environ 12 500 mètres carrés. La structure à deux niveaux s'élève à 18 mètres, ce qui a permis de créer des salles à plafonds de 10 mètres de haut à l'étage des expositions. Elle reste cependant assez basse pour respecter les proportions des monuments historiques voisins. Au rez-de-chaussée se trouvent des bureaux, des installations éducatives, des salles de recherche, des boutiques, un café, un théâtre et le hall d'accueil, les salles d'archives et les lieux de stockage et de livraison. La toiture en porte-à-faux et la façade à éléments mobiles recouvrent la quasi-totalité de la jetée. Un jardin paysager en bandeau occupe la partie sud de la jetée qui se termine au nord par un vaste bassin réfléchissant. Celui-ci, qui utilise de l'eau pompée dans la baie pour refroidir la structure, donne aux visiteurs l'impression que le musée flotte. Une fois utilisée, l'eau filtrée est rejetée dans la baie. Le bâtiment orienté nord-sud est décentré par rapport à l'axe longitudinal est-ouest de la jetée « maximisant l'effet de l'aménagement paysager continu qui regroupe de superbes jardins, des cheminements et des zones de loisirs sur toute la longueur de la partie sud de la jetée ».

MARINHA DO BRASIL

Sketches and a photo show the forward-leaning structure (below) but might also bring to mind a series of sails in the wind.

Zeichnungen und ein Foto zeigen das sich nach vorn neigende Bauwerk (unten), lassen aber auch an Segel im Wind denken.

Les croquis et la photo montrent la structure inclinée vers l'avant (ci-dessous), qui peut faire penser à une multitude de voiles sous le vent.

Here, as in other buildings, the architect favors dramatic cantilevered forms. The sketch below emphasizes the kind of extreme lightness that Calatrava's mastery of engineering allows.

Wie auch in anderen seiner Bauten zeigt der Architekt hier seine Vorliebe für dramatisch auskragende Formen. Die Skizze betont die extreme Leichtigkeit, die Calatrava dank seiner Ingenieurskunst erzielt.

Ici, comme dans d'autres réalisations, l'architecte a pris le parti de formes en porte-à-faux spectaculaires. Le croquis ci-dessous illustre bien l'extrême légèreté que sa maîtrise de l'ingénierie autorise à Calatrava.

Santiago Calatrava's sketches relate the design to human forms in a rather unexpected way. His watercolors have a lyrical quality but are always clearly based on his knowledge of architecture and engineering.

In Santiago Calatravas Skizzen nimmt der Entwurf auf überraschende Weise Bezug auf menschliche Formen. Seine Aquarelle haben eine lyrische Qualität, basieren aber stets auf seinen fundierten Kenntnissen der Architektur und des Ingenieurwesens.

Les croquis de Santiago Calatrava renvoient à des formes humaines de façon assez inattendue. Si ses aquarelles possèdent une qualité lyrique, elles s'appuient toujours clairement sur sa connaissance de l'architecture et de l'ingénierie.

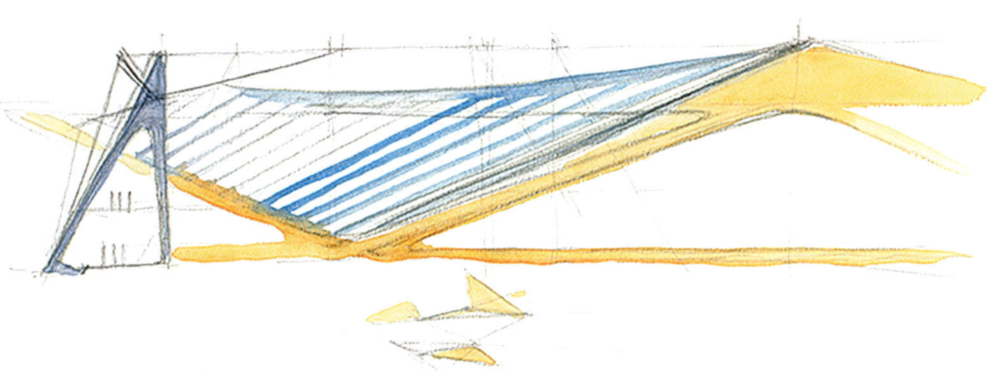

SHARQ CROSSING

Doha, Qatar. 2011–.

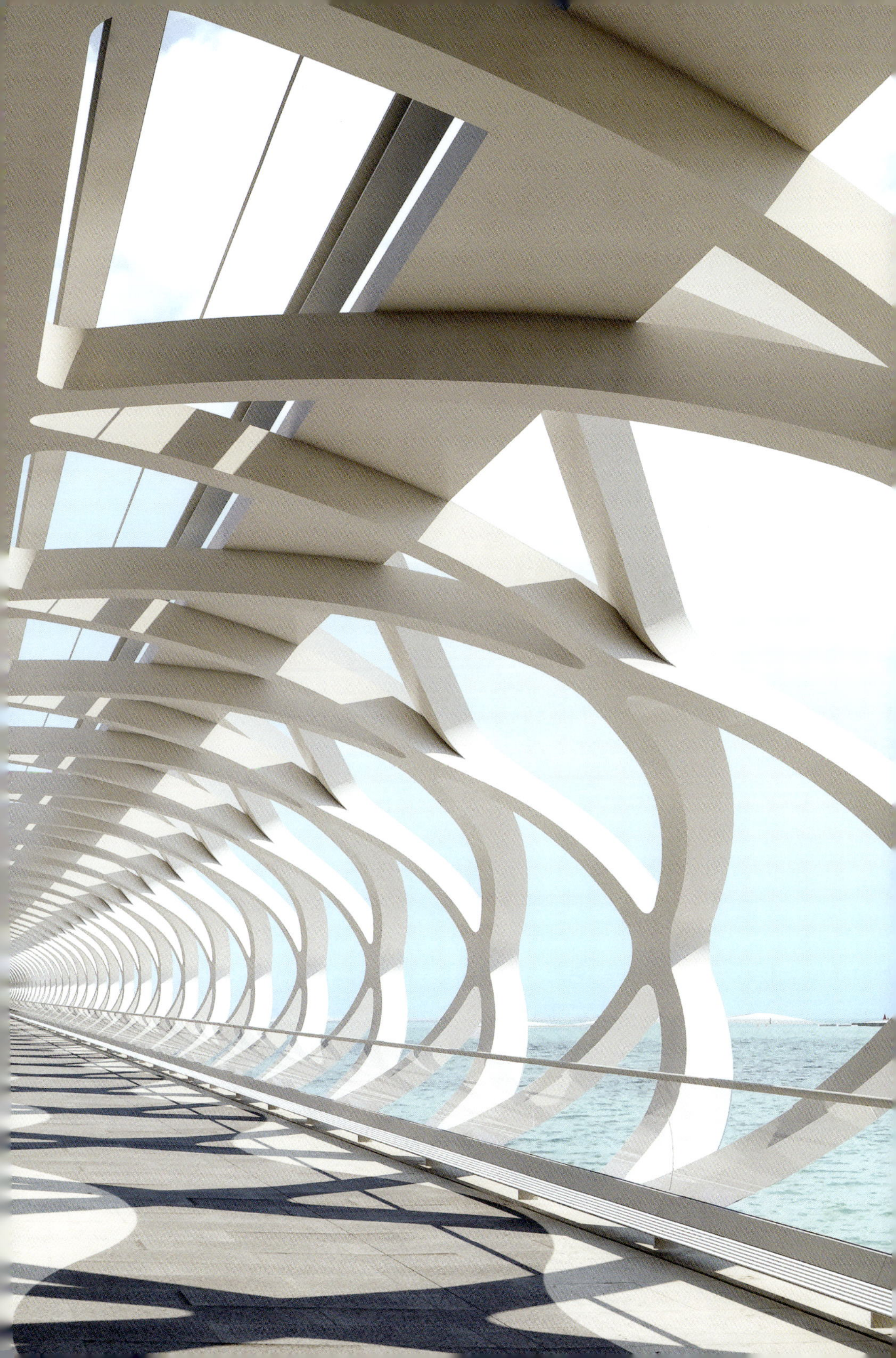

Project
SHARQ CROSSING

Location
DOHA, QATAR

Client
MINISTRY OF MUNICIPALITY AND URBAN PLANNING (MMUP)

Total fixed link length
12 KILOMETERS

Immersed Tube Tunnels
5.1 KILOMETERS IN TOTAL

A sketch by Calatrava likens a bridge to a curving, jumping fish. Left, the futuristic form of one of the bridges.

Auf einer Zeichnung Calatravas ähnelt eine Brücke einem gekrümmten, springenden Fisch. Links: Die futuristische Form einer der Brücken.

Un croquis de Calatrava rapproche le pont de l'image d'un poisson volant. À gauche, la forme futuriste de l'un des ponts.

The Sharq Crossing was designed by Santiago Calatrava at the request of the Ministry of Municipal Affairs and Urban Planning (MMUP) of Qatar. Rather than a simple tunnel, which was the originally planned solution, Calatrava proposed bridges at each of the three ends of the crossing. The Sharq area of Doha, not far from Jean Nouvel's National Museum of Qatar, is also relatively close to the Hamad International Airport. The main business area of Doha, at West Bay, is across the water, hence the need for this crossing, intended to relieve the Corniche Road of some of its heavy traffic, and to reduce transit times to the city center. West Bay is also near to the Lusail development zone, a substantial urban project that is part of Doha's current rapid development. In the style of Santiago Calatrava, each of the bridge segments is "iconic" and different in design. The West Bay Bridge is an arched structure incorporating a "longitudinal park" extending from the proposed Corniche Park along the bridge's length on an elevated walkway. The Cultural City Bridge is, in fact, formed by a series of cable-stayed bridges that "skims across the bay in a pattern of descending scales creating a long bridge dramatically reducing the lengths of the submerged tunnel links." The Sharq Bridge is a tubular structure located close to Hamad International Airport. In a city where such architects as I. M. Pei and Jean Nouvel have marked the horizon, Calatrava will thus take a substantial role in forming the cityscape.

Sharq Crossing wurde von Calatrava auf Wunsch des Ministeriums für städtische Angelegenheiten und Stadtplanung (MMUP) von Katar geplant. Anstelle des ursprünglich vorgesehenen einfachen Tunnels schlug Calatrava Brücken für alle drei Überquerungen vor. Der Bezirk Sharq in Doha, nicht weit von Jean Nouvels National Museum of Qatar entfernt, liegt auch relativ nahe am Hamad International Airport. Das Hauptgeschäftszentrum Dohas, West Bay, befindet sich am gegenüberliegenden Ufer. Daher soll die Brücke der Entlastung der Corniche Road vom Schwerverkehr dienen und die Fahrzeiten verkürzen. West Bay liegt auch hinter dem Bebauungsgebiet Lusail, einem wichtigen städtischen Bauprojekt, das zu Dohas schneller Entwicklung beitragen wird. Im Stil Calatravas ist jeder Brückenabschnitt „ikonisch" und unterschiedlich gestaltet. Die West Bay Bridge ist eine Bogenkonstruktion, die auch einen „Längspark" aufnimmt, der sich vom geplanten Corniche Park auf einer erhöhten Fußgängerebene über die ganze Länge der Brücke erstreckt. Die Cultural City Bridge besteht eigentlich aus mehreren Schrägseilbrücken, die „in einem System abnehmender Größe über die Bay führen und eine lange Brücke bilden, die die Länge der unterirdischen Tunnelverbindungen entscheidend verkürzt". Die Sharq Bridge ist eine Stahlrohrkonstruktion nahe dem Hamad International Airport. In dieser Metropole, in der Architekten wie I. M. Pei und Jean Nouvel die Silhouette geprägt haben, wird Santiago Calatrava eine wichtige Rolle bei der Gestaltung des Stadtbildes spielen.

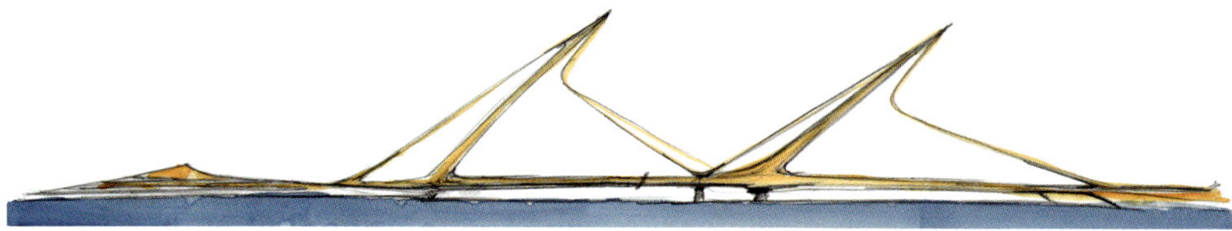

Above, a watercolor with the successive angled towers of the bridges. Below, a computer view of one of the arches.

Oben: ein Aquarell mit der Reihe schräger Brückentürme. Unten: Computerdarstellung eines Bogens.

Ci-dessus, une aquarelle montrant les piliers inclinés des ouvrages. Ci-dessous image de synthèse de l'une des arches.

Sharq Crossing est un projet conçu par Santiago Calatrava à la demande du ministère des Affaires municipales et de l'Urbanisme (MMUP) du Qatar. Au lieu du simple tunnel – solution prévue à l'origine –, Calatrava a proposé des ponts à chacune de ses trois extrémités. Le quartier Sharq de Doha, non loin du Musée national du Qatar par Jean Nouvel, est proche de l'aéroport international d'Hamad. La principale zone d'affaires de Doha, West Bay, est située de l'autre côté de la baie, d'où la nécessité de ces ouvrages qui doivent soulager la route de la Corniche d'une partie de sa circulation et réduire les temps de transit vers le centre-ville. West Bay est également située non loin de la zone de développement de Lusail, vaste projet urbain prévu dans le cadre du développement rapide de la capitale. Dans le style caractéristique de Calatrava, chacun de ces ouvrages de qualité fortement iconique est de conception différente. Le West Bay Bridge est un pont en arc intégrant un « parc longitudinal » s'étendant tout au long de l'ouvrage et accessible par une passerelle surélevée à partir du parc de la Corniche. Le Cultural City Bridge est en fait constitué d'une série de ponts suspendus qui « glisse sur la baie vers une succession d'écailles de dimensions décroissantes pour créer un pont allongé réduisant spectaculairement la longueur des segments de tunnel ». Le Sharq Bridge est une structure tubulaire proche de l'aéroport international. Dans cette cité dont des architectes tel que I. M. Pei et Jean Nouvel ont marqué l'horizon, Santiago Calatrava joue ainsi un rôle d'importance.

West Bay, visible in the background of the image below, is presently reachable only by following the long Corniche around the edge of the Bay.

Die im Hintergrund der Abbildung oben sichtbare West Bay ist gegenwärtig nur über die lange, am Rande der Bucht entlangführende Corniche erreichbar.

West Bay, visible dans le fond de l'image ci-dessus, n'est aujourd'hui joignable qu'en empruntant la longue route de la Corniche en bordure de la baie.

Above, a view of West Bay with Jean Nouvel's Doha Tower to the left, the Sheraton Doha Hotel (William Pereira, 1982) in the center and Calatrava's dramatic bridge on the right.

Oben: Ansicht der West Bay mit Jean Nouvels Doha Tower links, dem Sheraton Doha Hotel (William Pereira, 1982) in der Mitte und Calatravas eindrucksvollem Brückendesign rechts.

Ci-dessus, une vue de West Bay avec la tour de Doha par Jean Nouvel, à gauche, le Sheraton Doha Hotel de William Perreira (1982), au centre, et le spectaculaire ouvrage de Calatrava à droite.

Calatrava's drawings and the images below emphasize the almost dunelike nature of the design, inspired by local topography.

Calatravas Aquarelle und die Abbildungen unten betonen die dünenähnliche, von der örtlichen Topografie inspirierte Wirkung seines Entwurfs.

Les dessins de Calatrava et les images ci-dessous mettent en valeur le profil de dune du projet, inspiré de la topographie locale.

DUBAI CREEK TOWER

Dubai, UAE. 2016–.

Project

DUBAI CREEK TOWER

Location

DUBAI, UAE

While Calatrava's buildings have often taken on a quite present or substantial physical form, in this instance, he seeks an almost ethereal lightness.

Während Calatravas Bauten häufig eine sehr eindrückliche oder auffällige physische Gestalt aufweisen, bemüht er sich hier um fast ätherische Leichtigkeit.

Les créations de Calatrava possèdent souvent une forte présence physique, mais ici, il semble rechercher une légèreté presque éthérée.

Located in Dubai Creek Harbor, this observation tower is a project being carried forward by the renowned local developer Emaar Properties. It is the focal point of a vast six-square-kilometer development area that is to include a yacht club, marina, harbor, 22 hotels, and vast residential and retail spaces. Though its precise height is not clearly indicated, the tower is slated to be the tallest building in Dubai, surpassing the 830-meter Burj Khalifa Tower. It was due to be completed for Dubai's Expo 2020, for which the architect also designed the UAE Pavilion (see page 426). Calatrava states: "The building's design is inspired by the Islamic tradition, evoking the same history that brought the world the Alhambra and the Mosque of Cordoba. These architectural marvels combine elegance and beauty with mathematics and geometry. The design of the Dubai Creek Tower is rooted in classical art and the culture of Dubai itself. It is also a major technological achievement. Throughout my career I have used technology and engineering as a vehicle for beauty and art. This project is an artistic achievement, inspired by the goal of making this space a meeting point for citizens, not only from Dubai and the UAE, but from all across the world. It is a symbol of belief in progress." The building's observation decks are part of an elongated oval-shaped form at the top of the tower. The slender spine of the structure and the cables linking the building to the ground are "reminiscent of the delicate ribbing of the lily's leaves." The structure will also serve as a beacon at night, with lighting "that will emphasize the flower-bud design..."

Dieser Aussichtsturm im Hafen Dubai Creek ist ein Projekt des ansässigen renommierten Investors Emaar Properties. Er ist das Zentrum einer weiträumigen, 6 x 6 km großen Bebauung, zu der auch ein Jachtklub, eine Marina, der Hafen, 22 Hotels und große Wohn- und Einkaufsbereiche zählen. Der Turm soll, obgleich seine exakte Höhe noch nicht angegeben wurde, zum höchsten Gebäude in Dubai werden, das den 830 m hohen Burj Khalifa Tower übertrifft. Seine Fertigstellung war zur Expo 2020 in Dubai geplant, zu der der Architekt auch den Pavillon der Vereinigten Arabischen Emirate (siehe Seite 426) beitrug. Calatrava erklärt: „Der Entwurf dieses Gebäudes wurde von der islamischen Tradition inspiriert und ist Ausdruck derselben Geschichte, die der Welt die Alhambra und die Moschee von Cordoba bescherte. Diese architektonischen Wunderwerke zeigen eine Verbindung von Eleganz und Schönheit mit Mathematik und Geometrie. Der Entwurf für den Dubai Creek Tower wurzelt in der klassischen Kunst wie auch in der Kultur Dubais, aber er ist auch eine gewaltige technologische Leistung. In meiner gesamten Laufbahn habe ich Technologie und Ingenieurwissenschaften eingesetzt, um Schönheit und Kunst zu erzielen. Dieses Projekt ist eine künstlerische Leistung mit dem Ziel, einen Ort der Begegnung für Menschen nicht nur aus Dubai und den Emiraten, sondern aus der ganzen Welt zu schaffen. Es ist ein Symbol des Glaubens an den Fortschritt.“ Die Aussichtsplattformen des Gebäudes sind in die verlängerte, ovale Form an der Spitze des Turmes integriert. Das schlanke Tragwerk des Bauwerks und die Kabel, die es mit dem Boden verbinden, „erinnern an die feinen Rippen von Lilienblättern“. Das Gebäude wird bei Nacht auch als Leuchtturm fungieren, dessen Lichter „das Design in Form eines Blütenknospe betont …“.

Située dans le Dubai Creek Harbor, cette tour d'observation est un projet porté par le célèbre promoteur local Emaar Properties. Il est le point focal d'une vaste zone d'intervention urbanistique de six kilomètres carrés qui devrait comprendre un yacht-club, une marina, un port, 22 hôtels et de nombreux logements et commerces. La hauteur précise de la tour n'est pas encore communiquée, mais elle devrait être l'édifice le plus haut de Dubaï, dépassant les 830 mètres de la tour de Burj Khalifa. Elle devait être achevée pour l'Expo 2020 de Dubaï, manifestation pour laquelle l'architecte a aussi conçu le pavillon des ÉAU (voir page 426). Pour Calatrava : « Le concept de ce projet s'inspire de l'Alhambra et de la mosquée de Cordoue. Ces merveilles architecturales combinent l'élégance et la beauté avec les mathématiques et la géométrie. La conception de la Tour s'enracine dans l'art classique et la culture de Dubaï. C'est aussi une prouesse technique majeure. Tout au long de ma carrière, j'ai utilisé la technologie et l'ingénierie comme des véhicules d'art et de beauté. Ce projet est aussi un geste artistique inspiré par la volonté de faire de ce lieu un point de rencontre pour les citoyens, non seulement de Dubaï et des ÉAU, mais aussi du monde entier. C'est le symbole d'une croyance dans le progrès. » Les plates-formes d'observation se situeront dans une capsule ovale allongée au sommet de la Tour. La structure élancée de cette structure et les câbles qui le relient au sol « rappellent les délicates nervures des feuilles de lys ». La nuit, la tour servira également de phare et sera dotée d'un éclairage « mettant en valeur son dessin en bouton de fleur… »

As is often the case in the cities of the Gulf, a shopping or residential district is developed around the base of iconic buildings. In an environment where oddly shaped towers are the rule, Calatrava finds a way to differentiate his work from anything around it.

Wie so oft in den Städten der Golfregion wird ein Einkaufs- oder Wohnbezirk um ikonische Bauten herum geplant. In einem Umfeld, in dem ungewöhnlich gestaltete Hochhäuser die Regel sind, findet Calatrava einen Weg, um seine Entwürfe von allen übrigen abzuheben.

Comme souvent dans les villes du Golfe, un quartier résidentiel ou de commerces se développe autour d'immeubles iconiques. Dans un environnement où les tours de forme étrange sont la règle, Calatrava a trouvé une façon de différencier son œuvre de tout ce qui l'entoure.

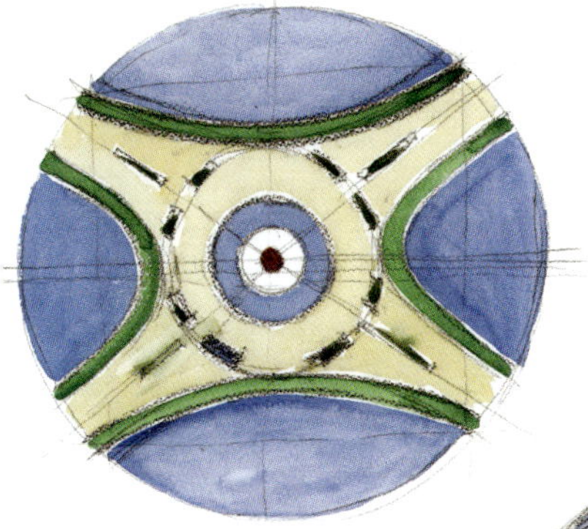

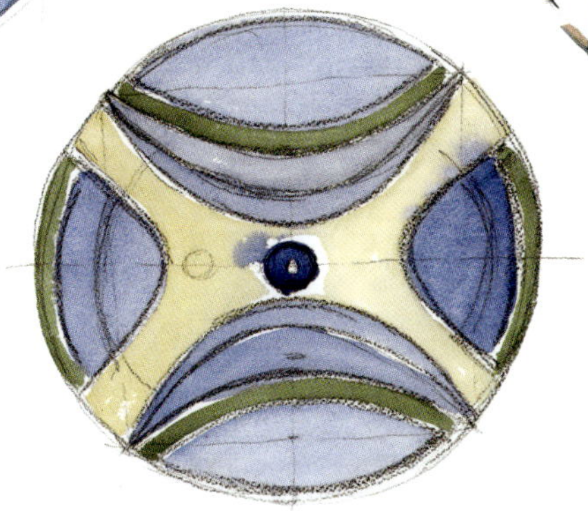

Computer-generated images show the soaring interior space of the building. Sketches by the architect (above) combine the simple circular form with variations on the internal structure.

Computergenerierte Bilder zeigen den hohen Innenraum des Gebäudes. Skizzen des Architekten (oben) verbinden die einfache Kreisform mit verschiedenen Möglichkeiten der Innengestaltung.

Ces deux images de synthèse montrent l'élévation des volumes intérieurs du bâtiment. Les croquis de l'architecte (ci-dessus) marient une forme circulaire simple à des variations sur la structure interne.

UAE PAVILION AT EXPO 2020 DUBAI

Dubai, UAE. 2016–2021.

Project

UAE PAVILION AT EXPO 2020 DUBAI

Location

DUBAI, UAE

Client

UAE NATIONAL MEDIA COUNCIL

Site area

15 064 m²

Floor area

15 000 m²

The UAE Pavilion is located near the center of Expo 2020, next to the dome of Al Wasi Plaza which was designed by Adrian Smith + Gordon Gill.

Der UAE-Pavillon befindet sich nahe des Zentrums der Expo 2020, neben der Kuppel der von Adrian Smith + Gordon Gill entworfenen Al Wasi Plaza.

Le pavillon des ÉAU est proche du centre de l'Expo 2020, à côté du dôme de l'Al Wasi Plaza, créé par Adrian Smith + Gordon Gill.

The UAE Pavilion designed by Santiago Calatrava stands at the heart of Expo 2020, which was delayed by one year because of Covid, opening on October 1, 2021. Inspired by the falcon, which is the national bird of the UAE, the 15 000-square-meter pavilion has no less than 28 movable carbon-fiber composite wings powered by 46 hydraulic actuators. The wings protect a surface grid of photo-voltaic panels in their closed position while allowing as much sunlight as possible to reach them when they are open. As is most often the case, Calatrava worked on many watercolor sketches to define the forms of the building, which were then converted into architectural drawings. The UAE Pavilion is LEED Platinum Certified (based on LEED 2009 standards for New Construction). According to the architects: "Passive cooling, ventilation, and shading strategies are central to ensuring that energy consumed by the building is both reduced and managed. Sunken, shaded gardens that are oriented to channel wind and air flow create comfortable outdoor environments that are further cooled by large pools flanking pedestrian walkways. Shaded arcades, protected by the sheltering form of the floating wings, allow for outdoor environments that are host to native and regionally adapted species of trees and plants to be highly functional and responsive to the hot climate of the region." The structure is made up of approximately 21 000 cubic meters of concrete and 1800 tons of steel. An auditorium at the center of the pavilion is marked by a faceted sphere with an outer diameter of 25 meters and a height of 20 meters. A fixed 12-meter-diameter oculus brings natural light into the exhibition spaces and tops the structure, bringing it to a total height of 27.8 meters. Landscaped areas around the pavilion are planted with 12 different species, of which eight are endemic.

Der von Santiago Calatrava entworfene Pavillon der Vereinigten Arabischen Emirate (VAE) ist das Herzstück der Expo 2020, deren Eröffnung sich Covid-bedingt um ein Jahr auf den 1. Oktober 2021 verschoben hatte. Inspiriert vom Falken, dem Nationalvogel der VAE, verfügt der 15 000 m² große Pavillon über nicht weniger als 28 bewegliche Flügel aus Kohlefaserverbundwerkstoff, angetrieben von 46 hydraulischen Aktuatoren. In geschlossenem Zustand schützen die Flügel die Oberflächenstruktur aus Fotovoltaikpaneelen, während sie geöffnet ein Maximum an Sonnenlicht ins Pavilloninnere einladen. Wie so oft schuf Calatrava zur exakten Formfindung zahlreiche Aquarellskizzen, die anschließend in Architekturzeichnungen umgewandelt wurden. Der VAE-Pavillon ist LEED-Platin-zertifiziert (basierend auf den LEED-2009-Standards für Neubauten). „Passive Kühlungs-, Belüftungs- und Beschattungsstrategien sind von zentraler Bedeutung, um den Energieverbrauch des Gebäudes sowohl senken als auch gezielt steuern zu können", so die Architekten. „Schattenreiche Senkgärten kanalisieren durch ihre Ausrichtung Wind- und Luftströmungen und schaffen eine angenehme Umgebung, die durch großflächige Wasserbecken entlang der Fußgängerwege zusätzlich gekühlt wird. Beschattete Arkaden, über die sich die Dachflügel schützend beugen, bieten einheimischen und regional angepassten Baum- und Pflanzenarten eine Heimat im Freien, sodass sie sich im heißen Klima entfalten können." Die Struktur besteht aus etwa 21 000 m³ Beton und 1800 t Stahl. Im Zentrum des Pavillons befindet sich ein Auditorium, in dem eine facettierte Kugel mit einem Außendurchmesser von 25 m und einer Höhe von 20 m die Blicke auf sich zieht. Ein Oculus von 12 m Durchmesser, durch den natürliches Licht in die Ausstellungsräume fällt, krönt die Struktur und markiert ihre Maximalhöhe von 27,8 m. Die Grünflächen rund um den Pavillon sind mit zwölf verschiedenen, davon acht endemischen Pflanzen- und Baumarten bepflanzt.

Le pavillon des ÉAU créé par Santiago Calatrava est au cœur de l'Expo 2020 qui a ouvert ses portes le 1er octobre 2021, après avoir été reportée d'un an en raison de la Covid. Inspiré par le faucon, l'oiseau national et emblème des Émirats, le bâtiment de 15 000 mètres carrés présente pas moins de 28 ailes mobiles en fibre de carbone composite, actionnées par 46 vérins hydrauliques. Elles abritent en position fermée une surface recouverte de panneaux photovoltaïques et permettent l'absorption maximale des rayons du soleil en position ouverte. Comme souvent, Calatrava a travaillé sur plusieurs esquisses à l'aquarelle pour mieux définir les formes du bâtiment avant de les convertir en dessins d'architecture. Le pavillon des ÉAU est certifié LEED platine (certification basée sur les normes LEED de 2009 pour les nouvelles constructions). Les architectes expliquent : « Les stratégies passives de refroidissement, ventilation et ombrage sont essentielles pour garantir à la fois une réduction et un contrôle de l'énergie consommée par le bâtiment. Des jardins surbaissés et ombragés ont été orientés de manière à canaliser le vent et le débit d'air, créant des espaces extérieurs agréables que rafraîchissent encore de vastes bassins le long des allées piétonnes. Des arcades ombragées, à l'abri des ailes qui les protègent, accueillent des espèces d'arbres et de plantes indigènes et adaptées à la région pour une fonctionnalité et une sensibilité au climat chaud optimales. » La construction a nécessité environ 21 000 mètres cubes de béton et 1 800 tonnes d'acier. Au centre du pavillon, un auditorium abrite une sphère à facettes de 25 mètres de diamètre et 20 mètres de haut. Un oculus de 12 mètres de diamètre fait entrer la lumière du jour dans les espaces d'exposition et couronne la structure principale qui atteint ainsi une hauteur totale de 27,8 mètres. Les espaces paysagers qui entourent le pavillon sont plantés de 12 espèces différentes, dont 8 endémiques.

Photos show the building with its carbon-fiber wings entirely open (next double page) and in the process of opening, in about four minutes, right.

Fotos zeigen das Gebäude mit vollständig geöffneten Kohlefaserflügeln (folgende Doppelseite) und im Öffnungsprozess, der etwa vier Minuten dauert (rechts).

On voit sur les photos le bâtiment et ses ailes en fibre de carbone entièrement ouvertes (double page suivante) ou en train de s'ouvrir, ce qui dure environ quatre minutes (à droite).

Left, a drawing by Calatrava of a Bedouin tent, another source of inspiration. Below, a model shows the complexity of the structure.

Links: Calatravas Zeichnung eines Beduinenzelts, einer weiteren Inspirationsquelle. Unten: Ein Modell offenbart die Komplexität der Struktur.

À gauche, dessin de Calatrava représentant une tente de bédouins, une autre de ses sources d'inspiration. Ci-dessous, maquette montrant la complexité de la structure.

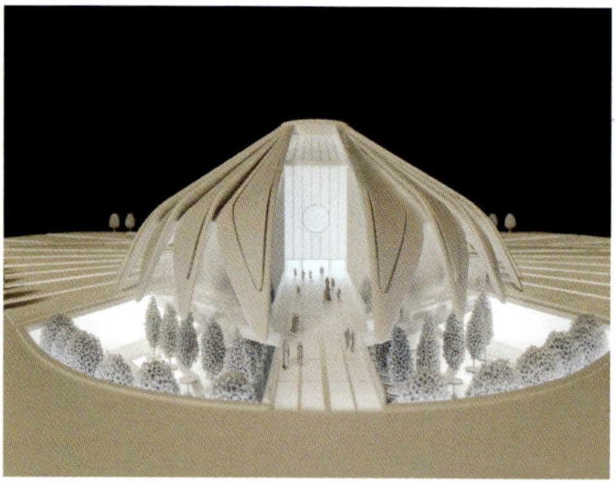

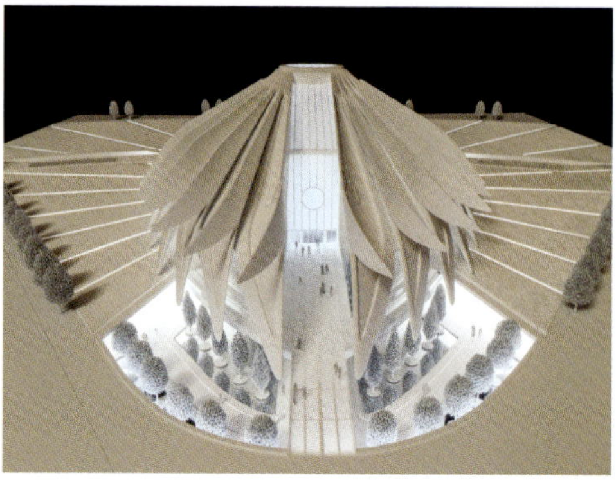

Above, a sketch of the interior structure with the central theater that was clad in Krion.

Oben: eine Skizze der Innenstruktur mit dem zentralen, mit Krion verkleideten Theater.

En haut, dessin de l'intérieur avec au centre l'auditorium qui a été revêtu de Krion.

Below, a Calatrava sketch of the entire building seen from above.

Unten: eine Calatrava-Skizze des gesamten Gebäudes von oben gesehen.

En bas, dessin de Calatrava du bâtiment vu d'en haut.

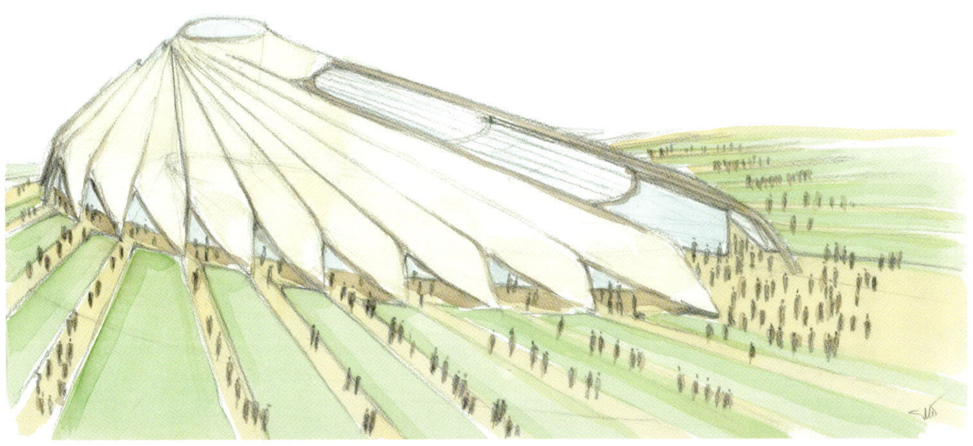

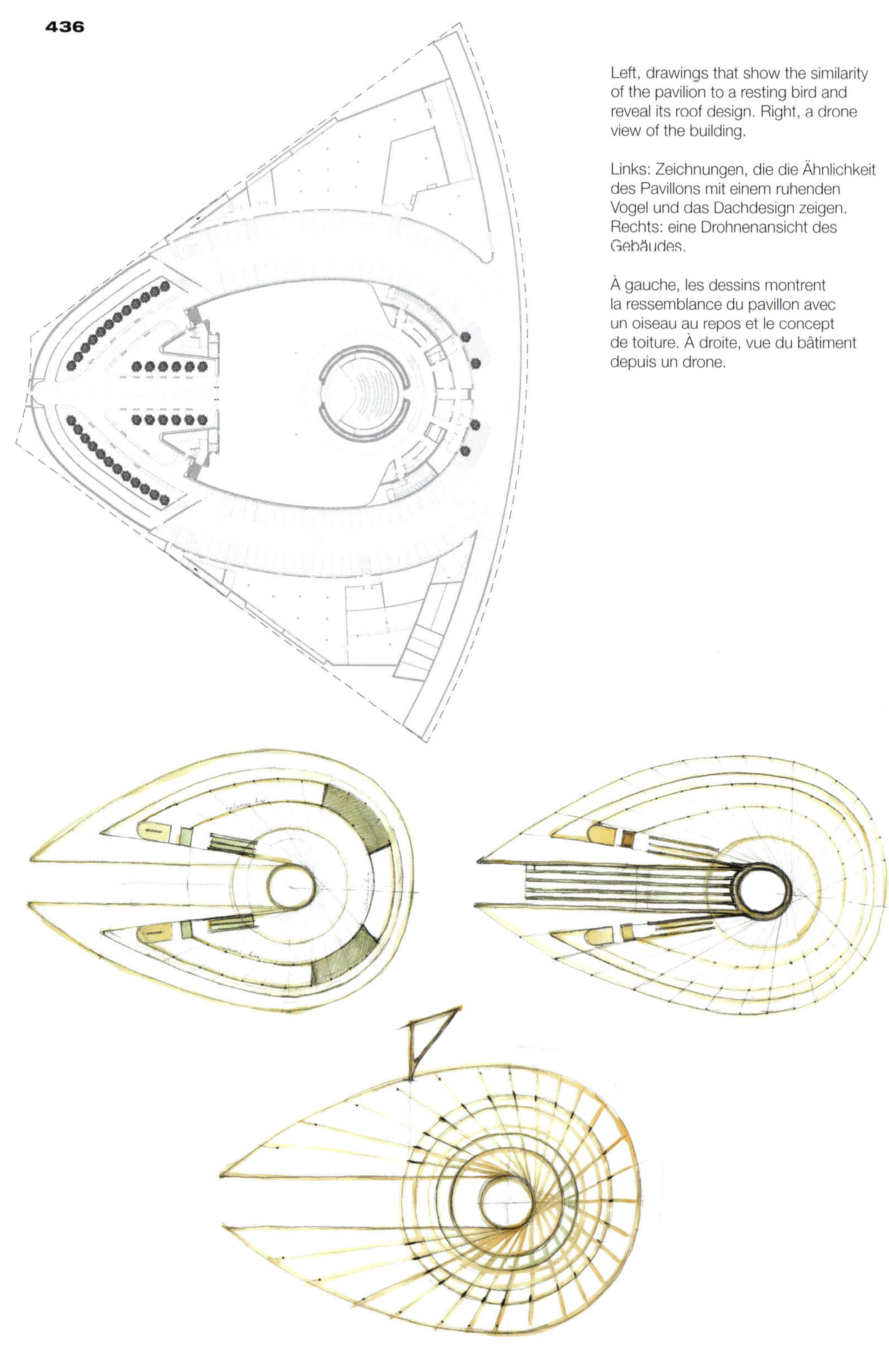

Left, drawings that show the similarity of the pavilion to a resting bird and reveal its roof design. Right, a drone view of the building.

Links: Zeichnungen, die die Ähnlichkeit des Pavillons mit einem ruhenden Vogel und das Dachdesign zeigen. Rechts: eine Drohnenansicht des Gebäudes.

À gauche, les dessins montrent la ressemblance du pavillon avec un oiseau au repos et le concept de toiture. À droite, vue du bâtiment depuis un drone.

The interiors exude the same wrapping and folding movement as the exterior, as seen in these images which include stairways and internal lighting design. Below, a section watercolor shows the sculptural cantilever design.

Diese Bilder der Treppen und der internen Lichtgestaltung zeigen, dass die Innenräume die gleiche umhüllende und faltende Bewegung wie das Äußere aufweisen. Unten: ein Aquarellquerschnitt des skulpturalen auskragenden Designs.

L'intérieur reproduit le mouvement drapé et plissé de l'extérieur, comme on le voit sur ces photos des escaliers qui montrent le concept d'éclairage interne. En bas, vue en coupe à l'aquarelle qui montre la construction sculpturale en porte-à-faux.

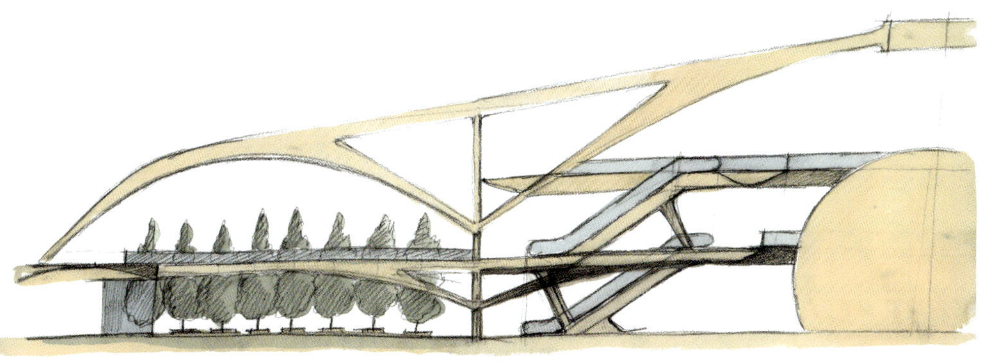

INSTALLATION IN THE CHURCH OF SAN GENNARO

Royal Park of Capodimonte, Naples, Italy, 2020–2021.

Project

INSTALLATION IN THE CHURCH OF SAN GENNARO

Location

ROYAL PARK OF CAPODIMONTE, NAPLES, ITALY

Client

MUSEO E REAL BOSCO DI CAPODIMONTE, NAPLES

Working within the confines of the old church, Calatrava added the dark-blue coloring seen here as well as the objects and artworks seen around the altar, all specially created for the occasion of his exhibition in Naples.

Umgeben von den alten Kirchenmauern fügte Calatrava dem Raum das dunkelblaue Farbkonzept sowie die rund um den Altar platzierten Objekte und Kunstwerke hinzu, die speziell für seine Ausstellung in Neapel geschaffen wurden.

Dans le cadre de son travail dans l'ancienne église, Calatrava a ajouté le bleu sombre des murs et du plafond qu'on voit ici, ainsi que les objets et œuvres d'art autour de l'autel, tous spécialement créés pour son exposition à Naples.

This multimedia installation (porcelain, textiles, glazing, painting, etc.) was created for the reopening of the Church of San Gennaro after 50 years of closure. The church was built in 1745 by the architect and stage designer Ferdinando Sanfelice at the behest of Charles of Bourbon in the Real Bosco (or Royal Park) of Capodimonte. The project was designed on a pro bono basis by the architect. The walls and ceiling of the church were painted in ultramarine blue "in order to highlight the structural and ornamental elements in the chapel and give it a greater sense of depth." Calatrava intervened on the totality of the space and sought to transform it visually, chromatically, and spiritually, paying homage to the historical artisan traditions of Campania: including the porcelain of the Manifattura di Capodimonte, the silks of San Leucio, and the stained glass of Vietri sul Mare. Calatrava donated all the works involved to the Capodimonte Museum and Real Bosco. For the ceramics (800 stars for the ceiling, 600 flowers and 600 leaves for the side niches, 6 vases, and 6 candelabra), the architect worked with the master ceramists and students of the Real Fabbrica di Capodimonte-Istituto Superiore ad Indirizzo Raro Caselli. Two semicircular panels were created, each composed of 47 terracotta plates, decorated with a mixed technique of majolica and a third firing. A crucifix is formed by gold leaves on a background entirely covered by olive branches and a cross composed of red flowers inserted into a dense network of yellow ochre flowers and biscuit branches. Stained glass for the chapel was created with the master glassmaker Antonio Perotti (Vietri sul Mare, Salerno). Silk vestments for the three altars were made according to Calatrava's designs by Anna Maria Alois (San Leucio, Caserta). Santiago Calatrava also painted the doves in the niches on either side of the main altar during his stay in Naples in October 2020. The work on San Gennaro was presented as part of a major 2019–21 exhibition entitled "Santiago Calatrava. In the Light of Naples".

Diese Multimediainstallation (u. a. mit Porzellan, Textilien, Glasur und Malerei) begleitete die feierliche Wiedereröffnung der Kirche von San Gennaro, die 1745 von dem Architekten und Bühnenbildner Ferdinando Sanfelice auf Geheiß Karls III. im Real Bosco (bzw. Königlichen Park) von Capodimonte errichtet worden und mehr als 50 Jahre lang unzugänglich war. Der Architekt stellte seine Leistung für dieses Projekt unentgeltlich zur Verfügung. Kirchenwände und -decke wurden ultramarinblau gestrichen, „um die strukturellen und ornamentalen Elemente der Kapelle hervorzuheben und ihr eine größere Tiefe zu verleihen". Calatrava arbeitete mit der Gesamtheit des Raums, um ihn visuell, chromatisch und spirituell zu transformieren und die historischen Handwerkstraditionen Kampaniens zu ehren: das Porzellan der Manifattura di Capodimonte, die Seidenstoffe von San Leucio und die Glasmalerei von Vietri sul Mare, um nur einige lokale Produkte zu nennen. Sämtliche Skizzen und Entwürfe des Projekts stellte Calatrava dem Museum von Capodimonte und dem Real Bosco zur Verfügung. Für die Keramiken (800 Sterne an der Decke, 600 Blumen und 600 Blätter für die Seitennischen, sechs Vasen sowie sechs Kandelaber) arbeitete er mit Keramikmeistern und Studenten der Real Fabbrica di Capodimonte-Istituto Superiore ad Indirizzo Raro Caselli zusammen. Sie schufen zwei halbrunde Tafeln aus jeweils 47 Terrakottaplatten, verfeinert mit einer Mischtechnik aus Majolika und Dreiphasenbrand. Das Kruzifix ist aus goldenen Blättern geformt, die auf einem vollständig von Olivenzweigen bedeckten Hintergrund angebracht sind. Rote Blumen in einem dichten Netz aus ockergelben Blumen und Zweigen bilden ein Kreuz. Die Glasmalerei für die Kapelle wurde von dem Glasermeister Antonio Perotti (Vietri sul Mare, Salerno) geschaffen. Die Seidengewänder für die drei Altäre nach Entwürfen Calatravas stammen aus der Werkstatt von Anna Maria Alois (San Leucio, Caserta). Die Tauben in den Nischen zu beiden Seiten des Hauptaltars schuf Calatrava während seines Aufenthalts in Neapel im Oktober 2020, als er unter anderem vor der Kirche Seminare mit Studenten des Caselli-Instituts veranstaltete. Die Arbeiten an San Gennaro wurden 2019–2021 in der Ausstellung „Santiago Calatrava. In the Light of Naples" präsentiert.

L'installation multimédia (porcelaine, textiles, vitrage, peinture, etc.) devait célébrer la réouverture, après une fermeture de cinquante ans, de l'église de San Gennaro, construite en 1745 par l'architecte et décorateur de théâtre Ferdinando Sanfelice sur ordre de Charles de Bourbon dans le Real Bosco (parc royal) de Capodimonte. Les murs et le plafond de l'église ont été peints en bleu outremer « afin de mettre en valeur les éléments structurels et ornementaux de la chapelle et de lui donner plus de profondeur ». Calatrava est intervenu sur la totalité de l'espace qu'il a voulu transformer visuellement, chromatiquement et spirituellement en rendant hommage aux traditions artisanales historiques de Campanie – la porcelaine de la manufacture de Capodimonte, les soies de San Leucio et les vitraux de Vietri sul Mare. Calatrava a fait don de ses travaux au musée de Capodimonte et du Real Bosco. Pour les céramiques (800 étoiles au plafond, 600 fleurs et 600 feuilles pour les niches des côtés, 6 vases et 6 candélabres), il a collaboré avec les maîtres céramistes et les étudiants de la Manufacture royale de Capodimonte-Istituto Superiore ad Indirizzo Raro Caselli. Deux panneaux semi-circulaires ont été créés, composés chacun de 47 plaques de terre cuite et décorés selon une technique mixte de majolique et de troisième cuisson. On y voit un crucifix de feuilles dorées sur un fond entièrement recouvert de branches d'olivier et une croix de fleurs rouges dans un dense réseau d'autres fleurs ocre jaune et de branches en biscuit. Les vitraux de la chapelle ont été réalisés avec le maître verrier Antonio Perotti (Vietri sul Mare, Salerne). La soie pour les parures des trois autels est l'œuvre d'Anna Maria Alois (San Leucio, Caserta), sur la base des modèles de Calatrava. Il a également dessiné lui-même les colombes des niches de chaque côté du maître-autel pendant un séjour à Naples en octobre 2020 au cours duquel il a aussi organisé des séminaires avec les étudiants de l'institut Caselli devant l'église. Le projet de San Gennaro a été présenté en 2019–21 dans une grande exposition intitulée « Santiago Calatrava. À la lumière de Naples ».

Some of Calatrava's watercolor sketches (above) show his personal implication in the project. Right, a vase and a candlestick of his design.

Einige von Calatravas Aquarellskizzen (oben) spiegeln sein persönliches Engagement in diesem Projekt wider. Rechts: Vase und Kerzenhalter nach seinen Entwürfen.

Certaines esquisses à l'aquarelle de Calatrava (ci-dessus) témoignent à quel point il s'est impliqué personnellement dans ce projet. À droite, un vase et un chandelier créés par lui.

Vestments, stained glass, vases, and the overall scheme of the decoration of the chapel were handled by the architect.

Die Gewänder, das Buntglas, die Vasen sowie das gesamte Dekorationskonzept der Kapelle wurden vom Architekten gestaltet.

Les parures d'autel, les vitraux, les vases et l'ensemble de la décoration de la chapelle ont été pensés par l'architecte.

Santiago Calatrava has long approached his work from a multidisciplinary point of view, especially through his watercolors and sculptures: here, he is also involved in paintings and textiles.

Calatrava verfolgt seit jeher einen multidisziplinären Ansatz in seiner Arbeit, insbesondere durch seine Aquarelle und Skulpturen: Hier bringt er sich auch in Malerei und Textilkunst ein.

Santiago Calatrava a longtemps abordé son travail sous un angle multidisciplinaire, notamment dans ses aquarelles et sculptures. On voit ici qu'il s'est aussi intéressé aux peintures et aux tissus.

Above, sketches and drawings of scenes from the Crucifixion and Deposition from the Cross animate the space, which also has a vegetal theme.

Oben: Skizzen und Zeichnungen von Szenen der Kreuzigung und der Kreuzabnahme beleben den Raum, den auch ein vegetabiles Thema prägt.

Ci-dessus, esquisses et dessins de la crucifixion et de la descente de croix qui animent l'espace également orné d'un motif au thème végétal.

Left, the starry pattern on the ceiling and liturgical elements are blended into the existing forms of the chapel.

Links: Das Sternenmuster der Decke und die liturgischen Elemente integrieren sich harmonisch in die vorhandenen Strukturen der Kapelle.

À gauche, le motif étoilé du plafond et du mobilier liturgique n'a pas été repris dans la chapelle actuelle.

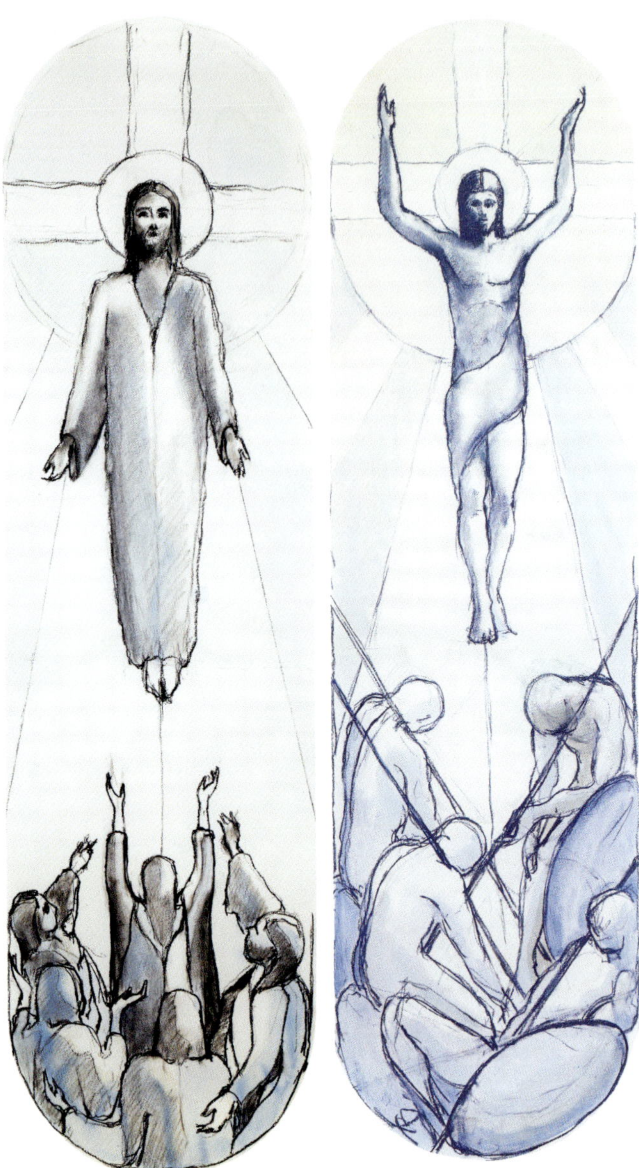

The stylized figures of Christ seen here succeed in bringing modernity to the designs for the chapel, while underlining the continuity of the Church.

Diese stilisierten Figuren Christi bringen Moderne in die Entwürfe der Kapelle und unterstreichen zugleich die Kontinuität der Kirche.

Les représentations stylisées du Christ qu'on voit ici apportent un peu de modernité au concept de la chapelle, tout en en soulignant la continuité.

The vegetal designs used for textiles and paintings are part of a carefully orchestrated intervention that approaches the idea of the Gesamtkunstwerk.

Die vegetabilen Designs der Textilien und Gemälde sind Teil eines sorgfältig orchestrierten Eingriffs, der die Idee des Gesamtkunstwerks aufgreift.

Les motifs végétaux de étoffes et des peintures font partie d'un travail d'ensemble orchestré avec soin, proche de l'idée d'œuvre d'art totale.

Liturgical vestments are also part of Santiago Calatrava's work for the chapel. All his interventions are modern and yet respectful of tradition.

Liturgische Gewänder gehören ebenfalls zu Santiago Calatravas Arbeiten für die Kapelle. Seine modernen Einfügungen respektieren dabei stets die Tradition.

Le travail de Santiago Calatrava comprenait aussi les vêtements liturgiques. Ses interventions manifestent toutes un respect de la tradition, malgré leur modernité.

More than architect in the case of San Gennaro, Calatrava intervenes in almost every imaginable way, including for the furnishings and obviously the decorative patterns.

Bei San Gennaro gestaltet Calatrava weit mehr als nur die Architektur und widmet sich nahezu allen denkbaren Aspekten, einschließlich der Möbel und dekorativen Muster.

Plus qu'en simple architecte, Calatrava est intervenu à San Gennaro à presque tous les niveaux imaginables, y compris le mobilier, et, visiblement, les motifs ornementaux.

Right, Calatrava's watercolors are unusual in that they do have an artistic element, coupled with the precision that an architect brings to the conception of objects in this instance.

Rechts: Calatravas Aquarelle sind ungewöhnlich, da sie künstlerische Elemente mit der Präzision eines Architekten bei der Gestaltung von Objekten verbinden.

À droite, les aquarelles de Calatrava étonnent par leur qualité artistique, associée à la précision de l'architecte dans la conception des objets qu'on voit ici.

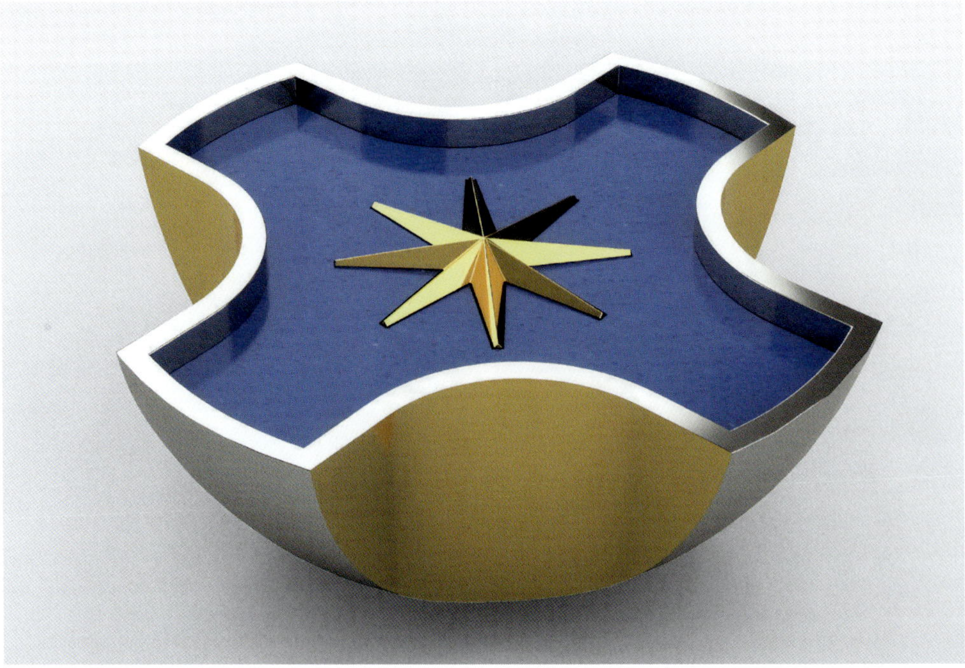

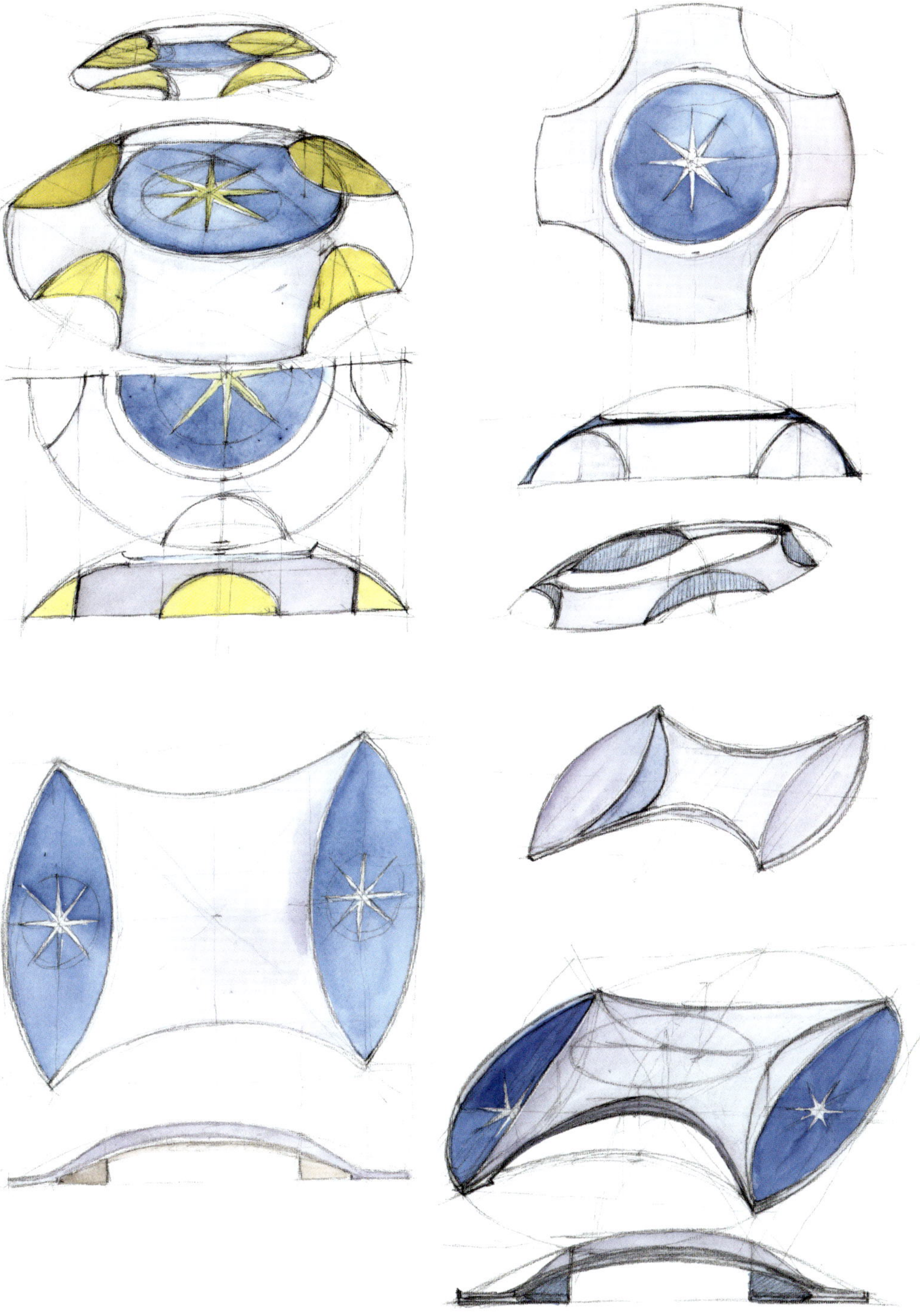

A-A
A
A

A lectern (above) or a cross (left) are approached with the same care as the other elements designed by the architect, whom one is tempted to call the artist in this case.

Der Architekt, der hier vielmehr als Künstler bezeichnet werden kann, widmet einem Pult (oben) oder einem Kreuz (links) dieselbe Sorgfalt wie allen anderen Details.

Le lutrin (ci-dessus) ou la croix (à gauche) ont fait l'objet de la même attention que les autres éléments créés par l'architecte – qu'on est ici tenté d'appeler artiste.

Appendix

MAIN PROJECTS

BIOGRAPHY

EXHIBITIONS, AWARDS, AND ACADEMIC ACKNOWLEDGMENTS

Einleitung

DAS GEHEIMNIS DER PHILANTHROPIE

Introduction

LE SECRET DE LA PHILANTHROPIE

CREDITS AND ACKNOWLEDGMENTS

MAIN PROJECTS

ALPINE BRIDGES
Switzerland, 1973–79

CABLE-STAYED BRIDGE STUDIES
1979

IBA SQUASH COMPLEX
Berlin, Germany, 1979

ZÜSPA EXHIBITION HALL
Zurich, Switzerland, 1981

LETTEN MOTORWAY BRIDGE
Zurich, Switzerland, 1982

MÜHLENAREAL LIBRARY
Thun, Switzerland, 1982

RHINE BRIDGE
Diepoldsau, Switzerland, 1982

SCHWARZHAUPT FACTORY
Dielsdorf, Switzerland, 1982

BAUMWOLLHOF BALCONY
Zurich, Switzerland, 1983

THALBERG HOUSE BALCONY EXTENSION
Zurich, Switzerland, 1983

JAKEM WAREHOUSE
Münchwilen, Switzerland, 1983–84

ERNSTING'S WAREHOUSE
Coesfeld-Lette, Germany, 1983–85

PTT POSTAL CENTRE CANOPY
Lucerne, Switzerland, 1983–85

ST. FIDEN BUS SHELTER
St. Gallen, Switzerland, 1983–85

WOHLEN HIGH SCHOOL ROOFS AND HALL
Wohlen, Switzerland, 1983–88

LUCERNE STATION HALL
Lucerne, Switzerland, 1983–89

STADELHOFEN STATION
Zurich, Switzerland, 1983–90

CABALLEROS FOOTBRIDGE
Lérida, Spain, 1984

DE SEDE COLLAPSIBLE EXHIBITION PAVILION
Zurich, Switzerland, 1984

DOBI OFFICE BUILDING
Suhr, Switzerland, 1984–85

BACH DE RODA-FELIPE II BRIDGE
Barcelona, Spain, 1984–87

BÄRENMATTE COMMUNITY CENTRE
Suhr, Switzerland, 1984–88

FELDENMOOS PARK & RIDE FOOTBRIDGE
Feldenmoos, Switzerland, 1985

STATION SQUARE BUS TERMINAL
Lucerne, Switzerland, 1985

AVENIDA DIAGONAL TRAFFIC SIGNAL GANTRY
Barcelona, Spain, 1986

RAITENAU OVERPASS
Salzburg, Austria, 1986

ST. GALLEN MUSIC SCHOOL CONCERT ROOM
St. Gallen, Switzerland, 1986

BLACKBOX TELEVISION STUDIO
Zurich, Switzerland, 1986–87

TABOURETTLI THEATER
Basel, Switzerland, 1986–87

9 D'OCTUBRE BRIDGE
Valencia, Spain, 1986–88

BANCO EXTERIOR
Zurich, Switzerland, 1987

BASARRATE METRO STATION
Bilbao, Spain, 1987

CASCINE FOOTBRIDGE
Florence, Italy, 1987

PONTEVEDRA BRIDGE
Pontevedra, Spain, 1987

THIERS PEDESTRIAN BRIDGE
Thiers, France, 1987

OUDRY-MESLY FOOTBRIDGE
Créteil-Paris, France, 1987–88

ALAMILLO BRIDGE & LA CARTUJA VIADUCT
Seville, Spain, 1987–92

BCE PLACE: GALLERIA AND HERITAGE SQUARE
Toronto, Canada, 1987–92

BUCHEN HOUSING ESTATE
Würenlingen, Switzerland, 1987–96

BAUSCHÄNZLI RESTAURANT
Zurich, Switzerland, 1988

COLLSEROLA COMMUNICATIONS TOWER
Barcelona, Spain, 1988

GENTIL BRIDGE
Paris, France, 1988

LEIMBACH FOOT-BRIDGE AND STATION
Zurich, Switzerland, 1988

PRÉ BABEL SPORTS CENTER
Geneva, Switzerland, 1988

WETTSTEIN BRIDGE
Basel, Switzerland, 1988

LUSITANIA BRIDGE
Mérida, Spain, 1988–91

EMERGENCY SERVICE CENTER
St. Gallen, Switzerland, 1988–99

BAHNHOFQUAI TRAM STOP
Zurich, Switzerland, 1989

CH-91 FLOATING CONCRETE PAVILION
Lake Lucerne, Switzerland, 1989

GRAN VIA BRIDGE
Barcelona, Spain, 1989

MIRAFLORES BRIDGE
Cordoba, Spain, 1989

MURI CLOISTER OLD AGE HOME
Muri, Switzerland, 1989

PORT DE LA LUNE SWING BRIDGE
Bordeaux, France, 1989

REUSS FOOTBRIDGE
Flüelen, Switzerland, 1989

SWISSBAU CON-CRETE PAVILION
Basel, Switzerland, 1989

LA DEVESA FOOTBRIDGE
Ripoll, Spain, 1989–91

MONTJUÏC COMMU-NICATIONS TOWER
Barcelona, Spain, 1989–92

LYON-SAINT-EXUPÉRY AIRPORT RAILWAY STATION
Colombier-Saugnieu, France, 1989–94

PUERTO BRIDGE
Ondarroa, Spain, 1989–95

BOHL BUS AND TRAM STOP
St. Gallen, Switzerland, 1989–96

ZURICH UNIVER-SITY LAW FACULTY LIBRARY
Zurich, Switzerland, 1989–2004

BELLUARD CASTLE THEATRE
Fribourg, Switzerland, 1990

EAST LONDON RIVER CROSSING
London, UK, 1990

NEW BRIDGE OVER THE VECCHIO
Corsica, France, 1990

SPITALFIELDS GALLERY
London, UK, 1990

CAMPO VOLANTÍN FOOTBRIDGE
Bilbao, Spain, 1990–97

SONDICA AIRPORT
Bilbao, Spain, 1990–2000

BETON FORUM STANDARD BRIDGE
Stockholm, Sweden, 1991

CALABRIA FOOTBALL STADIUM
Reggio Calabria, Italy, 1991

CATHEDRAL OF ST. JOHN THE DIVINE
New York, NY, USA, 1991

GRAND PONT
Lille, France, 1991

KLOSTERSTRASSE RAILWAY VIADUCT
Berlin, Germany, 1991

MÉDOC SWING BRIDGE
Bordeaux, France, 1991

SALOU FOOTBALL STADIUM
Salou, Spain, 1991

SPANDAU RAILWAY STATION
Berlin, Germany, 1991

VALENCIA COMMUNICATIONS TOWER
Valencia, Spain, 1991

KUWAIT PAVILION
Seville, Spain, 1991–92

ALAMEDA BRIDGE AND SUBWAY STATION
Valencia, Spain, 1991–95

KRONPRINZEN BRIDGE
Berlin, Germany, 1991–96

OBERBAUM BRIDGE
Berlin, Germany, 1991–96

CITY OF ARTS AND SCIENCES
Valencia, Spain, 1991–2000/1996–2005/2005–09

TENERIFE AUDITORIUM
Santa Cruz de Tenerife, Spain, 1991–2003

JAHN OLYMPIC SPORTS COMPLEX
Berlin, Germany, 1992

LAKE BRIDGE
Lucerne, Switzerland, 1992

MODULAR STATION
London, UK, 1992

REICHSTAG CONVERSION
Berlin, Germany, 1992

SERPIS BRIDGE
Alcoy, Spain, 1992

SHADOW MACHINE
New York, NY, USA, 1992

SOLFERINO FOOTBRIDGE
Paris, France, 1992

RECINTO FERIAL DE TENERIFE
Santa Cruz de Tenerife, Spain, 1992–95

REMODELING OF PLAZA DE ESPAÑA
Alcoy, Spain, 1992–95

L'ASSUT DE L'OR BRIDGE
Valencia, Spain, 1992–2008

ALICANTE COMMUNICATIONS TOWER
Alicante, Spain, 1993

LA RADE BRIDGE
Geneva, Switzerland, 1993

GRANADILLA BRIDGE
Tenerife, Spain, 1993

HERNE HILL STADIUM
London, UK, 1993

ILE FALCON VIADUCT
Sierre, Switzerland, 1993

ÖRESUND LINK
Copenhagen, Denmark, 1993

ROOSEVELT ISLAND SOUTHPOINT PAVILION
New York, NY, USA, 1993

TRINITY FOOTBRIDGE
Salford, Manchester, UK, 1993–95

SONDICA CONTROL TOWER
Bilbao, Spain, 1993–96

ORIENTE STATION
Lisbon, Portugal, 1993–98

HOSPITAL BRIDGES
Murcia, Spain, 1993–99

MICHELANGELO TRADE FAIR AND CONVENTION CENTRE
Fiuggi, Italy, 1994

QUAYPOINT PEDESTRIAN BRIDGE
Bristol, UK, 1994

ST. PAUL'S FOOTBRIDGE
London, UK, 1994

MANRIQUE FOOTBRIDGE
Murcia, Spain, 1994–99

MILWAUKEE ART MUSEUM
Milwaukee, WI, USA, 1994–2001

BILBAO FOOTBALL STADIUM
Bilbao, Spain, 1995

EMBANKMENT RENAISSANCE FOOTBRIDGE
Bedford, UK, 1995

KL LINEAR CITY
Kuala Lumpur, Malaysia, 1995

SUNDSVALL BRIDGE
Sundsvall, Sweden, 1995

VELODROME FOOTBALL STADIUM
Marseille, France, 1995

ZURICH STATION ROOF
Zurich, Switzerland, 1995

CATHEDRAL SQUARE
Los Angeles, CA, USA, 1996

CHURCH OF THE YEAR 2000
Rome, Italy, 1996

CITY POINT
London, UK, 1996

OLYMPIC STADIUM
Stockholm, Sweden, 1996

POOLE HARBOUR BRIDGE
Poole, UK, 1996

PORTE DE LA SUISSE MOTORWAY SERVICE AREA
Geneva, Switzerland, 1996

MIMICO CREEK PEDESTRIAN BRIDGE
Toronto, Canada, 1996–98

BRIDGE OF EUROPE
Orléans, France, 1996–2000

OPERA HOUSE
Valencia, Spain, 1996–2006

LIÈGE-GUILLEMINS RAILWAY STATION
Liège, Belgium, 1996–2009

BARAJAS AIRPORT
Madrid, Spain, 1997

PORT DE BARCELONA
Barcelona, Spain, 1997

PFALZKELLER GALLERY
St. Gallen, Switzerland, 1997–99

SUNDIAL FOOTBRIDGE
Redding, CA, USA, 1997–2004

PENNSYLVANIA RAILWAY STATION
New York, NY, USA, 1998

TORONTO ISLAND AIRPORT BRIDGE
Toronto, Canada, 1998

PONT DES GUILLEMINS
Liège, Belgium, 1998–2000

BODEGAS YSIOS
Laguardia, Spain, 1998–2001

MUJER BRIDGE
Buenos Aires, Argentina, 1998–2001

JAMES JOYCE BRIDGE
Dublin, Ireland, 1998–2003

PETAH-TIKVA FOOTBRIDGE
Tel Aviv, Israel, 1998–2006

SAMUEL BECKETT BRIDGE
Dublin, Ireland, 1998–2009

CRUZ Y LUZ
Monterrey, Mexico, 1999

LEUVEN STATION
Sint-Niklaas, Belgium, 1999

NOVA PONTE SOBRE O RIO CAVADO
Barcelos, Portugal, 1999

PEDESTRIAN BRIDGE
Pistoia, Italy, 1999

REINA SOFÍA NATIONAL MUSEUM OF ART
Madrid, Spain, 1999

RESIDENTIAL HOUSE
Phoenix, AZ, USA, 1999

ROUEN BRIDGE
Rouen, France, 1999

THE CORCORAN GALLERY OF ART
Washington D.C., USA, 1999

WILDBACHSTRASSE
Zurich, Switzerland, 1999

ZARAGOZA STATION
Zaragoza, Spain, 1999

THE NEW YORK TIMES CAPSULE
New York, NY, USA, 1999–2001

BRIDGES OVER THE HOOFDVAART
Hoofddorp, the Netherlands, 1999–2004

TURNING TORSO
Malmö, Sweden, 1999–2004

FOURTH BRIDGE ON THE CANAL GRANDE
Venice, Italy, 1999–2008

CHRIST THE LIGHT CATHEDRAL
Oakland, CA, USA, 2000

CIUDAD DE LA PORCELANA
Valencia, Spain, 2000

DALLAS FORT WORTH AIRPORT
Dallas, TX, USA, 2000

DARSENA DEL PUERTO, CENTRO MUNICIPAL
Torrevieja, Spain, 2000

KORNHAUS
Rorschach, Switzerland, 2000

OPERA HOUSE PARKING
Zurich, Switzerland, 2000

RYERSON POLYTECHNIC UNIVERSITY
Toronto, Canada, 2000

STADIUM ZURICH
Zurich, Switzerland, 2000

BRIDGE OVER THE RIVER CRATI
Cosenza, Italy, 2000–18

UNIVERSITY CAMPUS BUILDINGS AND SPORTS CENTER
Maastricht, the Netherlands, 2000

SMU'S MEADOWS MUSEUM WAVE SCULPTURE
Dallas, TX, USA, 2000–02

CONFERENCE AND EXHIBITION CENTER
Iedo, Spain, 2000–11

LAKE PROMENADE
Rorschach, Switzerland, 2001

NERATZIOTISSA METRO AND RAILWAY STATION
Athens, Greece, 2001

PRIVATE RESIDENCE QATAR
Qatar, 2001

QUEEN'S LANDING PEDESTRIAN ACCESS IMPROVEMENT
Chicago, IL, USA, 2001

STAGE SETTING LAS TROYANAS
Valencia, Spain, 2001

THE AMERICAN MUSEUM OF NATURAL HISTORY
New York, NY, USA, 2001

KATEHAKI PEDESTRIAN BRIDGE
Athens, Greece, 2001–04

OLYMPIC SPORTS COMPLEX
Athens, Greece, 2001–04

VITTORIA BRIDGE
Florence, Italy, 2002

RECONSTRUCTION OF THE MUSEUM OF THE OPERA DI S. MARIA DEL FIORE
Florence, Italy, 2002

80 SOUTH STREET TOWER
New York, NY, USA, 2002

ATLANTA SYMPHONY ORCHESTRA
Atlanta, GA, USA, 2002

GREENPOINT LANDING
New York, NY, USA, 2002

PHOTOGRAPHY MUSEUM DOHA
Doha, Qatar, 2002

STAGE SETTING ECUBA
Rome, Italy, 2002–03

REGGIO EMILIA BRIDGES
Reggio Emilia, Italy, 2002–07

LIGHT RAIL TRAIN BRIDGE
Jerusalem, Israel, 2002–08

NEW FLORENCE AV STATION
Florence, Italy, 2002–13

REGGIO EMILIA AV – MEDIOPADANA STATION
Reggio Emilia, Italy, 2002–14

LAKE SHORE DRIVE
Chicago, IL, USA, 2003

WORLD TRADE CENTER TRANSPORTATION HUB
New York, NY, USA, 2003–16

RAILWAY AND AUTOMOBILE BRIDGE
Kiev, Ukraine, 2004

TOWERS
Valencia, Spain, 2004

OBELISK PLAZA CASTILLA
Madrid, Spain, 2004–09

MONS STATION
Mons, Belgium, 2004–24

INTERNATIONAL FAIR WORLD EXPO
Thessaloniki, Greece, 2005

CHICAGO SPIRE
Chicago, IL, USA, 2005 (design)

AGORA
Valencia, Spain, 2005–09

CITY OF SPORTS TOR VERGATA
Rome, Italy, 2005–

UNIVERSITÀ DEGLI STUDI DI ROMA
Tor Vergata, Rome, Italy, 2005–

GOVERNORS ISLAND GONDOLA CARS
New York, NY, USA, 2006

SCIENCE HOUSE
Zurich, Switzerland, 2006–08

THE NEW YORK CITY BALLET COLLABORATION
New York, NY, 2008–10

PEACE BRIDGE
Calgary, Canada, 2008–12

MARINA D'ARECHI
Salerno, Italy, 2008–

YUAN ZE UNIVERSITY CAMPUS NEW BUILDING COMPLEX
Taipei, Taiwan, 2008–

UNIVERSITY OF SOUTH FLORIDA POLYTECHNIC
Lakeland, FL, USA, 2009–14

MARGARET HUNT HILL BRIDGE
Dallas, TX, USA, 2010–12

MUSEUM OF TOMORROW
Rio de Janeiro, Brazil, 2010–15

MARGARET MCDERMOTT BRIDGE
Dallas, TX, USA, 2011–21

SHARQ CROSSING
Doha, Qatar, 2011–

RIO BARRA BRIDGE
Rio de Janeiro, Brazil, 2012 (design)

ST. NICHOLAS GREEK ORTHODOX CHURCH AND NATIONAL SHRINE
New York, USA, 2012–22

HAUS ZUM FALKEN
Zurich, Switzerland, 2014–25

HUASHAN BRIDGES
Wuhan, Hubei, China, 2015–

DUBAI CREEK TOWER
Dubai, UAE, 2016–

LONDON PENINSULA PLACE
London, UK, 2016–

UAE PAVILION AT EXPO 2020 DUBAI
Dubai, UAE, 2016–21

UAE EMBASSY IN BEIJING
Beijing, China, 2019–

CONSTELLATION
Chicago, IL, USA, 2020

INSTALLATION IN THE CHURCH OF SAN GENNARO
Naples, Italy, 2020–21

QATAR PAVILION AT EXPO 2020 DUBAI
Dubai, UAE, 2021

THREE SWISS BRIDGES
Eglisau, Zurich/Grüningen/Chur, Switzerland, 2026–

BIOGRAPHY

Architect, Artist and Engineer, Santiago Calatrava was born in 1951 in Valencia, Spain. He attended primary and secondary school in Valencia and, from the age of eight, he also attended the Arts and Crafts School, where he began his formal instruction in drawing and painting. Upon completing high school in Valencia and following a period spent in Paris, he enrolled in the Escuela Técnica Superior de Arquitectura in Valencia, where he received a degree in Architecture and took a postgraduate course in Urbanism.

Attracted by the mathematical rigor of certain great works of historic architecture, Calatrava decided to pursue postgraduate studies in Civil Engineering and enrolled in 1975 at the ETH (Swiss Federal Institute of Technology) in Zurich. He received his Ph.D. in 1981, presenting a thesis concerning the Foldability of Space Frames.

After completing his studies, he opened his first office in Zurich in 1981 and took on small engineering commissions. He also began to enter competitions, with his first winning proposal in 1983 for the design and construction of Stadelhofen Railway Station in Zurich. In 1984, Calatrava designed the Bach de Roda Bridge in Barcelona. This was the first of the bridge projects that established his international reputation. Among other notable bridges that followed were the Alamillo Bridge and Cartuja Viaduct, commissioned for the World's Fair in Seville (1987–92); the Campo Volantín Footbridge in Bilbao (1990–97); and the Alameda Bridge and Metro Station in Valencia (1991–95). Other large-scale public projects from the late 1980s and 1990s include the BCE Place: Galleria & Heritage Square in Toronto (1987–92) and the Oriente Railway Station in Lisbon (1993–98), commissioned for Expo '98.

Calatrava established his firm's second office in Paris in 1989 when he was working on the Lyon-Saint-Exupéry Airport Station (1989–94). In 1991, he won a competition in Valencia for a large cultural complex and urban intervention—the City of Arts and Sciences, a 35-hectare complex of arts facilities, a science museum, a planetarium, an opera house, the Ágora, two bridges and gardens—and started working in Spain. His project changed the face of a very underdeveloped and depressed area of Valencia.

In 2004, following Calatrava's first building in the United States—the expansion of the Milwaukee Art Museum in 1994—he opened an office in New York City. Further projects in the United States include the Sundial Bridge in Redding, California (his first bridge in the United States), the bridges over the Trinity River in Dallas, Texas, and the World Trade Center Transportation Hub in New York City. Later commissions in the USA include the first building for the Florida Polytechnic University's new campus in Lakeland and the St. Nicholas Greek Orthodox Church at the World Trade Center in New York City.

Selected projects completed since 2000 include Sondica Airport, Bilbao (2000); Bridge of Europe, Orléans (2000); Bodegas Ysios Winery, Laguardia (2001); Mujer Bridge, Buenos Aires (2001); James Joyce Bridge, Dublin (2003); Tenerife Auditorium, Santa Cruz (2003); Three Bridges over the Hoofdvaart, Hoofdoorp (2004); Athens Olympic Sports Complex (2004); Zurich University Law Faculty (2004); Turning Torso Tower, Malmö (2005); Petah Tikva Bridge (2006); Opera House, Valencia's City of Arts and Sciences (2006); Three Bridges in Reggio Emilia (2007); Bridge of Strings – LRT Bridge, Jerusalem (2008); Fourth Bridge on the Canal Grande, Venice (2008); Assut de l'Or Bridge, Valencia (2008); Liège-Guillemins TGV Railway Station (2009); Samuel Beckett Bridge, Dublin (2009); New York City Ballet Collaboration (2010); Palacio de Congresos, Oviedo (2011); Calgary's Peace Bridge (2012); Margaret Hunt Hill Bridge, Dallas (2012); Reggio Emilia AV – Mediopadana Station (2013); Museum of Tomorrow, Rio de Janeiro (2015); the World Trade Center Transportation Hub, New York (2016); Margaret McDermott Bridge, Dallas (2021); UAE Pavilion at Expo 2020 Dubai (2021); Qatar Pavilion at Expo 2020 Dubai (2021); and St. Nicholas Greek Orthodox Church, New York (2022).

Other projects currently being designed or under construction elsewhere in the world include the Sports City, Rectorate and Campus Master Plan for Roma II University in Tor Vergata, Rome; Marina d'Arechi, Salerno; Yuan Ze University Performing Arts Center, Arts and Design School and Y. Z. Hsu Memorial Hall, Taipei; Mons Railway Station; London Peninsula Place, UK; Kreuzbühlstrasse, Zurich; and the Sharq Crossing master plan in Doha, Qatar—three inter-connected bridges, between 600 and 1310 metres in length, connecting eight kilometers of subsea tunnels.

Doha's Sharq Crossing will be one of the most ambitious engineering projects ever undertaken in the Middle East, linking Doha's Hamad International Airport with the city's cultural district of Katara in the north and the downtown central business district of West Bay—at a total of 12 kilometers. The Sharq Crossing features an unsurpassed combination of an efficient civil engineering solution and the design of three unique bridges—which will provide an iconic skyline for the city of Doha to the world.

The Dubai Creek Tower is an iconic structure that will combine modern, sustainable design with the rich culture and heritage of the United Arab Emirates. The building's numerous observation decks are part of an elongated, oval-shaped bud at the top of the tower. The slender stem serves as the spine of the structure and the cables linking the building to the ground are reminiscent of the delicate ribbing of a lily's leaves. The structure also provides a beacon of light at night, with lighting that will emphasize the flower-bud design of the building.

A couple of other ongoing projects are the UAE Embassy in Beijing, China; and the Sohar Bank International Headquarters in Muscat, Oman—both of innovative design.

EXHIBITIONS, AWARDS, AND ACADEMIC ACKNOWLEDGMENTS

EXHIBITIONS

Exhibitions of Calatrava's work were first mounted in 1985 with the display of nine sculptures in a Zurich gallery. A new level of recognition was marked by two solo exhibitions: a retrospective at the RIBA in London in 1992, and the exhibition "Structure and Expression" at the MoMA in New York in 1993, while in the same year "Santiago Calatrava: Bridges" was exhibited at the Deutsche Museum in Munich. In 1994, "Santiago Calatrava: The Dynamics of Equilibrium" was staged in Tokyo's MA Gallery. "Santiago Calatrava: Artist, Architect, Engineer", an exhibition of architectural models, sculpture and drawings, was presented at Palazzo Strozzi in Florence in 2000. "Santiago Calatrava: Wie ein Vogel" (Like a Bird) was held at Vienna's Kunsthistorisches Museum in 2003. In 2005, an exhibition of his artistic body of work was mounted at the Metropolitan Museum of Art titled "Santiago Calatrava: Sculpture into Architecture". In 2010, "Santiago Calatrava: Sculptectures" was shown at the Museum Le Grand Curtius in Liège. Together with Frank Stella he exhibited their joint work "The Michael Kohlhaas Curtain" at Berlin's New National Gallery in 2011. In 2012, Calatrava's "The Quest for Movement" was staged at the State Hermitage Museum in St. Petersburg. The exhibition "Santiago Calatrava. Le metamorfosi dello spazio" was mounted at the Vatican Museum in the Vatican City in 2013. "Sculptures, Ceramics and Paintings" was held at the Marlborough Gallery in New York in 2014. "The Renaissance of the Church of St. Nicholas at Ground Zero" was presented at the Benaki Museum in Athens and at the Teloglion Foundation of Arts AU Th., Greece. The same exhibition "The Renaissance of the Church of St. Nicholas at Ground Zero" was also shown at the Municipal Art Gallery of Larissa G.I. Katsigras Museum in Greece, in 2016. In 2017, "Santiago Calatrava: Recent Works" was staged at the Marlborough Gallery in New York, as well as "Santiago Calatrava: Exploring the Art of Construction" at the Georgia Institute of Technology in Atlanta. In 2018, "Santiago Calatrava: Art & Architecture" was held at the Prague City Gallery. 2019–2021, "Santiago Calatrava. Esculturas/ Cerámicas/Dibujos" took place at the Marlborough Gallery Madrid, and a great show that marked the 40 years of Santiago Calatrava's career "In the Light of Naples" was staged in the Museo e Real Bosco di Capodimonte, Naples, Italy. In 2022, he exhibited his sculpture and graphic work in "Beyond Hellas. Santiago Calatrava in the Glyptothek" in Munich.

AWARDS AND RECOGNITION

Calatrava has received numerous prizes and awards from renowned institutions and organizations such as the UIA Auguste Perret Prize in 1987, the Gold Medal of the Institution of Structural Engineers, the Royal College of Art "Sir Misha Black Medal" (2002), the Principe de Asturias Art Prize, Oviedo, SEFI's Leonardo da Vinci medal, and the MIT "Eugene McDermott Award in the Arts" (2005), for his artistic achievements. He also received the Fritz Schumacher Prize for Urbanism, Architecture and Engineering (1998), Médaille d'Argent de la Recherche et de la Technique from the Fondation Académie d'Architecture (1990), Il Principe e l'Architetto, Architettura e Design per la Cittá (2002), the AIA Gold Medal (2005), the Premio Nacional de Arquitectura (2005), the Grande Médaille d'Or d'Architecture, Académie d'Architecture (2003) and the AIA National Medal (2012).

His buildings, such as the Milwaukee Art Museum, received the SEAOI 2002 Excellence in Design Award for Best Large Structure, the 2004 IABSE Outstanding Structure Award, the 2004 Outstanding Project Award from the NCSEA; while the Turning Torso Tower in Malmö received the MIPIM Award (2005), the fib 2006 Award for Outstanding Concrete Structures, and the Ten Year Award (2015) from the CTBUH. His railway stations, such as the Zurich Stadelhofen Railway Station and the Oriente Station in Lisbon received the Brunel Award in 1992 and 1998 respectively, and the Liège-Guillemins High-Speed Railway Station received the ESCN 2006 European Award for Excellence in Concrete. He also received numerous ECCS European Steel Design Awards for his projects, such as the reconstruction of the Berlin's Kronprinzenbrücke, the Bridge of Europe in Orléans, the University of Zurich Law Library, Three Bridges over the Hoofdvaart, Athens Olympic Stadium OAKA, Three Bridges in Reggio Emilia, and the Margaret Hunt Hill Bridge, Dallas, in 2012. He received the CISC-ICCA 2013 Steel Design Award of Excellence and the 2014 National Steel Design Award of Excellence for the Peace Bridge in Calgary, Canada. The Florida Polytechnic University project in Lakeland, completed in 2014, received the Award of Merit for Quality Concrete and was the winner of the ENR's National Best of the Best Project in the Higher Education/Research and Specialty Construction categories. The same project won the American Institute of Steel Construction IDEAS Award of 2015. In 2015, The PATH Station Transportation Hub, New York, was awarded the SARA Special Award for Excellence in Urban Infrastructure. He also received the "European Prize of Architecture 2015", The Chicago Athenaeum and the European Centre for Architecture Art Design and Urban Studies Design of the Year for the World Trade Center Path Station, Commercial Observer, New York. Museu do Amanhã, Rio de Janeiro, received the best Innovative Green Building MIPIM Award, in 2017. In 2018, the Mujer Bridge was declared Monument and Cultural Heritage of the City of Buenos Aires. In 2022, the UAE Pavilion at the Expo 2020 Dubai received the Sustainable Project of the Year Award from the Design Middle East—Architecture Leader Awards 2022. Calatrava received the Leonardo da Vinci Lifetime Achievement Award for Design at the XIV Florence Biennale 2023. In the past 35 years, Santiago Calatrava has participated in over 80 design competitions.

Calatrava's personal contribution has been recognized by many renowned institutions and organizations. He was named a "Global Leader for Tomorrow" by the World Economic Forum in 1993 and was named as one of the 100 most influential people by *Time* magazine in 2005.

ACADEMIC ACKNOWLEDGMENTS

Calatrava is a permanent guest lecturer at universities such as the ETH (Swiss Federal Institute of Technology Zurich), MIT School of Architecture and Design, University of Yale, Azrieli School of Architecture in Tel Aviv, and the New York Columbia University. In his career so far, he has received over 20 honorary doctorates (Doctor Honoris Causa) from universities around the world. Heriot-Watt, Salford, Strathclyde and Oxford universities in the UK, the European universities of Delft, Liège, Cassino, Ferrara, Lund, Valencia, Seville, Madrid and the Aristotle University of Thessaloniki alongside Israel's Technion Institute in Haifa and Tel Aviv's University. Honorary Doctorates have also been forthcoming from the United States from the Milwaukee School of Engineering, the Columbia University and Rensselaer Polytechnic Institute in New York, the Southern Methodist University in Dallas, the Pratt Institute in New York City, and the Georgia Institute of Technology. Besides being a Member of the Pontifical Council for Culture of the Vatican since 2011, Calatrava was also nominated in 2019 Ordinary Academic of the Pontifical Academy of Fine Arts of the Vatican.

Page 472:
Santiago Calatrava by
Thomas Hoeffgen

Page 473:
Santiago Calatrava in the garden
of his Zurich office, 2005

DAS GEHEIMNIS DER PHILANTHROPIE

„Anfangs wollte ich eine Kunstakademie besuchen“, erinnert sich Santiago Calatrava. „Dann ging ich eines Tages los, um etwas in einem Schreibwarenladen in Valencia zu kaufen, und sah ein kleines Buch mit wunderbaren Farben. Es hatte gelbe und orangefarbene Ellipsen auf blauem Untergrund, und ich kaufte es auf der Stelle. Es handelte von Le Corbusier, dessen Werk für mich eine Offenbarung war. Ich sah Bilder von den Treppenhäusern aus Beton in der Unité d'Habitation, und ich dachte bei mir, was für ein außerordentliches Formgefühl! Das Buch sollte die künstlerischen Aspekte im Werk des Architekten veranschaulichen. Die Folge dieses Kaufs war, dass ich an die Architekturfakultät wechselte.“[1]

Calatrava wurde 1951 in der Nähe von Valencia geboren und besuchte dort die Grund- und Oberschule. Ab 1959 war er zudem Schüler an der Escola d'Art i superior de disseny de Valencia, wo er mit methodischem Unterricht in Zeichnen und Malen begann. Als er 13 Jahre alt war, schickte seine Familie ihn als Austauschschüler nach Frankreich, da die spanischen Grenzen kurz zuvor von Franco geöffnet worden waren. Nach Abschluss der Oberschule in Valencia ging er nach Paris, um dort die École des Beaux-Arts zu besuchen, geriet jedoch 1968 mitten in die Studentenunruhen jener Zeit. Er kehrte nach Valencia zurück und schrieb sich unter dem Eindruck eines kleinen, farbenprächtigen Büchleins an der Escuela Técnica Superior de Arquitectura ein. Nach Abschluss des Architekturstudiums belegte er weiterführende Kurse in Städtebau.

Angezogen von der mathematischen Strenge, die er in bestimmten Werken historischer Architektur erkannte, und mit dem Gefühl, dass die Ausbildung in Valencia ihm keine klare Richtung vorgegeben hatte, entschied er sich für weiterführende Studien im Fach Bautechnik und schrieb sich 1975 an der ETH (Eidgenössische Technische Hochschule) in Zürich ein. 1981 wurde er dort promoviert. Diese Entscheidung sollte sein Leben in vieler Hinsicht verändern. So lernte er während dieser Züricher Zeit die Jurastudentin Robertina Marangoni kennen und heiratete sie. Auch in beruflicher Hinsicht sind die Schlüssel zu Calatravas gegenwärtigem Tun in Zürich zu finden. Laut eigener Einschätzung verspürte er „das starke Bedürfnis, wieder ganz von vorne anzufangen. Ich war entschlossen, alles, womit ich in der Ausbildung gearbeitet hatte, zur Seite zu legen und zu lernen, wie ein Ingenieur zu zeichnen und auch wie einer zu denken. Ich war fasziniert von der Vorstellung der Schwerkraft und spürte deutlich, dass es notwendig war, mit einfachen Formen zu arbeiten. Ich kann sagen, dass mein Hang zu technischer Einfachheit zum Teil auf mein Studium der Arbeit des Schweizer Ingenieurs Robert Maillart zurückzuführen ist. Mit einfachen Formen zeigte er, dass es möglich ist, starke Aussagen zu machen und gefühlsmäßige Reaktionen hervorzurufen. Mit der richtigen Kombination von Kraft und Masse lässt sich Emotion erzeugen.“

INGENIEUR, ARCHITEKT, KÜNSTLER

Auch Calatravas frühes Interesse an Kunst und sein ästhetisches Gespür, das ihn das Büchlein über Le Corbusier erstehen ließ, sollten Konstanten in seinem Werk bleiben und ihn darüber hinaus in der Welt der zeitgenössischen Architektur zu einer herausgehobenen Erscheinung machen. In Bezug auf eine Ausstellung über seine Kunst und Architektur, die 2005 im Metropolitan Museum of Art in New York stattfand, sagte Calatrava: „Ich glaube, der zuständige Kurator Gary Tinterow verstand meine Art zu arbeiten, weil er der Schau den Titel ‚Sculpture into Architecture‘ gab und nicht umgekehrt.

Architekturkritiker reagieren auf meine Arbeiten nach wie vor eher mit Verwirrung." Und in der Tat registrierte Nicolai Ouroussoff in der *New York Times* zwar, dass man im Metropolitan zuletzt 1973 das Werk eines lebenden Architekten ausgestellt hatte, fuhr dann aber fort: „Niemand würde behaupten, Calatravas Skulpturen gehörten an und für sich betrachtet in das Met; in künstlerischer Hinsicht sind sie überwiegend vom Werk toter Meister wie Brancusi inspiriert", um mit der recht harschen Ansicht zu schließen: „Er hätte die Skulpturen besser in seinem Atelier gelassen."[2] Diese Bemerkung scheint vor allem einen Mangel an Verständnis für Calatravas bildhauerisches Werk zu offenbaren. „Bei den Skulpturen", sagt er, „verwende ich Kugeln und Kuben, einfache Formen, die häufig mit meinen Kenntnissen als Ingenieur zu tun haben. Es war die Bildhauerei, die mich zum Turning Torso (Malmö, Schweden, 1999–2004, siehe Seite 276) anregte. Ich muss gestehen, dass ich die Freiheit eines Frank Gehry oder eines Frank Stella als Bildhauer sehr bewundere. Stellas Werke sind von solcher Freude und Freiheit erfüllt, die in meinen Skulpturen, die stets auf den festen Regeln der Mathematik fußen, nicht präsent sind."[3] Calatrava ließ keinen Zweifel daran, dass ihm der Galerienzirkus stets zuwider war und er folglich seine Skulpturen nahezu nie ausstellte. Auch betonte er die Tatsache, dass „die Reaktionen, die ich von Künstlern erhalte, sehr positiv sind. Kunst ist viel freier als Architektur, weil, wie Picasso sagte, einige Künstler mit Marmor und andere mit Scheiße arbeiten." Dies soll jedoch keineswegs heißen, dass sich Santiago Calatrava über die Schwierigkeit seiner Aufgabe irgendwelche Illusionen machte. 1997 schrieb er: „Architektur und Bildhauerei sind zwei Flüsse, in denen dasselbe Wasser fließt. Man kann sich die Bildhauerei als ungehinderte Plastizität vorstellen, während Architektur Plastizität ist, die sich einer Funktion und der offenkundigen Vorstellung menschlicher Maßstäblichkeit (durch Funktion) unterwerfen muss. Wo die Bildhauerei Funktion außer Acht lässt, ungebrochen ist von profanen Fragen der Verwendung, ist sie als reiner Ausdruck der Architektur überlegen. Allerdings ist die Architektur aufgrund ihrer engen Beziehung zum menschlichen Maß und zur Umgebung sowie durch den Umstand, dass wir in sie eindringen und sie betreten können, in diesen spezifischen Bereichen der Bildhauerei überlegen."[4]

Calatrava schlug sogar vor, die Kunst als Ideenpool für Architektur zu betrachten. „Weshalb fertige ich Zeichnungen von der menschlichen Figur an? Künstler und Architekt können ihre Botschaft unabhängig von der Zeit durch die schiere Macht von Form und Schatten senden. Rodin schrieb: ‚Harmonie bei lebenden Körpern ist das Ergebnis des Ausgleichs sich bewegender Massen. Die Kathedrale wurde nach dem Beispiel des lebenden Körpers erbaut.'[5] Ich möchte ein Beispiel anführen für die Bedeutung der Kunst für die Architektur des 20. Jahrhunderts. Als Le Corbusier 1923 schrieb: ‚Architektur ist das kunstvolle, korrekte und großartige Spiel der unter dem Licht versammelten Baukörper',[6] wie vielen war da bewusst, dass er Anleihen bei dem Bildhauer Auguste Rodin machte? 1914 schrieb Rodin in seinem Buch *Les cathédrales de France*: ‚Der Bildhauer erreicht nur dann großen Ausdruck, wenn er seine ganze Aufmerksamkeit dem harmonischen Zusammenspiel von Licht und Schatten widmet, so wie es der Architekt tut.'[7] Die Tatsache, dass einer der berühmtesten Sätze der modernen Architektur nicht von einem Architekten, sondern von einem Bildhauer inspiriert wurde, unterstreicht die Bedeutung von Kunst."

---

1 Santiago Calatrava im Gespräch mit dem Autor, Zürich, 22. Februar 2006.

2 Nicolai Ouroussoff, „Buildings Shown as Art and Art as Buildings", *The New York Times*, 25. Oktober 2005.

3 Santiago Calatrava im Gespräch mit dem Autor, Zürich, 22. Februar 2006.

4 „L'architecture et la sculpture sont deux fleuves dans lesquels coule une même eau. Imaginons que la sculpture est plastique pure et que l'architecture et plastique soumise à la fonction et avec une évidente fonctionnalité, elle es étrangère à la servitude dérivée des questions d'utilisation et donc elle est, pour ainsi dire, supérieur à l'architecture en tant qu'expression purement plastique. L'architecture au contraire soumet son expression plastique et à ces exigence. Par contre, celle-ci, de par son rapport à l'échelle humaine, à l'échelle de l'environnement de par son intériorité et sa pénétrabilité, elle l'emporte dans ces domains spécifique sur la sculpture." In: Julio González, *Zeichnen im Raum. Dessiner dans l'espace*, Mailand: 1997.

5 „L'harmonie, dans les corps vivants, resulte du contrebalancement des masses qui se déplacent: la Cathédrale est construite à l'example des corps vivants." In: Auguste Rodin, *Les cathédrales de France*, Paris: 1914.

6 Le Corbusier, *Vers une architecture*, Paris: 1923. [dt. *Ausblick auf eine Architektur*, Braunschweig: 1982, S. 38].

7 „Il n'atteint à la grande expression qu'en donnant toute son étude aux jeux harmoniques de la lumière et de l'ombre, exactement comme fait l'architecte." In: Auguste Rodin, 1914.

Neben seinem anhaltenden Interesse für Kunst fügte Calatrava seiner sehr persönlichen Definition von Architektur eine weitere verwandte Leidenschaft hinzu: Bewegung, und zwar in implizierter wie realer Ausprägung, das heißt als naturgesetzliche Bewegung. Von den frühen Falttüren des Lagerhauses der Firma Ernsting's (Coesfeld-Lette, 1983–85, siehe Seite 36) bis zu dem neueren, 115 t schweren Sonnensegel des Kunstmuseums in Milwaukee (Wisconsin, 1994–2001, siehe Seite 232) kommt er mit seinen Skulpturen und seiner Architektur immer wieder auf das ungewöhnliche Element der sich wiederholenden, realen Bewegung zurück. Weshalb? „In der Kunst des 20. Jahrhunderts spielt Kinetik eine Rolle", erwidert Calatrava. „Künstler wie Alexander Calder, Naum Gabo oder Moholy-Nagy schufen Skulpturen, die sich bewegen. Ich liebe ihre Arbeit, und sie berührt mich emotional sehr stark. Meine Doktorarbeit ‚Über die Faltbarkeit von Tragwerken' beschäftigte sich mit der Tatsache, dass man eine dreidimensionale, geometrische Figur auf zwei und schließlich auf eine Dimension reduzieren kann. Nehmen Sie ein Polyeder, und klappen Sie es flächig zusammen. Eine weitere Wandlung reduziert es auf eine Linie und damit auf eine Dimension. Sie können das als eine mathematische oder topologische Frage betrachten. Sämtliche Mysterien der allgegenwärtigen platonischen Körper sind im Polyeder versammelt. Nachdem ich über diese Fragen nachgedacht hatte, sah ich antike Skulpturen in einem anderen Licht. Werke wie der Diskobol des Myron erzeugen eine Spannung, die von einer Augenblicksbewegung abhängt. So begann ich, mich für das Problem der Zeit zu interessieren, Zeit als Variable. Einstein sagte: ‚Gott würfelt nicht mit dem Universum', und so wurde mir klar, dass alles mit Mathematik und der einzigartigen Dimension der Zeit zu tun hat. Dann dachte ich über Statik nach (den Zweig der Physik, der sich mit physikalischen Systemen in statischem Gleichgewicht beschäftigt) und erkannte, dass daran nichts statisch ist. Alles ist potenzielle Bewegung. Im zweiten Newton'schen Axiom heißt es, dass die Beschleunigung eines Objekts von zwei Variablen abhängt: der auf das Objekt einwirkenden reinen Kraft und der Masse des Objekts. Masse und Beschleunigung stehen in Verbindung, und somit gibt es Zeit in der Kraft. Ich begriff, dass Architektur voller beweglicher Dinge ist, von den Türen bis zum Mobiliar. Architektur selbst bewegt sich auch und wird mit etwas Glück zu einer schönen Ruine. Alles verändert sich, alles stirbt, und zyklische Bewegungen bergen eine existenzielle Bedeutung. Ich wollte eine eigene Tür schaffen, eine, die poetische Bedeutung haben sollte und sich in eine Figur im Raum verwandeln konnte, und so entstand das Ernsting's-Projekt."

DAS WESEN DER ARCHITEKTUR

Die Tatsache, dass es manchen Menschen angesichts der von Calatrava gewählten vielfältigen Ausdrucksformen unbehaglich wird, ist vermutlich der beste Indikator dafür, dass er etwas Bedeutsames erkannt hat. 2016 stellte er eines der komplexesten und in den USA politisch denkbar heikelsten Projekte fertig: den Verkehrsknotenpunkt am World Trade Center (siehe Seite 320) in dem von den New Yorkern jetzt als Ground Zero bezeichneten Gebiet. „Wir halten ihn für den da Vinci unserer Tage", sagte Joseph Seymour, der frühere leitende Direktor der Port Authority von New York und New Jersey und Auftraggeber dieses Bahnhofs. „Er vereint Licht, Luft und konstruktive Eleganz mit Stärke." Umgeben von neuen Wolkenkratzern und neben dem 9/11 Memorial gelegen, behauptet sich der Bahnhof deutlich als Santiago Calatravas ureigene Vision im Zentrum des amerikanischen Gedenkens eines der prägendsten Ereignisse der jüngeren Geschichte. Selbst in der verschlossenen Welt der Architektur mangelt es Calatrava nicht an Auszeichnungen. 2005 war er nach Josep Lluís Sert 1981 der zweite Spanier, der mit der renommierten Goldmedaille des American Institute of Architects (AIA) ausgezeichnet wurde. Das Committee on Design des AIA erklärte: „Santiago Calatravas Schaffen spürt das Wesen der Architektur

---

8 Sigfried Giedion, *Raum, Zeit und Architektur. Die Entstehung einer neuen Tradition*, Zürich: 1992. S. 139 f. und 158 f.

9 Matilda McQuaid, *Santiago Calatrava, Structure and Expression*, The Museum of Modern Art, New York: 1993.

10 Ebd.

auf. Seine Architektur erweitert den Horizont und bringt die Energie des menschlichen Geistes zum Ausdruck, sie bezaubert die Fantasie und erfreut uns mit den Wundern, die plastische Form und dynamische Konstruktion hervorbringen können. Santiago Calatrava verkörpert den Anlass für diese Goldmedaille. Seine Vision erhebt den menschlichen Geist, indem er Umgebungen schafft, in denen wir leben, spielen und arbeiten."

Das Nebeneinander von Kunst, Architektur und Technik in seinem Denken scheint Santiago Calatrava nicht zu verwirren. Und dennoch rührt er mit seinen vielfältigen Interessen tatsächlich an den Kern einer der intensivsten Debatten der jüngeren Zeit von Konstruktion und Design. Sigfried Giedion schrieb in seinem zukunftsweisenden Buch *Raum, Zeit und Architektur*: „Das Eindringen des Ingenieurkonstrukteurs bedeutete zugleich das Eindringen rascherer, industrieller Gestaltungsmittel, die erst die Möglichkeit gaben, Grundlagen für das heutige Leben zu schaffen. Unbewusst übernahm der Konstrukteur im 19. Jahrhundert eine Wächterrolle. Durch die neuen Mittel, die er immer wieder dem Architekten in die Hand drückte, zwang er diesen, sich nicht völlig im luftleeren Raum zu verlieren. Der Konstrukteur drängte zu einer Gestaltung, die zugleich anonym und kollektiv war." Giedion verfolgte die Debatte über die Rolle des Ingenieurs zurück, indem er eine Reihe wichtiger Daten und Ereignisse anführte, darunter „1877: Die Akademie stellt eine Preisfrage über ‚L'union ou la separation des ingénieurs et des architectes'. Davioud, der Architekt des Trocadéro, erhält den Preis für die Antwort: ‚Die Union zwischen Architekt und Ingenieur muss untrennbar sein. Die Lösung wird erst dann wirklich, vollständig und fruchtbar sein, wenn Architekt und Ingenieur, Künstler und Wissenschaftler in einer Person vereint sind … Wir leben seit Langem in der einfältigen Überzeugung, dass die Kunst eine Wesenheit sei, die sich von allen anderen Formen der menschlichen Intelligenz unterscheide, durchaus unabhängig habe sie ihre Quellen und ihre einzige Geburtsstätte in der kapriziösen Fantasie der Künstlerpersönlichkeit.'"[8] Da weder Giedions Beharren auf der „Anonymität" der Arbeit des Ingenieurs noch Daviouds Verweis auf die „kapriziöse Fantasie" der Künstler zu Calatravas machtvoller Originalität zu passen scheinen, erfüllt er wohl die Forderung Daviouds nach dem Einklang von Kunst, Technik und Architektur. In diesem Zusammenhang kommt einem auch Joseph Seymours Bemerkung von Calatrava als dem „da Vinci unserer Tage" in den Sinn.

Der Katalog von Santiago Calatravas Ausstellung im Museum of Modern Art in New York von 1993 unterstreicht die enge Beziehung seiner Arbeit zu der anderer wegweisender Ingenieure: „Calatrava ist Teil des ruhmreichen Vermächtnisses der Ingenieure des 20. Jahrhunderts. Wie die Vertreter vorhergehender Generationen – Robert Maillart, Pier Luigi Nervi, Eduardo Torroja und Felix Candela – sucht Calatrava mit seiner Arbeitsweise mehr als nur die Lösung technischer Probleme. Konstruktion bedeutete für diese Ingenieure das Abwägen zwischen dem wissenschaftlichen Kriterium der Effizienz und der Einführung neuer Formen. Calatrava betrachtet die Arbeit von Ingenieuren als ‚die Kunst des Möglichen' und sucht nach einer neuen Formensprache, die auf technischem Wissen basiert und doch keine Hymne an die Technik ist."[9] Der zuerst genannte Maillart (1872–1940) schloss 1894 sein Studium an der ETH Zürich ab und schuf in der Folgezeit einige der spektakulärsten modernen Brücken. Darüber hinaus verwendete er Beton auf innovative Weise. Bei seinem Lagerhaus Giesshübel in Zürich (1910) kam erstmals eine „Pilzdecke" aus Betonplatten zum Einsatz, die es ihm ermöglichte, ohne Balken auszukommen. Matilda McQuaid führte aus: „Maillart war einer der ersten Ingenieure dieses Jahrhunderts, der vollständig vom Mauerwerksbau abkam und für das Bauen mit armiertem Beton eine technisch geeignete, elegante Lösung anwendete. Obgleich bei Calatravas Arbeit die technische Idee weder wie bei Maillart die primäre Motivation noch völlig untergeordnet ist, bestimmt sie den Gesamteindruck des Bauwerks. Sein Werk wird zu einer Verflechtung plastischen Ausdrucks und konstruktiver Offenbarung und zeitigt Ergebnisse, die man am ehesten als Synthese von Ästhetik und konstruktiver Physik beschreiben kann."[10]

Auch wenn Calatrava die Bauten Maillarts bewundert, stellt er doch schnell klar, dass sich seine Brücken stark von denen seines Vorgängers unterscheiden, und sei es nur aufgrund ihrer Standorte.

„Maillarts Brücken“, sagt Calatrava, „stehen oft in herrlicher Berglandschaft. Seine Leistung bestand darin, erfolgreich ein künstliches Element in solch großartige Standorte zu integrieren. Heute“, fährt er fort, „glaube ich, dass eine der wichtigsten Aufgaben darin besteht, die Peripherie der Städte neu zu überdenken. Die meisten öffentlichen Bauten in solchen Bereichen sind rein funktional, aber selbst in der Nähe von Eisenbahngleisen oder über verschmutzten Flüssen können Brücken eine bemerkenswert positive Wirkung haben. Indem sie ein passendes Umfeld schaffen, können sie eine symbolische Wirkung entwickeln, deren indirekte Folgen weit über ihren unmittelbaren Standort hinausreichen.“[11]

Calatravas Arbeit wurde zweifellos von der Felix Candelas beeinflusst. Der 1910 in Madrid gebürtige Candela emigrierte 1939 nach Mexiko, wo er eine Reihe bemerkenswerter dünnschaliger Betonbauten schuf, wie die Iglesia de la Virgen Milagrosa (Narvarte, Mexiko, 1955), deren Formgebung zur Gänze auf hyperbolischen Paraboloiden basiert. Ein weiterer Spanier, der Madrider Ingenieur Eduardo Torroja (1899–1961), war fasziniert von der Verwendung organischer oder vegetabiler Formen, deren skulpturale Präsenz sehr wohl vom Vorbild Gaudís herrühren mag. Calatrava bezieht viele seiner Anregungen von spanischen, genauer gesagt von katalanischen Architekten oder Künstlern. „Was mich beispielsweise an der Person Goyas fasziniert“, sagt Calatrava, „ist die Tatsache, dass er, wie Rembrandt vor ihm, zu den ersten Künstlern gehört, die sich von der Vorstellung lossagten, irgendeinem Meister zu dienen. An Mirós Werk bewundere ich dessen außerordentliche Stille, ebenso wie seine radikale Absage an jegliche Konvention.“ Obgleich Gaudí, ähnlich wie Maillart, für ihn ein Vorbild war, scheint Calatrava lieber über den Bildhauer Julio González zu reden. „González’ Vater und Großvater waren als Schmiede für Gaudí an Projekten wie dem Parque Güell tätig. Dann gingen sie nach Paris, und hier findet sich die Quelle für Julio González’ Arbeit mit Metall. Bei aller gebotenen Bescheidenheit“, schließt Calatrava, „lässt sich sagen, dass unsere Arbeit die natürliche Fortführung des Wirkens Gaudís und González’ darstellt, die Arbeit von Kunsthandwerkern auf dem Weg zur abstrakten Kunst.“[12]

Die Art von Kunst, auf die Calatrava sich bezieht, zeigt sich in seinen erfolgreichsten Brücken und Gebäuden, und doch ist sie schwer in Worte zu fassen. Ein anderer wegweisender Ingenieur des 20. Jahrhunderts, der Italiener Pier Luigi Nervi, wagte eine solche Definition in einer Reihe von Vorlesungen, die er 1961 in Harvard hielt: „Es ist äußerst schwierig zu erklären, warum wir bestimmte Formen unmittelbar akzeptieren, die aus einer physischen Welt zu uns kommen, zu der wir scheinbar keinerlei direkte Verbindungen unterhalten. Weshalb befriedigen und bewegen uns diese Formen in der gleichen Weise wie natürliche Dinge wie Blumen, Pflanzen und Landschaften, an die wir uns seit zahllosen Generationen gewöhnt haben? Es lässt sich weiterhin feststellen, dass diese Errungenschaften ein struktureller Kern eint, ein notwendiges Fehlen jeglicher Verzierung, eine Reinheit von Linie und Form, die mehr als ausreichend ist, um einen authentischen Stil zu definieren – einen Stil, den ich den *wahren Stil* nenne. Ich bin mir darüber im Klaren, wie schwierig es ist, die richtigen Worte zur Erklärung dieser Gedanken zu finden. Wenn ich Freunden gegenüber diese Bemerkungen mache, höre ich häufig, diese Auffassung von der nahen Zukunft sei schrecklich traurig, und es wäre vielleicht besser, freiwillig auf das weitere Festigen der Bande zwischen unseren Werken und den physikalischen Gesetzen zu verzichten, falls uns diese Bande zu einer tödlichen Monotonie führen müssen. Ich finde diesen Pessimismus nicht angebracht. Wie bindend technische Anforderungen auch sein mögen, es bleibt immer genügend Freiraum, um die Persönlichkeit des jeweiligen Urhebers erkennen zu lassen und, wenn es sich um einen Künstler handelt, zu gewährleisten, dass seine Schöpfung, ungeachtet ihrer strikten technischen Verpflichtung, zu einem wahrhaften Kunstwerk wird.“[13]

---

11 Santiago Calatrava im Gespräch mit dem Autor, Zürich, Juni 1997.
12 Ebd.
13 Pier Luigi Nervi, *Aesthetics and Technology in Building, The Charles Eliot Norton Lectures, 1961–1962*, Cambridge, Mass.: 1965, S. 186.
14 Santiago Calatrava im Gespräch mit dem Autor, Zürich, Juni 1997.
15 Ebd.

ENTLANG DER STÄHLERNEN GLEISE

Calatravas langer Aufenthalt in Zürich hat eine Reihe von Gründen. Nach Abschluss seines eigenen Studiums blieb er zunächst dort, weil seine Frau Robertina das ihre noch nicht beendet hatte. Wie es der Zufall wollte, gewann er 1982 einen offenen Wettbewerb für den neuen Bahnhof Stadelhofen (1983–90, siehe Seite 52). Zu behaupten, dieses ungewöhnliche Gebäude befinde sich in zentraler Lage, käme fast einer Untertreibung gleich.

Hineingebaut in einen begrünten Hang nahe dem Bellevueplatz an der Theaterstraße, unweit des Zürichsees, ist es in ein größtenteils traditionelles Stadtgefüge integriert. „Um den Bahnhof Stadelhofen zu verstehen", sagt Calatrava, „muss man ihn als urbanes Projekt betrachten, eines, bei dem es um die Instandsetzung des urbanen Gefüges ging. Es besteht ein eindeutiger Gegensatz zwischen der radikalen Natur der gewählten technischen und architektonischen Lösungen und der äußerst freundlichen Haltung zur Stadt hin. Es wurden unzählige Verbindungen geschaffen – nicht nur Brücken und Zugänge, sondern auch Verbindungen zu umliegenden Straßen, die es vorher nicht gab. Es entstanden kleine Parks, wie die Grünanlage auf der oberen Ebene." Tatsächlich trifft der Besucher, nähert er sich der Station von der Stadt aus, zuerst auf einen sehr traditionellen Pavillon, der ursprünglich den Bahnhof beherbergte, bevor er die von Calatrava entworfenen Bereiche betritt bzw. hinabsteigt. „Es war von Anfang an klar", so der Architekt, „dass der Respekt, den in der Schweiz Bauten genießen, die 100 Jahre oder älter sind, jeden Versuch ausschloss, das alte Bahnhofsgebäude abzureißen oder wesentlich zu verändern. Ich fand diesen Standpunkt allerdings nicht unlogisch, weil er zu einer intakten Stadt passt."[14] Hat der Reisende allerdings den alten Pavillon durchschritten, betritt er eine ganz andere Welt, die eher der Fantasie Gaudís verbunden scheint als dem Phlegma Züricher Bürger. Während Calatrava darauf verweist, dass Zürich mit Häusern von Leuten wie Marcel Breuer eine gewisse Tradition radikaler Architektur aufweist, ist es offensichtlich, dass er mit dem Bahnhof Stadelhofen zum ersten Mal in seiner Laufbahn in großem Maßstab die Art innovativer Gestaltung ausführte, die ihn berühmt gemacht hat.

Auf dem geschwungenen, 40 x 240 m großen Gelände musste bei laufendem Betrieb der Pendlerzüge gebaut werden; außerdem war eine großflächige unterirdische Einkaufszone hinzugekommen. Das Ganze zeichnet sich durch eine organische Einheit aus, die die Umstände nicht hätten vereinfachen können. Wie ein fantastischer Flugsaurier, der sich an diesem Abhang niedergelassen hat, wird der Bau durch ein Muster sich wiederholender Elemente gegliedert; riesige zoomorphe Tore führen zu der unterirdischen Einkaufszone, in der man schnell den Eindruck gewinnt, sich im steinernen Bauch des Tieres zu befinden. Es besteht eine Kontinuität zwischen dem oberirdischen dunklen Metall und dem rippengleichen Beton unten, die eine klare Hierarchie von Räumen und Formen festlegt, während gleichzeitig die Lesbarkeit und funktionelle Klarheit des Bahnhofs größte Bedeutung haben.

Obwohl der Bahnhof Stadelhofen insgesamt den Eindruck erweckt, er sei einer Art Dinosauriermetapher entsprungen, ist die Substanz von Calatravas Gestaltung komplexer oder andersartig. „In Wirklichkeit habe ich etwas versucht, das ich als dialektische Transgression bezeichnen würde, die auf der Formensprache konstruktiver Kräfte basiert. In Stadelhofen gibt es beispielsweise eine Reihe geneigter Pfeiler. Diese anscheinend ästhetische Entscheidung hat in Wahrheit mit der Notwendigkeit zu tun, den Bau zu stützen. Natürlich gab es verschiedene Lösungen für dieses Problem. Ich hätte zum Beispiel schlichte Zylinder wählen können, aber ich entschied mich, sie in Form einer Hand zu gestalten. Hier wird die Frage der Metaphern interessant. Wie lässt sich die Funktion von Pfeilern besser zum Ausdruck bringen, als sie mit der Empfindung der physischen Geste des Tragens auszustatten?"[15]

Obgleich Calatravas Name häufig im Zusammenhang mit Brücken genannt wird, ist er auch ein anerkannter Spezialist für Bahnhöfe, wie der Bahnhof Oriente in Lissabon oder der Komplex in Liège-Guillemins in Frankreich belegen. Einer der Bauten, die am meisten zu seinem wachsenden Renommee beitrugen, war allerdings der Bahnhof am Flughafen Lyon-Saint-Exupéry, ehemals Flughafen Lyon-Satolas (1989–94, siehe Seite 104). Dieser 5600 m^2 große Bahnhof gehörte damals zu einer neuen Generation von Bahnhöfen, die eigens für das wachsende Netz von Hochgeschwindigkeitszügen (TGV) in Frankreich errichtet wurden. Das Nebeneinander von Bahn-, Luft- und Lokalverkehr am selben Ort gewährleistet ein besonders leistungsfähiges Verkehrssystem. Das 120 m lange, 100 m breite und 40 m hohe Passagierterminal, das am 7. Juli 1994 eröffnet wurde, hat ein 1300 t schweres Dach aus Stahl. Mit seiner Anmutung eines fliegenden Vogels scheint Calatravas Bahnhof auf Eero Saarinens TWA-Terminal am Kennedy Airport (1957–62) zu verweisen, ist aber extravaganter als sein amerikanischer Vorfahr. Der Grundriss der Anlage erinnert dank seiner Verbindung zum Flughafen auch an einen Mantarochen. Unter dem Hauptgebäude verkehren insgesamt sechs Bahnlinien und halten an einem ebenfalls von Calatrava entworfenen 500 m langen, überdachten Bahnsteig. Die mittleren Gleise, die Zügen mit einer Geschwindigkeit von über 300 km/h vorbehalten sind, sind von einem Betongehäuse umschlossen, bei dessen Errichtung es galt, die Druckwellen sorgfältig zu berechnen, welche die Hochgeschwindigkeitszüge umgeben. Die Gesamtkosten dieser Einrichtung, die von der französischen Eisenbahngesellschaft (SNCF), der Region Rhône-Alpes und dem Département Rhône gemeinsam aufgebracht wurden, betrugen umgerechnet mehr als 91,5 Millionen Euro.

Auf das Bild des prähistorischen Vogels angesprochen, erwidert Calatrava in gewohnt indirekter, gleichwohl informativer Art: „Ich bin bloß ein Architekt, kein Künstler oder einer, der eine Revolution entfachen will. Interessanterweise hat Victor Hugo in seinem Roman *Der Glöckner von Notre-Dame* die Kathedrale mit einem urzeitlichen Monster verglichen. Obwohl er über gute Kenntnisse der Architektur verfügt haben mag und ein äußerst gewissenhafter Autor war, zögerte er nicht, zur Beschreibung von Notre-Dame eine derart unvermutete Metapher zu verwenden. Ich bin ehrlich gesagt nicht auf der Suche nach Metaphern. Ich hatte nie einen Vogel im Sinn, sondern eher die Vorstudien, die ich bisweilen etwas anmaßend als Skulpturen bezeichne.“[16] Tatsächlich rekurrieren die Zeichnungen und die Skulptur Calatravas, die sich am deutlichsten auf den Bahnhof in Lyon beziehen, anscheinend nicht auf die Vogelmetapher, sondern auf eine Studie des Auges und des Augenlides, ein in seinem Werk immer wiederkehrendes Motiv. „Das Auge“, so Calatrava, „ist das wahre Werkzeug des Architekten, und das ist eine Vorstellung, die sich bis auf die Babylonier zurückverfolgen lässt.“

Die gebogene Vorderseite des Bahnhofs Lyon-Saint-Exupéry, die in die Erde hineinzustoßen scheint, wurde mit dem Schnabel eines Vogels verglichen, aber einmal mehr scheint Calatrava an etwas gänzlich anderes gedacht zu haben. „Der ‚Schnabel‘ entstand als Ergebnis komplizierter Berechnungen der auf den Bau einwirkenden Kräfte. Außerdem laufen hier sämtliche Wasserabflüsse zusammen. Natürlich habe ich mich bemüht, die Masse dieses Punktes so gering wie möglich zu halten, ohne allerdings an irgendwelche zoomorphen Bezüge zu denken“, erklärte Calatrava. „Nennen Sie es irrational, aber ich würde sagen, dass es keinen Pfad gibt, dem ich folge. Ich möchte sein wie ein Schiff auf See. Es hinterlässt eine Spur, aber davor gibt es keinen Pfad.“[17]

BÄUME AUF DEM HÜGEL

Calatravas Arbeit an dem aufsehenerregenden Bahnhof Oriente (siehe Seite 212) in Lissabon ist ein vielsagendes Beispiel für seine Vorgehensweise und erklärt einen Gutteil seines frühen Erfolgs. In der Folge des verheerenden Erdbebens von 1755 orientierte sich Lissabon stärker zum Land hin und kehrte, nahezu im Wortsinn, der Tejomündung mit ihren weiten Ausblicken den Rücken zu. Diese Tendenz verstärkte sich in der Zeit danach, weil sich auf Aufschüttungen am Flussufer Industrieanlagen ansiedelten. Das 340 ha umfassende Sanierungsgebiet, in dessen Zentrum das Gelände der Expo ’98 und der Bahnhof Oriente liegen, hatte man bis in die 1990er-Jahre für Brennstofftanks, Containerlager, den städtischen Schlachthof sowie für Kläranlagen und Einrichtungen zur Abfallverwertung genutzt.

---

16 Santiago Calatrava im Gespräch mit dem Autor, Zürich, Juni 1997.

17 Ebd.

Obgleich viel von Lissabons glorreicher Vergangenheit in seinen Straßen und Plätzen noch erkennbar ist, ging sein inniges Verhältnis zum Tejo, einstmals die Quelle unvorstellbaren Reichtums, in den Zeitläufen beinahe verloren.

Vor diesem Hintergrund führte der portugiesische Architektenbund 1988 einen Ideenwettbewerb zur Gestaltung der Uferzone durch. Der Bau des Kulturzentrums von Belém (1988–92) in Ufernähe war der erste wichtige Schritt hin zu einer Wiederbelebung der historischen Bindungen Lissabons an den Tejo. Eine noch bedeutsamere politische und kulturelle Entscheidung begann im November 1993 Gestalt anzunehmen, als die Parque Expo '98 SA den Architekten Luís Vassalo Rosa mit einer ersten „Planung zur Urbanisierung des Sanierungsgebiets" betraute. Von Anfang an beabsichtigten die Bauträger, hier etwas entstehen zu lassen, das über die typisch kurzlebige Architektur einer Weltausstellung hinausging. Das am Ostrand der Stadt gelegene Gebiet, das 5 km Flussufer des Tejo umfasst, befindet sich in der Nähe der Vasco-da-Gama-Brücke. Die am 29. März 1998 eröffnete, 45 m hohe, imposante Brücke überspannt den hier 12 km breiten Tejo. Die Fertigstellung der nach dem berühmten Entdecker benannten Brücke und die Vergabe der Expo '98 hätten nicht symbolträchtiger sein können: Lissabon und mit ihm ganz Portugal waren entschlossen, ihr historisches Erbe wieder geltend zu machen und sich erneut dem Tejo und darüber hinaus der Welt zu öffnen.

Nach einem geschlossenen Wettbewerb, an dem sich auch Terry Farrell, Nicholas Grimshaw, Rem Koolhaas und Ricardo Bofill beteiligten, erhielt Santiago Calatrava den Auftrag zum Bau des Bahnhofs Oriente. Neben Álvaro Sizas portugiesischem Pavillon ist dieser Bahnhof zweifellos der architektonisch bedeutsamste Bau der Expo '98. Mit seinen 200 000 Besuchern pro Tag stand er eindeutig im Zentrum der Planung zur Wiederbelebung der Uferzone im Osten der Stadt. Das eindrucksvollste Element des Projekts ist dabei sicherlich die 78 x 238 m große Überdachung der acht erhöhten Bahngleise, die an ein lichtes Gehölz denken lässt. Anstatt die vom Bahnhof vorgegebene Zäsur zwischen Stadt und Fluss zu betonen, war Calatrava hier wie andernorts bestrebt, Durchgänge zu öffnen und Verbindungen wiederherzustellen. Deshalb schnitt der Architekt in den erhöhten Erdwall, auf dem die Gleise verlaufen, ein, um den Bahnhof unter die Erde zu verlegen. Über den Eingängen befinden sich zwei großflächige Schutzdächer aus Stahl und Glas, von denen das eine in der Länge nicht weniger als 112 m und in der Breite 11 m misst. Es gibt einen Busbahnhof und einen Parkplatz, darunter eine nicht von Calatrava konzipierte U-Bahn-Station sowie eine längs verlaufende Ladengalerie, die Bestandteil der Ausschreibung war. Die Fahrkarten- und Serviceschalter befinden sich 5 m unterhalb der Gleise, während unter der Galerie ein Atrium entstand, das die als Hauptzugang gedachte Öffnung zum Fluss hin markiert.

Aus der Entfernung oder auch von innen betrachtet, ist der augenfälligste Aspekt des Bahnhofs Oriente die an Bäume erinnernde Gestaltung. Mindestens zwei weitere Projekte Calatravas machten mit ihrer konstruktiven Typologie Anleihen bei Bäumen oder Wäldchen: sein nicht realisierter Entwurf für die Kathedrale St. John the Divine in New York (1991) und das Projekt BCE Place: Galleria und Heritage Square in Toronto (1987–92, siehe Seite 74). St. John the Divine, eine der bekanntesten Kirchen New Yorks, war 1892 von Heins & La Farge im Stil der Neoromanik erbaut und 1911 von Cram & Ferguson „gotisiert" worden. Calatravas Entwurf zufolge wären ein neues, südliches Querschiff und ein Bio-Shelter in 55 m Höhe ergänzt worden. Das offenkundig sinnbildlich mit dem Paradies verwandte „Bio-Shelter" hätte von konstruktiven Elementen gestützt werden sollen, deren Gestaltung von Bäumen inspiriert war. Dieser im vorhandenen Dachgeschoss des Langhauses untergebrachte Garten hätte zwar den Umriss des Bauwerks nicht verändert, aber Tageslicht in die Kirche einfallen lassen. Philip Johnson, der der Jury angehörte, wies auf den Zusammenhang von Calatravas Entwurf mit dem Stil der Kirche hin, und in der Tat ruft das Bild des Baums die Ursprünge der Gotik in Erinnerung. Auch dem Projekt BCE Place: Galleria und Heritage Square liegt das Bild des Baums zugrunde. In Zusammenarbeit mit dem New Yorker Büro von Skidmore, Owings & Merrill entwarf Calatrava einen sechsgeschossigen, 115 m langen Durchgang aus weiß lackiertem Stahl und Glas, der zwei Türme miteinander verbindet. Der Kommentar der *New York Times* dazu lautete: „Diese Galerie erinnert stark an Gaudí."

Sie erinnert außerdem an einen metaphorischen Waldweg. Der Gebrauch von weiß gestrichenem Stahl und Glas nimmt darüber hinaus die baumartige Gestaltung der Bahnsteige im Bahnhof Oriente vorweg.

Ob nun in Toronto oder in New York, Santiago Calatrava griff aus verschiedenen Gründen auf die Baummetapher zurück – im ersten Fall in Verbindung mit einem großflächigen städtischen Raum inmitten von Hochhäusern, im zweiten mit Bezug auf den neogotischen Stil von St. John the Divine. Die Tatsache, dass der Baum eine der offenkundigsten Vorlagen für Säulen oder die Formen früher Kirchenschiffe ist, bekräftigt nur seine starke biologische Präsenz. Dazu fallen einem die Worte Nervis ein, dass „wir bestimmte Formen unmittelbar akzeptieren, die aus einer physischen Welt zu uns kommen". Im Fall des Bahnhofs Oriente erläuterte Calatrava, dass mit seinem eigenen Verständnis von Lissabon in Zusammenhang stehende besondere Umstände zu dem ungewöhnlichen Entwurf der Überdachung führten. „Während des Wettbewerbs für den Bahnhof Oriente fuhr ich mindestens fünfmal nach Lissabon, und wenn es nur war, um die Atmosphäre der Stadt in mich aufzunehmen. Es mag unnötig sein, das zu sagen, aber Lissabon ist eine sehr schöne Stadt. Wie Rom ist sie auf Hügeln erbaut, sodass sich häufig denkwürdige Aussichten ergeben. Man befindet sich in der Stadt und kann sie doch gleichzeitig betrachten. Hinzu kommt der majestätische Tejo, der an diesem Punkt der breiteste Fluss Europas ist. Das sogenannte Mar da Palha (Strohmeer) ist unglaublich riesig. Die Stadtgeschichte Lissabons reicht weit in die Antike zurück, und doch zeichnet sich ihre Anlage durch große Klarheit aus."[18]

Wenn Calatrava von der Gestaltung der Bahnsteige des Bahnhofs Oriente redet, spricht er von „Bäumen auf einem Hügel". Mit „Hügel" ist der hohe Damm gemeint, auf dem die Gleise verlaufen. Zur Erklärung der Baummetapher verweist er wiederum auf seine Besuche in Lissabon während des Wettbewerbs. „In der Stadt gibt es zahlreiche Parkanlagen mit Bäumen", sagt er. „Ich spürte sofort, dass die erhöhten Gleise einen bewaldeten Hang brauchten. Ich hatte da eine sehr deutliche Vorstellung im Kopf. Für den Wettbewerb zitierte ich ein sehr düsteres Gedicht von Fernando Pessoa, das die Vorstellung heraufbeschwört, in den ‚arvoredo', den Wald, zu gehen. Ich wollte die Transparenz des Bahnhofs betonen. In einem urbanen Kontext, der sich zweifellos noch stärker verdichten wird, soll der Bahnhof Oriente einer Oase gleichen. Die Leute werden diesen Ort aufsuchen, um Ruhe zu finden!" Als er gefragt wurde, weshalb er in diesem Fall eine Pflanzenmetapher statt der vom ihm ansonsten geschätzten zoomorphen Gestaltungen bevorzugte, antwortete er: „Stellen Sie sich vor, Sie gestalten einen erhöhten Platz. Das ist offensichtlich keine introvertierte Art von Architektur. Ich stehe auf einem Hügel in Lissabon und schaue mich um. Was fehlt? Schutz vor der Sonne und dem Regen."[19]

Der Entwurf Calatravas für den Bahnhof Liège-Guillemins (siehe Seite 254) offenbart einige Änderungen in seiner Denkweise und veranschaulicht Gründe für die Unterschiede zwischen der schmucklosen Schlichtheit seiner Brücken und der komplexeren Anmutung seiner größeren Gebäude. „Brücken erfordern gerade aufgrund ihres Charakters eine strikte Sparsamkeit der Mittel. Man hat die Brückentafel, den sie tragenden Bogen und den Unterbau, die jeweils etwa ein Drittel der Kosten ausmachen. Angesichts der funktionalen Eindimensionalität einer Brücke gibt es nur begrenzten Raum für Abweichungen. Andererseits sind bei einem Bahnhof mindestens 16 Arten von Entscheidungen zu treffen, die sich ästhetisch auswirken können, angefangen bei der Wahl der Metallfensterrahmen bis hin zur Gestaltung der Beleuchtung und so weiter. Es hängt vom Geschick des Designers ab, innerhalb der wirtschaftlichen Zwänge eines solchen Projekts das von ihm intendierte Ergebnis zu erzielen." Ungeachtet dieser grundlegend anderen Situation ist leicht zu erkennen, dass Calatravas Neigung zu „Transgression" oder Innovation ihn gleichermaßen dazu bringt, ungewöhnliche Brücken und überraschende Bahnhöfe zu entwerfen. „Nehmen Sie den Fall des TGV-Bahnhofs in Liège", so Calatrava. „Wir erfanden

---

18 Santiago Calatrava im Gespräch mit dem Autor, Paris, September 1998.
19 Ebd.
20 Santiago Calatrava im Gespräch mit dem Autor, Zürich, Juni 1997.
21 Santiago Calatrava im Gespräch mit dem Autor, Zürich, 22. Februar 2006.

die Fassade vollständig neu. Beziehungsweise, es gibt keine Fassade. Das ist meiner Ansicht nach eine grundlegende Transgression. Anstelle einer herkömmlichen Fassade wird es nur große Öffnungen geben, durch Markisen aus Metall markiert, die den Bahnhofsvorplatz überdachen." Wie Calatrava betont, hat diese Designentscheidung wichtige Folgen für die funktionale Anlage des Bahnhofs. Bildlicher gesprochen, ließe sich fragen, wie ein Bahnhof ohne Fassade als solcher identifiziert werden kann. „Der Kontext ist urban, mir schien der erste Eindruck wichtig zu sein, den die Reisenden oder Besucher von der Station erhalten", erklärte Calatrava. „Meine Lösung war eine zweifache. Da sie sich auf einem Hügel befindet und von oben erreicht wird, bietet sich ein Blick auf die Stadt und das Layout der Anlage. Somit wird der Grundriss zur eigentlichen Fassade. Um die Beziehung zwischen Stadt und Bahnhof zu verbessern, schlugen wir vor, einen Platz davor anzulegen."[20] Es scheint, dass der Bahnhof von Liège mit dieser Strategie des Fehlens oder einer Art von Minimalismus in seinem Konzept den Brücken nähersteht als einige von Calatravas früheren Bauten. Was seinen Hang zur „Transgression" betrifft, wird ersichtlich, dass Calatravas sorgfältige Methoden Rücksicht auf die ökonomischen und funktionalen Bedingungen eines Projekts nehmen und aus der Skala verfügbarer technischer Möglichkeiten eine spezifische Schlussfolgerung ziehen. Seine Ideen funktionieren und fesseln das öffentliche Interesse, weil die fruchtbare Vorstellungskraft des Ingenieurarchitekten sie hervorbringt, aber auch, weil sie von Anfang an die beteiligten grundlegenden Kräfte berücksichtigen.

FLÜGEL UND EIN GEBET

Zweifellos war Calatravas Gespür für Stadtplanung ausschlaggebend für seine erfolgreiche Teilnahme an den Wettbewerben in Lissabon wie auch in Liège oder in jüngerer Zeit in Manhattan, wo es um den symbolisch bedeutsamen Verkehrsknoten am World Trade Center ging. Er ist anscheinend zutiefst davon überzeugt, dass der Architekt einen Ort wie einen Bahnhof überhöhen und mit einer sakralen Anmutung ausstatten kann. Gefragt, ob es ihm eher darum gehe, dem Menschen angemessene Räume zu bauen, oder ob er etwas anstrebe, was darüber hinausreiche, offenbart seine Antwort viel über sein kreatives Vorgehen. „Alles fußt auf dem Menschen, aber die Vielschichtigkeit des Menschen beinhaltet auch das Sakrale, sonst gäbe es nicht so viele Leute, die sich in Rom ins Pantheon drängen, um die runde Öffnung in der Kuppel zu sehen. Wie sieht es mit Bahnhöfen aus? Wenn Sie das Beispiel der modernen Bahnhöfe in der Schweiz nehmen – in Zürich oder Basel zum Beispiel –, haben Sie das Gefühl, sich in einem Einkaufszentrum zu befinden. Das Grand Central Terminal in New York scheint von einem anderen Planeten zu stammen. Indem sie abstrakte Werte sublimiert, kann die Architektur als Katalysator für gewaltige Ereignisse fungieren. Wenn man sie allerdings in rein funktionalistischer Absicht in Angriff nimmt, katalysiert man gar nichts, sondern landet in einem mittelprächtigen Einkaufszentrum. Das Gefühl, das sich bei mir in der zentralen Halle des Grand Central Terminals einstellt, sagt mir, dass ich es mit einem Werk großer Einsicht zu tun habe. Es verleiht dem Kommerz ein spezielles Empfinden, ja sogar eine sakrale Anmutung. Während an der Funktionalität des Bahnhofs keine Abstriche nötig sind, wird er zu einem Festakt. Schauen Sie sich an, was darum herum alles entstanden ist – das Seagram Building und die Park Avenue selbst. In dieser Hinsicht gleicht in Amerika kein Gebäude so sehr dem Pantheon. Schauen Sie, was die Architekten ins Zentrum der großen Halle gestellt haben: eine Uhr und einen kleinen Stand, an dem man Fahrpläne bekommt – zwei Elemente, die den Reisenden nichts nehmen, sondern ihnen etwas geben. Wir brauchen Schönheit, und Schönheit kann große Dinge in Gang setzen."[21]

Wenn Calatrava den Verkehrsknotenpunkt am World Trade Center (siehe Seite 320) beschreibt, führt er die Materialien „Glas, Stahl, Beton, Stein und Licht" auf. Calatrava hat begriffen, dass genau in den Brennpunkt eines der dunkelsten Geschehnisse der jüngeren amerikanischen Geschichte Licht fallen muss. Damit erreichte er das Empfinden der New Yorker, noch ehe sich die Flügel der Station aus dem Boden erhoben. Wenngleich die Form des Glasdachs Motive aus vielen Kulturen andeutet (byzantinische Mandorla, Engelsflügel über der Bundeslade, Schutzgötter auf ägyptischen Kanopen), lässt sie sich Calatrava zufolge in dem Bild eines Vogels zusammenfassen, der befreit aus der Hand eines Kindes aufsteigt. Ungeachtet seiner Symbolik geht der Komplex auch auf die übermäßig komplizierte Schichtung des Nahverkehrssytems in Lower Manhattan ein, die aus einem Jahrhundert ständiger Erweiterungen, Vergrößerungen und Richtungsänderungen resultiert. Da Calatrava auch hier, wie schon bei anderen Einrichtungen der Bahn, mit erfahrenen Spezialisten zusammenarbeitete, gelangen ihm elegante Lösungen für hochkomplexe technische Probleme. Die von Calatrava bei der Gestaltung des Grand Central Terminal beschworene Großzügigkeit liegt auch seinem WTC-Projekt zugrunde, und sie findet in erster Linie Ausdruck durch Raum und Licht. In der offiziellen Beschreibung heißt es: „Der auf Straßenhöhe sichtbare Teil der Anlage besteht aus einem gewölbten Oval aus Glas und Stahl, das etwa 107 m lang, an seinem breitesten Punkt 35 m tief und, zusammen mit der unterirdischen Halle, an der höchsten Stelle 49 m hoch ist. Die Stahlrippen, die diesen Bau stützen, verlängern sich nach oben zu zwei Kragdächern, die ausgebreiteten Flügeln ähneln und eine Höhe von 51 m erreichen. Von dem etwa 10 m unter dem Straßenniveau und 40 m unter der Spitze des Glasdachs gelegenen Hauptbahnsteig aus können Besucher zu einem stützenfreien, durchsichtigen Dach aufschauen."

Der ehemalige Bürgermeister von New York Michael Bloomberg griff bei der Präsentation Calatravas Gedanken über die Bedeutung einer erhebenden Gestaltung auf, als er sagte: „Heute zeigen wir den Entwurf für die neue zentrale PATH-Station, und wir stellen uns vor, dass künftige Generationen dieses Bauwerk als wahres Zeugnis unseres heutigen Lebens betrachten werden, da wir dabei sind, unsere Stadt wieder aufzubauen. Was werden sie in Calatravas sensationellem Bauwerk erkennen? Sie werden eine kreative Gestaltung und eine tragfähige Bauweise erkennen. Sie erkennen Zutrauen zu unserer Investition in ein fantastisches Tor zu dem, was immer die ‚Finanzkapitale der Welt' sein wird. Sie erkennen eine nahtlose Verbindung zu den Pendlerzügen von PATH, den städtischen Untergrundbahnen und schließlich zu unseren Regionalflughäfen. Und sie erkennen Optimismus – ein Gebäude im Begriff abzuheben, genau wie das umliegende Stadtviertel."

ÜBER DEN FLUSS UND DURCH DIE BÄUME

Wie Calatrava selbst erläutert, bringt das Entwerfen einer Brücke eine Reihe sehr spezifischer Fragestellungen mit sich, nicht zuletzt solche der Symbolik. „Betrachten wir die Geschichte der Brücken im 19. und 20. Jahrhundert", sagt Calatrava, „so finden sich darunter ganz besondere, bemerkenswerte Konstruktionen. Sie wurden mit Stein verkleidet, mit Löwenskulpturen und Brüstungen ausgestattet oder sogar, wie zum Beispiel auf der Alexander-III.-Brücke in Paris, mit Lampen tragenden Putti. Als Folge des Zweiten Weltkriegs verflüchtigte sich diese Einstellung zum Brückenbau. Hunderte von Brücken in ganz Europa mussten schnell wieder aufgebaut werden, und aus purer Notwendigkeit entstanden rein funktionalistische Brückenentwürfe. Eine gute Brücke war eine schlichte und vor allem kostengünstige Brücke." Calatrava ist der Meinung, diese funktionalistische Schule der Brückengestaltung habe schon lange ausgedient. „Heute gilt es, das Potenzial von Brücken wiederzuentdecken", erklärt er und führt das Beispiel europäischer Städte wie Florenz, Venedig oder Paris an, um zu veranschaulichen, welche Schlüsselrolle historische Brücken dank ihrer Nützlichkeit und Dauerhaftigkeit bei der Prägung von Stadtbildern spielten. Um seine Behauptung zu untermauern, geht Calatrava so weit zu sagen, eine Brücke könne eine überzeugendere kulturelle Aussage darstellen als ein Museumsneubau. „Eine Brücke ist effizienter", sagt er, „weil sie jedem dient. Auch ein ungebildeter Mensch kann Freude an einer Brücke haben. Eine einzige Maßnahme verwandelt die Natur und gibt ihr Ordnung. Etwas Effizienteres gibt es nicht."[22]

Calatravas erfolgreiches Bemühen, Brücken eine neue Bedeutung zu verleihen, lässt sich am besten anhand der Alamillo-Brücke und des La-Cartuja-Viaduktes (Sevilla, 1987–92, siehe Seite 80) darstellen. Der am Eingang zur Expo '92 stehende imposante, 142 m hohe Pylon ist in einem Winkel von 58 Grad (dem gleichen wie der der Cheopspyramide) geneigt und ist von einem Großteil der Altstadt von Sevilla aus zu sehen. Die von 13 Seilpaaren getragene Alamillo-Brücke überspannt mit 200 m den Meandro San Jeronimo, einen nahezu stehenden Nebenarm des Guadalquivir. Neben den 13 doppelten Spannseilen reicht „vor allem der mit Beton gefüllte Pylon als Gegengewicht für die Brückentafel aus und macht weitere Verstrebungen entbehrlich".[23] Zwar hatte Calatrava ursprünglich eine in die Gegenrichtung geneigte zweite Brücke vorgesehen, die wie ein Spiegelbild der ersten den nahen Guadalquivir überqueren sollte, wegen der Knappheit des Budgets entschied sich jedoch der Auftraggeber, die Junta de Andalucia, für nur eine Brücke und das mehr als 500 m lange La-Cartuja-Viadukt.

Abgesehen von den reich bebilderten Aufzeichnungen, die den Denkprozess bei der Entwicklung der innovativen Form des Alamillo-Pylons verdeutlichen, griff Calatrava hier ganz direkt auf das Vorbild des *Running Torso* zurück, einer 1986 von ihm geschaffenen Skulptur, bei der schräg gestapelte Marmorkuben von einem Spanndraht gehalten werden. Tatsächlich zeigen viele der Zeichnungen, die an den Wänden von Calatravas Züricher Wohnung hängen, Figuren in Bewegung. Wie der Titel sagt, ist auch der *Running Torso* von der Spannung und den Kräften eines sich nach vorne bewegenden Körpers inspiriert. Wenngleich die Art, wie Calatrava diese Analyse umsetzt, sehr persönlich ist, ist dem Ergebnis doch etwas von dem von Pier Luigi Nervi beschworenen „wahren Stil" eigen.

Obwohl es auch einem Laien nicht schwerfällt, die Schönheit einer Brücke zu würdigen, sind die Verfahren, die zu diesen Formen führen, durchaus komplex. Calatrava zufolge ist es „ein intuitiver Prozess, soll heißen, ein System, das auf der Synthese einer Reihe von Faktoren beruht". Seine Beschreibung des Entwurfsverfahrens verdient ausführlich zitiert zu werden: „Ich glaube, dass an allererster Stelle der künftige Standort einer Brücke bedacht werden muss. So kann man beispielsweise an bestimmten Orten keine Bögen bauen, weil sich die Lasten nicht in angemessener Weise auf das Ufer ableiten lassen. Außerdem muss der Schiffsverkehr berücksichtigt werden. Die Höhe einer Brücke kann von der Art der Schiffe abhängen, die sie passieren müssen. Darüber hinaus ist auch die Wahl des Materials wichtig – Holz, Stahl oder Beton können entsprechend den lokalen Gegebenheiten und der Kostenplanung verwendet werden. Diese Faktoren führen neben anderen durch ein Ausschlussverfahren zu bestimmten konstruktiven Lösungsmöglichkeiten. An diesem Punkt beginnt nicht nur der Brückentyp selbst, sondern auch seine Wirkung auf die Umgebung die Form vorzugeben. Schließlich muss der Ingenieur die nötigen Berechnungen anstellen, um sicherzugehen, dass die ihm vorschwebende Gestaltung tatsächlich realisierbar ist. Ich fertige ein Modell an, das mathematische Gesetze mit der Natur verbindet und mit dessen Hilfe es möglich ist, das Verhalten der Natur zu begreifen. Wir sind beständig mit den Kräften der Natur konfrontiert", fügte er abschließend hinzu.[24]

Eine weitere Brücke Calatravas, die Campo-Volantín-Fußgängerbrücke in Bilbao (Spanien, 1990–97, siehe Seite 118), ist beispielhaft für die Einbeziehung peripherer oder industrieller Stadtareale sowie ein technisches Glanzstück, das zu einer überraschenden Formgebung führte. Die Brücke überquert die Ría de Bilbao und verbindet das Stadtzentrum mit einem Uribitarte genannten heruntergekommenen Geschäftsviertel. Calatrava hatte diesen Brückentyp mit einem geneigten Bogen zum ersten Mal 1988 bei einem nicht realisierten Projekt einer neuen Seine-Brücke zwischen dem 12. und 13. Arrondissement vorgeschlagen, die den Gare de Lyon mit dem Gare d'Austerlitz verbinden sollte. Der insgesamt 71 m überspannende, geneigte Parabelbogen trägt einen geschwungenen Fußweg, ein optisch reizvolles Bild. Diese Biegung geht jedoch über reine künstlerische Freiheit hinaus. Sergio Polano erläuterte: „Die Torsion, die an den Aufhängungspunkten der Stützen durch die exzentrische Lage des Gewichts entsteht, wird durch die gegenläufige Kurve des Fußwegs ausgeglichen, die Last

22 Santiago Calatrava im Gespräch mit dem Autor, Zürich, Juni 1997.

23 Dennis Sharp (Hrsg.), *Santiago Calatrava*, London: 1996.

24 Santiago Calatrava im Gespräch mit dem Autor, Zürich, Juni 1997.

somit auf die Betongründung übertragen.“ Das Ganze erinnert an „ein im Schwung angehaltenes Pendel“.[25] Wo tatsächliche physische Bewegung nicht Teil des Entwurfs ist, erinnert Calatravas Schaffen häufig an die Art von Spannung, die er in einer Skulptur wie dem Diskuswerfer hervorruft.

Viele Brücken Calatravas konfrontieren extrem unterschiedliche Standorte mit der schlichten Formensprache und Effizienz, die für seine Fluss- oder Kanalüberführungen typisch geworden sind. Viel heikler im Hinblick auf den historischen Rahmen verhält es sich in Venedig, wo Calatrava die passend benannte Fourth Bridge on the Canal Grande (1999–2008, siehe Seite 248) baute. Es ist in der Tat erst die vierte Überquerung des berühmten Kanals seit dem 16. Jahrhundert. Die 94 m lange Brücke, die den Bahnhof mit der Piazzale Roma verbindet, zeichnet sich durch einen sehr hohen zentralen Bogen und eine transparente gläserne Brückentafel aus, die kontrovers diskutiert wurde. Wiederum haben Eleganz und Geschick im Umgang mit Lokalstolz und politischen Verflechtungen es Calatrava ermöglicht zu bauen, wo in der Vergangenheit andere scheiterten.

DIE VERTIKALE HERAUSFORDERUNG

Aus der horizontalen Welt der Brücken wagte sich Calatrava in seiner Tätigkeit bei zahlreichen Gelegenheiten in die Vertikalität von Türmen vor; gegenwärtig scheint er sich noch stärker auf Projekte dieser Art zu konzentrieren. Der bekannteste seiner frühen Türme ist der Fernmeldeturm auf dem Montjuïc in Barcelona (Spanien, 1989–92, siehe Seite 86), der im Vorfeld der Olympischen Spiele errichtet wurde. Mit seinen mehr als 130 m Höhe und dem geneigten Schaft wurde der Turm mit einem Speer im Flug verglichen, aber wie gewöhnlich war Calatravas eigener Gedankengang ein überraschend anderer. Aus seinen Zeichnungen geht hervor, dass die geneigte Form von einer knienden menschlichen Figur inspiriert ist, die ein Opfer darbringt. In ähnlicher Weise scheint der Grundriss des Turms auf den ersten Blick von freimaurerischen Symbolen wie dem Kompass inspiriert. Calatrava beteuert hingegen, dieser Eindruck treffe nicht zu, sondern ihn habe wiederum das menschliche Auge angeregt. Natürlich gehört auch das Auge zu den Symbolen der Freimaurer, aber Logik und Substanz des Montjuïc-Turms sind offensichtlich mehrdimensional, ebenso wie seine Konstruktionsweise eine überraschend dynamische Form ergab. Im Katalog der 1993 gezeigten Ausstellung im MoMA heißt es dazu: „Der Turm verweist sinnbildhaft auf die Rituale der Olympischen Spiele. Seine eigentümliche Form widerspricht nicht den Gesetzen der Statik, weil der Massenschwerpunkt an der Basis mit der sich ergebenden Senkrechten seiner Eigenlast übereinstimmt. Der Neigungswinkel des Schafts fällt zusammen mit dem Einfallswinkel der Sommersonnenwende in Barcelona. So fungiert der Turm als Sonnenuhr, wenn die Sonne über die kreisrunde Plattform am Sockel der Treppe wandert. Diese Eigenschaften heben die Existenz der beiden Prachtstraßen Barcelonas, La Meridiana und El Paralelo, hervor, unterstreichen die avantgardistische Ausrichtung dieser Stadt und verweisen auf die technischen Fortschritte der Zeit.“[26]

In den letzten fünfzehn Jahren entwarf Calatrava drei sehr unterschiedliche Türme: den Turning Torso (Malmö, Schweden, siehe Seite 276), der auf seinen Zeichnungen eines männlichen Torsos basiert, den 80 South Street Tower in New York, der aus zwölf auskragenden gläsernen Kuben besteht, die von einer Gruppe bis zu 20 Jahre früher entstandener Skulpturen des Architekten inspiriert wurden, sowie den erstaunlichen Chicago Spire (siehe Seite 344), einen 160-geschossigen, 610 m hohen Turm, der zum höchsten Gebäude der USA hätte werden können. Bei all diesen Projekten hat der Architekt gezeigt, dass er Hochhäuser als Symbole oder als funktional wirksame Formen keineswegs für überholt hält. Sowohl der Turning Torso als auch der 80 South Street Tower verkörpern seine Absicht, die Gesetze der Statik zu nutzen, um den Ausdruck der Bewegung im Konzept der Masse zu vermitteln. Diese auf mathematischen Berechnungen basierenden Hochhäuser verlassen den Bereich der trockenen Wissenschaft und vermitteln körperliche oder erhebende Empfindungen, die nur großartige Bauwerke hervorrufen können. Der Turning Torso wurde 2005 eröffnet, während der Chicago Spire und der 80 South Street Tower wegen der Finanzkrise von 2008 nicht zur Ausführung gelangten.

Bei der Beschreibung von Calatravas Skulpturen berief sich die *New York Times* auf Brancusi, an sich kein abschätziger Vergleich, und es ist vielleicht zutreffend, dass der Ingenieurarchitekt eher auf Gedanken und Kunst aus dem frühen 20. Jahrhundert als auf solche aus neuerer Zeit zurückgreift. Calatrava zitiert Einsteins berühmten Satz, Gott würfele nicht mit dem Universum. Damals reagierte der Vater der modernen Physik auf den Vormarsch der Quantentheorie und im Besonderen auf die Heisenberg'sche Unschärferelation, in der es in Bezug auf subatomische Teilchen heißt, dass die Kenntnis des Orts eines Teilchens sich komplementär zu seiner Geschwindigkeit verhält und umgekehrt. Wenn so viele Künstler und Architekten seither (1927) der Denkweise unsicherer Zeiten in ihrer Arbeit Form gaben, wie kommt es, dass Calatrava anscheinend fest in einer anderen Ära verankert ist – einer, in der platonische Körper bestimmend sind statt der beispielsweise von den Theorien Benoît Mandelbrots beschriebenen Komplexität? „In den 1980er-Jahren“, sagt Calatrava, „wurde in der Architektur tatsächlich mit der Chaostheorie und der Sorte Mathematik experimentiert, mit der man die Bewegungen am Aktienmarkt oder das Wetter voraussagen kann. Aber in Einsteins berühmtem Satz ist ein programmatisches Element enthalten, das ich gerne unterstreichen möchte. Ordnung existiert, und ich bin versucht zu sagen, dass wir die Chaostheorie bereits hinter uns gelassen und damit begonnen haben, an die Ordnung des Entwurfs zu denken. Ich persönlich wollte mit Architektur nie etwas anderes als Ordnung wiedergeben. Tatsächlich habe ich mich immer auf reine Geometrie und beherrschte Bewegung bezogen. Die einzige Gelegenheit, bei der in meiner Arbeit der Zufall eine Rolle spielen könnte, ergibt sich, wenn ich Skizzen anfertige. Wo es um aktuelle Architektur geht, stelle ich fest, dass diejenigen, deren Entwürfe auf Ungewissheit in Form von Unordnung oder Dekonstruktion fußen, sehr stark auf Bautechnik angewiesen sind, wenn sie für ihr Schaffen eine gewisse Ausgereiftheit anstreben. Leute wie Daniel Libeskind verweisen stolz auf ihre Erfahrung mit Mathematik, und es ist offenkundig, dass die Ingenieurwissenschaften für ihre Architektur unentbehrlich sind. Ich möchte so weit gehen zu behaupten, dass ich immer aus dem Zentrum heraus begonnen habe. Sogar das Dach der Bodegas Ysios (Laguardia, Álava, Spanien 1998–2001, siehe Seite 264) basiert auf einer Sinuskurve. Bei meinen Skulpturen habe ich offensichtlich einfache Formen verwendet, und 20 Jahre später lieferte eine mit der Vorstellung des menschlichen Körpers verwandte Skulptur die Grundlage für den Turning Torso.“[27]

EINE PAVILLON WIE EIN FALKE, EINE KAPELLE WIE EIN GEBET

Für Calatrava hatte inzwischen die Reifephase seiner Laufbahn begonnen, aber seine Projekte kündeten davon, dass er keineswegs beabsichtigte, als Tribut an die Zeit weniger Spannungsreiches zu planen. Bei dem Projekt in seiner Heimatstadt Valencia wurde mit dem Opernhaus (Palau de les Arts, 1996–2006, siehe Seite 198) der Schlusspunkt des 1991 begonnenen Kulturkomplexes gesetzt. Das Auditorio de Tenerife (Santa Cruz de Tenerife, 1991–2003, siehe Seite 146) bestätigte in ähnlicher Weise die Kühnheit seiner Entwürfe und greift das immer wiederkehrende Leitmotiv des menschlichen Auges auf. Unter enormem Zeitdruck und in riesigen Dimensionen stellte Calatrava außerdem die Sportanlagen der Olympischen Spiele in Athen (OAKA, Athen, 2001–2004, siehe Seite 292) fertig, darunter 199 000 m² Platzanlagen, ein Wegenetz von 94 000 m², 61 000 m² Grünflächen, 29 000 m² Wasserflächen, 130 000 m² Serviceeinrichtungen sowie 178 000 m² Parkplätze und Straßen. Es ist leicht zu sehen, wo Calatrava gewesen ist, aber es ist nicht ganz so einfach zu sagen, wohin er sich künftig wenden wird. Genau dies könnte der Schlüssel zum Verständnis seiner Gedankengänge sein.

---

25 Sergio Polano, *Santiago Calatrava, Complete Works*, Mailand: 1996.

26 *Santiago Calatrava, Structure and Expression*, MOMA, New York, März–Mai 1993.

27 Santiago Calatrava im Gespräch mit dem Autor, Zürich, 22. Februar 2006.

„Stellen Sie sich vor, Sie wissen nicht, wohin Sie gehen", sagt er, „das mitgeführte Gepäck ist das, was man im Inneren mit sich trägt. Für mich bedeutet das beinahe eine paranoide oder schizophrene Situation. Ich habe ein Formgefühl, das in 14 Jahren Universitätsstudium entstanden ist – ich habe Mathematik kennengelernt, und ich liebe sie. Wenn ich das Werk von Picasso, Cézanne oder Matisse betrachte, das mich tief bewegt, muss ich feststellen, dass sie sich, abgesehen von begrenzten Details in ihren Werken, nie auf die Abstraktion einließen. Sie wollten Emotionen hervorrufen, ich fühle mich darin als ihr Bruder im Geiste. Mich hat lange Zeit ein einfacher Satz Michelangelos inspiriert, ‚*l'architettura dipende dalle membra dell'uomo*'. Den menschlichen Körper als Ausdrucksmittel zu nutzen ist und bleibt wichtig." In einem kürzlich geführten Gespräch zeigte sich Santiago Calatrava begeistert von den Plänen für eine umfassende Ausstellung seiner Kunstwerke. In seinem Haus und Atelier in Zürich malt und zeichnet er unter anderem Figurenstudien nach lebenden Modellen. Außer seinem weithin bekannt gewordenen Projekt am World Trade Center hat Santiago Calatrava vor 2020 das Museum of Tomorrow in Rio de Janeiro (2010–2015, siehe Seite 394). Die Formen jedes dieser Projekte bezeugen den Wunsch und die Fähigkeit des Architekten, die konventionellen Grenzen zeitgenössischer Gebäude herauszufordern. Seine Arbeiten stechen aus ihrer Umgebung hervor und beweisen, dass Modernität immer noch erstaunen und aufregend sein kann.

Für diese Auflage seiner Monografie traf sich Santiago Calatrava mit dem Autor, um über einige seiner jüngsten Arbeiten zu sprechen, darunter eine monumentale Skulptur in Chicago sowie eine überraschend kleine Kapelle in Neapel, die komplett renoviert und mit von ihm entworfenen und von lokalen Kunsthandwerkern ausgeführten Werken ausgestattet wurde. Seine Arbeit in der Kirche San Gennaro (Neapel, Italien) stellt ein Eintauchen in die Vergangenheit dar, was im Kontrast zu den laufenden Plänen des Architekten steht: einer bemerkenswerten Tunnel-Brücken-Überquerung im West-Bay-Distrikt (Doha, Katar) sowie einem mindestens ebenso außergewöhnlichen Turm in Dubai – zwei Projekte, die momentan noch auf Eis liegen.

PJ *Was hat Sie dazu bewogen, eine großformatige Skulptur in Chicago zu schaffen?*

SC Es war mir schon immer ein Anliegen, nicht nur Architektur, sondern parallel dazu auch Kunstwerke zu schaffen. 2015 installierte ich auf Einladung des Fund for Park Avenue sieben großformatige Skulpturen auf dem Mittelstreifen der Park Avenue zwischen der 52. und 65. Straße. Daraufhin kontaktierte man mich aus Chicago, und ich war begeistert von der Idee, für diese Stadt eine große, 8,8 m hohe Skulptur (siehe Seite 352) zu entwerfen. Chicago genießt zu Recht den Ruf, eine der Geburtsstätten der modernen Architektur zu sein. In den letzten 50 Jahren wurde seinem Stadtbild eine Reihe bedeutender öffentlicher Kunstwerke hinzugefügt, darunter eine 15 m hohe Skulptur von Picasso (1967), Anish Kapoors *Cloud Gate* (2004), Jaume Plensas *Crown Fountain* (2004), Joan Miros *Chicago* (1981), Jean Dubuffets *Monument with a Standing Beast* (1984) und Alexander Calders leuchtend roter *Flamingo* (1973). Meine *Constellation* hat an der Flussgabelung des Chicago River einen hervorragenden Standort gefunden: Auch wenn hinter ihr ein gewaltiges Hochhaus emporragt, strahlt sie eine gewisse Autonomie aus. Es war eine Herausforderung, ein Werk im Kontext so vieler großer Gebäude zu schaffen. Ich hätte natürlich gefärbten rostfreien Stahl, Aluminium oder Bronze verwenden können, aber die Größe der Skulptur schloss Bronze als Option aus. Ich entschied mich für leuchtend rotes Aluminium, schon allein deshalb, weil ich Alexander Calders Werke bewundere, vor allem die Bewegungen seiner Mobiles. 2015 gestalteten mein Sohn Gabriel und ich das Design einer Ausstellung kleinformatiger Calder-Werke (*Multum in Parvo*, Dominique Lévy Gallery, New York). Das leuchtende Rot meiner Chicagoer Skulptur soll außerdem den Kontrast zu dem hinter ihr stehenden grünlichen Glasturm verstärken.

PJ *Wie steht es um andere Arbeiten, die Sie in der Golfregion durchführen?*

SC Wir arbeiten an zwei Projekten in der Region, die jedoch momentan stagnieren: an der Sharq Crossing, die zwei Teile des West-Bay-Distrikts in Doha miteinander verbinden soll (siehe Seite 408), und am Dubai Creek Tower (siehe Seite 416). Die Projektentwicklung verzögert sich, da die beteiligten

Länder mit dringenderen Arbeiten befasst sind: der bevorstehenden Fußballweltmeisterschaft in Katar und der Expo 2020 in Dubai in den VAE. Fertiggestellt sind bereits die Fundamente des Towers.

PJ *Sie sind derzeit dabei, ein erstaunliches Projekt in Neapel abzuschließen, die Renovierung einer Kapelle aus dem 18. Jahrhundert. Es scheint, als hätten Sie sich dieser Arbeit eher mit der Seele eines Künstlers als der eines Architekten genähert.*

SC Der Direktor des Museums von Capodimonte in Neapel ist der Franzose Sylvain Bellenger, der zuvor in den Museen von Cleveland und Chicago gearbeitet und das Chateau de Blois in Frankreich (1992–99) geleitet hat. Ende 2019 hatte er „Im Lichte Neapels“ organisiert, eine Ausstellung über mein Werk. Darüber hinaus veranlasste er die Sanierung des 134 ha großen Real Bosco (bzw. Königlichen Parks) von Capodimonte. Zum Park gehören auch rund 10 Gebäude, darunter die Porzellanfabrik Real Fabbrica di Capodimonte-Istituto Superiore ad Indirizzo Raro Caselli und die Kirche San Gennaro (siehe Seite 442) von 1745, die von dem bedeutenden Architekten und Bühnenbildner Ferdinando Sanfelice auf Geheiß Karls III. erbaut wurde. Sylvain Bellenger kam auf die Idee, anlässlich und während meiner Ausstellung die seit mehreren Jahrzehnten geschlossene Kapelle zu renovieren. Ich stellte mir vor, an der Installation in der Kapelle, oder eher: an ihrer Restaurierung, lokale Handwerker und Künstler zu beteiligen. Die benachbarte Porzellanfabrik war die Erste, die wir dafür anfragten, anschließend wandten wir uns auch an die Königliche Seidenmanufaktur in Caserta, San Leucio, und den Meisterglaser Antonio Perotti von Vietri sul Mare. Derzeit arbeiten wir noch an einem neuen Altar, der von ansässigen Kunsthandwerkern aus Bronze gefertigt wird, und an den liturgischen Gewändern. Sämtliche Zeichnungen meiner Entwürfe, zu denen mich weitgehend die umliegende Park- und Waldlandschaft inspirierte, habe ich dem Museum zur Verfügung gestellt. Finanziert wurde das Projekt im Wesentlichen von der Region Kampanien.[28]

EINE HYMNE AN DIE LEBENDIGE WELT

Ganz gleich, welch maßgebliche Rolle Mathematik und Ingenieurwissenschaften in Calatravas Werk spielen, es sind Kunst und Emotion, die ihn Werke schaffen lassen, die über die nüchterne Berechnung von Kräften hinausgehen. „Das Leben ist wie eine Sammlung Perlen“, so Calatrava. „Du findest hier und da eine auf deinem Weg. Was ist der Sinn von Funktion in der Architektur? Es ist Liebe, die Liebe, die man anderen schenkt, die Freigiebigkeit des Architekten. In der Architektur gibt es ein großes Geheimnis, und das ist ihre philanthropische Natur, und diese Philanthropie kann man im Sinne von Funktion verstehen. Ein Gebäude funktioniert gut aus Liebe zu den Menschen. Das Geheimnis der Philanthropie in der Architektur ist in ihrer Funktion zu finden. Schönheit entsteht durch Intelligenz oder Intuition. In der Architektur muss man jedes Detail zeichnen. Jede Tat außer der dich antreibenden Emotion ist eine rationale Tat. Architektur ergibt schöne Ruinen; sie ist die abstrakteste der Künste.“[29] Doch trotz der Schönheit dieser Ruinen wandte sich Santiago Calatrava verstärkt jenen weniger abstrakten Kunstformen zu, wie er sie in Form von Porzellan und Textilien auch für die Kapelle in Neapel verwandte. Seine großformatigen Skulpturen zeigen sich in der Tat abstrakter als seine Zeichnungen oder Aquarelle. All diese Werke zeugen von einer unermüdlichen Liebe zum Leben selbst in seinen vielfältigen Formen. Seine Architektur, die sich oft buchstäblich bewegt, ist auch eine Hymne an die lebendige Welt.

---

28 Santiago Calatrava im Gespräch mit dem Autor, Zürich, 17. Januar 2022.

29 Santiago Calatrava im Gespräch mit dem Autor, Zürich, 22. Februar 2006.

LE SECRET DE LA PHILANTHROPIE

« J'ai commencé par vouloir étudier dans une école d'art, se souvient Santiago Calatrava. Puis un beau jour, dans une papeterie de Valence, j'ai aperçu un petit livre aux superbes couleurs. On yvoyait des ellipses jaunes et orange sur fond bleu et je l'ai acheté immédiatement. C'était un ouvrage sur Le Corbusier, dont l'œuvre m'était inconnue. J'y ai découvert des images des escaliers en béton de l'*Unité d'habitation* et j'ai été émerveillé par cet extraordinaire sens de la forme. L'objet du livre était de montrer les aspects artistiques du travail de l'architecte. Après l'avoir acheté et étudié, j'ai choisi de m'inscrire à l'école d'architecture[1]. »

Né en 1951 près de Valence, Calatrava y a fait ses études primaires et secondaires et, dès 1959, a commencé à suivre des cours de dessin et de peinture à l'école des Arts appliqués. Lorsqu'il a 13 ans, sa famille profite de l'ouverture récente des frontières de l'Espagne franquiste pour l'envoyer en France dans le cadre d'un échange. À la fin de ses études secondaires, il part pour Paris et l'École nationale supérieure des beaux-arts, mais arrive en 1968 au beau milieu des événements étudiants. Il rentre donc à Valence et, séduit par un opuscule plein de couleurs, s'inscrit à l'Escuela Técnica Superior de Arquitectura, où il passe son diplôme d'architecte, puis fait des études supérieures d'urbanisme.

Quand d'autres auraient pu décider de s'en tenir là, il décide de poursuivre sa formation. Attiré par la rigueur mathématique qu'il perçoit dans certaines réalisations historiques et sentant que ses études à Valence ne lui offrent aucun débouché précis, il décide d'entamer des études supérieures de génie civil et, en 1975, intègre l'ETH (Institut fédéral de technologie) de Zurich, d'où il sortira docteur en 1981. Cette décision modifie le cours de sa vie à maints égards. C'est au cours de cette période qu'il rencontre et épouse Robertina Marangoni, étudiante en droit à Zurich également. Sur le plan professionnel, la clé des activités actuelles de Santiago Calatrava se trouve aussi en Suisse. Comme il l'explique : « Le désir de recommencer à zéro était très fort chez moi. J'étais déterminé à mettre de côté tout ce que j'avais fait à l'école d'Architecture pour apprendre à dessiner et à penser comme un ingénieur. J'étais fasciné par le concept de la pesanteur et persuadé qu'il fallait travailler à partir de formes simples. Je peux dire que mon goût pour la simplicité en ingénierie vient en partie de mon observation du travail de l'ingénieur suisse Robert Maillart. À l'aide de formes simples, il montrait qu'il était possible de créer un contenu puissant et de susciter une réponse émotionnelle. Avec une combinaison adéquate de force et de masse, vous pouvez créer l'émotion. »

INGÉNIEUR, ARCHITECTE, ARTISTE

L'attrait précoce de Calatrava pour l'art et l'esthétique qui le poussa vers le petit livre sur Le Corbusier allait rester un facteur permanent dans son œuvre, et l'un des éléments qui font de lui une figure à part dans le monde de l'architecture contemporaine. Évoquant une exposition organisée en 2005 par le Metropolitan Museum of Art de New York sur son travail architectural et artistique, il explique : « Je pense que Gary Tinterow, conservateur et commissaire de l'exposition, avait compris ma façon de travailler car il a intitulé la manifestation *Sculpture en architecture* plutôt que l'inverse. Les critiques d'architecture n'ont pas encore dépassé le stade de la perplexité devant mon travail. » En effet, tout en notant que la dernière fois que le Metropolitan a présenté l'œuvre d'un architecte vivant remontait à 1973, Nicolai Ourousoff écrit dans le *New York Times* : « Personne ne contestera que les sculptures de M. Calatrava pourraient être présentées au Metropolitan pour leurs mérites propres. En tant qu'objets d'art, elles dérivent essentiellement des œuvres de maîtres disparus comme Brancusi. » Mais il conclut sur un mode moins agréable : « On aurait préféré qu'il laissât ses sculptures dans son atelier[2]. » Ce commentaire montre avant tout une incompréhension de la sculpture de l'architecte. « En sculpture, dit celui-ci, j'ai utilisé des sphères, des cubes et des formes simples souvent liées à ma connaissance de l'ingénierie. C'est une sculpture qui a donné naissance à la Turning Torso (Malmö, Suède, 1999–2004, page 276). Je dois admettre que j'admire énormément la liberté de Frank Gehry ou celle de Frank Stella en tant que sculpteurs. On trouve une joie et une liberté dans l'œuvre de Stella qui sont absentes de mes sculptures qui, elles, partent toujours de la matière brute des mathématiques[3]. » Il explique par ailleurs qu'il n'a jamais apprécié le milieu des galeries d'art et n'a presque jamais présenté ses sculptures. Et il souligne : « La réaction que je reçois des artistes est très positive. L'art est beaucoup plus libre que l'architecture car, comme le disait Picasso, certains artistes travaillent avec le marbre et d'autres avec la merde. » Ceci ne veut pas dire qu'il est naïf devant la difficulté de sa tâche. En 1997, il écrivait : « L'architecture et la sculpture sont deux fleuves dans lesquels coule une même eau. Pensons la sculpture comme une plastique pure et l'architecture comme une plastique soumise à la fonction, avec la prise en considération nécessaire de l'échelle humaine (à travers la fonctionnalité). La sculpture, elle, ignore le cadre de la fonctionnalité, elle est étrangère à la servitude issue de l'utilisation, ce qui la rend donc, d'une certaine façon, supérieure à l'architecture en tant qu'expression purement plastique. L'architecture au contraire soumet son expression plastique à ces exigences. Par son rapport avec l'échelle humaine et son environnement, par sa pénétrabilité et son intériorité, elle l'emporte sur la sculpture dans ces domaines spécifiques[4]. »

Calatrava va jusqu'à suggérer que l'art doit être considéré comme une source d'idées pour l'architecture. « Pourquoi fais-je des dessins du corps humain ? L'artiste, ou l'architecte, peut transmettre son message dans le temps par la seule force de la forme et de l'ombre. Rodin a écrit : "L'harmonie dans les corps vivants est le résultat de l'équilibrage des masses qui se déplacent ; la cathédrale est construite à l'exemple des corps vivants[5]." Laissez-moi vous donner un exemple de l'importance de l'art pour le XXe siècle architectural. Lorsque Le Corbusier écrivait, en 1923, "L'architecture est le jeu savant, correct et magnifique des volumes assemblés sous la lumière[6]", combien savaient qu'il l'empruntait à la pensée du sculpteur Auguste Rodin ? En 1914, dans son livre *Les Cathédrales de France*, ce dernier écrivait en effet : "Le sculpteur n'atteint à la grande expression qu'en concentrant son attention sur les jeux harmoniques de la lumière et de l'ombre, exactement comme le fait l'architecte[7]." Le fait que l'une des plus célèbres citations de l'architecture moderne ait été inspirée non pas par un architecte mais par un sculpteur me semble souligner l'importance de la signification de l'art. »

---

1 Entretien de l'auteur avec Santiago Calatrava, Zurich, 22 février 2006.

2 Nicolai Ourousoff, « Buildings Shown as Art and Art as Buildings », *The New York Times*, 25 octobre 2005.

3 Entretien de l'auteur avec Santiago Calatrava, Zurich, 22 février 2006.

4 Julio González, *Dessiner dans l'espace*, Skira, Kunstmuseum, Berne, 1997. « L'architecture et la sculpture sont deux fleuves dans lesquels coule une même eau. Imaginons que la sculpture est plastique pure et que l'architecture est plastique soumise à la fonction et avec une évidente notion de l'échelle humaine (à travers la fonctionnalité). Tandis que la sculpture ignore le cadre de la fonctionnalité, elle est étrangère à la servitude dérivée des questions d'utilisation et donc elle est, pour ainsi dire, supérieure à l'architecture en tant qu'expression purement plastique. L'architecture au contraire soumet son expression plastique et à ces exigences. Par contre, celle-ci, de par son rapport à l'échelle humaine, à l'échelle de l'environnement de par son intériorité et sa pénétrabilité, elle l'emporte dans ces domaines spécifiques sur la sculpture. »

5 Auguste Rodin, *Les Cathédrales de France*, Armand Colin, Paris, 1914. « L'harmonie, dans les corps vivants, résulte du contre-balancement des masses qui se déplacent : la Cathédrale est construite à l'exemple des corps vivants. »

6 Le Corbusier, *Vers une architecture*, 1923. « L'architecture est le jeu savant, correct et magnifique des volumes assemblés sous la lumière. »

7 Auguste Rodin, *Les Cathédrales*, *op. cit.* « Il n'atteint à la grande expression qu'en donnant toute son étude aux jeux harmoniques de la lumière et de l'ombre, exactement comme fait l'architecte. »

En dehors de cet intérêt permanent pour l'art, Santiago Calatrava apporte également une vraie passion à sa définition très personnelle de l'architecture, soit le mouvement, implicite mais également bien réel, autrement dit le déplacement physique. Des premières portes articulées de son entrepôt Ernsting's (Coesfeld-Lette, Allemagne, 1983–85, page 36) au plus récent « Burke Brise Soleil » de cent quinze tonnes du Milwaukee Art Museum (Milwaukee, Wisconsin, 1994–2001, page 232), il revient sans cesse dans sa sculpture comme dans son architecture sur le concept original de mouvement physique répétitif. Pourquoi ? « Il existe un élément cinétique dans l'art du XXe siècle, réplique-t-il, des artistes comme Alexander Calder, Naum Gabo ou Moholy-Nagy ont créé des sculptures qui bougent. J'aime leur travail et il déclenche en moi une grande émotion. Ma thèse de doctorat sur "La flexibilité des structures tridimensionnelles" étudie le fait qu'une figure géométrique peut passer de trois à deux dimensions et terminer en une seule. Prenez un polyèdre et pliez-le pour en faire une surface plane. Une autre manipulation le réduit à une simple ligne, donc à une seule dimension. Vous pouvez considérer ceci comme un problème de mathématique ou de topologie. Tout le mystère des solides platoniciens se résume dans le polyèdre. Après avoir réfléchi à ces questions, j'ai regardé la sculpture ancienne sous un jour différent. Des œuvres comme le *Discobole* de Myron créent une tension qui repose sur un instant de mouvement et c'est ainsi que j'en suis venu à m'intéresser au problème du temps, du temps en tant que variable. Einstein disait : "Dieu ne joue pas aux dés avec l'univers." Et il m'est apparu que tout est lié aux mathématiques et à la dimension unique du temps. Puis, j'ai réfléchi à la statique (la branche de la physique qui traite des systèmes physiques en équilibre statique) et j'ai compris qu'il n'y a rien de statique. Tout est en mouvement potentiel. La seconde loi du mouvement de Newton dit que l'accélération d'un objet dépend de deux variables, la force nette qui agit sur l'objet et la masse de cet objet. La masse et l'accélération sont liées et ainsi le temps est présent dans la force. J'ai réalisé que l'architecture est pleine d'éléments mobiles, des portes aux meubles. L'architecture elle-même bouge, et, avec un peu de chance, devient une ruine magnifique. Tout change, tout meurt et les mouvements cycliques possèdent une signification existentielle. Je voulais faire une porte qui serait mienne, qui aurait un sens poétique et se transformerait en figure dans l'espace, et c'est ainsi qu'est né le projet Ernsting. »

L'ESSENCE DE L'ARCHITECTURE

Le fait qu'un certain nombre de gens ne se sentent pas à l'aise avec les diverses formes d'expression choisies par Santiago Calatrava est probablement la meilleure preuve qu'il touche à quelque chose d'important. En 2016, il a achevé l'un des projets les plus complexes et les plus politiquement sensibles que l'on puisse imaginer, puisqu'il s'agit de la gare de transit du World Trade Center (page 320), à New York, au milieu de cette zone que les New-Yorkais ont appelée Ground Zero. « Nous pensons qu'il est le Vinci de notre époque », a dit Joseph Seymour, ancien directeur exécutif de la Port Authority de New York et du New Jersey, commanditaire de cette gare. « Il associe lumière, air, élégance structurelle et puissance. » S'élevant au milieu des tours et juste à côté du mémorial du 9/11, ce *hub* place la vision originale de Santiago Calatrava au cœur de la mémoire américaine de l'un des événements les plus traumatiques de l'époque récente. Ce type de louange n'est pas rare, même dans le cercle restreint de l'architecture. En 2005, Santiago Calatrava est devenu le second Espagnol (après Josep Lluís Sert en 1981) à remporter la prestigieuse médaille d'or de l'American Institute of Architects. Le comité de l'AIA a déclaré à cette occasion : « L'œuvre de Santiago Calatrava exprime l'essence de l'architecture. Elle enrichit la vision de l'esprit humain et exprime son énergie, captivant l'imagination et nous émerveillant devant ce qu'une forme sculpturale et une structure dynamique peuvent accomplir. Santiago Calatrava justifie et définit à la fois la raison d'être de cette médaille d'or. Sa vision élève l'esprit humain par la création d'environnements dans lesquels nous vivons, nous nous divertissons et nous travaillons. »

Calatrava ne semble pas perturbé par cette coexistence dans sa pensée de l'art, de l'architecture et de l'ingénierie, qui le plonge au cœur d'un des débats les plus intenses de l'histoire récente de la construction et du design. Comme l'écrivait Sigfried Giedion dans son œuvre fondamentale *Espace, temps et architecture* : « L'arrivée de l'ingénieur structurel et de composants industriels à mise en œuvre rapide et générateurs de formes a brisé le pathos artistique, bousculé la position privilégiée de l'architecte et jeté les bases des développements actuels. L'ingénieur du XIXe siècle assumait inconsciemment le rôle de garant des éléments nouveaux qu'il fournissait aux architectes. Il développait des formes qui étaient à la fois anonymes et universelles. » Giedion retrace le débat sur le rôle de l'ingénierie en citant un certain nombre de dates et d'événements essentiels, dont : « 1877 : cette année-là, la question fit son entrée à l'Académie lorsqu'un prix fut offert pour la meilleure communication sur "L'union ou le divorce entre l'ingénieur et l'architecte". Davioud, l'un des architectes du Trocadéro, remporta le prix avec cette réponse : "L'accord ne sera jamais réel, complet et fructueux tant que l'ingénieur, l'artiste et le savant n'auront pas fusionné dans la même personne. Nous avons longtemps vécu avec la folle conviction que l'art est un type d'activité distinct de toutes les autres formes d'intelligence humaine, qui prendrait sa source et son origine dans la personnalité de l'artiste et les caprices de son imagination[8]." » Même si l'insistance de Giedion sur « l'anonymat » du travail de l'ingénieur ou la référence de Davioud aux « caprices de l'imagination » de l'artiste ne semblent pas correspondre à la puissante originalité de Calatrava, ce dernier pourrait bien incarner ce désir de l'architecte français d'un accord entre l'art, l'ingénierie et l'architecture. Et l'on ne peut s'empêcher de penser à la référence faite par Joseph Seymour au « Vinci de notre époque ».

Le catalogue de l'exposition de Santiago Calatrava au Museum of Modern Art de New York en 1993 souligne l'étroite relation entre son œuvre et celle d'autres grands ingénieurs : « Calatrava appartient au remarquable patrimoine de l'ingénierie du XXe siècle. Comme ses prédécesseurs – Robert Maillart, Pier Luigi Nervi, Eduardo Torroja et Felix Candela –, il va au-delà d'une approche qui se contenterait de résoudre des problèmes techniques. Pour ces ingénieurs, la structure résulte d'un équilibre entre le critère scientifique d'efficacité et l'innovation dans la recherche formelle. Calatrava considère l'ingénierie comme "l'art du possible" et cherche un nouveau vocabulaire formel, reposant sur un savoir-faire technologique qui ne soit pas pour autant un hymne à la technique[9]. » Le premier personnage cité, Robert Maillart (1872–1940), diplômé de l'ETH de Zurich en 1894, a créé quelques-uns des ponts modernes les plus spectaculaires et fait un usage novateur du béton. Son entrepôt de Giesshübel à Zurich (1910) faisait appel pour la première fois à un « plancher-champignon » en dalles de béton, permettant de se passer de poutres. Comme l'écrit Matilda McQuaid : « Maillart fut l'un des premiers ingénieurs de ce siècle à rompre complètement avec la construction en maçonnerie et à appliquer une solution élégante et techniquement appropriée à la construction en béton armé. Bien que, comme pour Maillart, la trouvaille technique chez Calatrava ne soit ni sa première motivation ni la dernière, elle nourrit l'expression générale de la structure. Son œuvre devient une imbrication d'expression plastique et de mise en valeur structurelle, aboutissant à des résultats qui peuvent parfaitement se décrire comme une synthèse de l'esthétique et de la physique structurelle[10]. »

Bien qu'il admire, naturellement, l'œuvre de Maillart, Santiago Calatrava s'empresse de faire remarquer que ses propres ponts sont très différents de ceux de ses prédécesseurs, ne serait-ce que par leurs sites. « Les ponts de Maillart, dit-il, sont souvent implantés dans de magnifiques paysages de montagne. Sa réussite est d'avoir su introduire un élément artificiel dans des lieux aussi splendides. Aujourd'hui, je crois que l'une de nos tâches les plus importantes est de reconsidérer la périphérie des

---

8 Sigfried Giedion, *Space, Times and Architecture*, Harvard University Press, Cambridge, Massachusetts, 5e édition, 1976.

9 Matilda McQuaid, *Santiago Calatrava, Structure and Expression*, The Museum of Modern Art, New York, 1993.

10 *Ibid.*

villes. La plupart du temps, les réalisations publiques dans ces zones sont purement fonctionnelles alors que les ponts, même près de voies ferrées ou au-dessus de rivières polluées, peuvent exercer un effet formidablement positif. En créant un environnement approprié, ils peuvent avoir un impact symbolique dont les ramifications vont bien au-delà du site immédiat[11]. »

L'œuvre de Calatrava a sans nul doute été influencée par celle de Felix Candela qui, né à Madrid en 1910, avait émigré au Mexique en 1939 où il conçut un certain nombre de remarquables structures en voiles minces de béton, comme l'église de la Vierge miraculeuse (Iglesia de la Virgen Milagros, Narvarte, Mexico, 1955), projet reposant entièrement sur des paraboloïdes hyperboliques. Un autre Espagnol, l'ingénieur madrilène Eduardo Torroja (1899–1961), était fasciné par les formes organiques ou végétales dont la présence sculpturale indéniable vient sans doute de l'influence de Gaudí. Nombre des références de Santiago Calatrava sont espagnoles et plus spécifiquement liées à des architectes ou des artistes catalans. « Ce qui me fascine dans la personnalité de Goya, par exemple, dit-il, c'est qu'il a été l'un des premiers artistes, comme Rembrandt avant lui, à renoncer à l'idée de servir un maître. Ce que j'admire dans l'œuvre de Miró, poursuit-il, c'est son remarquable silence et son rejet radical de tout ce qui est conventionnel. » Bien que Gaudí lui offre un exemple voisin de celui de Maillart, il semble plus à l'aise lorsqu'il évoque le sculpteur Julio González. « Le père et le grand-père de González étaient ferronniers pour Gaudí et ils ont travaillé sur des projets comme le parc Güell. Puis ils se sont installés à Paris et c'est de là qu'est venu le goût du travail du métal chez Julio González. Avec toute la modestie qui s'impose, on pourrait dire que ce que nous faisons est la continuation naturelle du travail de Gaudí et de González, un travail d'artisans s'orientant vers l'art abstrait[12]. »

Si le type d'art auquel Calatrava se réfère est bien apparent dans ses ponts et ses bâtiments les plus réussis, il reste cependant difficile à décrire avec des mots. Une autre des figures essentielles de l'ingénierie du XXe siècle, l'Italien Pier Luigi Nervi, en a tenté une définition dans une série de conférences données à Harvard en 1961 :

« Il est très difficile d'expliquer pourquoi nous approuvons instantanément des formes qui nous viennent d'un monde physique avec lequel nous n'avons apparemment pas le moindre lien direct. Par quel biais ces formes nous satisfont-elles, pourquoi nous touchent-elles de la même façon que des choses naturelles comme les fleurs, les plantes et les paysages auxquels nous sommes accoutumés depuis d'innombrables générations ? On doit aussi noter que ces réussites possèdent en commun une essence structurelle, la nécessaire absence de toute décoration, une pureté de lignes et de formes plus que suffisante pour définir un style authentique, un style que j'ai baptisé le *style véridique*. Je comprends à quel point il est difficile de trouver les mots justes pour exprimer ce concept. Lorsque je fais ces remarques à des amis, ils me disent souvent que cette vue d'un futur proche est terriblement triste, qu'il serait peut-être préférable de renoncer volontairement à resserrer plus encore les liens entre nos créations et les lois de la physique, si en effet ces liens doivent nous mener à une monotonie fatale. Mais je ne pense pas que ce pessimisme soit justifié. Aussi contraignantes que soient les exigences techniques, il reste toujours une marge de liberté suffisante pour permettre à la personnalité du créateur d'une œuvre de s'exprimer et, s'il est un artiste, pour faire en sorte que sa création, même dans sa stricte orthodoxie technique, devienne une œuvre d'art véritable et authentique[13]. »

LE LONG DES RAILS D'ACIER

La raison de la présence prolongée de Calatrava à Zurich tient beaucoup aux circonstances. Après y avoir achevé ses études, il y demeura d'abord parce que son épouse, Robertina, n'avait pas encore fini les siennes, puis – signe du destin – il remporta le concours pour la conception de la nouvelle gare de Stadelhofen (1983–90, page 52). Dire que ce curieux bâtiment est « central » serait un euphémisme. Implanté sur le flanc d'une colline boisée près de Bellevueplatz et de la Theaterstrasse, non loin du lac, il est étroitement intégré à un environnement urbain essentiellement traditionnel. « Pour comprendre la gare de Stadelhofen, explique Calatrava, il faut la voir comme un projet extrêmement urbain, qui a entraîné une intervention sur le tissu de la ville. Il existe un contraste clair entre la nature radicale des solutions architecturales et techniques choisies et l'attitude envers la ville, qui est extrêmement respectueuse. Un certain nombre de liens ont été créés, pas seulement des passerelles et des accès, mais également des connexions avec des rues, qui n'existaient pas auparavant. De petits espaces verts, comme le voile de verdure surmontant le niveau supérieur, ont été créés. » En effet, lorsque, venant de la ville, le visiteur approche de la gare, il tombe d'abord sur un pavillon très traditionnel – la gare d'origine – avant de pénétrer ou de descendre dans les espaces imaginés par Calatrava. « Il était évident dès le départ, poursuit l'architecte, que le respect accordé à tout bâtiment vieux de plus de cent ans en Suisse interdisait toute tentative de démolition ou de modification substantielle de l'ancienne gare. Néanmoins, je n'ai pas trouvé cet aspect illogique, car il s'intégrait à une lecture de la ville qui reste intacte[14]. » Sans compter qu'après avoir traversé l'ancien pavillon, le voyageur entre dans un univers très différent, qui semble plus proche de l'imagination de Gaudí que de celle des tranquilles bourgeois zurichois. Même si Calatrava fait remarquer que Zurich possède une tradition d'architecture radicale avec des maisons réalisées par des figures comme Marcel Breuer, il est clair que la gare de Stadelhofen lui a permis pour la première fois de sa carrière de se livrer, à grande échelle, au type de conception novatrice qui allait le rendre célèbre.

Le terrain en légère courbe de 40 mètres de large par 240 mètres de long fut aménagé pour permettre l'implantation d'une vaste surface commerciale en sous-sol. Par ailleurs, les travaux ne devaient pas interrompre le passage des trains de banlieue. L'ensemble présente une unité organique que le contexte ne favorisait pas particulièrement. Tel un ptérodactyle qui serait venu faire son nid au flanc de cette colline, la structure s'articule dans un système d'éléments répétés et d'énormes portes anthropomorphiques qui mènent au centre commercial souterrain où l'on a rapidement l'impression de se trouver dans les entrailles de la bête. On note une continuité entre la structure en métal sombre à l'air libre et les nervures en béton du sous-sol, qui crée une hiérarchie claire de volumes et de formes tout en renforçant la lisibilité et la clarté fonctionnelle de l'ensemble.

Si cette gare donne l'impression d'être conçue autour d'une métaphore de dinosaure, la substance de la conception de Calatrava est plus complexe, ou peut-être différente. « En réalité, ce que j'ai tenté est ce que j'appellerais une dialectique de transgression, qui repose sur le vocabulaire des forces structurales. À Stadelhofen, par exemple, se trouve une série de colonnes inclinées. On peut imaginer qu'il s'agit d'une décision esthétique, mais elle vient en fait de la nécessité de soutenir la structure. Il existait bien sûr plusieurs solutions pour ce type de support. On aurait pu n'avoir que de simples cylindres, par exemple, mais j'ai choisi de les articuler comme une main. C'est là que la question des métaphores devient intéressante. Comment mieux exprimer la fonction des colonnes qu'en les investissant du sens du geste physique de porter quelque chose[15] ? »

Si Santiago Calatrava est souvent cité dès qu'il est question de ponts, il est également un spécialiste reconnu des gares et l'auteur, notamment, de la gare de l'Orient à Lisbonne et de la gare de Liège-Guillemins, construite peu après. L'une des réalisations qui ont le plus contribué à sa réputation croissante reste cependant la gare ferroviaire de l'aéroport de Lyon-Saint-Exupéry (1989–94, page 104). Cette gare de 5 600 mètres carrés a incarné en son temps la nouvelle génération d'installations ferroviaires intégrées au réseau français des trains à grande vitesse (TGV). Elle assure une correspondance efficace entre le TGV, les transports locaux et le terminal aérien. Inauguré le 7 uillet 1994, le hall central de 120 mètres de long, 100 mètres de large et 40 mètres de haut s'articule

---

11 Entretien de l'auteur avec Santiago Calatrava, Zurich, juin 1997.
12 *Ibid.*
13 Pier Luigi Nervi, *Aesthetics and Technology in Building, The Charles Eliot Norton Lectures, 1961–1962*, Harvard University Press, Cambridge, Massachusetts, 1965, p. 186.
14 Entretien de l'auteur avec Santiago Calatrava, Zurich, juin 1997.
15 *Ibid.*

autour d'un élément central pesant 1 300 tonnes. La gare de Calatrava rappelle un peu le terminal TWA conçu par Eero Saarinen pour l'aéroport Kennedy (New York, 1957–62) par sa ressemblance avec un oiseau en vol, tout en étant plus exubérante que son ancêtre américain. Le plan du complexe et de sa liaison avec le terminal de l'aéroport évoque, lui, une raie manta. Le bâtiment principal, prévu pour six voies, possède des quais couverts de 500 mètres de long également conçus par Calatrava. Les voies centrales sont prises dans une coque de béton pour permettre aux trains qui ne s'y arrêtent pas de traverser la gare à 300 km/h. Ce système a nécessité des calculs approfondis de l'onde de choc générée par le TGV. Le budget de cette réalisation financée par la SNCF, la région Rhône-Alpes et le département du Rhône a atteint cent millions d'euros.

Interrogé sur la référence à un oiseau préhistorique, Calatrava répond à sa façon, assez détournée, mais néanmoins informative : « Je suis avant tout un architecte, pas un artiste ni quelqu'un qui essaye de fomenter une révolution. Il est intéressant de noter que Victor Hugo, dans *Notre-Dame de Paris*, compare la cathédrale à un monstre préhistorique. Bien qu'il possédât sans doute une bonne connaissance de l'architecture et fût un écrivain très consciencieux, il n'a pas hésité à user d'une métaphore aussi inattendue que celle-ci pour décrire cet édifice. Honnêtement, je ne cherche pas la métaphore. Je n'ai jamais pensé à un oiseau, mais plutôt à une recherche que j'ai parfois la prétention d'appeler sculpture[16]. » En fait, les dessins et la sculpture de Calatrava qui se rapprochent le plus du projet de Lyon-Saint-Exupéry semblent trouver leur origine non pas dans l'image d'un oiseau, mais dans une étude de l'œil et de la paupière, thème récurrent dans son œuvre. « L'œil, dit-il, est le vrai outil de l'architecte, et cette idée remonte aux Babyloniens. »

L'avancée en plongée vers le sol de la gare de Saint-Exupéry a été comparée au bec d'un oiseau, mais l'architecte, une fois encore, avait en tête une idée fort différente. « Ce "bec" est le résultat d'un calcul complexe des forces jouant sur la structure. C'est également le point où se regroupent les écoulements des eaux pluviales. Naturellement, j'ai fait de mon mieux pour minimiser la masse en ce point, mais sans aucune intention zoomorphique. » Admettant que l'utilisation de ses propres sculptures comme point de départ du projet représente autant un choix esthétique qu'un concept métaphorique voulu, il ajoute : « Vous pouvez juger cela irrationnel, mais je dirais qu'il n'y a là aucune piste à suivre. Je veux être comme un navire en mer : derrière, il y a bien le sillage, mais devant, rien qui indique la voie[17]. »

DES ARBRES SUR LA COLLINE

Le travail de Calatrava sur la spectaculaire gare de l'Orient à Lisbonne (page 212) est un exemple significatif de sa méthode et explique en grande partie ses premiers succès. À la suite du catastrophique tremblement de terre de 1755, Lisbonne se réorienta vers l'intérieur des terres, tournant pratiquement le dos à l'estuaire du Tage. Ce mouvement s'est amplifié à une époque plus récente, lorsque des installations industrielles ont pris possession de remblais en bordure du fleuve. Les 340 hectares de la « Zone de redéveloppement » centrés autour d'Expo '98 et de la gare de l'Orient étaient occupés jusque dans les années 1990 par des dépôts d'essence et des entrepôts de conteneurs, les abattoirs municipaux et des installations de traitement des eaux usées. Si le glorieux passé de la capitale reste inscrit dans ses rues et ses places, sa relation intime avec le Tage, source de sa richesse, s'était presque perdue dans les brumes du temps.

C'est dans ce contexte que l'Association des architectes portugais lança, en 1988, un « concours d'idées pour la zone du fleuve ». La construction du Centre culturel de Belém (1988–92) sur la rive du fleuve représentait une première grande étape vers la réhabilitation des liens historiques de la ville avec le Tage. Une décision politique et culturelle encore plus importante fut prise en novembre 1993 lorsque Parque Expo '98 SA confia un premier « plan d'urbanisation de la zone de redéveloppement » à l'architecte Luís Vassalo Rosa. Dès le départ, l'intention des promoteurs était de créer quelque chose qui apporte davantage à la capitale que l'architecture éphémère typique des expositions universelles. Située à l'extrémité est de la ville, avec cinq kilomètres de quais sur le Tage, la zone de redéveloppement jouxte le pont Vasco de Gama. Inaugurée le 29 mars 1998, cette structure impressionnante enjambe le fleuve sur douze kilomètres et atteint jusqu'à 45 mètres de hauteur. Symboliquement, l'achèvement de ce pont qui porte le nom du grand explorateur et l'implantation d'Expo '98 n'auraient pu représenter un signal plus clair. Lisbonne et le Portugal manifestaient leur intention de reprendre en main leur héritage historique et de s'ouvrir de nouveau sur le Tage et sur le monde.

Santiago Calatrava a été choisi pour le projet de la gare de l'Orient à l'issue d'un concours sur invitation organisé entre lui, Terry Farrell, Nicholas Grimshaw, Rem Koolhaas et feu Ricardo Bofill. Ce projet, avec celui du Pavillon portugais d'Álvaro Siza, fait incontestablement partie des constructions les plus significatives suscitées par Expo '98. La gare et ses 200 000 voyageurs quotidiens étaient le point central du programme de réaménagement des quartiers est. L'aspect le plus spectaculaire est constitué par la couverture (238 x 78 m) des huit quais surélevés dont la typologie évoque une forêt. Plutôt que de faire ressortir la rupture entre la ville et le fleuve qu'impliquait la gare, Calatrava a cherché, ici comme ailleurs, à ouvrir des passages et à rétablir des liens. Cette volonté se manifeste dans sa décision de couper dans le tertre sur lequel passent les voies pour construire la gare proprement dite en dessous. Le complexe comprend, au-dessus des entrées, deux vastes auvents en verre et acier mesurant chacun 112 mètres de long par onze de large. On trouve également une gare routière, un parking, une station de métro (non conçue par Calatrava) et une longue galerie qui comprend des espaces commerciaux prévus dans le cahier des charges. Les services et le hall de vente des billets sont situés à cinq mètres sous les voies et un atrium signale la galerie tout en longueur cinq mètres plus bas. L'accès côté fleuve constitue l'entrée principale.

De loin comme de l'intérieur, l'aspect le plus visible de la gare est son évocation d'une forêt. Au moins deux autres projets de Calatrava se sont appuyés sur la typologie structurelle de l'arbre ou de la forêt : le projet, non réalisé, pour la cathédrale St. John the Divine à New York (1991) et celui de Gallery and Heritage Square pour BCE Place à Toronto (1987–92). St. John the Divine, construite à l'origine en style néo-roman par Heins & La Farge en 1892 et « gothicisée » en 1911 par Cram & Ferguson, est l'une des plus célèbres églises new-yorkaises. Le projet de Calatrava consistait à lui ajouter un nouveau transept sud et un « bio-abri » perché à 55 mètres du sol. Lié au symbolisme du jardin d'Éden, ce dernier aurait été complété par des éléments structurels dérivés de la forme des arbres. Implanté dans l'attique au-dessus de la nef, ce jardin n'aurait pas modifié la silhouette du bâtiment mais permis de faire entrer plus de lumière naturelle dans l'église. Philip Johnson, l'un des membres du jury, fit remarquer la relation entre le projet de Calatrava, le décor de l'église et la typologie de l'arbre qui rappelle les origines de l'architecture gothique. L'image de l'arbre est également au centre de la Bell Canada Entreprises (BCE) Place (page 74), à Toronto. Calatrava a travaillé ici avec l'agence new-yorkaise de Skidmore, Owings & Merrill, pour créer, entre deux tours de bureaux, un passage de six étages de haut et 115 mètres de long à structure en acier laqué blanc et verre. Comme le *New York Times* l'a alors écrit alors, « Cette galerie est pour le moins gaudiesque ». Elle évoque aussi, métaphoriquement, un cheminement en forêt. L'utilisation de l'acier peint en blanc et du verre annonce également les projets arboricoles des quais de la gare de l'Orient.

À Toronto comme à New York, Santiago Calatrava a fait appel à la métaphore de l'arbre pour différentes raisons, liées dans le premier cas à un vaste espace urbain pris entre deux tours de grande hauteur et dans le second au style néo-gothique de St. John the Divine. Que l'arbre soit l'un des modèles évidents de la colonne et des nefs des premières églises ne fait que confirmer son indéniable présence biologique. Mais dans un cas comme dans l'autre, les mots de Nervi – « … notre approbation

---

16 *Ibid.*

17 *Ibid.*

instantanée des formes qui nous viennent du monde physique » – remontent jusqu'à nous. Concernant la gare de l'Orient, Calatrava explique que ce sont des circonstances très spécifiques tenant à sa vision personnelle de Lisbonne qui l'ont conduit à proposer cet auvent de forme si curieuse : « Je suis allé à Lisbonne au moins cinq fois pendant la préparation du concours pour la gare, ne serait-ce que pour ressentir l'atmosphère de la ville. Il est évident que c'est une très belle ville. Comme Rome, elle est construite sur des collines, ce qui offre des perspectives remarquables. Vous êtes dans la ville tout en vous trouvant en position de la regarder. Il y aussi la monumentalité du Tage, qui est à cet endroit le fleuve le plus large d'Europe. Cette "mer de Paille" est incroyablement vaste. L'histoire urbaine de Lisbonne est très ancienne et a pourtant conservé sa clarté de composition[18]. »

Lorsque Calatrava parle de la conception des quais de la gare, il fait référence à « des arbres sur une colline ». Ici, la « colline », c'est le petit tertre sur lequel passent les voies. Il repense à ses visites à Lisbonne : « Il y a dans cette ville de nombreux parcs boisés, dit-il, et j'ai senti immédiatement que ces voies surélevées appelaient un flanc de colline planté d'arbres. C'était très clair dans mon esprit. Pour le concours, j'ai cité un poème plein de mélancolie de Fernando Pessoa qui évoque l'idée d'aller à l'Arvor Edo, aux bois. Je voulais accentuer la transparence de la gare. Dans un environnement urbain, qui deviendra très certainement de plus en plus dense, la gare de l'Orient ressemblera à une oasis. Ce sera un lieu où les gens viendront se reposer ! » Si on lui demande pourquoi il a préféré, dans ce cas précis, une métaphore végétale plutôt qu'anthropomorphique (avec laquelle il semble plus à l'aise), il réplique : « Imaginez que vous créez une place surélevée. Ce n'est, à l'évidence, pas un type d'architecture introvertie. Je suis sur une colline de Lisbonne et je regarde autour de moi. Que manque-t-il ? De quoi se protéger du soleil et de la pluie[19]. »

Un projet plus récent, pour la gare de Liège-Guillemins (page 254) cette fois, illustre certaines évolutions dans sa pensée et les raisons des différences entre la simplicité épurée de ses ponts et l'impression d'une plus grande complexité que donnent ses grands bâtiments. « Les ponts, par leur nature même, nécessitent une stricte économie de moyens. Vous avez le tablier, l'arche qui le soutient et les fondations, chaque élément représentant environ un tiers du coût. Étant donné la simplicité de la fonction d'un pont, la marge d'intervention est limitée. D'un autre côté, dans une gare, au moins seize types de décisions peuvent exercer un impact esthétique, depuis le choix des huisseries métalliques jusqu'au mode d'éclairage. Obtenir le résultat voulu tout en respectant les contraintes économiques d'un tel projet met à l'épreuve le savoir-faire du concepteur. » Même si les deux situations sont fondamentalement différentes, on constate que le goût de l'architecte pour la « transgression » ou l'innovation le pousse néanmoins à dessiner des ponts inhabituels et des gares qui le sont tout autant. « Prenez le cas de la gare TGV de Liège, poursuit-il. Nous avons totalement réinventé la façade. Ou plutôt, il n'y a plus de façade. C'est, à mon avis, une transgression fondamentale. Au lieu d'une façade traditionnelle, il n'y aura que de grandes ouvertures signalées par des auvents métalliques au-dessus de la place devant la gare. » Comme il le fait remarquer, cette décision entraîne des conséquences importantes sur le plan fonctionnel. Au niveau du symbole, on peut se demander comment une gare sans façade peut être identifiée comme telle. « L'environnement est urbain et il m'a semblé que la première vision que les voyageurs ou les visiteurs auraient de la gare était importante, explique-t-il. Ma solution est en deux volets. Comme le bâtiment est situé sur une colline et qu'on en approche par le haut, on a une vue sur la ville et sur le plan de la gare. Le plan devient ainsi la vraie façade. Pour améliorer le rapport avec la ville, nous avons proposé de créer une place juste devant[20]. » Il peut sembler que cette stratégie d'absence ou d'un certain minimalisme rapproche davantage, dans son concept, la gare de Liège des ponts que de certains bâtiments réalisés auparavant par l'architecte. Pour ce qui est de son goût pour la « transgression », il est clair que ses méthodes prudentes impliquent un vrai respect du contexte fonctionnel et économique d'un projet et la recherche d'un raisonnement spécifique parmi la gamme des possibilités techniques disponibles. Ses idées fonctionnent et suscitent l'intérêt du public parce qu'elles sortent de l'imagination fertile de l'architecte ingénieur, mais aussi parce qu'elles respectent, dès l'origine, les forces fondamentales qui sont en jeu.

DES AILES ET UNE PRIÈRE

La sensibilité de Calatrava à l'urbanisme est certainement ce qui lui a valu de remporter le concours de Lisbonne mais aussi celui de Liège et, plus récemment, celui de Manhattan pour le *hub* du World Trade Center. Il est sincèrement convaincu qu'un architecte peut donner un sens du sacré à un lieu tel qu'une gare. À la question de savoir si son but est de réaliser des espaces confortables et humains ou bien d'atteindre à quelque chose de supérieur, il répond : « Tout repose sur l'homme mais, dans la complexité de l'homme, le sacré existe, ou bien il n'y aurait pas tant de gens pour venir voir, au Panthéon de Rome, l'oculus de sa coupole. Et les gares ? Si vous prenez l'exemple des gares suisses modernes, à Bâle ou à Zurich par exemple, vous avez l'impression de vous retrouver dans un centre commercial. Celle de Grand Central, à New York, semble appartenir à une autre planète. En exaltant les valeurs abstraites, l'architecture est capable de catalyser d'immenses événements. Mais si vous l'abordez avec une attitude purement fonctionnaliste, vous ne catalysez rien du tout. Vous vous retrouvez avec un centre commercial médiocre. Le sentiment que j'éprouve dans le hall principal de Grand Central est le produit d'une grande intelligence. Le lieu donne au commerce un sens particulier, presque sacré. Tout en ne sacrifiant rien de sa fonction, la gare devient un acte de célébration. Regardez tout ce qui a surgi autour du vide au cœur de Grand Central, le Seagram Building et Park Avenue… De ce point de vue, en Amérique, rien ne ressemble autant au Panthéon. Voyez ce que ses architectes ont placé au centre du grand hall – une horloge et un petit tourniquet pour donner les horaires –, deux éléments qui sont là pour offrir quelque chose aux voyageurs et non pour leur prendre. Nous avons besoin de la beauté et la beauté peut générer de grandes choses[21]. »

Lorsqu'il décrit ses plans pour le hub du World Trade Center (page 320), Calatrava énumère ses matériaux : « Le verre, l'acier, le béton, la pierre et la lumière. » Il a compris que la lumière doit briller au cœur même de ce qui rappellera toujours l'un des plus sombres événements de l'histoire récente des États-Unis et en cela il a su toucher la sensibilité des New-Yorkais avant même que les ailes de sa gare ne surgissent du sol. Bien qu'empruntant à l'iconographie de civilisations variées (la mandorle byzantine, les ailes du chérubin au-dessus de l'arche de l'Alliance, les ailes protectrices sur les urnes canopes égyptiennes), la forme de son toit de verre représente plutôt, selon lui, un oiseau s'échappant des mains d'un enfant. Mais au-delà de ce symbolisme, ce projet résoudra également les problèmes que pose l'accumulation des strates de systèmes de transport de Manhattan, aboutissement d'un siècle d'extensions, d'agrandissements et de changements de direction. Calatrava, en collaborant avec des spécialistes comme pour ses autres projets ferroviaires, a su trouver des solutions élégantes à des problèmes techniques d'une extrême complexité. La générosité dont parle l'architecte à propos de la conception de la gare de Grand Central est au centre de son projet pour le WTC et s'exprime avec ampleur dans l'espace et la lumière : « La partie du bâtiment visible au niveau de la rue est un arc ovale de verre et d'acier, d'environ 107 mètres de long, 35 de large à son maximum et 49 de haut à son apex. Les nervures d'acier qui soutiennent la structure se prolongent en un couple d'auvents qui ressemble à des ailes déployées et s'élève jusqu'à 51 mètres. Dans le hall principal, à quelque dix mètres sous le niveau de la rue et à 40 mètres du sommet de la couverture de verre, les visiteurs pourront regarder vers le haut, vers une immense aile sans pilier. » Faisant écho au sentiment de Calatrava sur l'importance d'une conception qui élève l'âme, Michael Bloomberg, l'ancien maire de

---

18 Entretien de l'auteur avec Santiago Calatrava, Paris, septembre 1998.

19 *Ibid.*

20 Entretien de l'auteur avec Santiago Calatrava, Zurich, juin 1997.

21 Entretien de l'auteur avec Santiago Calatrava, Zurich, 22 février 2006.

New York, a déclaré : « Aujourd'hui, nous dévoilons le projet de la nouvelle gare PATH (Port Authority Trans-Hudson) du centre-ville et nous pouvons penser que les générations futures regarderont ce bâtiment comme un authentique témoignage de notre vie au moment où nous reconstruisons notre ville. Que verront-elles dans l'œuvre enthousiasmante de Santiago Calatrava ? Elles y verront la créativité de la conception et la force de la construction. Elles y verront la confiance dans notre investissement pour cette étonnante "porte" de ce qui restera toujours la "capitale financière du monde". Elles y verront une connexion parfaite entre les trains, le métro et, enfin, nos aéroports régionaux. Et elles y verront un signal d'optimisme – un bâtiment qui semble prendre son envol –, comme tout le quartier du WTC qu'elle dessert. »

DE L'AUTRE CÔTÉ DE LA RIVIÈRE, À TRAVERS LES ARBRES

Comme le dit Santiago Calatrava lui-même, concevoir un pont entraîne un ensemble de défis très spécifiques dont les moindres ne sont pas ceux qui concernent les symboles. « Si vous considérez l'histoire des ponts des XIXe et XXe siècles, beaucoup sont des structures très spéciales et chargées de sens. Ils ont reçu des habillages de pierre, des lions sculptés ou même des anges soutenant les lampadaires, comme sur le pont Alexandre III à Paris. Cette attitude a disparu après la Seconde Guerre mondiale, poursuit-il, des centaines de ponts devaient alors être reconstruites rapidement dans toute l'Europe et c'est de la nécessité qu'est née cette école de conception de ponts purement fonctionnels. Un bon pont était un pont simple et, surtout, peu coûteux à construire. » Calatrava pense que cette école fonctionnaliste a perdu de son utilité après-guerre. « Aujourd'hui, nous devons redécouvrir le potentiel des ponts », ajoute-t-il, citant les exemples de villes européennes comme Florence, Venise ou Paris pour souligner qu'à travers leur fonction, mais aussi leur permanence, les ponts du passé ont joué un rôle clé dans la formation de l'image des villes. Il va jusqu'à dire que la construction d'un pont peut être un geste culturel plus fort que l'édification d'un nouveau musée. « Le pont est plus efficace, affirme-t-il, parce qu'il est accessible à tous. Même une personne analphabète peut apprécier un pont. Un simple geste transforme la nature et l'ordonne. Il n'y a rien de plus efficace[22]. »

Le succès de ses efforts pour donner un sens nouveau aux ponts est brillamment illustré par l'exemple du pont Alamillo et du viaduc de La Cartuja à Séville (1987–92, page 80). À l'une des entrées de l'Expo '92, le spectaculaire pylône de 142 mètres de haut incliné à 58° (le même angle que celui de la pyramide de Khéops près du Caire) de l'Alamillo le rend visible d'une grande partie du vieux Séville. Soutenu par treize paires de haubans, ce pont de 200 mètres de portée franchit le Meandro San Jeronimo, un bras vigoureux du Guadalquivir. « Le poids du pylône rempli de béton suffit à équilibrer celui du tablier et évite de recourir à des haubans arrière[23]. » Bien que l'architecte ait à l'origine pensé à un second pont incliné dans le sens opposé – telle une image en miroir du premier – pour franchir le Guadalquivir tout proche, des considérations budgétaires ont poussé les autorités andalouses à ne retenir qu'un seul franchissement et le viaduc de 500 mètres de long de La Cartuja.

Parallèlement à ses propres carnets de notes, abondamment illustrés, qui éclairent sa réflexion sur la forme novatrice du pylône sévillan, Calatrava s'est appuyé ici assez directement sur *Running Torso*, une sculpture qu'il créa en 1986, composée d'un empilement de cubes de marbre inclinés maintenus en équilibre par un câble en tension. De fait, nombre des dessins accrochés aux murs de sa maison de Zurich représentent des figures en mouvement. *Running Torso* est clairement inspiré, comme son titre l'indique, par la tension et les forces d'un corps se déplaçant vers l'avant. Malgré l'utilisation spécifique et très personnelle que l'architecte fait de cette analyse, le résultat conserve quelque chose du « style véridique » évoqué par Pier Luigi Nervi.

Bien qu'une personne non informée puisse apprécier aisément la beauté d'un pont, la méthode qui conduit à ces formes est assez complexe. « C'est un processus intuitif, c'est-à-dire un système qui s'appuie sur la synthèse d'un certain nombre de facteurs », affirme Calatrava. Son explication mérite d'être citée *in extenso* : « Je pense qu'avant tout, la localisation du pont doit être prise en considération. Sur certains sites par exemple, vous ne pouvez pas utiliser d'arche parce qu'il est impossible de transférer les charges aux rives de façon adéquate. Ensuite, il faut tenir compte du trafic fluvial. La hauteur d'un pont peut être déterminée par le type de bateaux qui vont passer dessous. Le choix des matériaux est tout aussi essentiel : le bois, l'acier ou le béton peuvent être utilisés en fonction du contexte local et du cadre budgétaire.

Ces éléments, et d'autres encore, mènent par un processus d'élimination à un certain nombre de solutions structurelles. C'est ainsi que le type de pont, mais aussi son impact sur l'environnement, commencent à prendre forme. Dès lors, l'ingénieur doit faire les calculs nécessaires pour être sûr que son projet est totalement viable. Je crée une maquette qui fait le lien entre les études mathématiques et la nature, pour permettre de mieux comprendre le comportement de celle-ci. Nous sommes toujours confrontés aux forces de la nature[24] », conclut-il.

Un autre pont, la passerelle de Campo Volantín (Bilbao, Espagne, 1990–97, page 118), est tout aussi exemplaire de sa réflexion sur les espaces urbains périphériques ou industriels et d'un exercice approfondi de l'ingénierie permettant d'aboutir à une forme inattendue. Franchissant le fleuve de Bilbao pour relier le centre-ville à un quartier commercial en déshérence appelé Uribitarte, il fait appel au principe de l'arche inclinée que Calatrava avait utilisé une première fois en 1988 pour le projet (non réalisé), à Paris, d'un pont sur la Seine entre les gares de Lyon et d'Austerlitz. À Bilbao, une arche parabolique inclinée de 71 mètres de haut soutient la passerelle en courbe, dessinant une silhouette étonnante. Mais cette courbe est bien plus qu'un caprice esthétique. Comme l'explique Sergio Polano, « La torsion créée aux points de suspension des montants par la position excentrée du poids est équilibrée par la contre-courbe de la passerelle, transférant ainsi la charge vers les fondations en béton, l'ensemble suggérant un pendule arrêté dans son mouvement[25] ». Même lorsque le mouvement physique ne fait pas partie du propos, les projets de Calatrava font souvent penser à la tension évoquée dans une sculpture comme celle du *Discobole*.

Beaucoup des ponts construits par l'architecte confrontent des sites radicalement différents avec le langage de la simplicité et de l'efficacité qui caractérise désormais ses passages sur les rivières ou les canaux. Le pont construit par Calatrava à Venise, le bien nommé Quarto Ponte sul Canal Grande (1999–2008, page 248), n'est que le quatrième pont construit sur le fameux canal depuis le XVIe siècle. Reliant la gare à la Piazzale Roma, cet ouvrage de 94 mètres de long possède une arche centrale de très grand rayon et un tablier en verre transparent qui a suscité quelques critiques. Là encore, l'élégance et la capacité à se plier à la fierté et aux complexités politiques locales ont permis à Santiago Calatrava de réussir à construire là où d'autres l'avaient tenté en vain dans le passé.

LE DÉFI VERTICAL

À maintes occasions au cours de sa carrière, Calatrava est audacieusement passé de l'univers des ponts, essentiellement horizontal, à la verticalité de celui des tours, et il semble aujourd'hui se concentrer sur ce type de projet. La plus connue de ses premières réalisations dans ce domaine est la Tour de communications de Montjuïc (Barcelone, 1989–92, page 86), édifiée à l'occasion des Jeux

---

22 Entretien de l'auteur avec Santiago Calatrava, Zurich, juin 1997.
23 Dennis Sharp (dir.), *Santiago Calatrava, Architectural Monographs* n° 46, Academy Editions, Londres, 1996.
24 Entretien de l'auteur avec Santiago Calatrava, Zurich, juin 1997.
25 Sergio Polano, *Santiago Calatrava, Complete Works*, Gingko, Electa, Milan, 1996.

olympiques. Avec ses quelque 130 mètres de haut, son fût incliné l'a fait comparer à un javelot lancé, bien qu'une fois encore, l'approche de l'architecte soit déroutante. Ses dessins montrent qu'il s'est inspiré d'une figure agenouillée en position d'offrande. À première vue, le plan de la tour pourrait aussi paraître inspiré de symboles maçonniques comme le compas, mais Calatrava réfute cette remarque et avoue qu'une fois de plus, son inspiration vient en fait de l'œil humain. Certes, l'œil est également l'un des emblèmes maçonniques, mais la conception comme le contenu de la tour de Montjuïc ont de multiples significations et sa technique de construction crée une forme étonnamment dynamique. Comme l'explique le catalogue de l'exposition du MoMA (1993) : « Symboliquement, la tour se réfère à l'événement rituel des Jeux olympiques. Sa forme singulière ne contredit pas les lois de la statique, car son centre de gravité coïncide à la base avec la verticale de son poids mort. Son fût a une inclinaison qui correspond à l'angle du solstice d'été à Barcelone, et il agit comme un cadran solaire lorsque le soleil se déplace à travers la plate-forme circulaire au pied de ses escaliers. Ces caractéristiques rappellent la résence des deux grandes avenues de Barcelone, la Meridiana et El Paralelo, qui expriment la vocation d'avant-garde de cette ville et se réfèrent aux progrès techniques de l'époque[26]. »

Une quinzaine d'années plus tard, Calatrava a conçu trois tours très différentes, la Turning Torso (Malmö, Suède, 1999–2004, page 276), d'après ses dessins d'un torse masculin ; la 80 South Street Tower à New York, faite de douze cubes de verre en porte-à-faux inspirés d'une série de sculptures qu'il réalisa vingt ans plus tôt et, plus surprenante encore, la Chicago Spire (Chicago, 2005, page 344), une tour de 160 étages et 610 mètres de haut qui devrait être l'immeuble le plus haut des États-Unis. Dans chaque cas, l'architecte montre qu'il ne pense évidemment pas que les tours sont des symboles dépassés ni de simples formes efficaces qui seraient démodées. La Turning Torso comme la tour de 80 South Street incarnent son idée d'utiliser sa maîtrise de la statique pour évoquer un mouvement inhérent à son concept de masse. Reposant sur des calculs mathématiques poussés, ces projets échappent au domaine de la science pure pour évoquer le corps ou un sentiment d'élévation que seule une grande œuvre architecturale peut susciter. Si le Turning Torso a été inauguré en 2005, les projets de la Chicago Spire et de la 80 South Street Tower ont été abandonnés du fait de la crise financière de 2008.

Le *New York Times* citait le nom de Brancusi pour décrire les sculptures de Calatrava, ce qui en soi n'est pas une comparaison désavantageuse, mais de fait, il est vrai que l'architecte-ingénieur se réfère plus volontiers à l'art de la première moitié du XXe siècle qu'aux développements plus récents de l'art et de la pensée. Il cite Einstein, pour lequel « Dieu ne joue pas aux dés avec l'univers ». Mais en même temps, le maître de la physique moderne réagissait aux progrès de la Théorie des quanta et en particulier au *Principe d'incertitude* de Werner Heisenberg qui, faisant référence aux particules infra-atomiques, écrivait que « Plus la position est déterminée avec précision, moins la mesure du moment de mouvement est précise, et *vice versa*. » Alors que beaucoup d'artistes et d'architectes depuis lors (1927) ont exprimé dans leurs œuvres l'incertitude du moment, pourquoi Calatrava semble-t-il si fermement ancré dans l'époque du règne des solides platoniciens plutôt que dans la complexité décrite par les théories de Benoît Mandelbrot par exemple ? « Dans les années 1980, dit-il, il existait en effet des expérimentations architecturales en rapport avec la théorie du chaos et les mathématiques servant à prédire les mouvements de la bourse ou de la météo. Mais il existe dans la célèbre phrase d'Einstein un élément programmatique que j'aimerais souligner. L'ordre existe, et je suis tenté de dire que nous avons déjà dépassé la théorie du chaos et commencé à penser à l'ordre de la conception. Personnellement, je n'ai jamais souhaité rendre explicite, dans mon architecture, autre chose que l'ordre. Je me suis toujours référé à la géométrie pure et au mouvement contrôlé. Le seul moment où le hasard peut apparaître dans mon travail est l'instant du croquis.

Pour ce qui est de l'architecture actuelle, je note que ceux qui choisissent des modèles basés sur l'incertitude, en forme de désordre ou de déconstruction si vous préférez, doivent se rapprocher de l'ingénierie lorsqu'ils cherchent à donner quelque maturité à leur travail. Des architectes comme Daniel Libeskind, par exemple, font état avec fierté de leur expérience des mathématiques et il est évident que la science des ingénieurs est indispensable à leur architecture. Je pourrais aussi me vanter et dire que j'ai toujours joué au centre du terrain. Même le toit du chai des Bodegas Ysios (Laguardia, Álava, Espagne, 1998–2001, page 264) part d'une courbe sinusoïdale. Dans ma sculpture, j'ai toujours utilisé des formes simples et, vingt ans plus tard, une sculpture sur l'idée de corps humain a été la base de la tour Turning Torso[27]. »

UN PAVILLON TEL UN FAUCON, UNE CHAPELLE TELLE UNE PRIÈRE

Alors que sa carrière entrait dans une phase de maturité, Santiago Calatrava n'a cessé de témoigner d'une vitalité créative qu'il n'a jamais eu l'intention d'assagir. À Valence, sa ville natale, son Opéra (1996–2006, page 198) a marqué la phase finale de son énorme complexe culturel dont les travaux avaient débuté en 1991. L'Auditorium de Tenerife (Santa Cruz de Tenerife, îles Canaries, Espagne, 1991–2003, page 146) confirme également l'audace de ses projets et reprend le thème récurrent de l'œil, objet de sa passion. Travaillant contre la montre et à une échelle énorme, il a également achevé le Complexe sportif olympique d'Athènes (OAKA, Athènes, Grèce, 2001–04, page 292) qui ne comprend pas moins de 199 000 mètres carrés de places, 94 000 mètres carrés d'allées, 61 000 mètres carrés d'espaces verts, 29 000 mètres carrés d'installations aquatiques, 130 000 mètres carrés d'équipements de service et 178 000 mètres carrés de voies d'accès et de parkings. S'il est facile de voir d'où vient l'architecte, il est moins aisé de prédire où il sera demain. « Imaginez que vous ne savez pas où vous allez, dit-il, votre bagage, c'est ce que vous portez en vous. Pour moi, c'est presque une situation de paranoïa, ou de schizophrénie. Je possède un sens des formes issu de quatorze ans d'études universitaires, j'ai fait la rencontre des mathématiques et je les aime. Lorsque je regarde l'œuvre de Picasso, de Cézanne ou de Matisse, artistes qui m'émeuvent, je suis obligé de remarquer qu'ils ne se sont jamais engagés dans l'abstraction, à quelques détails près. Ils ont travaillé pour créer une émotion et c'est de cet univers-là que je viens. J'ai longtemps été inspiré par une petite phrase de Michel-Ange : « *L'architettura dipende dalle membra dell'uomo* (L'architecture dépend des membres de l'homme). Utiliser le corps humain comme moyen d'expression est et restera important pour moi. » Dans une discussion récente, Santiago Calatrava a paru enthousiasmé par les plans d'une future grande exposition de ses œuvres d'art. En effet, il peint et il dessine chez lui et dans son studio de Zurich, parfois aussi des études à partir de modèles vivants. Avant 2020 et en dehors du très visible projet du World Trade Center, Calatrava a également achevé le Musée de demain à Rio de Janeiro (2010–15, page 394) et Peninsula Place, à Londres, qui fait partie du vaste projet de rénovation urbaine de la péninsule de Greenwich. La forme de chacun de ces projets confirme le désir et la capacité de l'architecte à défier les limites conventionnelles de la construction contemporaine. Ses œuvres se distinguent fortement de leur environnement et donnent le sentiment que la modernité reste toujours aussi exaltante.

Pour cette édition de la monographie chez TASCHEN, Santiago Calatrava a discuté avec l'auteur de certains de ses travaux les plus récents, parmi lesquels une sculpture monumentale à Chicago et une étonnante petite chapelle à Naples, entièrement rénovée et redécorée avec des œuvres que l'architecte a conçues et fait exécuter par des artisans locaux. Le saut dans le passé que représente la chapelle San Gennaro contraste avec les projets en cours de traversée de la baie de Doha (Doha, Qatar) par un ensemble remarquable de tunnels et de ponts ou d'une tour encore plus étonnante à Dubaï, tous deux en attente depuis quelque temps déjà.

---

26 *Santiago Calatrava, Structure and Expression*, MoMA, New York, mars–mai 1993.

27 Entretien de l'auteur avec Santiago Calatrava, Zurich, 22 février 2006.

PJ *D'où est venue l'idée de cette immense sculpture à Chicago ?*

SC J'ai toujours aimé créer des œuvres d'art en même temps que mes travaux en architecture. Quelqu'un de Chicago m'a contacté après mon exposition de sculptures en 2015 à New York. J'ai été invité par le Fonds pour Park Avenue à installer sept œuvres de grande envergure sur l'ilôt central de Park Avenue, entre la 52ème et la 65ème Rue. J'ai été enchanté par l'idée de créer une sculpture aussi grande (8,8 mètres de haut) à Chicago (page 352), ville qui est connue à juste titre comme l'un des berceaux de l'architecture moderne. Depuis une cinquantaine d'années, bon nombre d'œuvres d'art publiques reconnues ont déjà été installées dans la ville, notamment une sculpture sans titre de 15 mètres de haut par Picasso (1967), *Cloud Gate* d'Anish Kapoor (2004), *Crown Fountain* de Jaume Plensa (2004), *Chicago* de Joan Miro (1981), *Monument à la bête debout* de Jean Dubuffet (1984) et le *Flamingo rouge* vif d'Alexander Calder (1973).

L'emplacement de mon œuvre *Constellation* à la fourche de la rivière Chicago est excellent car elle a beau être placée devant un gratte-ciel, elle garde une certaine autonomie. C'était difficile de créer quelque chose au milieu de tant de grands immeubles. J'aurais pu utiliser de l'acier inoxydable coloré naturellement, de l'aluminium ou du bronze. Mais la taille de l'œuvre rend l'utilisation du bronze très difficile. J'ai donc choisi l'aluminium et la couleur rouge vif parce que j'admire le travail d'Alexander Calder, surtout l'emploi qu'il fait du mouvement dans ses mobiles. Mon fils Gabriel et moi, nous avons conçu une exposition du travail à petite échelle de Calder en 2015 (*Multum in Parvo*, galerie Dominique Lévy, New York). J'ai aussi choisi le rouge vif pour Chicago, pour que l'œuvre contraste avec le vert de l'immeuble de verre derrière lui.

PJ *Où en sont vos autres réalisations dans la région du Golfe ?*

SC Nous avons deux projets en attente dans la région : le Sharq Crossing qui doit traverser la baie de Doha et relier les deux côtés de West Bay (page 408) et la tour Dubai Creek Tower (page 416). Ils ont été reportés car les pays où ils se trouvent ont privilégié des travaux plus urgents : la prochaine coupe du monde de football pour le Qatar et l'Expo 2020 de Dubaï pour les ÉAU. Mais ils vont reprendre tous les deux. Les fondations de la tour sont terminées.

PJ *Pendant ce temps, vous avez presque terminé un projet étonnant à Naples : la rénovation d'une chapelle du XVIIIe siècle. Il semble que vous y avez plus réalisé un travail d'artiste que d'architecte.*

SC Le directeur du musée de Capodimonte, à Naples, est le Français Sylvain Bellenger qui a travaillé auparavant aux musées de Cleveland et de Chicago et a dirigé le château de Blois, en France (1992–99). Il a organisé une exposition de mon travail intitulée « À la lumière de Naples » fin 2019, dans le cadre de la remise en état des 134 hectares du Real Bosco (parc royal) de Capodimonte. Le parc compte une dizaine de bâtiments, parmi lesquels la Manufacture royale de Capodimonte-Istituto Superiore ad Indirizzo Raro Caselli, une manufacture de porcelaine. La chapelle San Gennaro (page 442) en est un autre, construite en 1745 par le grand architecte et décorateur de théâtre Ferdinando Sanfelice sur ordre de Charles de Bourbon. Sylvain Bellenger a pensé que mon exposition pourrait être l'occasion de rénover la chapelle, fermée depuis plusieurs dizaines d'années. J'ai eu l'intuition qu'il devait être possible de faire appel aux artisans de la région pour une installation dans la chapelle, ou plutôt sa restauration. Le premier a été la manufacture de porcelaine voisine. Nous nous sommes ensuite adressés à la manufacture textile royale de Caserta, San Leucio, encore en activité, et au maître verrier Antonio Perotti de Vietri sul Mare, pour les inviter à participer au projet. Nous travaillons encore à un nouvel autel avec des artisans locaux qui travaillent le bronze et aux vêtements liturgiques. J'ai donné tous les dessins de mes projets au musée. Ils sont en grande partie inspirés par le parc et la forêt environnants, tandis que le projet a été financé pour l'essentiel par la région de Campanie[28].

UN HYMNE AU MONDE VIVANT

Quelle que soit l'importance des mathématiques et des sciences de l'ingénierie dans l'œuvre de Santiago Calatrava, c'est l'art et l'émotion qui le poussent à créer des œuvres qui dépassent le prosaïque calcul des forces. « La vie est comme une collection de perles, dit-il. Vous en trouvez une ici, une autre là, sur votre chemin. Quel est le sens de la fonction en architecture ? C'est l'amour, l'amour que l'on donne aux autres, la générosité de l'architecte. Il existe un grand secret en architecture, c'est sa nature philanthropique, qui doit être comprise en termes de fonction. Un bâtiment fonctionne bien grâce à l'amour des hommes. Le secret de la philanthropie en architecture est dans sa fonction. La beauté est perçue par le biais de l'intelligence ou de l'intuition. En architecture, il est nécessaire de dessiner chaque détail. Chaque acte, à part l'émotion qui guide votre vie, est un acte d'intelligence. L'architecture est ce qui fait que les ruines sont magnifiques, c'est le plus abstrait de tous les arts[29]. » Même lorsqu'il évoque les « magnifiques ruines », Santiago Calatrava a progressivement privilégié de plus en plus les formes d'art moins abstraites, notamment la porcelaine et le textile, pour la chapelle à Naples. Il faut dire que ses sculptures monumentales sont plus proches de l'abstraction que ses dessins ou aquarelles. Tous parlent cependant d'un amour inlassable de la vie sous toutes ses formes. Son architecture, qui souvent bouge littéralement, est aussi un hymne au monde vivant.

28 Entretien de l'auteur avec Santiago Calatrava, Zurich, 17 janvier 2022.

29 Entretien de l'auteur avec Santiago Calatrava, Zurich, 22 février 2006.

CREDITS AND ACKNOWLEDGMENTS

CREDITS

All drawings by Santiago Calatrava. All photographs, renderings and plans by Archive Calatrava unless otherwise noted.

© **Architekturphoto** 96/97, 103 top; © **Nathan Beck** 464, 473; © **Amedeo Benestante** 442/443, 444, 447, 449, 450, 453, 454, 459 bottom left, 459 bottom right; © **Robert Burley** 76, 79; © **Collection Tom F. Peters/Courtesy of Lehigh University Art Galleries (LUAG)** 31, 32 top, 32 bottom; © **Ionut David/Alamy Stock Photo** 152/153; © **Hans Ege** 193; © **James Ewing** 254/255, 259, 260 top, 261 bottom, 263; © **Sarah Hadley/Alamy Stock Photo** 232/233; © **Roland Halbe** 266, 270/271, 273, 274, 275, 428; © **Heinrich Helfenstein** 27, 30 top, 30 center, 30 bottom, 35, 80/81, 100, 102; © **Thomas Hoeffgen** 472; © **Hufton + Crow** 320/321, 322, 326 top, 327 top left, 327 top right, 327 bottom left, 327 bottom right, 328, 325; © **Alan Karchmer / OTTO** 146 top, 151, 156, 157, 158, 159, 161, 162/163, 164, 165, 166, 167, 234, 239 top, 238, 240, 243 top, 247, 286/287, 288, 290 left, 292/293, 294, 298 top, 301, 302/303, 304, 305, 306/307, 309, 311 top, 432/433, 330/331, 332, 337 bottom, 228/229, 340, 342/343; 360/361, 362, 366 bottom, 367 bottom, 386/387, 388 top, 388 bottom, 391, 393, 392 top, 392 bottom; © **Thales Leite** 394/395, 399, 400/401, 402 bottom, 403 top, 406/407; © **Angie McMonigal Photography LLC** 352/353, 354, 358/359; © **Bachir Moukarzel** 437; © **Palladium Photodesign/Oliver Schuh+Barbara Burg** 43 bottom, 44, 45 top, 45 center, 45 bottom, 52/53, 47, 55 bottom, 58, 59, 62/63, 68, 71, 93, 110, 111, 112 top, 113, 114/115, 116/117, 119 bottom, 125, 129, 135 above, 136 top, 136 bottom, 138 bottom, 139 bottom, 141, 142 top left, 142 top right, 144/145, 173 top, 173 bottom, 176 top, 176 bottom, 181, 186/187, 188, 189, 190/191, 192 top, 194, 195, 197, 198, 201, 202, 203 top, 203 bottom, 204, 205, 206, 207, 208, 209, 210, 211, 220/221, 226/227, 229, 248/249, 250, 253, 262 bottom, 279, 282, 285, 308, 310, 311 top, 313/314, 314 top, 314 bottom, 315 top, 315 bottom, 368/369, 370, 372, 374/375, 376 top, 376 bottom, 377 top, 378/379, 416, 417 top, 417 bottom, 418/419, 426/427, 431 top, 431 bottom, 432/433, 439, 440, 441 top; front and back cover; © **Paolo Rosselli** 56, 61, 64 bottom left, 64 bottom right, 65, 69, 73 bottom, 91, 122, 123, 126/127, 128 bottom, 212 bottom, 214, 222 bottom, 223 bottom, 225, 230, 242 bottom, 245 bottom; © **Spektra Imaging** 357; © **Hisao Suzuki** 72, 82, 85, 86/87, 90 top left, 90 top right, 89.

ACKNOWLEDGEMENTS

The author would like to thank Santiago and Tina Calatrava for their patience and kindness, and for the efforts they made for this book.

ALSO AVAILABLE BY THE SAME AUTHOR

TADAO ANDO
COMPLETE WORKS 1975–TODAY

SHIGERU BAN
COMPLETE WORKS 1985–TODAY

NORMAN FOSTER
COMPLETE WORKS 1965–TODAY

ZAHA HADID
COMPLETE WORKS 1979–TODAY

KENGO KUMA
COMPLETE WORKS 1988–TODAY

JEAN NOUVEL

RENZO PIANO
COMPLETE WORKS 1966–TODAY

EACH AND EVERY TASCHEN BOOK PLANTS A SEED!
Each year, we offset our annual carbon emissions with carbon credits at the Instituto Terra, a reforestation program in Minas Gerais, Brazil, founded by Lélia and Sebastião Salgado. To find out more about this ecological partnership, please check: www.taschen.com/institutoterra.
Inspiration: unlimited. Carbon footprint: (almost) zero.

Want to see more? Visit taschen.com to view our current publications, browse our latest magazine, and subscribe to our newsletter.

Hohenzollernring 53, D–50672 Köln
www.taschen.com

German translation: Christiane Court, Frankfurt/Main;
Nora von Mühlendahl, Ludwigsburg; Barbara Thoma, St. Moritz
French translation: Jacques Bosser, Montesquiou; Claire Debard, Freiburg

Printed in Bosnia-Herzegovina
ISBN 978-3-7544-0461-4